MW00834948

Growing FREE: Financially Resilient and Economically Empowered
Building Regenerative Wealth Without Losing Your Soul or Destroying the Planet

Michael Hoag and Laura Oldanie

With Eric Brown, Jenny Nazak, and Jason Padvorac

Transformative Adventures Cooperative

Change your life * Change the World

Fort Wayne, Indiana

Published in the United States in 2021, by
Transformative Adventures
1407 Spy Run
Fort Wayne, IN 46805

Inquiries:
269 350 3407
TransformativeMike@gmail.com

Introduction: A Money Book for Artists, Activists, Small Holders, Permaculturists, and Anyone Who Wants to Build a Better Life and a Better World—WHY?!

Many of my best friends and the people I respect most in this life happen to be exactly these sorts of people. They're regenerating our soils and ecosystems, fighting for social justice, cleaning up the environment, filling the world with beauty, teaching us, and taking care of us all. And of course that includes other professions I couldn't fit on the cover of this book, including teachers, journalists, social workers, and many more.

To me, it's these sorts of people who are doing the most important work in the world.

And yet, more often than not, it appears these good, hard-working people are plagued by "money problems." They may struggle to make ends meet, get burned out, have to quit their real work for day jobs they hate, live paycheck to paycheck, or self-exploit by working endless hours just to get by. The thought of having enough money to truly support their work the way they'd like, or support the work of others seems completely impossible. The path to escape the "rat race" trap of our exploitive economy remains elusive. And often, when they come to their later years, they have few options and few resources to support the kind of lives in retirement they want.

Let's face it, folks in *our* circles tend to take things like eating weeds (or painting pictures of them) far more seriously than talking about money! We think about what is good, and what is important first, and think of money second or third, if at all.

Meanwhile, other people think of money first, second, third, and in many cases it appears they think of little else!

Guess which group ends up with all the money. (And the political power that goes with it.)

But imagine if the right folks had the money for a change. Imagine if you, and others like you, could afford to devote your time and energy to supporting your life-enhancing work, AND live a good, wealthy, vibrant life while doing so. Imagine if we had the resources to defend our neighborhoods and communities from the people who would wreck them to make a little money. Imagine if we had the resources to ensure that our friends and families were taken care of, and to finally secure a measure of political power to match those people that are too preoccupied with money to ever get the big questions right.

That would be a game changer.

"But surely there are 10,000 best selling books about money at the local bookstore already? Couldn't these help us become better with money?"

There are indeed many books about money, but most are written by those people who think mostly of money, instead of the things that folks like us care about.

Those books say people like us are just "bad with money." They try to guilt us out to reduce our spending, only so we can spend more on the corporate stocks that support the companies that are destroying the planet and everything we care about. They'll tell us to "run our lives like a business" using the exact same thinking that corporations are using to destroy the planet ever more efficiently. They tell us to work harder, hustle more, and sacrifice all the things that really matter, so that we can be "good with money."

Then after telling us we need to invest in the stock market, the very same books tell us that 90% of investors lose money in the stock market!

Worse, these books give the "same old" advice for an economy that disappeared decades ago. But today, we're living in an increasingly chaotic world—with climate shocks, global conflicts, pandemics, and economic instability—that requires a new degree of resilience. As we'll see in this book, even mainstream financial institutions are being forced to rethink conventional investing and retirement advice based on the idea of an "infinite growth" economy.

So we need a different sort of money book, a revolutionary's money book. We need a money book that understands that climate change, soil loss, and resource limits are real, and that these, too, will have an impact on our financial futures. Yet, this massive carbon-fueled elephant in the room is rarely addressed in personal finance books.

At the same time, the books many of us turn to to escape the rat race—books on alternative lifestyles like "homesteading," farming, arts, and Permaculture —rarely give us frank talk on money and livelihoods. This is especially true when it comes to the reality of our later years when we may no longer be able to do the work that our young bodies once reveled in.

So it's time for an entirely different kind of money book, one that puts our values, quality of life, and care for the earth first. We need a book that will give us alternatives to destructive stocks and soul-sucking business practices. We need a book that will help us change the whole economy, not just our personal finances. We need a book that will help guide us from wherever we are, to wherever we want to be.

That is what we have tried to create in this book. We believe the patterns and adventures in this book will help you create a plan for the future, and transform your life from exactly where you are now, whether you're:
—Looking for right livelihood ideas;
—Looking for regenerative ways to invest your savings;
—A young person trying to find your way in this mad world;
—A recent graduate caught in the trap of student loans and the corporate grind;
—Seeking to support your life's work, when it isn't valued by society;
—Stuck in the corporate rat race and you want to be FREE to focus on what's really important to you;
—Struggling to make ends meet as a farmer, artist, activist or other career you love;
—Running your own business and trying to figure out how to make it work;

—Stuck in a low-income job with few resources, and little idea of how to escape your situation;

—Already on the path to Financial Independence, but looking for ways to achieve your goals without sacrificing your values, or better yet, while working to build a better world.

—Someone moving into eldership, and looking for ways to support the younger generation in your family and community in building more FREE lives.

We will not give you more one-sized-fits-all "advice" as though there's only one corporate-approved path to dealing with money. But as you read this book, and skim the "patterns and adventures," we hope it will give you many ideas you can take and replicate, and action items we call "adventures" you can follow. And hopefully we'll provide you with inspiration to create your own unique, life-enhancing relationship with money.

A Brief Overview and Disclaimer

We just said this book will not give you "one-sized" or conventional financial advice, but really, it will not give financial advice at all.

Because, we, the authors of this book, are not financial advisors or planners. We are—for the purposes of this book—Permaculture designers, here to lead you through a life-design process.

Besides that, "advice" is being told what to do by some expert, when we want you to get deeply interested in setting your own path. You're the best expert of your own life.

Permaculture is a system of nature-inspired design for human habitats and lives in general. Most people know Permaculture as a specific formal design system for landscapes and gardens. But since its earliest days (since Permaculture Two was published in 1979, to be exact) people have been applying the design system to all aspects of life and livelihood, including our money systems and family economies. Indeed, Permaculture's founder Bill Mollison often called this financial aspect of Permaculture "the most important part of Permaculture." In his final interview, he characterized this work of designing money systems as the defining aspect of Permaculture, and without designing for money, he said, it's not Permaculture.

And many people who have studied Permaculture have agreed with many of its leaders, that the most important and impactful part of Permaculture is what happens when we apply its tools to money.

Laura and I, along with our contributors Jenny, Jason, and Eric, have been leading people through applying this design process to their financial lives for over a decade, and it's certainly the most transformative teaching I have personally seen. Just as it has changed my life, students have often told me that this material has "given them their lives back," and "set them free."

And this book will be leading you through that personal Permaculture design process. It's a process that doesn't offer advice or easy answers. Permaculturists famously never give a straight answer, but instead offer up "it depends" as the answer to most questions. Because this is an invitation to do the work ourselves, consider the topic deeply, educate ourselves, seek out resources, and come up with the right answer for our own lives.

We hope that process will inspire you, raise your financial literacy, change your relationship with money, lead you on learning "adventures" that will transform your financial understanding, expose you to new "patterns" for financial resilience and right livelihood, introduce you to resources to continue your learning, and help you design a more **Financially Resilient and Economically Empowered (FREE)** life.

Chapter 1. Growing Free

"When you clear out your life of all the unnecessary junk we think we need, all sorts of real abundance starts to appear. Even this right here is a form of abundance."

The abundance co-author Eric Brown was talking about was the five of us having the ability to meet together on a Tuesday morning to work on this book, a labor of love for all of us that we believe could help a lot of people grow better lives.

"The fact that we can just have space for these conversations together, because none of us have jobs that we have to be at, is a huge form of abundance."

Everyone agreed. Jason was calling in from a quiet morning at home with his children, Jenny and Laura were both calling from their homes in their chosen sub-tropical paradise communities, Eric had welcomed the rising sun on the still lake in front of his summer home, and well, I was hosting the meeting from my garden at my new Victorian remodeling project—my next home paradise in the making.

Each of us had found our own ways to get FREE from the 9-to-5 rat race, to make space to do the kind of work and live the kind of lives that really mattered to us. Having these meetings together was a reminder that for each of us, this ability to call our own shots and be in control of our own lives was a phenomenal and immeasurable form of real wealth.

But this isn't a form of wealth we often see on social media, or celebrated by the financial gurus. Instead, we're taught that being "rich" means having sports cars, and big houses with enough rooms for an entire marching band, and flying around the world in jets. But for us, it's this illusory view of "wealth" that keeps us filling up our lives with the junk that keeps us from experiencing that true abundance of life. And so, it looks to me like Thoreau's saying that "the multitude of men live lives of quiet desperation" is as true today as it was in his time.

And yet, if one knows where to look, you can find people quietly growing beautiful, abundant lives in the cracks of the system, like thistles growing in the cracks of a sidewalk. Like *thistles*, they've found ways to be very resilient and get everything they need to thrive, without having to rely on a corporate mainstream job to make ends meet.

I've met many people living these secret dream lives. They have created situations where they get to spend part of their day doing some kind of rewarding, meaningful work in the world and the rest of their day they're free to spend with family, friends, or in healing solitude. Some of them are artists and musicians who've found ways to thrive while doing what they love, others are activists who've found the way to actually pay themselves a real livelihood for doing their good work. They may be the people in your community who are making the non-profits work and organizations actually function. And of course, I've met many people making beautiful livelihoods by living regeneratively with the land. They live like professional elves or hobbits from a fantasy novel, and that is their life! All of these people have found the true wealth of being masters of their own lives.

What's spectacular about all these people is that they've managed to accomplish this while so many others just like them stay stuck in the daily grind of bills and employment. I know many artists who are just as talented and hard working, yet they're stuck in jobs they hate, or struggling to make ends meet doing art. For them, the idea of feeling "free" seems elusive as they teeter back and forth into dead-end day jobs to pay bills. And of course I have dozens of activist friends in the same boat, who may drift from campaign to campaign, but work at fast food in the evenings. Many burn out and go back to work for the same companies they were campaigning against as activists. And of course, the vast majority of "homesteaders" who quit their jobs for the "good life" end up working longer, harder hours at some "profitable farming" scheme, doing hard physical labor during the day, and harder sales at night. Most fail in a few years time and end up back in the corporate grind anyway.

What's different about the ones living the dream is that they have all planned and designed for the dream to become a reality. They almost all have done a lot of things in common in order to manifest lives that are truly FREE, where they are actually Financially Resilient, and Economically Empowered to live the way they want to live. They almost always have a whole support system in place to allow them to live the way they want.

And in times of increasing chaos and economic instability, it needs saying that these models we'll talk about have all created truly "resilient" lives. "Resilience" is the ability to weather storms and bounce back from shocks, and the folks we'll be looking to for examples have all achieved an abundance of it. Whatever the future brings, they'll be better prepared for it than folks following the conventional advice.

After learning from these success stories, I believe they all have a similar path in common. And I think we've done a good job of laying out that path in this book. It begins by breaking down some of the standard delusions about money that keep us stuck in the paycheck-to-paycheck cycle. With the delusions cleared, all of these successes I've met were very clear about their goals and why they wanted what they wanted. And with a clear view and vision of what they wanted, they all went about creating a sort of holistic ecosystem that supported their vision to become a reality.

While others stay stuck in the mindset of working to pay their bills, what these people have discovered is a cheat code for that whole system, which allows them to opt out. Those stuck deeply in the mainstream job/bills mindset might not even have any idea what that even means!

So the very first step we'll take is to get clear about what exactly is keeping us "stuck," so that we can understand how we might get FREE.

Our Stories

As authors of this book, we thought we'd share our stories up front, so that you can see that real people out in the real world are building lives that are abundant and FREE.

But keep in mind, everyone's journey will be different. There's no "right" way to do it, no timeline for getting it done. We'll all have different starting points. But no matter where you are and what your situation, we believe we can all move towards greater financial resilience and freedom.

You'll find Laura's "escape plan" on page XXX
Eric's Income Stack on page XXX
Jason's story on XXX
And Jenny's story as a green living specialist on page XXX

Mike's Story

I spent the first decade of my life in a working class neighborhood in downtown Flint, Michigan, before moving out to a farm where my family tried different farming livelihoods, heated the house with firewood, and tried to make ends meet off a variety of income streams. I got to know other families in similar situations and sometimes worked on their farms and orchards. It wasn't an easy lifestyle, and money seemed like a constant source of stress for everyone. I saw that "farming" and "homesteading" lifestyles offered some beautiful aspects, but generally were difficult financially, and left people stressed about money and living paycheck to paycheck off low incomes.

Seeing good people struggle, it was not something I ever thought I'd end up doing!

Later as a young first-generation college graduate, I saw plenty of people stuck in corporate jobs they hated. They also seemed trapped, and stressed out from living paycheck to paycheck. They complained of spending their days in soul sucking environments under fluorescent lighting, working to make rich people richer while making the world worse off.

But I also started to find real people quietly living the alternative: artists, activists, writers, smallholders—all making their way by building community, making smart investments, and doing work they loved. After trying a few short-term jobs on the corporate path, I knew by the time I was in my 20s which path I wanted to take. I wanted to be FREE, even if it meant making less money than I could in the rat race.

While many models in the FIRE community "do hard time" in corporate American rat-race jobs to build up a nest egg for retirement, I've honestly never taken such a long-term corporate job. I've worked as an activist, a musician, teaching college classes here and there, and doing some jobs in farming, landscaping, and gardening that I was passionate about.

But it wasn't until I discovered Permaculture, and the tools you'll read about in this book, that I realized I really could live the life I wanted, with connection to community, culture, art, and nature, while also being financially resilient and economically empowered. And that I was already closer to it than I thought.

My first major Transformative Asset Stack (a concept you'll read about later in this book) completely transformed my life. The project, Lillie House Permaculture, helped me create a right livelihood selling produce, herbs, plants and seeds, and helping others transform their landscapes. I got to wake up and work in a literal paradise every day, with beauty in abundance all around me, in a landscape that grew most of my own food and provided my livelihood.

I quit my last "day job" about 12 years ago. My life's financial design is now "regenerative," which means that I will keep growing wealthier naturally over time, no matter how much I work or not.

Here's the thing: if I "retired" today, I'd still want to spend my retirement doing exactly—EXACTLY—what I'm doing right now. Each day I do something creative; I write, make art, or create garden designs. And each day I do rewarding physical work regenerating the land I'm on, restoring beautiful old houses, playing with plant devas, making amazing meals, and teaching other people about how to do these same things.

And this project completely transformed my personal "community," too. Almost every day, people would visit to pick up plants and produce, to take classes and tours, and often we'd sit around and have herbal tea or look around the garden. My garden grew amazing friends and a feeling of village for me. I became recognized as an information-rich part of the community, and was often invited to participate in projects and organizations to build a better city and region. And my whole life was surrounded with a padded feeling of abundance, knowing that my needs were taken care of by this system I'd created, so that I set my hours, I decided what to work on, or if or when I was even going to "work." I could make time to work on whatever seemed important to me and my community on that particular day. If I want, I can travel teaching people about Permaculture. If I want to take a week off to meditate, or visit friends, I can do that, too.

And if I wanted to take a job, I'm FREE to do that, too. That's right! Being my own boss is great, but I don't base my self worth off of it. If I was offered an opportunity to do fulfilling, fun, important work, I have the freedom to rearrange my life to do it. I probably wouldn't want to do it forever, but the point of being FREE ins't a cookie cutter lifestyle, it's "choose your own adventure." The point is we get to choose.

I have to say, life really does feel pretty easy, free, beautiful, and rewarding. I experience abundance every day. Now, some of this is because I actually make a deliberate practice of feeling happy, of appreciating my life, and building freedom into it! Perspective is huge part of it. I suppose someone else could have my exact life circumstances and still be a miserable wretch, if they worked at it. But, I have the "solid base" conditions and support (more concepts we'll teach in this book) to practice that gratitude and ease, and cultivate a sense that no matter what happens, it will all be workable.

And for me, it was possible to create this FREE lifestyle without inheriting any money or property, as a first generation college grad, and without ever "doing time" in the corporate rat race.

Chapter 2: Dispelling the Money Delusions that Keep Us Trapped

"In music one doesn't make the end of a composition the point of the composition. If that were so, the best conductors would be those who played fastest, and there would be composers who wrote only finales. People would go to concerts just to hear one crashing chord; because that's the end!

But that's not something we see in the Education system... Then when you wake up one day at about 40 years old you say "My God! I've arrived! I'm there". And you don't feel very different from what you've always felt.

And there's a slight let down because you feel there's a hoax. And there was a hoax. A dreadful hoax. They made you miss everything. We thought of life by analogy with a journey, with a pilgrimage which had a serious purpose at the end and the thing was to get to that end. Success or whatever it is, or maybe heaven after you're dead.

But we missed the point the whole way along. It was a musical thing and we were supposed to sing or to dance while the music was being played."

—*Alan Watts*

Wendigo Spirit

In my region, the Great Lakes and Great Plains region of North America, the native people of the Algonquin family of languages speak of the wendigo, a gaunt spirit with deep set eyes, emaciated skin stretched thin over its bones, and parched, cracked lips. It is cursed with a deep, endless hunger that cannot be sated. This spirit can possess humans with its insatiable hunger, leading us to devour and destroy all we hold dear. Overtaken by the Wendigo spirit, a poor soul may be driven to steal, to exploit, to sacrifice the health of the land, to sell out their own communities and environments, and may even crave to devour the flesh of their loved ones.

It is often seen as a metaphor used by native peoples—a warning that excessive greed can take hold of individuals, spread to infect entire peoples… driving us to betray our own highest values, and essentially devour the very things that sustain us. And with them, our own futures.

Many cultures around the world have similar parables.

Many Buddhist communities speak of "hungry ghosts," with large, swollen stomachs, always aching for food and drink, and large mouths to cram with food—yet small restricted throats incapable of swallowing but little nourishment. To many Buddhists, this is a fate that can befall any of us, if we become too enslaved to greed.

One could see our Western vampires and werewolves, beings condemned to destroy that which they love in an out-of-control search to consume, as a similar warning against the destructive power of greed and addiction.

But in today's Western world, we're more likely to put wendigos on magazine covers, celebrate our hungry ghosts in school, parade werewolves on television as role-models. We look to wendigos to learn how to "make money" and put our monsters in charge of our most important institutions. And what do you get when you put wendigos in charge of your institutions?

The Wendigo Economy

And what exactly does that look like?

For me, the most stunning example of wendigo economics is that we've built an entire wendigo food system of no-nutrition products consumers can gorge themselves upon, grow obese, yet remain chronically malnourished.

Many of our modern food products contain ingredients like high-fructose corn syrup which are known to keep us hungry as wendigos, despite our bellies being overstuffed. That's right, high fructose corn syrup—which is now in nearly everything—has been proven to short-circuit our body's mechanism for feeling satisfied, so that it actually makes us hungrier. At the same time, this universal sweetener is associated with weight gain, behavioral problems, tooth decay, type 2 diabetes, metabolic syndrome, high triglyceride levels, increased risk of heart disease, and colorectal cancer. And, according to Kiyah J. Duffey and Barry M. Popkin, this wendigo food has grown to be roughly 40% of all added sweetener in consumer products, accounting for a full 8% of the typical American's calories. ("High-Fructose Corn Syrup: Is this what's for dinner?")

As Bee Wilson documented in her classic book "Swindled, the History of the Food Cheats," high-fructose isn't the only no-nutrient food additive we've allowed the wendigos to sneak into our food. We bulk up food with sawdust (we call it "cellulose",) pad it with floor sweepings, and routinely allow adulterated ingredients in packages labeled "100% pure." The highly refined carbs in white flour and highly processed grains that have replaced our nutrient-rich old world breads, have the same overall effect as high-fructose. They actually leave us hungry, despite having less nutrition and more calories per bite. We're fed the image of food, but are left hungry for the substance.

In fact, the birth of the focus group phenomenon was associated with the snack chip industry (if you'll allow me to count snack chips as an example of "food.") In these early focus groups, snack companies found an odd phenomenon: if the snacks are too good, then they are "satisfying," and people stop eating them after a few. But if they make them just a bit off, a bit unpleasant, or unsatisfying, then the consumer will keep eating more. And even the size and colors of snack bags have been scientifically calculated to leave us dissatisfied to maximize our consumption.

"Once you pop, you can't stop."

Why, it's almost like the whole food system is designed to leave us hungry, unsatisfied consumers, to keep our corporations growing healthy and strong.

Many of us sense that today's consumer products all seem to work that way, keeping us always hungry for more even as we buy and buy and buy. That includes our cell phones, computers, electronics, appliances, clothes, cars, health care products, and virtually everything else.

We would be tempted to say "they don't make 'em like they used to," or to use the technical term "planned obsolescence". But of course, marketers, advertisers, and corporate tech-bro apologists scoff, wag their fingers and tell us our technology and products are always improving, not getting worse! This makes it seem like our lived experience of consumer crap breaking is nothing but a conspiracy theory. That's what most people think when I talk about "planned obsolescence," that it's just a conspiracy theory. In fact, the way our government calculates the real value of our money, the consumer price index, is based on this idea that our products are ever improving! Certainly then, it can't be true that corporations are intentionally making bad products!

What do we call "gaslighting" when it's being done by a whole economic system? As we'll see, perhaps we should call it "light bulbing."

Wendigobulbs

It doesn't help the "conspiracy theory" appearance that the man who coined the term "planned obsolescence" was a Freemason. Of course, that's the part that gets repeated the most. The rantings of conspiracy theorists get used to dismiss the real and actual—yet truly bizarre—facts of our economy. But when Bernard London published his pamphlet "Ending the Depression Through Planned Obsolescence" in 1932, he was only popularizing theories that corporations and business leaders were already putting into practice for over a decade. But London went so far as to suggest that the government itself should get involved in the fleecing of consumers, by encouraging products designed to self-destruct.

After the rise of the assembly line factory, and its whole suite of new consumer gadgets in the last decades of the 19th century, corporations began hitting a bottle neck in the 1920s. What happens when every consumer has all the refrigerators and light bulbs they need? Corporations can't get the endless growth they need to survive. This same bottleneck hit across industries, and the roaring 20s began to whimper, as consumers had enough light bulbs, appliances, tools, cars, and even housing.

And what made this all "worse" for capitalist profits was the overall ethic of frugality and thrift among the masses. Frugality is a sensible ethic in a world of insecurity, where a famine or war might disrupt supply lines. And to that point, consumers the world over valued thrift. It's also a wise ethic in a finite world of finite resources. A measured approach to consumption was seen as a measure of morality, while gluttony was considered a sin, especially when there were those in the world who still had so little.

Of course, this moralism was a nightmare for industrialists who wanted us to buy, buy, buy!

One of the first industries to "solve" this "problem" of thrifty consumers and durable consumer goods was the light bulb industry. Because the truth is indeed stranger than conspiracy theories, the "Phoebus Cartel," a secretive group of light bulb corporations including G.E. and Phillips, which began in 1921 and formally met in Geneva Switzerland in 1925. The "problem" for these corporations was that light bulbs were too damn durable, with an average lifespan of 2500 hours. Indeed, some pre-cartel lightbulbs from the 1900s are still functioning today, over 120 years later! The cartel's goal was to standardize lightbulb lifespans down to 1000 hours, to ensure higher turn-over and more bulb sales. When the new bulbs came out, corporations claimed the lower lives were necessary to make "better" bulbs, with brighter, safer lights, but it is well-documented that the only difference was the new bulbs self-destructed much sooner.

"Light-bulbing" indeed.

Wendigomobiles

By the 1920s, "market saturation" pressures began hitting the automotive industry. The head of marketing for Ford, Alfred P. Sloan Jr. created a rescue plan he called "dynamic obsolescence" in 1924. Under Sloan's direction, Ford began a strategy of "yearly models" and "manufactured demand" through heavy marketing, combined with decreasing durability over time. Americans would be taught to feel insecure about old cars, and jealous of those with this year's new model. This quickly became the status quo for all American car companies.

As a kid in the 1980s and 90s, I myself was always terribly embarrassed of being dropped off at school in my parents' old cars. The kids I saw on TV all had nice, new cars! Advertisers and TV producers called this "aspirational programming," by the way. Advertisers want shows with happy families getting complimented on the nicest, newest consumer products.

Not hiding a damn thing, in 1929, Charles Kettering, director of General Motors Research Laboratories, published an article titled "**Keep the Consumer Dissatisfied.**" In it, he described the new ideal economy and his plan for General Motors: "there is no place anyone can sit and rest in an industrial situation." The goal? Everyone constantly dissatisfied with the things they're essentially forced to buy as their old purchases self-destruct... sounds like a lovely way to design a culture. No wonder we feel like rats on treadmills. That was exactly the design: no place to sit.

Over time, durable metal parts that were long lasting and easy to fix were replaced by plastic parts that easily wore out, or were easily destroyed in crashes. Computerized parts that easily break replaced durable manual features. As with the 1000 hour light bulbs, all this cheap crap was installed in the name of "safety" and "consumer convenience." By the 1960s and 70s, the poor quality of American cars had become famous, and Japanese cars with much higher reliability and durability began to gain acceptance. Finally, American companies were forced to increase reliability to compete. But as quality increased, corporate profits began to sag yet again.

"Luckily," when the new bottle neck finally hit in 2008, the government followed one of Bernard London's suggestions: using our tax dollars to buy up and destroy perfectly good cars in the Cash for Clunkers program, to bail out our floundering car companies. This was a bi-partisan, tax-funded catastrophe for the environment and for low-income folks, who faced an overnight increase in car prices of thousands of dollars. Remember today in 2022, as cars are scarce, prices are ludicrous, and corporate profits are soaring, that a decade ago we used tax dollars to send perfectly good cars to the landfills.

The Wendigo Commissions for the Wendigo Way of Life

By 1929, when the US Government published its Hoover Commission Report on Recent Economic Changes, the idea of a consumer culture built on products designed for the landfill was already a tenant of religious faith for American industrialists and the ambitious middle class that ran the country. Hoover's report foreshadowed the approach that would later be championed in London's call for planned obsolescence, declaring that Americans must become consumers, and that the economy would be built on "insatiable wants," "a boundless field before us ... new wants that make way endlessly for newer wants, as fast as they are satisfied." And thus the US Government made it its mission to implement the industrialist dream of a wendigo economy.

"We need things consumed, burned up, replaced and discarded at an ever-accelerating rate." Victor Lebow, retail analyst, 1955. For Lebow, this was actually a good thing.

Hoover himself was the perfect diplomat to sell the wendigo way to Americans. By all accounts, he was certainly a true believer in the "progressivism" of his day, the idea that efficiency, industrialist barons, and corporations would build a true utopia! And the engine that would get us there would be consumption. And of course, the new wendigo science of consumer marketing: infecting the masses with insatiable wants.

Interestingly, Hoover himself was one of the first subjects of an explicit campaign for personal marketing, the Public Relations industry. Hoover was an intellectual, who had made openly racist and classist remarks. And he was associated with Europe and egg-headed elitism. Hoover's marketing firm famously created a plan to manufacture a demand for Hoover himself, remaking him the image of a real American. With its success, a newly remade Hoover went on to become President, and to lead commissions to "modernize" agriculture, culture, the economy, and the government itself. These "Hoover Commissions" were all led by teams *of the industrialists, by the industrialists, and for the industrialists.* Together, these corporate "experts" implemented our modern system where we all work for corporations, to buy goods from corporations.

When it came to that old-fashioned, Jeffersonian "yeoman farmer" way of life—frugal, self-reliant living on smallholdings—the industrialists had a clear answer. As the Hoover Commission on Agriculture clearly stated, "the problem of farmers is farming." There were too many farmers, and to the industrial perspective, we needed fewer, larger, more mechanized farms. The goal for a US farm policy then would be to consolidate land through aggressive credit and insurance schemes, kicking family farmers off their farms to free up cheap labor for industrial capitalists to build our shining utopia. Loans were only available to the wealthiest (and whitest [and male]) land owners, who were government-selected to become new gentleman land barons. Meanwhile the rest would go to work—Grapes-of-Wrath-style as low-paid labor—once their land was confiscated and redistributed to the wealthy. And so, the modern wendigo food system of factory farming and factory foods was created—not by the free market—but by industrialist utopian dreamers and heavy handed government "social engineers."

America went from having nearly 7 million farms to having just over 2 million today. Average farm size went from 142 acres at the start of the century to 445, today. The same "reforms" were made across industries, moving business ownership from Mainstreet to Wallstreet. 9000 American small banks were gobbled up in the depression alone, and since the 1950s, we've gone from having nearly 24,000 (mostly small) banks to only about 5,000, while the few largest banks take nearly 85% of the market. Small grocery stores have become nearly non-existent, being replaced almost entirely by big corporate chains.

And so, a huge swath of Americans went from running worker-owned community-based, small businesses, to being owned by—ahem, I mean being employed by—the capitalist class. We've gone from being producers to being workers and consumers.

And well-to-do American capitalists were eager to export our system of "progress" around the world. We dispatched teams of university-trained evangelists to sell our highly profitable economic and agricultural reforms to all nations, and everywhere they went, the well-to-do ruling castes ate it right up.

And as the *coup de grace*, our government has finally turned Bernard London's suggestion of government-backed planned obsolescence to housing. Media headlines practically scream that we have a housing shortage, driving up that lovely anxiety over one of our most basic needs, and they say the solution is "we need to build more houses (and of course use our tax dollars to help pay for it!) Indeed, rents are skyrocketing, rising more than 100-300% in many markets in just a few years. Housing prices relative to income are at an all-time high, with many now paying 40-50% of their incomes on housing.

Meanwhile, **we're continuing to use tax dollars to demolish high-quality, durable houses** in high-demand areas, just as we've been doing for the last decade or two. Privately owned, for-profit "Land Banks" and perversely named "affordable housing" corporations are using government powers to confiscate homes from citizens, then demolish them, during our supposed "housing crisis."

But building more and more new houses has never brought prices down in the decades we've been doing it. Why should it? We already have 16 MILLION vacant houses on the market, often in the same high demand urban areas we're building suburban sprawl around. 16 million vacant houses, by the way, is a little bit more than the 550,000 homeless we have in the US, if we wanted to solve that problem. Instead, we're using tax dollars to tear down houses to boost corporate profits. And new layers of code and ordinances keep us regular people from solving the problem the way we always have, with cohousing, "mother in law" apartments, and right-sized housing for small, young families, made of safe, sustainable, natural materials. An increasingly corporate housing system of over-sized houses meant to last 20-30 years, made of toxic, unsustainable materials is our only legal option.

We can detect this same apparent plan for obsolescence in so many of our modern consumer goods: appliances that last a fraction as long as they used to, plastic dish ware that looks "cute" new, but gets cloudy by the time next year's line comes out, fast fashion that's quickly off to the landfill, and don't get me started on electronics! In the documentary "The Light Bulb Conspiracy," from maker Cosima Dannoritzer exposes how printer manufacturers force updates that intentionally break your printer. These same companies' other products like phones and cameras seem to have a similar behavior, and many commentators have observed forced "security updates" making their devices dreadfully slow and wonky. It's as if corporate wendigos are breaking into our homes at night and destroying our personal possessions, and everyone thinks that's just perfectly normal. They say these updates are all for security and user experience. Riiiiight.

And so we now find ourselves at the natural end point of a wendigo economy: a world where our resources, our land, and even our time is all being *consumed*. Our consumption is driving climate change, mass extinctions, soil loss, ocean dead zones, deforestation, theft of indigenous lands, child sweatshops, islands of plastic in the oceans and oceans of plastic in our soil.

And that is the system we find ourselves stuck in. If you're reading this, you already felt this. Maybe you feel you spend your days doing mindless, meaningless work just to make people you will never meet richer than the highest kings of old. We may feel trapped into working away from home,

away from our families, away from our own passions and the work that is important to us. Many of us may even feel we are compelled to waste our energy—and our deeply precious brief time here with each other—toiling in unhappy conditions in support of systems that we know are harmful to people, destroy the environment, and kill our living planet.

They key insight here is that our "money" problems are a systemic issue. Most financial gurus guilt trip us into thinking it's just our consumer choices that are holding us back. We'd be rich if only we stopped buying pumpkin lattes. It's only our addiction to the malls, these experts say, that keep us from our goals. They're missing that the whole system is rigged to keep us trapped, so we'll need an escape plan based on that reality.

Radio and television have given way to even more sophisticated means of programming us with endless desire. If I make a joke about whisky, I'll get ads for 10 different brands pumped right into my feed the next time I go on social media. If my girlfriend shops for shoes, I'll start getting ads for these, too. If my eyes linger too long on a picture of a belt or a watch on my screen, modern advertisers will serve up ads for belts and watches. All of this again sounds like a conspiracy theory—and sure enough, tech companies deny it—but it's all well-documented fact. We today are constantly immersed in the most powerful tool for psychological manipulation marketing ever conceived of //, with its whole goal to make us feel dissatisfied, unfulfilled, incomplete, and empty. Your intentionally manufactured anxiety is the fuel the whole system runs on.

The first myth we need to dispel is that this is normal and natural.

This is not normal. This certainly is not natural.

In an era where we as a society appear driven to devour our own futures, to give up our freedom, to sacrifice our precious time with friends and family, to clear cut our ecosystems, sacrifice our children's inheritance, and destroy our only home in the universe in a quest to cram ever more consumer crap into our insatiable maws, one may wonder: Is there something to this wendigo myth after all?

If so, what deep magic can we summon to ward off this malevolent spirit, before we consume all we hold dear?

———————

As we start this adventure together, I'd like you to take a moment to think about the things you value most. Because that is what this book is about: growing the freedom to actually invest your time and resources in the things you value most, and live in alignment with your values and your dreams.

Probably a couple things flashed right into your mind—maybe people you care about, maybe your home, or your community. But go a little further, and think of 5 to 10 things. Name them. Say the words aloud. This—the things you truly value—is an incantation to ward off the wendigo.

Well done! If there were wendigos around, they're certainly running for the door. If there were other people around, they're probably looking at you like they're questioning your sanity. That's okay, we'll need to get used to strange looks if we're going to start questioning some of society's deepest taboos: our beliefs around money.

Over the last decade, I've led many workshops to help people transform their relationships with money, build right livelihood, and create more joyful, secure and abundant lives—and this is always where we start: *rooting ourselves deeply in that which truly matters.* Lately, I've been developing these courses with my friend and co-author Laura Oldanie. Since our courses are designed for permaculturists, earth warriors, activists, artists, and smallholders (a term for "homesteaders" without the potentially offensive connotations) our students reliably share the same sort of values around the earth, community, family, equality, peace, justice, beauty, etc.

Some folks may consider these hippie dippie ideas that mainstream people should laugh about.

When the superior mind encounters the truth they accept it instantly

When the average mind encounters the truth, they struggle to accept it.

When the fool encounters the truth, they laugh aloud! If they didn't, it would not be the truth.

-The Tao De Ching.

That's okay, the joke's ultimately on them. Most people thoughtlessly trade away the real and truly valuable things in life for mere symbols, like paper money, or worse, 1s and 0s in a computer somewhere. Inevitably, the punchline comes for us all sooner or later: when the computer's unplugged (literally or metaphorically) all those 1s and 0s don't mean much.

These "laughable, hippie dippie" goals and values our students talk about often include things like:
—"A life where I don't have to stress and worry constantly over our basic needs."

—"A life where I can spend time with the people who really matter to me, and where I have the resources to take care of them."

—"A life where I can contribute to my family and community in ways that are meaningful and satisfying to me."

—"A life where I am FREE to pursue my passions and interests."

—"A life where I can truly relax."

—"A life where I don't have to worry about what will happen in my later years, or who will take care of me."

—"Where I'm FREE to seek a spiritually rich, philosophically wealthy, creative, fulfilled life of art, culture, expression, and beauty."

—"I want to be FREE to live in a beautiful, connected community with deep, meaningful relationships."

—"…in a beautiful place, with a vibrant, healthy ecosystem, with a deep connection to nature."

—"Where I'm FREE to fight for a more just and sustainable world, where I can take my place among those who are building the future we all know we really deserve if we'd just stop trying to turn everything into money all the time."

—"I want the FREEdom to take responsibility for myself and build a life with rich relationships—without making life harder for others!"

—"I want to live in a place where we all have the FREEdom to seek our own self-actualization, and support everyone else around us in their own search for self-actualization, community actualization, and a more enlightened society."

Perhaps you have your own ideas to add to this list.

For many of our students, this vision—a life where we are economically empowered to spend our rare, precious time on the things that truly matter— sounds like true wealth.

In fact, when we understand what really matters, it finally puts "wealth" in context. Do you keep trying to inhale more air even when your lungs are full? Do you keep gulping down endlessly more water even once you've quenched your thirst? Do you keep telling the same joke over and over again, even once you know the punchline? If you have all of these real riches I mentioned above, why would you still waste your precious time trying to gulp down even more money? When is it *enough*?

So, this is another way of asking this question: what does true wealth mean to you? What would a truly wealthy life look like? What is enough?

That is what this book is about: helping you to transform your relationship with money, to build right livelihood, and create a truly wealthy, abundant life where you're more financially resilient, and economically empowered to spend your time on the things you value most.

———————————————-

"Normal is getting dressed in clothes that you buy for work and driving through traffic in a car that you are still paying for—in order to get to the job you need to pay for the clothes and the car, and the house you leave vacant all day so you can afford to live in it."
—Ellen Goodman

"Life is enriched by aspiration and effort, rather than acquisition and accumulation."

-Helen and Scott Nearing

Chapter Resources and Notes

Dannoritzer, Cosima. The Light Bulb Conspiracy. RTVE 2010.

Lebow, Victor. "Price Competition in 1955," Journal of Retailing, Spring 1955.

Pope, Kamila. Understanding Planned Obsolescence. Kogan Page, 2017.

Robin, Vicki, and Joe Dominguez. Your Money or Your Life 9 Steps to Transforming Your Relationship with Money and Achieving Financial Independence. Malmö: MTM, 2020.

Wilson, Bee. Swindled. John Murray Publishers Ltd, 2009.

Debt, David Graeber

Klein, Naomi. No Logo, Shock Doctrine

Korten , David

Hayes, Shannon. Radical Homemakers

Laura's Escape Plan

My financial freedom story really started right about the time I turned forty. It was then that I discovered three pivotal elements in my journey—permaculture, the financial independence community, and the concept of lifestyle design—a powerful trifecta indeed! As I devoured books and online content about people who had designed their financially solvent escapes from the rat race, I wanted that for myself. And I wanted it in a way that incorporated the regenerative ethics and design principles I found in permaculture.

I've never really had a conventional job or lifestyle as an adult - after college I spent almost eight years as a Peace Corps volunteer, student, and State Department fellow in Poland. When I came back to the U.S. I landed in

Washington, DC, where I worked for non-profits with domestic and international education missions so I found myself frequently traveling overseas and around the U.S. I was far from miserable in any of those jobs, but as enjoyable as visiting new places was, traveling ate up a good chunk of my life and was exacerbating some low-grade health issues. Then in my last job I ended up managing a program focused on an issue I wasn't particularly passionate about.

All of this led me to start thinking in some out of the box ways. Firstly, I realized that my position was largely funded by grants. Because I had a very good working relationship with my supervisor I was able to convince my employer to allow me to quit my full-time job and use some of that same grant funding to hire me as a well paid part-time consultant (in addition to a full-time staff person to replace me.) It was a win-win situation.

Secondly, to compensate for the reduction in income I moved into my basement and got a roommate, the rent from which almost completely covered my mortgage. I had always been relatively frugal and avoided debt (thanks for the positive money examples mom and dad!) other than student loans (which I'd paid off a few years before quitting my full-time job) and my mortgage so my financial situation was very stable.

Three years later, in search of a life in a more affordable location with better weather I sold my house and spent two years exploring the southwest. In the end, I landed right back where my journey started before I left for the Peace Corps 25 years ago in St. Petersburg, Florida. It was here I found the best bang for the buck given the amount of money I had to work with from the sale of my DC house and the quality of life I wanted to achieve.

These days I find myself deeply tapping the multiple forms of capital and cultivating a more holistic balance sheet. (We'll learn more about this on page XXX.) These building blocks of true wealth consist of a wide range of resources and assets beyond financial capital that fill our lives with meaning, richness, and resilience. Some examples from my life of what that involves include planting soap berry and olive trees in my yard as part of my climate resilient retirement plan; responsibly foraging the delicious subtropical fruits that litter the alleys and sidewalks of my neighborhood; dumpster diving for much of my food; building a diverse multi-generational circle of friends, and actively participating in my local time bank & Buy Nothing groups.

As I regularly stress with my coaching clients, tapping these multiple forms of wealth and capital helps us establish a "solid base" from which we can more confidently earn, spend, manage, and invest our money and lead our lives in ways that truly align with our values. In my case, I am single (in a committed long-term relationship), childless, in my early fifties, and debt-free with a home I own free and clear. I've opened up a self-directed IRA through which I'm making socially conscious investments off Wall Street and I'm pursuing financial freedom on my own terms with a strong emphasis on frugality, sustainable living, regenerative right livelihood, and the triple bottom line (people, planet, & profit.)

Adventures and Patterns (One way to use this book.)

This book is organized around two very useful tools for helping us meet our goals: "Patterns" and "Adventures." You'll notice the "patterns" pages are in light green, while the adventures are light blue.

The idea of the "patterns," as they are used in this book, comes from architect Christopher Alexander. In our context, a "pattern" is anything that we can understand, share, and replicate to solve problems. For example, "raised bed garden," "rain garden," and "fruit tree guild" are patterns you can replicate in your garden. Christopher Alexander used the idea of a "pattern language" to help communicate ideas about architecture across disciplines and to DIYers, who don't need a PhD in Architecture to build a garden shed. But looking at "patterns" is a research-based way to absorb a lot of information that can help a DIYer build a better shed.

Thus many of this book's chapters will provide "patterns" you can skim over, read if they're useful, and hopefully, they will be helpful in making better decisions about money.

But, the best patterns in the world don't help if you never put them into action! And glancing at patterns can give us an overview of a topic, but it cannot give us the expertise that actually "learning by doing" can. So this book also includes "adventures." In this context, our "adventures" are finite learning tasks you can complete over a brief period of time that will have a huge positive impact on increasing your outcomes (they'll improve your financial life) while also helping you develop real skills and expertise.

So to use this book, you may pick an area of financial life you need to improve on, select an "adventure" to work on, and also look over the related patterns for inspiration. If you complete even half the adventures in this book, you will have completely transformed your financial life plan. For more information on what makes a great "transformative adventure," see TransformativeAdventures.org.

ADVENTURE 1: Envisioning your new transformative financial life.

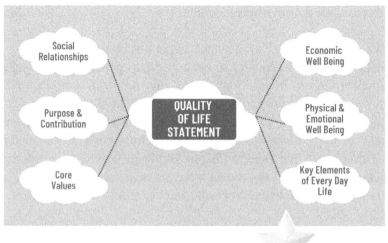

your new North Star

The first adventure in this book is to start envisioning the future you want. If you don't know where you want to go, how can you expect to get there? A Permaculture design process begins with deep goal-setting for our lives. Some designers call this step a "quality of life statement." The more fully we can imagine what we want, the more likely we are to find it on our path. This kind of visioning preps us to see opportunities we otherwise might have missed.

For this adventure, we recommend keeping a notebook or sketch book to write your ideas in as you read this book. Keep a section specifically on envisioning "your best life."

Time Commitment: Consider this adventure to last over your first read-through of this book. If you're just skimming the patterns, it could take an average reader about 7 hours, and if you're reading deeply and doing other brief adventures, it could take 12-15 total hours. If you're reading an hour a night, about 2 weeks.

Tips:
Don't think that you have to answer these questions in writing, use the method that works best for you. That may well be writing, or you may prefer a more creative, intuitive approach. You could try a "vision board." Use a pinboard online that you can share with friends. Answer each question with a poem and add to them as you read the book. Paint pictures. Make sketches. Simply sit in quiet meditation and give each question space. Nor do you have to do these with a sense of prudent homework. You can do them with a sense of adventure and/or daring, even if you aren't the daring type. You might as well be bold, this is your one and only life we're talking about here!

"If you can see it clearly enough in your head, when you wake up the next morning it will be there."

These questions may help you in contemplating your vision:

Relationships:
What do you want your family life to be like?
What do you want your social life to be like?
How many good friends would you like to have? How often will you spend time with them? What things will you do and where?
How big a family will you have? How much time will you spend with them? Where?
How many people will live in your house? Do you want to live in a small community or a big house full of people?

Community
What kind of community do you want to be in? A relaxed one, an energetic one? A big or small community? An engaged community? A diverse community? One with important problems to solve, or one without problems? One that's liberal or conservative? A place with a small town feel? A college town?

Home
What kind of place do you want to call home?
What do you want your home to be like and feel like?
What kind of surroundings do you want?

What kind of location do you want your home to be in? City? Country? Subdivision?

How much land do you want to live on?

What kind of climate do you want to live in?

Time

How will you spend your daily time?

What activities would make an idea day?

What things do you want to most invest your time in?

Self Actualization and Spiritual Fulfillment

What will you do for self actualization and spiritual fulfillment?

How often will you engage in these activities?

Will you do these alone or with other people?

What kind of resources do you need to pursue these activities?

What kind of person do you want to become?

What would you like to contribute to the world?

The Future

Where do you want to be in 5 years time?

Where do you want to be at the peak of your working life?

If you want a family, what kind of situation do you want for your family?

How do you want to spend your later years? (Note: there's a whole chapter about designing for your later years later in this book.)

Work

What kind of environment would you like to spend your days working in?

What kind of work would you like to be doing?

Would you like variety in your work? What types of tasks do you enjoy?

Would you like your work to make the world a better place, or leave it worse off?

Do you want to make money for your work? How much?

How many hours per week/day/year would you like to work?

Pattern 1 (P1): The Caveman Bucket List for Happy, Spiritually-Fulfilled Life

One of the other great delusions of money is that it is necessary to "truly live."

This is a delusion we even find in corners of the movements around Permaculture and anti-consumption. We may poo poo the idea that we can buy meaning at the shopping mall, but glorify buying carbon-drenched plane tickets to travel the world in search of "real life." Why can't we "really live" at home? Is life an amusement ride we need to buy a ticket for?

"Our Burdens are merely memories of what was that we gave significance and heaviness"

Society is an Amusement Park for the Ego, A Hall of Mirrors for our Illusion

These days, everyone is into "Paleo" diets and "caveman" fitness, convinced that we humans evolved to live, eat and exert ourselves in a certain way, and that despite all their backwards lack of air-conditioning, our ancestors just might have known *something* about how to be human. So why does nobody ever wonder what was on the Caveman and Cavewoman's bucket list?

Rather than argue over what our most human ancestors ate and drank, why not ask what the cavewoman LIVED FOR and how she LIVED?

For tens of thousands of years (and probably much, much longer) our ancestors went about living their lives, creating memories, discovering untold secrets, having adventures, building life-long deep relationships and romances, busting through personal limits, dancing with gods and goddesses, communing with the raw forces of the universe… often without ever even leaving their own villages. Instead, most of our human cultures marked their lives with journeys into dark, mysterious places, found the empty core of the universe in each other's souls, deconstructed the very meaning of life and put it back together in the form of something spectacular, achieved stunning magnificence in ritual and rite.

Somewhere way back in your family tree was a shaman great, great, great, great grandmother who dreamt of YOU and her fondest wish for your life was that you would learn to feel the heady power of the sacred grove as she did, and that over the chasm of great time and distance you and she would resonate in infinite one-ness there together.

These subtle yet profound life experiences our ancestors lived for are all but forgotten today. We ask: If a tree falls in the woods, but nobody posted it on social media, did it really happen?

Did all our human ancestors up to the advent of the zipline and iPhone 6 truly lead dull, meaningless, unfulfilling lives?

Or in contrast, would Henry David Thoreau look upon the jet-setting, world-travelling, mall-shopping elite of modern Concord, and still abandon their "lives of quiet desperation" in search of his simple hut in the woods?

"The mass of men lead lives of quiet desperation."
—Hennry David Thoreau

In my life I've been privileged to travel further than 99.999% of the humans that ever lived, spoken to people in 9 different languages in their own countries, sold original works of art, music and poetry, played in a punk-rock band, sung Opera on professional stages in Europe, starred in plays (good ones!) and movies (terrible ones!) written 3 novels (yup) slept in a castle, played in a marching band, visited some of the great gardens, art and architecture of the world...

But these are not the most profound moments, experiences, and lessons of my life. Nor do they mean that I have "lived" more than those who haven't had these experiences. Sure, I've had some profound experiences while visiting exotic places, but the profound parts could have just as likely (perhaps MORE likely) happened without ever leaving home. And what one discovers on a real adventure is found inside, and has little to do with the scenery.

Indeed, when I traveled the world, it was for work—both as a musician and as a permaculture designer. I have taken very few vacations in this life, because the idea of wasting jet fuel to sit with other Americans, eat American style food and American drinks in a resort just doesn't interest me much. And to be honest, I haven't prioritized the money to be able to go do that, so I couldn't afford to go spend a week in such a place, away from my life anyway. But, free from the rat race, I have had the ability to be able to go and live for a few summers working in Europe, or traveling to do Permaculture. And, in my opinion, that gave me a real immersive cultural experience with real connection to place and people. Most vacations, it seems to me, would have only been my same old life, just with a change in scenery. Here again, the search for money gets in the way of having a better, richer experience directly. For me, it's the difference between consuming life, and actually living it.

None of the following fundamental human experiences require money, consumption, belief, none require drugs, none of it requires meeting the Dalai Lama or attending expensive beach-side retreats in the tropics with world-renowned "gurus." These are not things to be bought at any price. And these are experiences that are found in all traditions, and are open to anyone, from Christians, to Pagans, to Muslims, to Buddhists, and Atheists. I can fully believe in these fundamental human "spiritual" experiences without having to believe in anything supernatural.

Don't get me wrong, I'm not kicking the bucket list idea entirely. At its best, the bucket idea taught a generation to live their lives, to value experiences over buying stuff, and being adventurers over being consumers. Rad. But at its worst, it makes us into consumers of our own lives, looking to buy experiences, approval and wisdom from our peers on social media.

So here's a new section for MY bucket: the vital human experience, the Caveman bucket list, aspirations most of our human ancestors could have shared in. I really don't ever need another selfie sipping umbrella drinks on an exotic beach, and neither did Captain Caveman. I want to journey to far darker, more mysterious, more hidden places: the room of the wolf-mother wallpaper, the room where the antler carved the drum… and shit. I've personally visited enough of these places to know that they are real, and well worth the price of admission. But I'm not gonna put a big check mark next to them to show off, because they're the sort of things you build a truly fulfilling life upon, not the kind you cross off once you've got the selfie.

What's the point of this chapter in this book? Simple: money can't buy us the experience of "really living." You don't need a "per diem" to "carpe diem." And no matter how much money someone else has, it absolutely doesn't mean that they're "living" any more than you or I, or Wilma Flintstone.

---

1. Being still enough long enough that the "world rolls in ecstasy at my feet," as Kafka said. This is a fundamental experience, sought after in all the world's mystic traditions, because it is both a profound experience in itself, but also something that is said to deepen every other potential experience. When one can quiet the mind, it is said we can experience our lives more directly, instead of having to squint to see reality through the tint of our own rose-colored glasses, and we can hear the song of the world without struggling over the noise of our own mental chatter. This is an experience that can be had both alone and with company, such as in the Japanese tea ceremony, or participating in contemplative arts.

2. The dissolution of the prison of time. Mystics across many traditions wrote about this experience and modern science is confirming the possibility. Some highlight destinations in the time-travelogues of mystic literature: "to see my own face before my father was born," to spend a "few eternities" as the god of the sea as the Buddha did, and to finally understand that line in Revelations about "a time, times and half a time." Seriously, wtf?

3. Sympathetic joy. To experience the joy of others opens us up to a whole world of joy! Infinite joy! For many of us, we're instead taught to envy the victories of others, especially our friends! So cultivating sympathetic joy also defends us from the boring grumpiness of jealousy when our friend gets a promotion. It can even deaden the sting of enmity and hate. But it is also said this deep form of compassion is the basis for experiencing the arts more fully. Imagine if we could feel what the great painters felt as they put the final touches on their masterpieces?

4. To co-evolve in my own forest garden. This is another fundamental human experience, intimately connected to spiritual traditions and religious rites in many cultures. It's an amazing thing to grow inside such a living system!

5. I am my ecology. My ecology is me. Sacred connection with nature.

6. The care of magical creatures. One of the lies we tell ourselves in our culture is that "animals" are not the same as us, they do not feel, do not have their own romances and adventures, hopes and dreams. And so we de-vitalize them. It takes a sort of renunciation (renouncing this lie) to begin to see our non-human animals as the vital, living, amazing creatures they actually are. Once we do, we're surrounded by magical creatures more magnificent than anything in Harry Potter. Look!

7. Deep, life-long relationships such as those formed in folk societies and horticultural villages. It would be amazing to share a cup of coffee with a friend over 50 years of time.

8. The Epicurean Life: Self-reliance, living with friends, Contemplation. Epicurus wanted to learn what made the ultimate human life. His bucket list was real simple, yet so profound that ideas about the good life still bear his name today!

9. Getting un-carved: Daoists call the human ideal "the Uncarved Block." How it's often described: To get up, stretch, breathe, eat while reading a few lines of a book for inspiration, mindfully practice some kind of useful, simple work, take a meal with friends, spend some time in quiet contemplation, walk in the garden....

10. Life in "Dunbar's village." According to the researchers of the Dunbar Group, humans evolved in folk villages of about 200 people, who were friends, relatives, and a real community. It would be an amazing accomplishment to get to experience a life where we're truly invested in the people around us and their stories! Every archetype of the human drama playing out in our own lives instead of a screen. For most of us, this will mean getting creative about how we engage in village building and community organizing.

11. A life-long path of spiritual development. It's said these tools of happiness can be sharpened over a lifetime of use, polished into sublime states of refinement and radiance. Most of us grow bored of the repetition of life. But what if in 10 years we were better at enjoying a strawberry than we are today?

12. Freedom from possessions. Hard work in the modern age, yet quite a worthy accomplishment! This might take me some time to fully get to. But I hope to work towards this the rest of my life, making a goal to own less, and less and less, to make room in my life for what's really valuable.

13. The freedom of self-reliance. To grow my own food, grow my own medicine, be able to live off the land, to be as trusting and carefree as the "lilies of the goddamn field."

14. True deep relaxation. To stop trying to control the world, to stop "aspiring" to exert "power" over others and over society, and instead lead by example. To fully "let go" into life and "trust" the world. That sentence has a bunch of words with a bunch of quotation marks, because our society has all sorts of bad ideas about these things. I've come to think that what I was taught was "power" is actually a complex of delusion, aggression and insecurity. "Aspiration" as we use it too often lacks any genuine self-knowledge, which leaves it as nothing more than settling for conformity to a sick society. Finding what it means to "trust" humans in such a sick society is its own challenging quest.

15. Deep trust and true love. Awe, I'm a romantic like that. But I'm also not limited by conventional ideas about what that means.

16. The Djanas. These are the states of concentration the word "zen" is derived from, and they've often been compared to mind-blowing orgasm, but timeless and infinite, and subtle. While this word comes from the Buddhist world, one can find similar descriptions of states of deep concentration and contemplation across many of the world's mystic traditions.

17. The outright ecstasy of creative, artistic revelry, to "lose myself" in song and dance. The great experiences of life lie along the extremes of the spectrum of "pleasures subtle and gross." According to the great mystics, it is the experiences at the "subtle" end, found through simplicity, that are the greatest experiences a human is capable of. But, surely there's something to be said for "gross," bold, hedonistic overwhelming pleasures, too!

18. To commit to and follow a culturally relevant spiritual tradition. Tough for a skeptic like me. But I wish to be more than a consumer of spiritual

products. I wish to experience that fundamental of following a spiritual path. Many paths lead to the top of the mountain. Only one moon shows in the sky.

19. To eat really, really good just-picked fruit at that magical moment before the sugar starts converting to starch and the complexity of flavor is so profound you literally see technicolor. Or at least I do.

20. Lucid dreaming. Anything is possible in the dream realm.

> *"Simplicity, serenity, utility and harmony are not the only values in life, but they are among the important ideals for the good life."*
>
> *-Helen Nearing*

Systems Thinking for Growing Wealthy and Creating a Healthier Economy

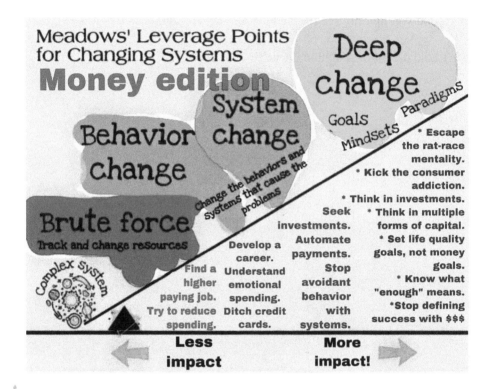

Here's a major way this book is different from most money books. We'll focus holistically on systems.

According to systems thinker Donella Meadows, when we want to change things, like our health, our soil, or our family finances, the standard way we do it is to look at we'll call "brute force" methods. That means we look at the numbers involved and just try to directly change them—without trying to understand why the numbers are what they are in the first place. For example, we might look at our income, see that it's smaller than our expenses, and try to change one end of the equation, either spend less or earn more.

It sounds very simple, but this is pretty much the standard advice in a lot of money books: spend less, earn more. If only it were so easy.

The problem is, as you may have already found for yourself, this usually doesn't work well. This is because 1, these brute force methods are almost always perceived as conflict and stress. Brute force. For example, if you're trying to lose weight, you could try to eat fewer calories. So you count calories and directly try to reduce them. But then you might stress about the conflict between your diet and that piece of cake that's flirting with you at the party. *Bad cake! Why is it looking at you so longingly, when it should know you're already taken by a commitment to self-punishment and anguish?* And so we'll have to use some "muscle," of self restraint to ward off that cake.

Brute force is for brutes. It means we're going to solve a problem by muscling through instead of by thinking things over and solving them with our minds. With things like diet, exercise, and finances, it means using our self discipline to solve the problem, but research has shown that our daily self discipline is a finite resource. It literally burns significant blood glucose to ward off the temptation of that naughty piece of cake. When blood glucose runs for resisting, that piece of cake will have you at last. So, brute force methods are about force, conflict.

The same can be said for "skip your cup of Starbucks" advice of "just spend less!" Sure, everyone knows that cup of Starbucks is the only thing keeping you from being the next Jeff Bezos. In reality, your daily cuppa might be a tiny tax on your income, but resisting it could be a huge tax on your self discipline reserves. We can only resist the cup of coffee so long, and if we're also resisting cake, meeting a work deadline, and trying to maintain an exercise program we hate, then we've set ourselves up to fail at at least one of those things, if not all.

Secondly, it doesn't work because we end up putting a lot of energy into making these weak brute force changes like skipping starbucks, but we leave all the STRONG big ideas and systems in place that are really keeping us from meeting our financial goals. Those might be things like being stuck in a whole exploitive consumer culture system with a dead-end job, being exploited by a big corporation that steals your time and energy so rich people can get richer.

Yet, these weak brute force methods are almost entirely where most of us focus when we try to improve our financial situations: we need to get a better dead end job, we need to spend even less, or maybe we just need to sell more units. It's certainly easier to understand how to do that than to change the whole system you're stuck in. (Or is it?)

But if you're making $20,000/year and just getting by on that, you might put literally hundreds of hours into trying to spend less, and even if you cut spending by a whopping 20%, that's still only $3500 extra a year. It would still take decades to meet any financial goal and all that additional time might not be sustainable, and that time sink might be standing in the way of real systems changes that could be worth ten times that amount.

But for busy people only spending $17k and working 50 hours a week to get there, it might take a lot of extra time and effort to cut an additional $2k! Even if that struggle was sustainable for our self discipline reserves, that $2k of savings still won't make you the next Warren Buffet.

According to Meadows, we use the same thinking on societal problems. For example, if we want to fix poverty, we'll struggle in protracted brute force conflict just to pass a law to track and better understand income and poverty. That alone won't do anything for poverty, but it could take years to get there, and use up finite reserves of political capital. Next, we may try to distribute a few thousand dollars from the wealthy in ways that will benefit the poor, yet we leave all the important powerful systems in place that are creating absurd wealth and tragic levels of poverty.

We could write every American a stimulus check for $3800, for example (which just coincidentally happens to be the amount a typical American individual received for Covid.) But then we leave in place larger economic systems that will just turn that into inflation that actually makes us poorer over the long term. If that causes 30% inflation (which is the amount the government is telling us to expect) then for the median American with an income of $31,000, their income will be worth $9,300 less this year, and every year thereafter. Meanwhile, all that money that disappeared from our wallets is getting hoovered upwards to the mega wealthy, who are doing better than ever, and the stuff they buy is far less affected by inflation. And they have most of their wealth tied up in assets that will just appreciate with inflation! They're actually selling us the stuff that prices have gone up on, making them pretty immune to rising prices.

And again, we leave all the big systems in place, like the fact that the wealthy own all the big businesses, have worked for generations to put small businesses out of business so that big corporations are the only providers, they have massive amounts of inherited wealth, get literally free money from the government, and essentially control the government, too. The tiny amounts of money we divert to the poor will quickly get sucked back up to the wealthy by these strong systems.

We could say the same for our efforts on climate change, which focus on weak brute force methods like distributing tiny carbon credits from one polluter to another, while we leave all the big systems—like a fossil fuel based consumer economy—intact.

According to Meadows, our actions become more effective as we move up towards larger systems. For example, if we move up to thinking about the common behaviors that basically keep systems going, that will be more powerful. And if we move up a step to changing the systems themselves, this will be even more powerful. And at the top of the list, we can access the most powerful leverage points by changing the goals and paradigms that create the systems to begin with, or ultimately by transcending those paradigms altogether.

This is why in this book, we repeat the old advice: *the poor focus on jobs (brute force), the middle class develop careers (a behavior change) while the wealthy invest (create wealth-generating systems.)* And that's why in this book, we'll set out to create societal change by taking aim at the economic systems that are actually causing the problems, and the underlying goals, paradigms, and ways of thinking that bring those systems into being.

The approach in this book will be about developing systems that will make you wealthy and FREE.

But we can go even further into even stronger leverage points. We can change our whole ideas about money, wealth, consumption and livelihood. We can focus on investing in life systems that will support us with abundance and grow naturally wealthier over time. Ultimately, we can organize to change the whole system we're all embedded in, which is creating inequality and destroying the planet.

In the BEST Permaculture courses, this is the kind of thinking we use. In Transformative Adventures, we're taking that approach to a whole new level, and providing the tools that have truly transformed our paradigms around money and allowed us to design lives around wealth generating systems that also transform society.

And in this book we'll show you DOZENS of real world examples and models of real people who've actually done it.

There's a Role for Brutes

But on balance, with that said, we need to also remind ourselves that there is a place for some brute force methods!

For example, dieting by counting calories (a brute force method of counting calories) is notoriously a horrible way to lose weight, and an even worse way to get truly healthy. Most people now agree the best way to get healthy is to commit to big systems change: changing our habitual behaviors, developing good habits, changing our whole way of thinking about health, using systems so that we're eating better and exercising appropriately, and so on.

But, with these big changes in place, now the brute force methods become much more effective! Folks with high levels of fitness swear by counting calories to dial in their weight, lose those last few pounds or meet a new fitness goal. Someone who has healthy exercise habits and a healthy way of eating could get a lot out of counting macros.

And so in this book, we'll hopefully be changing some of our big habits, our goals, and our whole ideas about money.

But with those big changes in place, there's nothing more effective in helping to meet our goals than to actually start tracking things like how much we're spending and how much we're saving and earning—and then using some brute force to make changes and meet our goals. And then we can know that we're making those brute force tweaks—not just for small changes—but as part of an effective, holistic plan.

So the best strategy will apply some pressure at all different leverage points, changing paradigms, changing goals, creating new systems, changing our behaviors, AND paying more attention to the numbers in our bank accounts.

Stocks and Flows
The Bathtub Analogy

In-flow

Stock

Out-flow

To control the stock level, we must change the flows in and out of the system. If the in-flow is greater than the out-flow, the tub will fill.

P2–System Stocks and Flows

In this book, we'll use a lot of charts that look like the illustration on the previous page, which is often called the "bathtub analogy" in systems thinking. This sort of chart invites us to think of our personal finances from a systems lens.

The most basic idea here is that a lot of problems around resources are about having a "stock" of a resource to meet needs. For example, when we're talking about poverty, we're talking about whether people have a large enough stock of money to pay their bills. To change the stock, we think we either have to increase the income or reduce the spending. The problem is usually we stabilize our financial situation by equalizing our inflows and outflows, so that we spend every dollar we make. If the spending is equal or higher than the income, then the money-tub will always be empty and we'll have very little resilience! Any unexpected bill is going to leave us unable to meet our needs.

And of course, if we have too much of a resource, then our problem is "pollution." For example, if we pump carbon into the atmosphere faster than we can store it in soil and trees and so on, then we have a carbon pollution problem that will cause climate change.

When we talk about "brute force" methods, we're talking about just directly trying to control one of those two spigots, the inflow or the outflow. Got a money problem? Just put more money in there! Hence that standard financial advice: "earn more, spend less." But when it comes to complex systems, stocks and flows are not so intuitive, for the reasons we've just discussed.

So the approaches in this book will be all about escaping this linear way of thinking, finding more sophisticated ways of impacting flows, and imagining a whole new sort of bathtub! For example, we can break down the delusions that are causing the tub to drain! Or, can we even create a money-tub where the flows are as important as the stocks, the tub is self-filling, and the water in the tub actually multiplies by itself?

The Money Delusions

A scheme as bizarre and self-destructive as the wendigo economy is clearly held together by some epic delusions. These are the delusions that keep us trapped, wasting away our time and lives. Following our systems thinking approach, one of our first goals will be to break down and transform these delusions that are getting in the way of the outcomes we want.

Delusion 1: If you just follow the rules and do what you're told, you'll end up rich!

This one key insight may be the birth of modern alternative money wisdom.

In the Fall of 2001, I (Mike) had decided to go back to university after taking a couple years off to perform as a musician full time. Though I had been making a decent income, I had been through a break-up, and had seen a brilliantly talented friend end up living out of his car when he stopped getting gigs. I was worried about my own future and where I was headed, and I turned back to the old, proven path: get an education, find a good job (in my case, a tenure position,) and live happily ever after. This was basically the path I was taught to follow in school. It's the path that we're all taught to follow.

And then, of course, the terrorist attacks on 9-11, and subsequent war happened. The world seemed a dangerous and unpredictable place. In the economic downturn, a couple of my mentors lost their tenure positions, once thought to be a golden ticket for life. Others were unhappy in theirs, but felt trapped by that golden ticket.

I just wanted to be able to do something positive in the world, support myself in doing it, and as I looked at the people around me, I was no longer confident that old path would lead in the right direction.

One day I was visiting one of my mentors, Jerry, who like me, was both a musician and an activist. He seemed to have a great life, mostly creating work as he went, teaching a little, and performing when he wanted. And compared to my friends working full-time inside institutions, he never appeared stressed out. He seemed to have created his own vibrant arts community, had time for a dedicated martial arts practice that kept him in great shape, and he performed more than any of the full-timers at the university.

I asked if he wouldn't rather have the security of one of those full-time tenure positions.

Jerry nearly spit out his drink.

"Hell no!" He said. "Give up this?" As though he would have to trade away the ability to sit around having a beer with a friend at 2:00 Tuesday for that supposed security. "These days, those jobs are such a hassle there's no time left over to make art *or a living.*"

He got up, and came back and handed me a book, "Your Money or Your Life," by Vicki Robin.

When I started reading, the first pages introduced the stories of other people like me, people who had come to understand that the "old road map," as Vicki called it, was no longer working. It told of a people who traded the things they held dear for the promises of that old road map: a musician who traded away music for it, a computer programmer who traded her enjoyment of daily life it, young professionals trading away their health for it, and they were all waking up to the fact that the trade wasn't worth it.

These days, there's a whole genera of "money" books about this exact moment of insight. For Rich Dad, Poor Dad co-author Sharon Lechter, the moment came during an argument with her son. She was still stuck to the old road map of a professional education and a corporate job, and her son pointed out that none of the wealthiest people in the world today followed that path! All of our wealthiest business people, athletes, artists, creatives all followed their own quite different roadmap to success.

Of course, many of these money books come with their own new delusions, but there must be some truth to the core idea here that the old life path society laid out for us simply is no longer the best one to follow for many of us.

My current opinion is that it probably has never been all it's cracked up to be. Workers during Victorian industrialism or in the days of the rail road barons certainly didn't have it all too great.

In a longer book, I might make the argument that there was really only a brief golden age of the "modernist" "progressive" economy. During the early days of the 20th century, the working class fought hard, and often gave their lives to secure higher wages, dignity, weekends, unions, labor laws, and vacations. Then, World War 2 mobilized a massive working class of men and women together to take on a massive project, freeing the world from fascism. They won that war. And when they came home, they took on the project of demanding a better deal than their parents and grandparents had. Thus began the golden age. It was defined by a "New Deal," that any one who wanted to work could get a job, and any American who worked would be able to afford a home, have a family, and retire prosperous.

And it appeared that was a wise deal for many of the greatest generation and the boomers who followed. But over time, the deal has become less and less of a bargain.

American Wages Haven't Gone Up in 50 Years

Then and Now

Comparing median costs around 1970 to today

	Around 1970.	In today's dollars. (If CPI were true)	Actual Amount Today.
Median income:	$9,870	$44,229	$44,229
University Tuition:	$358	$1,611	$9700
Car:	$3542	$16,200	$47,000
Gas:	$.36	$1.62	$5.01
Monthly groceries:	$50	$225	$611
Wedding:	$2000	$9,000	$27,000
Child birth, full:	$1,500	$6750	$30,000
(Delivery only).	$256	$1152	$11,000
Cost of an education, House, car, wedding, And 2 kids:	$8950	$40,536	$144,311

To afford this stuff as easily as the median worker in 1970, here's how much you'd have to make:

Compared to 1970, it's simply much, much harder to make the deal work out.

As we stand now in 2022, wages have not gone up in over 50 years. Half a century! Meanwhile, many important costs have out-paced inflation.

And that's because we use the "consumer price index," which we've already said is widely attacked for being skewed in favor of the wealthy. For example, the median income in 1970 was $9870, which according to the CPI, would be $44229 in today's dollars. But looking at our list above, the median cost for many of our most important life expenses has gone up far above the CPI inflation rate! According to CPI, median monthly groceries should only cost $225, but in the real world we're paying $611. A year of university tuition should only be $1611, while students today are paying $9700. If CPI inflation were right, the median new car would only cost $16,000 in today's dollars, when instead the median new car costs about $47,000!

We could call this list of items above the "major life expenses index." To afford these major life expenses associated with the "old deal"—an education, a car, a wedding, and 2 children—the median worker in 1970 could pay for them all with less than 1 year of income. The same would take over 3 years of work today. For a worker today to afford these major life expenses as easily as the median worker in 1970, we'd have to make about $150,000/year. Is it any wonder our debt is now sky high?

Of course, CPI isn't completely wrong! Some costs have come way down, like yachts, personal jets (which were once an unheard of luxury) and plastic surgery. These days our movie stars can all afford great abs, which CPI essentially counts as a trickle-down benefit to all of us movie-watchers.

In seriousness, our "major life expenses index" is not a scientific way of measuring inflation, but for me it is a real measure of the economic realities we face today.

And perhaps it helps explain why research shows that fewer and fewer people are now getting the promise of the New Deal.

According to Pew research, 95% of Americans born in the 1940s earned more than their parents. For the boomers, it was about 90%. For the most part, only those whose parents were at the tip top of earners would generally earn less than their parents. For those of us born around or after 1980, that number has gone down from 90% or higher to just 45%. And yes, that's still using the CPI numbers. If you wanted to use our "major life expenses index," this number would be abysmally low, except for those at the top of the scale.

Meanwhile, we're now working longer hours than ever, and reporting lower levels of job satisfaction for it. In 1970, the average worker reported putting in 39-41 hours of work per week. Fast forward to today, the Average American puts in 47 hours of work per week. And when it comes to the professionals who are more likely doing as well as their parents, they're often working 70 hours per week. All this and we're still failing to keep up with our parents.

And all these trends seem to only be intensifying, not getting better.

So what all this means is that the old road map no longer works for many of us. What we can expect with that path is that we'll have to continually work longer hours with less job security for wages that don't keep up with inflation. If we want to have the same kind of lifestyles that our parents had, then the new money wisdom is right: we are simply going to have to do something different to get there. The map they used to get there is simply not going to reliably get us to the same place.

And if we want to do it without destroying the planet, then we'll also have to redefine what that lifestyle even looks like.

Delusion 2: Anyone can get rich, if they only…

Usually that line ends with "buy my program, class, or business." "Get rich quick" scams are likely as old as, well, getting rich. And yes, the very point is they prey on people who have caught on to the problems of the rat race, and are looking for a way out.

These days, popular get rich quick scams include multi-level marketing cons, NFTs, cryptocurrencies, drop shipping, and various other online gambles.

Here's the thing, it's true that "anyone" might get rich using these techniques. But, these people all know very well that not "everyone" can. In fact, almost all these get rich quick schemes only work for some exactly because they don't work for everyone! The idea of a pyramid scheme is that one person at the top gets rich off many others further down. And "drop shipping" (a popular scheme for becoming an online middleman) only works if you somehow are the only person selling 100,000 toilet seats printed with a picture of Andrew Tate, or whatever is popular this week. If all 10,000 people taking that class ALSO start selling Toilet Tates, then nobody's going to make a million dollars.

And "anyone can get rich" also ignores the idea of privileges, different starting points, and systemic problems we've already discussed in this book. We can't just expect everyone to pull themselves up by the bootstraps and expect that if they don't that's their own fault.

So the truth is we can't all be rich. And another truth is that most people who read money books will never be rich, either. And going even further, trying to get "rich" is probably a terrible goal, and distraction from the kind of achievable goals we might make.

But that doesn't mean we can't create more beautiful, abundant lives, and even truly build a better world. It's absolutely possible for you to set the goal to be truly FREE and to achieve a beautiful and abundant life. But, first we need a holistic, comprehensive plan to get FREE, and then we have to work diligently to create those circumstances. And second, if we're serious about creating a better economy for everyone, then we'll need to work directly on dismantling those systemic problems.

Delusion 3: The key to getting rich is to just invest in the stock market!

While writing this book I've been slogging through a massive number of "money" books, and the active ingredient in EVERY. SINGLE. ONE. boils down to:
1. Stop buying pumpkin lattes.
2. Make more money.
3. YOU MUST THEN INVEST SAID MONEY IN THE STOCK MARKET.

In fact, few of these books even mention any kind of investment other than the stock market (beyond MAYBE becoming a slum lord for profit.)

And then we wonder why those very companies we're blindly investing in are rampaging around destroying the planet like murderous comic book super villains.

AND then those same exact books turn around and say that 90% of people who invest in the stock market actually lose money! In fact, while these "get rich so you can retire when you're 32" books tout the stock market as the way, the average age of people who've made $1 million in the stock market is 70. The stock market is at best a long-term plan.

There's got to be a better way!

The truth is, most of the people I've met who have grown truly beautiful FREE lifestyles have done so (mostly) outside of the stock market. I've actually met many people who have achieved beautiful, abundant lives by investing in things that actually heal the earth and dismantle destructive, oppressive systems. We can do this by finding ways to invest in improving the old economy or by investing in the means of production for a new just and sustainable economy.

Delusion 4: Money Can Buy Happiness.

One of the biggest delusions that keeps us trapped in less than ideal circumstances is that money can buy us happiness. And so, we keep trading away our lives in search of money, so we can finally buy that happiness we're looking for.

We could think of this as the ultimate example of "penny wise, pound foolish." We stress out "pinching pennies" over our pay and purchases, and will drive an extra block if the gas is $0.03 cheaper at the next station! But this whole system is just plain a terrible deal when it comes to getting the things we really want: happiness, security, freedom, peace, vibrant communities, and meaningful connection.

We're like a captive audience at one of those amusement parks that charge $10 of actual legal cash for $7 worth of "park dollars," to buy mediocre items so overpriced you wouldn't pay $5 for them outside the park!

We may groan at the bad deal of the amusement park economy, yet each day we thoughtlessly trade away the very things that we all know (and research confirms) have the biggest impact on obtaining happiness: like free time, time with family, time pursuing our hobbies, time spent in beautiful happy environments. We exchange these riches for cash, then attempt to buy back a little taste of it on vacation each year.

At this point, we have countless studies that demonstrate the bad deal we've all bought into. A 2019 meta analysis found that more free time was more important to happiness than more money, in several studies of thousands of participants.

Psychologists have calculated the value of a happy marriage and family relationships, and found these to be worth the equivalent of $100k/year in terms of happiness. Yet, many of us will sacrifice our family time in pursuit of money and careers. Speaking of careers, having work you love has also been calculated at a value of $100k/year. 9/10 people would be willing to earn less to have more meaningful work. So, if you have happy work, and a happy family, you're already very wealthy! Yet, we'll pass up these tens of thousands of dollars of happiness value in search of a raise to get another couple grand.

Many critics have noted that the American healthcare system is the most expensive in the world, where we spend $12,000/year per person for a quality of care that would cost less than $5000 in any other developed nation. That's a bad deal!

But nobody is talking about our "happiness care" system. American consumers (and this is similar for those of us in the rest of the Western world) only make an average of $31,000/year, yet spend an average of $61k/year on consumer items! No wonder we live in constant debt! But for all that spending we still only come in 16th in "happiness." That's right, we actually use credit cards to spend money we don't have on stuff we don't need, that doesn't even make us happy.

"You buy furniture. You tell yourself, this is the last sofa I will ever need in my life. Buy the sofa, then for a couple years you're satisfied that no matter what goes wrong, at least you've got your sofa issue handled. Then the right set of dishes. Then the perfect bed. The drapes. The rug. Then you're trapped in your lovely nest, and the things you used to own, now they own you."

— *Chuck Palahniuk, Fight Club*

Compare that to the happiest country in the developed world, Finland, where the average income is only $45k USD, but consumer spending is only $26k, allowing each family to save and grow wealthier over time. They get a far better deal, getting much more real satisfaction out of each dollar they spend, and get more financial security in the bargain.

No wonder countless studies have found that once our basic needs are met, more income does not buy more happiness. Using debt, and the stress—and loss of freedom that go with it—to try to buy our happiness is surely a terrible plan.

And if you're reading this from pretty much any country other than the US, you're probably already financially better off, and have better health care, and a better basic safety net. But watch out! The wealthy are keen to export the American system world wide. And no matter where we live, most of us in fields like art, activism, and land-based livelihoods can still benefit by working to build more financially resilient and economically empowered lives. And all of us who want to build a better world should start thinking about how we can build durable power to create change.

If you can't buy happiness, how can you get it?

Alternatively, let's compare the consumption plan to some of the happiest individuals in the world.

To understand happiness, researchers at the University of Wisconsin began conducting brain scans of people around the world. They found that different cultures and different countries had different baselines, such as we've already discussed.

But then they scanned a Buddhist monk. They thought they had found an anomaly: a man so happy that something had to be wrong. This man must have had "happy brain damage," because his happiness was off the charts, despite hardly having any possessions and no "wealth" to speak of.

Then they began looking at other similar monks and found that these folks, often with absolutely no money or financial wealth at all, all had the same happy brain damage!

Don't worry, I'm not going to tell you to join my religion to be happy.

But it appears that when it comes to our actual experience of life, happiness is a skill we can practice and develop, and—once our basic needs are secured —money has little to do with it. They key here is that if you want to be happy, then set aside time and develop some way of practicing it. Practice gratitude. Practice simplicity. Practice a good attitude and upbeat outlook.

Delusion 5: We don't have the Right to Right Livelihood

OR:

It's Okay to Not Die Broke in a Gutter

One of the very first delusions that we need to dispel on our path to a balanced right relationship with money is the notion that money is evil, gross, icky, and something we feel very uncomfortable even thinking about, let alone having.

Many of my farmer, activist and artist friends are notorious for self exploitation. Since money itself feels bad, they subconsciously avoid anything that might be associated with having any.

So, I want to give you some ethical basis for why it's okay to not die of self-imposed poverty in a gutter. And I want to even give you some activist reasons why I actually want you to have enough money to become FREE (Financially Resilient/Economically [and Ethically] Empowered.) Within our particular circles, where "capitalism" often has a very bad name and money is viewed very suspiciously, it's entirely necessary for us to take on this discussion directly.

If you are one of these folks I'm talking about, then I think you are doing some of the most important work out there, finding sustainable ways to feed people, protecting people, advocating for those whose voices aren't heard, creating joy and beauty, documenting the truths of our era... so why do such good people often feel absolutely guilt-stricken over the idea of making a living for doing their work, even though they're doing good things? They may feel like evil "capitalists" for accepting pay, even though in a literal sense no capitalism has actually occurred.

Or, like me, you may have seen folks on social media admonishing such folks for daring to make a living instead of dying broke in a gutter.

Let's be clear: Making a living is not evil. It's not harmful. It's not even "capitalism," not that I'm convinced all capitalism at every scale is inherently evil. Exchange is not "capitalism." Providing a good or service, and asking your community members to value your life, your contribution, and your service is certainly not harmful, nor is it any reasonable person's definition of "capitalism."

These days it's necessary to talk about capitalism, since many people are absolutely opposed to it, but rarely does anyone talk about what it actually is and why they think it's bad.

For the record, in this book "capitalism," is when someone (a "capitalist") "privately" owns some means of "collective" production. For example, if I own a computer company, or Facebook group, and make money off the work of other people laboring to build computers or provide content. I own the tool and profit from other people using it. That is what "capitalism" is.

Capitalism is considered by some to be unethical because there's an argument that if I own a car factory, I am essentially stealing the value of the labor of the folks working for me. I'm making money for not working, off of the work of other people. That is one common definition of "exploitation," and why some people consider capitalism unethical.

In other words, why is capitalism unethical? Because people who don't work steal money from those who do the work for them. Capitalism is bad because of the exploitation.

For me, this is a complicated subject, since I've seen ethical businesses that use hired labor. But I certainly believe that exploitation of labor is a real and unethical thing. I think there are many workers who feel exploited by their employers, and feel they have no choice but to unwillingly agree to the arrangement. I think this is a bad arrangement for workers, and ultimately for the exploitive employers, too, so this particular money book will try to avoid encouraging that kind of arrangement. In other words, this is a (mostly) non-capitalist money book, which is a very strange thing in our society.

So, right off the bat, if you own land and grow vegetables to sell, or make art to sell, or do landscaping work, or rent out a room to provide housing services by your own labor.... and you are not exploiting workers to make money, then there's no argument that you're doing "capitalism," let alone that you're necessarily doing something unethical.

What if you are hiring some labor? Well... you might be a capitalist, but— even though I'm no fan of capitalism—I'm still not convinced you're necessarily doing anything unethical.

While I personally prefer coops and sole proprietorships where possible (so that there's no exploited labor) I argue for giving a bit of leeway to the use of some consensual labor for some small local businesses. I also encourage local businesses to be honest and mindful about this dynamic. But I recognize a difference between a small business owner making a similar income to the happy employees they work beside, and Jeff Bezos making $200,000,000,000.00 off the labor of his miserable workforce. I would make the argument that if everyone is happy, and educated, and no one involved thinks that exploitation is happening, then exploitation probably isn't happening. I meet many artists who are happy to have flexible part time income, community, and respect from a supportive local cafe owner or restaurateur and proud to hang their art on the walls at their workplaces.

These artists working at cafes would never think of their cafe-owning friend making a living by providing a cool community space as doing something necessarily unethical!

Yet I've met many who judge themselves for selling art they themselves made or produce they themselves grew with their own hands! (Again: I say this as someone who has avoided hiring any labor for the last 10 years, and has instead encouraged peer to peer business. And yes, that is exactly the approach we'll emphasize in this book.)

One reason we have this guilt is actually that we have internalized the messages of capitalism: that only corporate produce has value, and only corporate work is "real" and should be paid. Most of us wouldn't think twice about accepting pay from Ronald McDonald for participating in real exploitation, and harming ecosystems to sell crap that makes people sick, yet we feel guilty paying ourselves for our good work! Just ask any hippie gardener "how much for this tomato" and watch the hemming and hawing as they convince themselves to sell you the tomato they'd be absolutely happy to just give you, if only they didn't have bills to pay. They certainly deserve pay for that beautiful tomato!

So here is an ethical basis for paying yourself well for your work: it is revolutionary. It is direct action toward rebuilding healthy, supportive local economies, which is the most important work of our generation. We need to build the kind of economies where people are valued for their contributions, and that means you.

Remember above, we discussed how "capitalism" is a system where "capitalists" own "the means of production" (the businesses and equipment) over practically everything we need to live.

So it is revolutionary for us as workers to directly take back ownership over the businesses in our communities.

And in a way… by giving our work away for free all the time, not only are we exploiting ourselves, we are amplifying this element of internalized capitalism, communicating that the produce of non-corporations has no value, and contributing to the exploitation of others. We may even be directly driving down wages for others when we devalue ourselves.

So in this book, we're asking you to cast off this dominant vague hippie notion that making a living is unethical. That idea has no revolutionary or transformative potential. It has no teeth!

Now this isn't to say we follow the path of certain boomer hippies who burned out on their guilty self-exploiting idealism and turned into yuppie capitalists! The opposite of a bad idea is often not a good idea, but another bad idea. There is a middle path. The path we lay out in this book is for us to directly regenerate our communities and our economies, and there is good money to be made doing it.

A serious, transformative and radical approach is to rebuild those ecosystems of mutual reliance, and directly regenerate control over the means of production of the system we rely upon to meet our needs. It's revolutionary to build a sun-powered, regenerative, solidarity economy, starting with ourselves. It's revolutionary to take care of ourselves so we can take care of others, invest in ourselves so we can invest in others, to grow our community wealth, social and political capital long term in ways that divest from the corporate system, so we can effect real change at the societal level.

Making a living doesn't have to be unethical. By transforming our livelihoods and lives, we can positively transform the world.

The ethic of Transformative Action:

Seek happiness skillfully.

If our holistic Quality of Life statement is our "guiding star," then getting there "skillfully" is our moon, showing us the path through the darkness. There are no simple one-sized solutions here, we must "do the best we can" to grapple our way through difficult terrain, doing the best we can as we go. It's a reminder to hold ourselves accountable, and to keep a deep understanding that if we create a worse world, then we ourselves, and our future generations will have to live in that world. And if our actions create a better world, then we get to live in that better, happier environment.

P3–Toxic Patterns: A Pattern Language for Unethical Ways of Making Money

Since we want people to feel empowered to make great livelihoods, we'll suggest a general rule for making money, that "if nothing unethical is being done, then it's probably ethical." If you're not doing harm, then have at it! Simple as that.

But how do we really know if we're causing harm?

There's a whole tradition of thought on this topic of economic ethics across cultures and going back to Ancient Greece. But it's not something I was ever taught in school. One might get the idea that those in charge don't want people thinking that money can be made in unethical ways!

These are some actions that most economic thinkers agree are ethically problematic. As you consider different investments and livelihoods, running through this checklist can help consider whether the options are truly in line with our values.

1. **Exploitation**. Discussed above, we may experience feeling exploited when others unfairly benefit from our labor against our consent. So, this may happen when we hire other people to do labor. Unfairly profiting off the work of others without fairly contributing ourselves may be exploitation. Of course, if everyone is happy, then in my opinion, probably no exploitation is happening. But if your employee "coworkers" seem unhappy, are unreliable, or have high turn-over, you very well may be engaging in exploitation. When I hear farmers complain about Wwoofers, I suspect exploitation is the reason everyone (including the farmers!) are unhappy.
2. **Resource/Earth Exploitation**. Profiting by using the earth, ecosystems, animals, or resources in a way that harms them, or degrades them for all. To whom does the earth "belong?" If we profit by destroying resources, it may be said that we have stolen from future generations.
3. **Self-exploitation**. Sometimes we exploit ourselves so that others can benefit. We may be doing this to try to help, but in many cases, self-exploitation leads to burnout and potentially other unethical

behavior. People self-exploiting often end up exploiting friends, family members, or "volunteers." Worse, other workers will have to compete with your self-exploitation, causing them to do the same. This contributes to a system where workers are exploited, so self-exploitation is almost always participating in causing the exploitation of others, even though it was done with good intentions.

4. **Over-charging/price gouging.** This is charging more than a fair price. This can be a matter of perspective, since buyers may often feel prices are too high, even while sellers are only barely getting by. Ethical sellers have to compete with the low prices of unethical corporations, which make money by exploitation, and so they don't need to make as much from customers. Ideally, a "free market" should set a fair price, since if someone is overcharging, others will be able to charge less.

5. **Collusion (price fixing.)** This is where businesses form a "cartel" and collude to fix prices, keeping the free market from setting a fair price.

6. **Theft (And appropriation.)** Theft is pretty clearly unethical, taking something that isn't yours and profiting by it. But theft is surprisingly common under the guise of "business." This can include the common activity where wealthy people use political connections to steal public assets like land, air, and water. "Privatization" has often been straight theft. That includes stealing intellectual property rights. I know a few permaculture activists who believe in stealing intellectual property to "liberate it" (for their own economic profit, of course!) Working people worked hard to create these works for us, and we should value their work, not steal it. Most often this is also done by privileged people from middle-class backgrounds. This harms working and low-income people, it doesn't help them. And it makes it harder for activists to honestly support good work. Appropriation is another form of theft where cultural or intellectual assets are taken and profited from.

7. **Profiteering.** This is profiting by the hardships of others. Many American fortunes were made by profiting from war, from natural disasters, and now from Covid. This is an affront to our basic sense of human solidarity and fairness, that we take care of each other when we're vulnerable, not use it to gain advantage and hoard wealth.

8. **Rent-seeking**. This sounds like charging rent, but it is not. Rent-seeking is attempting to gain money without contributing anything of value, and it's one of the top economic sins on this list. The classic example is a bridge troll who charges money to use a bridge built by the community. The troll contributes nothing, but simply charges money for something that was previously free. Some critics say this is the most common economic activity of the wealthy today: finding ever new ways to get money without contributing anything. This has nothing to do with charging rent for housing or tools, which by itself is a perfectly ethical, and helpful activity! Housing and tool rental provides a service of value. Market manipulation is a common form of rent seeking. This one usually goes with other unethical activities, like exploitation. A well-timed press release can cause stocks to soar or plummet, and when this happens, there are billions to be made. This steals money from those who lose in the bargain. Speculators engage in rent seeking when they intentionally invest with the aim of driving up values of things like housing or land. "Planned obsolescence" is a form of rent-seeking we'll discuss in depth later. Ponzi schemes and "credentialing rackets" are rent-seeking behaviors. "Multi-level-marketing" pyramid schemes are rent-seeking behavior that also includes worker exploitation.

9. **Lying/false advertising**. Telling customers that cigarettes are good for their health is clearly unethical. Subtler forms may include mislabeling plants, lying about products, or making exaggerated claims. Planned obsolescence is probably also an example of false advertising.

10. **Usury/loan-sharking/predatory lending**. Considered a crime and sin in many societies, including in the Judeo-Christian bible, usury is growing unreasonably wealthy by unethical or excessive lending. It's related to both exploitation and rent-seeking. Probably as with exploitation, my opinion is that if everyone is educated and happy, probably no usury is going on. Lending a gardener in your community the money to buy seeds and tools is probably not usury. Parents lending their kids money to buy a home probably isn't usury. But the fact that big banks are among our most ludicrously profitable institutions and that people are generally unhappy with them implies that a lot of usury is going on. In fact, we've built a whole economic system upon it! As a system, this unfairly drives up prices, making banks a necessary middle man in buying cars and houses. If people

couldn't get loans to buy houses or cars, then the market would have to price houses and cars such that customers could afford them without loans, and employers would have to pay wages high enough to make this possible. Like our bridge troll above, "credit" is "solution" that only solves the problem that credit itself creates!

11. **Wealth hoarding**? Many thinkers agree that this one may not be unethical by itself, and I tend to agree. This is because it's nearly impossible to accumulate enough wealth for it to be a real problem without doing one or more of the other 10 unethical activities to get there. For example, almost all hoarded wealth was built on exploitation, profiteering, slavery, theft, and/or collusion. But holding onto wealth built in such ways is deeply unethical, even if we ourselves were not the ones doing these crimes.

12. **Big data/data mining/data sales**. While this isn't really a separate violation, it has become so ubiquitous, and it's so problematic, that we're giving it its own number. Data mining is another combination of these unethical activities. Typically, there is deception involved, because people going to play a Facebook game are not really consenting to having their information sold. Then, this information gets used to manipulate people into buying things they don't really need (more deception and rent seeking,) exploiting their labor, and profiteering off of addictive behaviors and biological hacks. What a lousy, unethical way to make a dime.

Delusion 6: Money can buy security

Are we going to tell you that money can't buy security? Well… no.

An honest and balanced approach has to recognize that money indeed buys security—to an extent. As someone who grew up poor, this is something I must admit, and it's one of the reasons for this book. Poverty means we always have to fear our basic needs won't be met, and we may go hungry, we may go without clothes, without shelter, and without basic dignity. Taking responsibility for having our basic needs met isn't greed. In fact, it may make us better people and better activists. It means we will be a boon to our communities, rather than a burden.

But just as more water does us no good once we have enough to quench our thirst, more food makes us unhealthy, and more money doesn't make us any happier, there is a limit to how much security money can buy us. And pursuing more money past that point can actually make us less secure.

That's because there are alternative routes towards security, just as there are towards happiness. What happens if we lose all our hoarded cash in a stock-market crash or natural disaster? Well that depends on whether your neighbors love you or think that you're a money hoarding miser!

True security doesn't come from self-reliance and hoarding cash, it comes from a caring community and rich natural support system. Someone who loses all their money in an economic downturn may worry far less if they live in a supportive community where everyone's basic needs are taken care of, and people value each other based on their intrinsic worth rather than their bank accounts. Those who live in communities where people come together in mutual aid to help each other rebuild may worry far less about natural disasters.

This is how natural systems, natural communities, and communal organisms like ants store their wealth: they give it away. They "leak value" to the beings around them, so that the whole system grows wealthier. As the whole system grows more abundant, there's more excess cash for everyone. The community that grew wealthy off our generosity becomes the piggy bank we need in times of trial.

On the other hand, if we hoard money to the exclusion of investing in our ecosystems, in our family and friends, and in community sufficiency, then our pursuit of money has left us less secure! If through our greed we degrade our environment and communities, then we have depleted our most important natural emergency fund. We'll discuss these alternate modes of building real security in our upcoming chapters.

Beyond this, my friend, Permaculture Designer Dan Wapepah always points out that those who hoard money often end up being the ones who have to worry about having it taken away. Especially those who earn wealth through exploitation and theft. They have to constantly worry that the people they are stealing from may decide to steal something back.

And we have yet another mythological monster to warn us of this exact downfall: the dragon sitting guard of its hoard, earned in violence. Once great, the dragon now must hide in its cave away from the people it has abused, never to leave lest intruders come to take something back. And of course, such a hoard of wealth becomes the quest of many young knights looking to earn their own glory.

Upon his retirement, a great general became a collector of rare Ming Vases. Hearing of an especially rare and beautiful specimen, he traveled across the country to purchase it personally, to secure that the precious piece would be safely transported. Inspecting the piece, and verifying its authenticity, he was overcome… this piece would be the greatest in his collection. As he went to set it down, he slipped briefly and nearly dropped the vase. Terror flashed before him, and in that instant he understood that owning this piece, he would always worry about it and its safety… the vase would own him. With a light and carefree heart, he smiled, relaxed his fingers, and let the vase fall to the floor.

Security and Luna Moth Spirit

As I write this, a war has developed in the heart of Europe, where it was utterly unthinkable for many that there could be another war.

Seeing the images of homes destroyed, and planes crashed onto farm fields, I remember why I've always sought and respected a spirituality that looks bravely out on the world over spirituality that seeks to block out the world and turn inward for security.

We may run from the world but its chaos may crash down upon us at any time. What security does a hoard of money buy when disaster falls from the sky?

And, this is why I've always felt more secure with an approach that turns to community reliance and connection, over an approach that turns away from the world to grow a hoard in the dark. I'm reminded why in our money classes, as in this book, we teach community organizing: our real security, our real peace, our real LIFE is found in reaching out into the world, to each other, even when it's scary.

There once was a famous debate between two zen monks: one implored his students to turn from the world, to cut out the cares of the world, to surround themselves with an environment conducive to cultivating and experiencing deep peace. Just as many "back to the landers" move to the quiet country, away from the cares of the world.

The other monk acknowledged that there is a time and place for that, but said that when the students were truly ready, when they had cultivated a wisdom and inner peace that was true and unshakable, "they will be able travel to even the deepest hell realm, and make flowers there bloom."

We could see these as cocoon spirituality vs luna moth spirituality.

In building its cocoon, the caterpillar stays safe and warm, turned away from the dangers and cares of the world, so that it can grow and transform in peace. We all deserve to take breaks and return to the cocoon to heal and grow. It's okay to give ourselves that permission. And we all deserve to build personal financial security for ourselves, too.

But in leaving the cocoon, the true adventure of life begins. Yes, there are dangers, there will be fights that need fighting, but there are also the wonders of soaring above the garden, drinking the nectar of flowers, dancing with the sky spirits, surrendering to float on the wind, to wherever it may lead.

Imagine the caterpillar so afraid, or so attached to the stillness and security of the cocoon that it never leaves.

Yes, it is safer, but there are still no guarantees, and in the end the great black crow will come for all of us just the same. But safe in its cocoon it will have never felt the flutter of the breeze in its chest, tasted flower wine, felt the sun high over the earth, or learned to trust its life to the wind.

So if the world feels scary right now, it's okay to return to the cocoon, to grow in strength and focus, and to build financial security for ourselves. But for me, I will always do so with the intention to practice being still and happy in my own life OUT THERE in the madness of the world. That requires me to find a way to trust my life to the wind, to fully look at and acknowledge the chaos, the injustice, the wrongs of the world, and the anger and pain that come with them and then committing to righting them, to contributing something good and beautiful.

The only true and lasting peace is that which we can find on the chaos of the wind. In finding it, we may also return to dance with the sun, the flowers, and the other radiant beings of the sky.

P4–Patterns and Adventures for Growing Security

The Solid Base

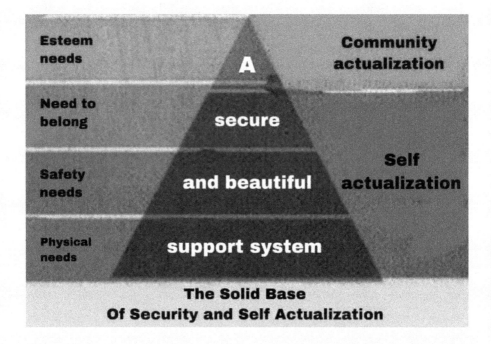

The Solid Base
Of Security and Self Actualization

We want you to succeed gloriously on your adventure to create a better life and a better world. To do that, one of our first jobs is to make sure you don't fail miserably before you've even begun.

This is the part of our journey where we tell you how to be prepared for when things don't go according to plan.

After setting goals and envisioning a better life, starting out with a "solid base" for our adventures is our very next important step.

The "solid base" is a vibrant and secure support system. It's what we get when we recognize the wisdom of founding our lives simultaneously on both having a secure situation that meets our physical needs, and setting the goal to create a better community for all. So any smart path of self-improvement can start with activities that work towards self-actualization and community permanence together. This gives us a truly strong foundation for following our dreams.

In Transformative Adventures programs, we always start with work on the "solid base," whatever we're doing. People in gardening or herbalism programs often ask "where do we start?" And over decades of teaching, it has become clear that if our families and personal situations aren't in order, any big project is likely to fail. So the solid base means getting ourselves ready for the project by spending some time on our support systems and networks. And of course, that means tuning into our own most basic financial situation, too. This will give us some basic financial security from which we can complete our quests and build our wealth, without the worry that we'll hit a disaster just out of the start.

A brief Solid Base self-assessment:

Rate your own situation on each of these areas on a 1-5, with 1 being poor and 5 being very secure. This will show you the areas you may wish to work on. We're rarely encouraged to be proactive about making sure our basic needs are being taken care of.

1. You basic physical needs:
___food access. ___ your housing. ___ Water access.

2. Your safety needs:
___ Do you feel safe in your location and work?

3. Your Self Actualization needs:
___ Do you have space for self actualization activities?

4. Community Actualization needs:
___ Do you have projects that bring you into community?

5. Belonging needs:
___ How are your family and friend relationships? Are there any that need attention?

Some adventures for building the solid base. Each of these grow our resources at the intersection of our personal needs and community actualization:

1. Start a Transformative Landscape like a food forest garden.
2. Start a community forest garden.
3. Start a Meet-up for something you enjoy, like board games, hiking, biking, gardening, etc.
4. Get involved in local organizations that are working on issues you care about.
5. Start a weekly family event like a game night or other activity.
6. Learn to forage, and start a monthly or weekly group foraging meal with friends.
7. Start a garden mutual aid group where you volunteer to help each other in your gardens 1 day a week, and share produce.
8. Start a meal-prepping club on Sunday nights, where you and some friends get together for a few hours, and prepare meals for the week to save time and money.
9. Start a coupon and sales sharing group where you all look out for local savings opportunities.
10. Start a Growing FREE reading group dedicated to helping each other on your paths to getting FREE.
11. Start a bulk buying club for groceries.
12. Get involved in some kind of community recreation like community theater, a sporting league, etc.
13. Start going to your neighborhood association meetings.
14. Start a blog about local politics and environmental news by going to local meetings, covering upcoming meetings, posting agendas and so on. This is sorely needed and can instantly make you an information rich part of the community.
15. Walk around your neighborhood and pick up garbage. Say hello to all your neighbors.
16. Start a club for home improvement. You might find opportunities to share tools, work together, learn about the same tasks, and share costs.

Adventure 2: Slush/Emergency Fund

One of the more important "bricks" in our secure base for our journey is having an emergency fund to help us deal with any bumps in the road.

The conventional financial advice is to have 3-6 months expenses on hand at all times. If you cut into this, then your first goal should be to save this up again.

This should be in a savings or checking account where it is fairly "liquid," meaning it's easily accessible and can be quickly converted to cash. Some people like to keep $1000 or so of this in easily accessible cash.

Keeping this emergency fund should always be a high priority. My first great financial mentor put a number on it: $5000. In today's dollars, that's probably $6000, but for many of us, $5000 will probably still do. But if $5000 is just one month's necessary expenses for you, then $15-30k will probably be better.

This is not just good financial advice. This is great emotional, relationship, and spiritual advice.

This most basic brick of our secure base does so much to allow us to relax, allow us to begin to feel FREE, and to be able to act out of a mindset of abundance, rather than one of scarcity and panic that is known to cause us to make poor long-term decisions.

Save $5000? That Seems Impossible. I Guess I Can Quit Reading This Book and Give Up Now

Well, don't give up!

But, being very honest, this first top priority of saving up about $5000, is not just important for our security.

It is also an important opportunity to take stock of our financial situation and where we're at on the path to our dreams.

Some people may be reading this and already have $5000 or more in savings. If that's you, congrats! You can skip ahead to the next section if you like.

Others may be reading this and thinking, "well, we'll have to tighten our belts for a while, but we should be able to save this much in a year if we do X, Y, and Z...." For these folks, this is the first important chance to start flexing the savings muscles, by looking at the patterns for frugality in this book. It will be the first chance to actually practice making a plan for saving, and following through. At the end, when you reach that $5000, you can throw a little party to celebrate, and it will feel great. If you can save up $5000, you know what you need to do to meet whatever goals you set.

But for others, saving up $5000 will seem impossible.

You may quickly go over your expenses and income, and figure that at best —with no emergencies and no pleasure spending— it would take 10 years to save $5000. Or perhaps even that seems impossible, stuck in a situation living paycheck to paycheck.

If that's the case, let that sink in for a minute. Ask yourself: if it will be such a struggle just to establish an emergency fund, is it realistic to meet your financial and other life goals, or prioritize your highest values? Will you have the resources to prioritize the quality of work you'd really like to do on the topics you're passionate about?

If this is you, you're not alone. I meet many folks in this situation in my classes.

Hope for the Self-Employed

Some folks I meet have jumped into farming or going full time as artists or self-employed activists, and now they're stuck working long hours and cutting corners each month just to make ends meet. They may have little hope of saving any money at all.

Their first step may be to ask whether they can realistically meet their career and work goals in this situation. Or do they need to step back from that work a little, and prioritize getting financially secure first? Perhaps they'll need to look for a part-time job, or a "side hustle," or a temporary full-time job, so that they can return to their real work from a more secure base.

Or perhaps you realize that even a side hustle or temporary influx won't change your long-term ability to meet your goals. There simply isn't enough income coming in, and—beyond wild experiments—you don't have a concrete plan to get that cash flowing in.

In that case, it may be time to evaluate your business or career, and give it a thorough economic feasibility assessment. (There's an adventure for that later in this book.) Then you may decide that it's time to try something else, whether that's trying new approaches to the business, or perhaps trying something else altogether.

It's important to realize that whether you're doing a land-based business, working as an artist, an activist, or some other "privileged" position, there are folks out there—who are no more talented than you are— doing exactly what you're doing and they're making lots of money doing it. I know self-employed artists out there, with no art education, no special training, and no special background, who work full time as artists and make hundreds of thousands of dollars a year just selling their art at art fairs on weekends. I know activists who make similar money off their work, working for themselves while tackling topics they're passionate about.

And I know plenty of folks doing regenerative land-based work who are also doing just as well, (though none of them are doing that with conventional approaches to "farming.")

Which brings us to the point of what these folks are doing differently: they're starting with the solid base and their financial goals first. They've figured out how to make money doing what they want to do.

If they're making big money selling art at fairs, it's usually because they're making a compromise with their communities, and prioritizing art that will sell. That doesn't mean "selling out," or that they're not also doing work they're passionate about, that is cutting edge and important. In fact, it could be that they've found a way to reach a significant audience with the message they want to get out, or they may even consider that audience part of their "terroir," that gives them their identity. But rather than living in poverty to do the work of their passion, they are prioritizing "solid base" first, then working on their passions from a resourced, and secure situation. Given the choice, where would you rather be?

And the same is true for these other endeavors. You can either keep banging your head against the wall in a financial dead end situation, simply hoping that somehow things will change, or you can make a plan to "profit first" with your endeavors, so you can work from a solid base. If you need to re-evaluate your business, you will find many tools at the end of this book to help you do so. But I hope you will decide to invest in yourself and your work this way, so that you can give your work the best possible chance of having an impact on the world, and yourself the best possible chance for succeeding.

Hope for Those Stuck in Gainless Employment

Still others I meet are stuck working dead-end, low wage jobs just to pay the bills, and see no way out. Or perhaps they are at the start of their journeys, stuck with degrees that have few opportunities, or just a high school education, and no interest in or ability to pursue the college path.

And now you are reading this book because you have goals or dreams for the future, and you want to build a realistic path to getting there, not just live off "hopes and prayers" that somehow your dreams will fall into your lap.

Michael Shuman's book *Put Your Money Where Your Life Is* is
It's your time to take stock. Do you see a realistic, concrete plan for how you'll get where you want to go and accomplish your goals? Can you even save up $5000?

If not, what are the options you have for moving forward?

—Can you simply get a better job? Can you ask for a raise? Can you establish a great work record, let your bosses know you want to work on being more valuable to the company and ask them what you can do to advance with the company? If not, how can you build the "social capital," networks, and good references you need to get a better paying job? The section in this book on "capitalism survival strategies" can help you make a concrete plan to do this, and get a better paying job. (XXX)

—Is going back to school your best option? You don't have to go to school for something you hate. Read this book and pay special attention to the section on "skill stacking," because you could get training in work that can both cash flow, and help you achieve your long-term life goals. For single parents and those with families, this is surprisingly sometimes the best option, as you may be eligible for grants and loans to help make ends meet while you retrain.

—Are there community programs to help? Many communities have programs especially for those in tough life situations, to help us get out of trouble and help us meet our goals. Are there people you can talk to about resources?

—Is a "side hustle" an option? See the section in this book on low-skill, part-time jobs that can make real money.

—Do you simply need to recognize that your life energy, your time, and your skill are worth more than what you are being paid for?

—Do you need to just demand better for yourself, and go to where your work will be rewarded with better compensation?

But whatever your situation, if you're stuck in gainless employment with no hope of achieving your goals, you either need to have a concrete action plan, or accept that you're not going to reach your goals. The choice is yours.

A Note for Artists, Entrepreneurs, Activists, and Others Who Don't Own Land (and Don't Want to)

Heads up: in this book we'll talk a fair bit about land-based incomes and things like self-reliance.

This is in part because self-reliance can be good for saving money and building wealth, and a lot of my mentors who were successful in art and activism fields used these techniques to secure the FREEdom to do their work. And of course, I think a lot of the audience for this book are probably already keen on exactly that idea.

But it's not necessary to have these land-based incomes or self-sufficiency techniques. And, more to the point, it's not necessary to own a house or land to be self reliant, grow food, or make money off of land-based investments! We will talk about these things a lot, but certainly don't think we consider them mandatory.

Basic Health Care for Americans

We'll go into more detail later (on pages XXX,) but if you're an American, congratulations, you have the world's most dysfunctional health care system. And while everyone else in the world either has more affordable costs or significant help from their countrymen, you'll have to plan for the world's highest health care costs and a government that seems determined to do everything possible to make accessing health care as difficult as possible. And if you don't get it right, you'll face a higher risk of losing everything than you would almost anywhere else. So health care has to be its own important consideration.

For now suffice it to say that as your personal wealth grows, and you have more to lose, the need for some sort of health insurance rises.

And because the American system is constantly shifting and changing, it's difficult to offer very concrete advice.

But for most of us pursuing Financial Resilience and Economic Empowerment, some minimum strategy to mitigate risks is important. Many choose a high deductible based on our "emergency fund," to minimize our healthcare overhead (and payments that go to support a bloated corporate bureaucracy with little service in return.)

CHART PATTERNS IN THIS BOOK FOR DIFFERENT BACKGROUNDS AND GOALS

We hope this book is about "transforming" your financial situation, which means starting wherever you are, with exactly what you have, and getting to where you want to go. We hope that whatever your background, you will find tools, patterns, and adventures that will help you do that. And there are a few common starting points and goals that folks may come to this book with, so we'd like to help direct you to some specific parts of this book.

Mike will create infographic: List the Patterns and Adventures for...

XXX
...those who don't own a home.
...those who don't want to own a home.
...those who want to own a home.
...artists.
...farmers, homesteaders, and others looking to live off the land.
...unemployed or underemployed folks
...those approaching retirement.
...those who don't want to run any kind of business.
...those who are deep in debt.

Delusion 7: Hoarding Money Makes Us Wealthy

One of our biggest delusions is that hoarding money makes us rich.

It doesn't.

In fact, hoarding money makes us lose wealth as inflation eats away at our earnings over time. Throughout this book, we'll see that those of us on the lower end of the economic spectrum focus almost entirely on income and accumulating money. But over time, our incomes, and money are worth less and less, keeping us stuck on the rat race treadmill.

Meanwhile, the wealthy certainly hoard wealth, but they don't hoard money! Again, this is a great myth. Instead, they hoard assets, which they use to finance loans to buy more assets. All this borrowing increases the money supply, which drives inflation, making your money worth less and their assets ever more valuable.

The whole system is like a pump that constantly distributes wealth from the lower classes who live off exchanging money, to the people who own the assets, or "means of production."

So a key strategy in this book for transforming our lives and our society is to stop thinking of jobs, income, and money, and start thinking of investing in "means of production."

We could see this as another "stocks and flows" system problem, where we over-emphasize the stocks and under-appreciate the flows. And so, it is not hoarding money that makes us wealthy, but letting it flow, or what our grandmothers called "sharing."

What would make you feel truly "wealthy:" having lots of money but living in a community with poverty, crime, disease, crumbling houses? Or having less spare cash, but living in a community with no poverty, no homelessness, little crime, and beautiful homes and neighborhoods?

Ecological research shows the most successful species do not hoard resources, they "leak" wealth to the beings around them. They collect resources in very inefficient ways in which the resources leak outwards to support a rich community network. Plants produce far more mass than they need to live, and more seeds than they need to procreate, and a myriad of beings flourish off that excess. Squirrels gather and bury far more nuts than they'll eat, helping to plant forests that will support more squirrels. Trees produce more calories through photosynthesis than they need, then secrete them through their roots to share with fungi and other trees. Successful beings in an ecosystem store energy in their community to grow wealthy.

And yet we humans get stuck in a mindset of hoarding money instead of sharing it, which impoverishes our communities and world. If plants, squirrels, and trees acted this way, the world would be a dessert! We cling to cash even while we create that degraded world that we then must live in. Imagine the positive good that could be done if someone like Elon Musk decided to just share a tiny amount of his billions of dollars.

Throughout this book, we'll explore different strategies to help us grow wealth by getting better at sharing, like investing in holistic forms of wealth (XXX,) and growing our personal gift economy (XXX).

Delusion 8: Buying Status and Respect with Money.

In Walden, Henry David Thoreau said "he who walks gets there first." He was doing an exercise familiar to folks in financial circles: calculating the "real costs" of a thing. For example, many people feel stuck in jobs they hate because they feel like they're making a lot of money. We call that "golden handcuffs." But when they calculate the costs of their job, like living in an expensive area, buying expensive clothes, expensive commutes, and long hours, they find that in reality they'd be making more money if they worked at a local cafe or book store. Especially if they figure in how much they'd pay for more free time, more time with family, or a livelihood they loved.

As it turned out, with the cost of a train ticket in Thoreau's time, one would have to work a month to cross the Eastern states. But one could walk anywhere and back in less time. So, "he who walks gets there first," before the person who got a job to take the train.

Now bear with me here, but I've come to think the same applies to achieving the real respect of our communities.

Of course, a certain amount of self-reliance is important, which is why we're writing this book. But once we have the resources to help ourselves and contribute to our communities, we're better served by showing up than spending money.

Yet again, using money to buy respect is just a poor deal!

When I think of the people I most admire in this life, none of them are ludicrously well-to-do. It appears money does not correlate with how much I respect people. Is the richest person you know the person you respect most?

The people I most respect are the people who showed up in my life, even when it was hard, and who lived well and taught me to live well and beautifully, too. They're people who have chosen to live, be creative, and care for people, instead of hoarding financial wealth. They're the people who inspired this book.

Why on earth do we look to wendigos to learn how to "make a livelihood?" As if Warren Buffet or whatever "get rich quick" influencer is trending on social media this week has any clue about how to help people like you and me to grow more financial resilience! Why would people who started off rich, famous, and well-connected, and then made obscene money as wendigos destroying the planet, have even the faintest idea of how to help somebody who started with nothing and who wants to become FREE while not making the world a worse place? Instead of respecting these wendigos, we should raise up the real people in our lives who have figured out how to have enough without becoming monsters. Those are the people I most respect, and they're the ones we'll learn about in this book.

Looking beyond my personal sphere, even at the heights of the most respected humans through history, few were phenomenally well-to-do with financial wealth. Think of Mother Theresa, of Ghandi, of Martin Luther King Jr. Nelson Mandela, the Dalai Lama, the world's great artists, musicians, and religious teachers. None of these had great riches!

Meanwhile, when most of us think of the mega wealthy—even on the scale of our own communities—there's mixed feelings about it.

As it turns out, most people around the world spontaneously rank the people in their communities with the greatest financial wealth right alongside those in the greatest poverty. On an instinctive level, we understand that mega-riches are usually a form of hoarding, more a mental illness than an accomplishment.

And Michael Shuman's book *Put Your Money Where Your Life Is* is almost always comes with an asterisk, (*how much was inherited wealth, privilege, and money gained via unethical activity? Did this wealth come from the slave trade? From blood diamonds, like Elon Musk? From war profiteering?) Most of our great hoards of wealth were accumulated through war profiteering, through theft of indigenous lands, through unethical treatment of labor, and then passed down through the ages.

Meanwhile, what really earns respect is showing up. It's being present in the lives of those around us, doing our part to help, doing our part to tune into our moral compass and do the right thing.

Which is all easier if we're not spending long hours "hustling" in pursuit of more excess wealth. And the kind of respect we earn by showing up is a kind that money just can't buy.

And yet, many of us will still have to overcome hangups around the delusion that money can buy us what we need in terms of respect.

P5–Patterns for Processing "Status"

Back to Henry David Thoreau. Henry's lifestyle of purpose, freedom, and simplicity has inspired countless people to grow FREE themselves, not to mention, being cited as an influence for civil rights movements in India, Africa, and North America. His choices had a major influence on the lives of all of us writers of this book! We're incredibly thankful for this genius.

And yet, there were certainly many who considered it an incredible waste for a Harvard man to plot an alternate course, instead of getting a mainstream job and home. Even today, there are still people who—despite his long-lasting accomplishments—think he was just a bum in a shack without a job.

The truth is, not everyone will understand the choice we're making to opt out of the mainstream dream of BUYING status with conspicuous consumption. In fact, some people in our lives may recoil strongly from it. Often, people flip flop from extremes, like *hippies* who went from teen-age dreams of extreme simple living and boomeranged back to the other extreme of *yuppie* consumption. This creates a strong cognitive dissonance for them. Our rejection of their choice may feel like a condemnation. And perhaps they themselves have doubts. Such friends and family members may give us heavy-handed feedback to "just get a regular job!" Even though many things have changed since the 60s. This may say more about their uncertainty over their own choices than about the choice we're making.

Family members who abandoned arts or music careers for the conformity of a banking job may feel the same exact cognitive dissonance, and express the same kind of judgment.

One of my deans at a college I taught at once ridiculed me for wearing a T-shirt for a rock band I played in on weekends. When I untangled this comment, he told me that he had actually been a music major in college with big dreams. It was clear that giving it up was painful for him. "We all have to grow up sometime," he said bitterly. Everyone in the department would remark about how bitter he seemed and how much he seemed to hate his job.

With people like this, the "money delusion" is theirs, not ours. And so we must face the very real repercussions of losing respect or getting criticized because of THEIR hangups.

"It feels like dying." That's how one friend put it. She was at the precipice of the FREE lifestyle she always wanted, but simply could not quit the "good job" that she absolutely hated. Her family and affluent friends considered it a "good job" and it paid for a "good home" and a "good car" that she felt bought her respect and status. And as much as she hated that job, the thought of losing that respect and status in the eyes of her network "felt like dying."

Try communicating your dreams and asking to be respected: If we have specific people we're dealing with, then an important step is to try communicating with them directly. Perhaps let them know that you hear their concern about your financial life, and that you also take that seriously, but that you are trying to design a life where you can have financial security and do work that is important and meaningful to you. Consider telling them directly that you need them to respect your decisions to follow your dreams.

Slacking is important work! Of course, I'm using that word "slacking" with a bit of sarcasm. But in a society with sick, addictive ideas about work—one where we work so much we're actually less productive because of it—then figuring out how to work less and model that is truly important work! We absolutely need people to boldly take this step and show others how to do the same. And just as people taking the leap before me have inspired me to do the same, someday our model will help set others FREE. That is one of the most vital "jobs" I can think of in the world today.

Focus on FREEdom. Remember why you're making your choice. Many people say they value freedom, but they don't actually take that very seriously. We're actually taking that seriously. We're prioritizing freedom, time, and good work over false status.

Don't judge others for lack of money. If we judge others for a lack of money, the same mental habit ends up coming back to us. Besides, when we judge others for not having money, we might miss out on the opportunity for their social capital! In this book, we'll discuss "non-monetary capital." Folks who lack money often have lots of time and skills that could be put to use in our community-building efforts! Similarly, keep in mind that when people judge you, they may lose out on your help, too. That's their loss!

You are joining the community of the truly FREE. "She who chooses not to compete—nobody can compete with her." Throughout human history, there has always been this brave community of the shamans, the hedge witches, sages, saints, and noble ones, who have lived at the margins to teach others the path to FREEdom and real riches. These are the people who have risen above the delusions of mainstream society, to find true wealth. We join the ranks of these noble ones.

You have my respect. You inspire and astonish me. With the rise of ever more manipulative social media, it is getting harder and harder to break free from conformity to consumer culture. And yet you are reading this book, plotting your escape. Every day, it is people just like you who inspire me and give me hope. You have my deepest respect.

Focus on your real community. Just as some people will always see Thoreau as an unemployed bum in a shack, some people will just never get our choice, no matter how much we'd like them to. They have their path, we have ours. But as you plot your own bold path, people who DO respect you will flock to you. People who see what you're doing and want the same will respect the hell out of you.

"I know there are some people in my family who will never understand my choices, but then I see my students, and my community members, and I know they have great respect for me." —Jason

Do your inner work, talk to people, therapy might help. In the end, this is part of your journey. You always knew that making your own way would mean breaking free from the expectations and projections of other people who are stuck in conformity. This is your life. And this is your work. Talk to others on the path. Talk to friends. Working through this kind of issue with a therapist may open up whole new ways of thinking and being in the world.

> *I shall be telling this with a sigh*
> *Somewhere ages and ages hence:*
> *Two roads diverged in a wood, and I—*
> *I took the one less traveled by,*
> *And that has made all the difference.*
> *—Robert Frost*

Wealth in the form of a full cabinet of home-grown herbs, spices, medicines, and seeds.

Delusion 9: "I'm Terrible with Money."

Somehow, most of us reading (and writing) this particular book have internalized the message that we're just plain bad with money. If we were "good" with money, and knew enough about it, then we wouldn't need this book and we'd already be loaded, right?

Meanwhile, we imagine there are all these other people out there who are just "good with money," they have loads of it and they're not worried about it. They must know some important truths about money that we just have never learned!

But take a closer look at this idea. The main idea here is that money is a measure of merit, that being "good" with money is the key to having loads of it. In other words, it's part of the belief that skill and wealth are correlated.

This faith in meritocracy is one of the leap-of-faith beliefs that makes the world of capitalism go 'round. Without it, we simply would not accept gross inequality. Without it, we would not simply accept the leadership of the "great men" with the money to make the decisions and impose them on the rest of us. Without this, we would not easily sacrifice our own life time and energy so that those above us on the social hierarchy can live in extravagance.

But in reality, this belief is ludicrously, demonstrably false.

These days, we have babies who are born with billion dollar trust funds and destined for inheritances bigger than most hard-working American neighborhoods will earn in their whole lives. It should be quite obvious to even the most devout believer in the faith of "meritocracy" that a billionaire baby was born with no more skill, work ethic, or market value than all the bankrupt babies out there. The inequality between a billion dollar baby and one with literally a billion times the wealth should be enough to dispel the idea that wealth correlates with merit. But consider the other examples in this chapter, folks who have done amazing life work like Ghandi and Mother Teresa who died with hardly any wealth to their names. Or perhaps think of great artists like Mozart or Van

Michael Shuman's book *Put Your Money Where Your Life Is* is Gogh, who died penniless despite outstanding skill.

So, let's be done with the myth of meritocracy. And further, let's look at the specific idea of skill with money.

Are the wealthy really "better with money?"

The media is filled with persistent stories that the wealthy are in reality just more frugal than all the spend-thrift poor in the world. We get the idea that every billionaire is an Ebenezer Scrooge, choosing to forgo winter heat and decent food to prudently save up some hard-won cash.

But the reality is that the top 20% of Americans spend an average of $31,000 a year on their rent or mortgage costs for their primary homes. That is more than folks in the bottom 80% spend on all their core needs (housing, food, transportation) combined. Prior to Covid, the lowest quintile Americans, whom the media casts as careless spendthrifts, spent around $4000/year on food. Meanwhile, the top 20% spent over $12,000, 3 times as much. What about transportation? According to Consumer Expenditure Research data, the lowest quintile spend about $3000/year on transportation. The wealthiest 20% meanwhile, spend about 5 times as much each year. And while nearly 60% of the lowest income Americans don't even have cars, about 50% of the upper crust have more than 2 cars.

So, are these folks with more rooms in their houses than they can use, and more cars than they need actually "better with money?" No! The data shows they're actually worse with money than the rest of us.

Meanwhile, those of us without loads of hoarded wealth likely use our money more frugally, and more beneficially. We are the ones who are "better with money," because we are not engaging in the wasteful and socially destructive behavior of hoarding wealth.

So we do not need to be "good" with money. We're not bad with money to begin with!

What we really need is to start thinking strategically about money, by recognizing that we live in a society that is inherently unequal, unfair, and classist. And what we need is a revolutionary strategy to claim our own financial rights and freedom for ourselves, our families, and communities, within a system that is rigged against us.

Wealth in the form of homegrown produce, *from a low-maintenance, low-work Permaculture forest garden that only takes a few hours of work per week to grow a complete diet.*

Delusion 10: Meritoracy—"We Make Money the Old-Fashioned Way, We Earn It."

If one myth is that we are poor because we simply deserve to be, then the opposite side of that mythical coin is that the wealthy are where they're at because they also deserve it.

As we already pointed out, we live in a society with billion dollar trust fund babies and those born with less than nothing. Some of us face economic barriers due to the way we look, our sexual orientation, identity, or color of our skin, and all of these have proven impacts on our ability to accumulate wealth in this culture.

A whole host of modern research now shows that the class we're born into is the biggest indicator of our earning potential, and upward mobility has largely reversed since the 1940s. In many countries, people are well aware of this fact, though many North Americans still believe otherwise. According to social scientist Fabian Pfeffer, "Especially in the United States, people underestimate the extent to which your destiny is linked to your background." (Mobility Regimes and Parental Wealth.) "Research shows that it's really a myth that the U.S. is a land of exceptional social mobility."

Today the top 10% of Americans own 70% of the total wealth, and just 1% own 32% of all wealth. The top 1% own 57% of all businesses, according to the Federal Reserve, and they gained $6.5 trillion last year alone.

And if you really want to go down the rabbit hole, do an internet search for "fractional reserve banking," which is the way money is created in the modern world (there are several good Youtube videos on this little-known truth.) The bizarre fact is that the wealthiest Americans, through ownership of banks, essentially get to create money when they need it. In a fractional reserve system, on paper, banks need to have 10% of a loan in the bank to write the loan. In other words, to write a $1,000 loan, they need to have $100 in the bank. So banks can create $900 to write a loan. But that $100 "in reserve" can be money that the bank or another bank itself created. According to the federal reserve, the 10% rule "does little to limit the money creation ability of banks."

Of course, it's not exactly like rich people are just printing off money to give to themselves, are they? Well, the system does follow rules, and the big rule is that this created money must be profitable. How profitable is creating money? Well, 4 of the 10 most profitable companies are banks, and even some of the others, like Apple and Amazon are getting involved in providing banking services, too.

More importantly, where does this money go? According to Bank of America, nearly 19% goes to corporate loans, which are mostly owned by the top 1%, another 19% goes to commercial loans, which are again mostly owned by the top 1%. About 10% goes to residential mortgages, and we just saw that the wealthy spend far more on mortgages than the rest of us. Only about 15% goes to credit cards and car loans, the most democratic, and also the most predatory, with the highest interest rates. Meanwhile, the wealthy typically don't take out high interest loans for cars! We give them big tax-break loopholes for buying them outright.

In other words, if you're wealthy, you're immersed in an environment where money is cheap and easy to come by, it's often given directly to you by the government, and if you need more, it can be made out of thin air by your acquaintances in the banks. If you're not wealthy, money is much harder to come by.

So the point of all this isn't to be discouraging. Any of us can indeed improve our financial resilience and freedom! But we do need to be realistic. Achieving our goals isn't just about "following the rules" and "being good with money." It means we may have to think about changing some of the rules, and thinking radically about changing the unfair systems we're trapped in. And if we care about the future and the wealth of our children, we may need to take political action to transform these systems for all, instead of thinking we can just "play the game." The game is rigged, and we need to play accordingly.

Adventure 3: Set the Goal to Really Transform

At this point in your journey, it is time to go beyond thinking you're just reading this book. In fact, that may be exactly the current goal you've set "finish this book." In a way, that's another brute force tactic, measured in the number of pages you turn.

Instead, we hope you'll set a more important and personal goal: to become more knowledgeable and wise about money.

That means if you want to change your outcomes with money, you need to think of consciously changing some of your current attitudes, goals, and paradigms around money. If these don't change, nothing else is likely to change. Just turning pages in a book isn't likely to do much.

You may also consciously think of how you can apply pressure at all different leverage points. What will you do to change your behaviors, your systems, your goals, your paradigms? Set a goal of finding ways to change all of these.

Good! Now that you've set that goal, consider doing something small to celebrate. And, when you complete this goal, by knowing that you've changed some of these important leverage points, that will also be worth celebrating.

Chapter Resources:

1. Meadows, Donella. Thinking in Systems. Chelsea Green. 2008

2. Story, David. Systems Thinking for Social Change. Chelsea Green, 2015.

Chapter 3: Our Strategy for Transforming our Lives and Communities

After talking about our society's money myths and all these conspiracy-sounding systemic issues, our main strategy for societal transformation should be pretty clear already: we believe in taking direct action to transform our destructive economic system right at its core, it's basic systems, assumptions, and even questioning the basic paradigms it's built upon. We believe that we together can recreate a new, holistic, healthy economy, and make the old, dystopian economy obsolete.

And that same is our strategy for transforming our lives.

But to do that, we must first get a better understanding of the nature of the trap that we as individuals, and collectively as a society are caught in. If we understand the trap, we may better understand how to get out.

So we must journey into the deep, dark heart of the wild wood, under old growth forest, with cool, quiet air, the caw of a crow, and soft moss underfoot. There, we may find the wisdom to set us free.

Because this is one of the few places left that make sense in a modern machine of "consumers" and "consumption" that seems to be doing its darndest to consume all of us.

Behind you now! This is a dangerous path we're on and it is guarded. Feel the claws gently scrape on your shoulders? Do not look! Feel its breath at your neck? Hear the rumble in its stomach? It's toying with you—don't look! You would never see it anyway, because it's only in your imagination.

And we wouldn't want to anger it.

So, quick! Forget it's there. Focus back on the path before us, to the wood, the crow, the sound of cold water flowing gently over stones and sand nearby. We must travel to the heart of the wildwood, to find imaginary allies to fight imaginary foes in an imaginary war, that—though it is only in our

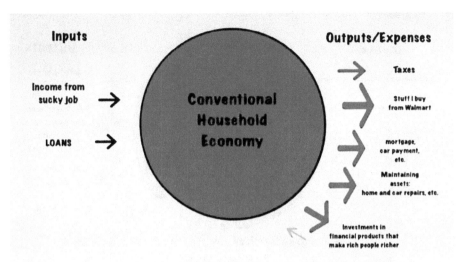

Money in one side, money out the other. Stuff on the right side keeps getting more expensive. If stuff on the left side doesn't go up too, we're screwed.

imaginations—is nevertheless heating the planet, polluting our waters and air, and killing us all.

We'll need a map.
Take up a stick and sketch into the sand.
Or, if you'd rather, a pen and paper will do.

How would you sketch the landscape of your own personal economy? What does your financial life look like? This is the map we'll need.

For me, several years ago it looked like this. Let's begin by drawing a circle in the sand. This represents "my money," my bank accounts, the cash in my wallet, and so on.

On one side of the circle, we'd have the money coming into my bank accounts, and on the other side, the money going out to pay for my wants and needs. This includes my taxes, the stuff I used to buy at Walmart, my mortgage or rent, and car payments, maintenance costs, and so on. If you'd like, you can be detailed about sketching out all your expenses, since we'll do that later on.

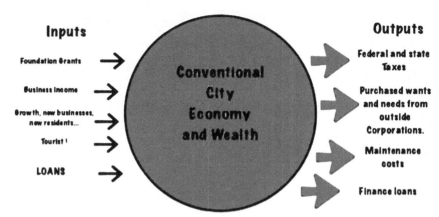

Inputs

Foundation Grants →

Business income →

Growth, new businesses, new residents... →

Tourist ! →

LOANS →

Conventional City Economy and Wealth

Outputs

Federal and state Taxes

Purchased wants and needs from outside Corporations.

Maintenance costs

Finance loans

If outputs are greater than inputs, the City is in decline. Basically, duh.

Remember the "bathtub analogy" diagram from our section on systems thinking? We've just sketched our financial life as a simple system.

This is the way most of us see our basic household economies. So, as we talk about societal change, it's important to realize that most of us would sketch our money design in ways that look just like this. If we can change our own landscapes, we have a map others in our society can use as well.

That's one important point of our strategy for societal transformation: our individual escapes, when put together collectively, become a mass exodus.

Moreover, this is also the way most of our communities function. The conventional city economy is conceived of as the city coffers, with inputs on one side, and outputs on the other.

What we are looking at is a sketch of the basic trap we all find ourselves in. Dependent on money from "the system" in order to meet our needs from "the system." This is a sketch of a sort of chain, which keeps us tied to lives we don't like, and keeps us from the things that really matter.

This is not really surprising, since even Adam Smith pointed out in Wealth of Nations, corporations (the main economic institution of our system) were created as instruments of colonial warfare and control. It's a strategy that goes back to the earliest days of colonialism.

Controlling people through violence is hard work. And well, it costs lives, which makes it politically difficult.

"Divide and conquer," as the Romans called it, is a much easier way to control people so that we can extract wealth and resources from them with less bother. If you want to control people, you give one, necessarily smaller, group of people rights to exploit all the resources necessary for the larger group to live. Then, the minority will defend their privileges, and the other people will be forced to work for them just to meet their needs. It's a neat system. The corporation was invented to incentivize getting citizens to take the initiative to be violent to each other, for surprisingly small amounts of reward.

What we've drawn is a sketch of the divide and conquer economy, the wendigo economy.

So, corporations were intentionally designed as a trap to keep people in. It's no surprise that as these imaginary beasts have grown, we all find ourselves in the trap today.

———————————

There's a reason why all the great saints and sages got their groove in the wilderness, the central epiphany of all wisdom traditions happens on a pilgrimage to wild nature, whether it's the Buddha, Moses, Mohammad, Jesus, or take your pick of dozens of others.

If you want to find the path to prosperity, the way to live a good life, you'd do well to look in the woods, or other wild ecosystems that naturally grow wealthier, more fertile, more diverse and more resilient over time. Ecologists and biologists call this characteristic of all living systems "syntropy, "negative entropy" or "negentropy."

These are systems that prosper but produce no waste, have no need to exploit or abuse, or "export entropy" on to others in the form of pollution, oppression or war. As we've already discussed, they do this in part by "leaking value," or storing energy in the beings around them.

Learn the wisdom found there in the wood, the patterns that allow ecosystems to generate increasing abundance over time, and apply them to our human systems and we'll be on the path to plenty, naturally growing wealth.

Designing this idea of "accumulating prosperity" into our lives is a deeply sensible thing to do.

And it can be applied to all the systems humans inhabit, whether they're tangible ones like a city or homestead, or invisible ones like a PTA or a co-op.

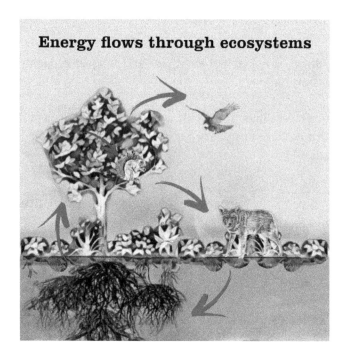

Energy flows through ecosystems

An ecosystem takes energy from multiple sources and converts them into a web of diverse beings, which in turn take energy from the sun, from the wind, from water, and invests it in new beings, which themselves transform energy into more growth…. Little is lost, as animals eat the fruit and nuts, reinvesting that energy into living beings. Their waste fertilizes the soil and grows new plants, endlessly reinvesting the energy into more complexity, resiliency, diversity and fertility.

Brilliant! What if we humans attempted to design our lives and communities like this?

But we humans generally make things in a much sillier way, like the sketches we drew of our economies, where our money doesn't get cycled, it's in one end and right out the other.

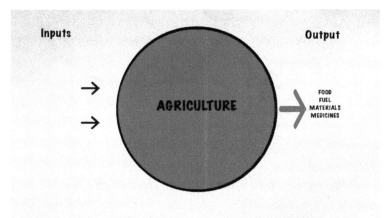

STUFF in one side, STUFF out the other. Hopefully, the stuff on the right side is worth more than the stuff on the left, otherwise, the situation is unsustainable.

You'll notice that this also looks like another system many of us are familiar with, farming.

Only what's important to understand, is that in this system, *we* are not the ones doing the farming.

Instead, this ever-growing insane suicidal global corporate system is there, giving us puny inputs in the form of cheap consumer junk, cheap low-quality food, wages, and grants, then extracting ever-greater mammoth "profits" from us.

Urban Death Spiral

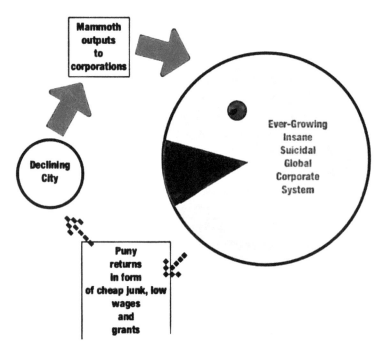

If this were a bathtub diagram, we'd all be drowning in it.

To make sure that the profits keep coming, the system feeds us products that are designed to fall apart. Moreover, they're often designed to be unsatisfying, infecting us with the wendigo spirit to consume ever more.

To say that we are being farmed would sound like another conspiracy theory, if we hadn't seen the quotes right from President Hoover and Titans of industry themselves, that this was exactly the plan: a system where consumers would be trapped in a rat race to power the economy.

And this is exactly what my own personal economy looked like 10 years ago.

As an environmentalist, I understood very well that these corporations were destroying the planet, causing climate change, driving mass extinctions, and harming people. And yet, everything I did all day long sucked away my life energy to support these very institutions I would oppose. When I woke up in

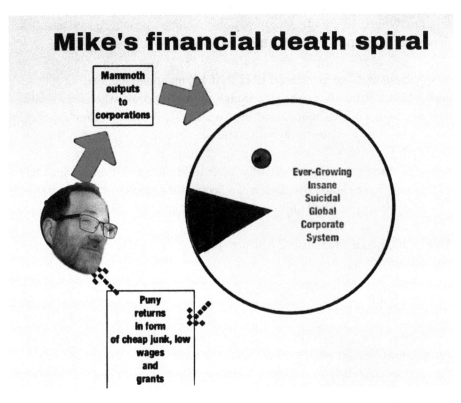

Mike's financial death spiral

Mammoth outputs to corporations

Ever-Growing Insane Suicidal Global Corporate System

Puny returns in form of cheap junk, low wages and grants

the morning my corporate alarm clock would play advertisements for more corporate consumer crap. I'd eat my corporate breakfast while reading morning news about how farm workers were kept in generational camps and paid too little to escape. I'd put on my corporate clothes made in sweatshops and go to my corporate job where I helped sell loans to farmers for corporate tools they didn't need. I had a forced retirement fund that went to support these companies, though it always lost more money than it made. When I went to the bathroom with corporate toilet paper, brushed my teeth with corporate toothpaste, and went to bed in corporate sheets, everything I did all day long supported this system I would oppose if only I could... and someday when I died, I knew even that would be phenomenally profitable to these corporate supervillains, while my grieving family would be obligated to give them more money.

This is because we are deeply silly beings with fantastically overactive imaginations, and we thought it would make life more fun and exciting if we brought all of our most horrible imaginary nightmare monsters into the real world in the form of "corporate persons," doomed to kill, ravage and mindlessly feed on the life energy of non-imaginary people and systems lest they violently implode causing massive amounts of collateral damage.

Think about that, we've created LITERALLY imaginary beings, corporations, that only exist in the imaginations of people when they come together to play make-believe and say "we are Shell Oil," yet they can steal, pillage, murder, and destroy whole communities and ecosystems in the real world. Being extra silly, we have famously made them legal "persons," (Google "corporate personhood" if you're unfamiliar with this strange fact) so that they have rights. But then when accountability comes calling, they can say "we are not Shell Oil" and vanish back into the realm of imagination.

This would make a fantastically bizarre plot for a sci-fi dystopia, if it were not actually real.

Humans, huh?

Since these imaginary corporate "persons" have to feed and grow and feed and grow or else perish, they have had to grow to take control over virtually every aspect of our lives, and manipulate us into buying things we simply don't need. One wonders what else is left for them to grow and consume to stave off their inevitable self-destruction, taking the whole economy with it as they vanish into smoke....

Humans of the Forest

Here, as we approach the heart of the wildwood, we can look around and see how these natural systems work... the tree leaves fall and are added to the soil, the fruit falls and is taken up by wildlings, when they fall, they too will be taken up by the tree, with no waste, no loss... energy caught and stored, cycled through the various beings in the system as it grows wealthier and more abundant each year.

This is the basic idealized way healthy human systems work, too, when humans are connected parts of the ecosystem.

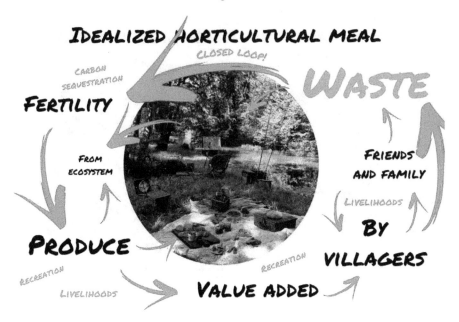

IDEALIZED HORTICULTURAL MEAL

CLOSED LOOP!

CARBON
SEQUESTRATION

FERTILITY

WASTE

FROM
ECOSYSTEM

FRIENDS
AND FAMILY

LIVELIHOODS

BY

PRODUCE

VILLAGERS

RECREATION

RECREATION

RECREATION

LIVELIHOODS

VALUE ADDED

Here is a sketch of the idealized meal in such a human society. It looks much like the ecological food web above. Our food, shelter, clothing and entertainment all come from our ecosystems. The fertility to grow these things also comes from the ecosystems. We get produce, which we can turn into food and products, which we can exchange with our friends and family, creating meaningful livelihoods. And all waste just goes back to fertilize the system, so there is no pollution, no waste, and no need for imports that harm other people and places.

As in the wildwood, everything here is based on connection.

The only problem is there is no room for insane corporate supervillain profits in such a system! There is no way for one person to become phenomenally more well-to-do than the others. Everyone naturally has access to what they need. There's no planned obsolescence, no manufactured demand.

So, here is where we see exactly how these imaginary beings feed. They feed by destroying our natural, life-enhancing connections to nature and community, such that profit is created on one side, and pollution and chaos is created on the other.

THE MODERN AMERICAN MEAL

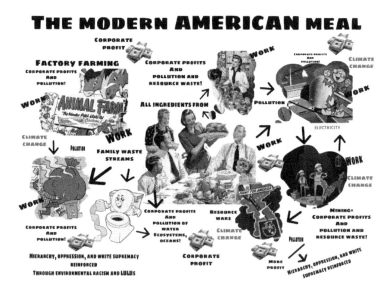

While we used to get food directly from connection with our ecosystems and community, the corporate persons destroy those connections, and insert themselves as middlemen at each step—just as colonial era corporations used to in their role of warfare. And so we must have a paycheck to get our food from grocery stores, which run off exploited labor and energy from energy corporations that destroy the planet and cause wars and oppression. The stores get the food from large corporate farms that destroy ecosystems, rely on heavily exploited labor, use animal cruelty, create massive amounts of pollution, and cause climate change. Each step of the way creates more social inequality, exploitation, pollution, and destruction, and each step is phenomenally profitable.

Remember, corporations were created as implements of colonial oppression, designed to do exactly this. "Divide and conquer" means destroy interconnection to extract profit. This is the institution we've made the cornerstone of our economy.

An Anti-Corporate Movement

In general, we'd like this book to be available to folks of all political philosophies. We all deserve a more abundant, beautiful life and world. We consider it our job to provide you with patterns and adventures to meet your own values, whatever they are. But, our huge modern corporations get treated as the principal villain in this book. So this book will provide a financial strategy that's based on combating these monsters, minimizing our support for them, and hopefully even aiming to crash some of the worst.

Is this a fair way to treat good ol' Ronald McDonald?

Well... all our major societal and environmental problems are caused by these large dystopian corporations. The largest 100 corporations (which are tightly interlinked, like heads of the hydra) are responsible for 71% of global carbon emissions. Large corporations are responsible for all our oil spills, and nearly all our chemical and plastics pollution. They're virtually the sole source of sweatshop labor, and drive displacement of farmers and indigenous communities. Corporations in the housing sector are the reason prices are going up for renters and home-owners alike. Just 12 corporations are responsible for most global deforestation. Corporations make the chemicals that are creating ocean dead zones and driving the decline in insect biodiversity globally. And it's no wonder that as the corporate economy has expanded and corporate profits have increased consistently, wages have stagnated for decades for virtually all of the working classes. Studies show that these corporations make workers miserable, as well, and that those working for themselves or in smaller companies have far higher job satisfaction.

And so virtually every problem we'd like to address, and every way we'd like to make the world better could be affected by turning back the dial on corporate expansion and having an economy less dominated by corporate supervillains, and more powered by people like you and me. This isn't our only strategy, but it's a big one.

The basic thing to understand is that these imaginary corporate persons get their energy from destroying our connections to nature and community. They don't care about you, your family or your city. Being imaginary, they didn't evolve, so they do not have cerebral cortexes, or the handy mammalian adaptations like empathy and love that are found there. According to the very silly rules of the game ("laws") in which we made up these imaginary beings, they **must** only care about one thing: converting your life energy and connection into "profit" and growth. They are literally, legally required to only care about that one thing. If a corporation were to prioritize "not being evil" for example, it could be found guilty of abusing its shareholders, either in a court of law, which would give it an imaginary slap on its imaginary wrist, or in the "market," which would rip it to shreds ruthlessly and feast on its bloody corpse.

Now, there are corporations that are trying to be better. There are corporations that have legally adopted a "triple bottom line," caring about the earth, people, and profit. We recognize that not all corporations are the same here, and a smart strategy is to target the worst of the worst, and encourage the best, which is what we'll try to do. We'll also recognize that as we create our financial designs, we may need to invest in "least worst" corporations as part of our strategy.

So, whether you want to save yourself, your family, your city, your country or the world, fighting off these imaginary, but very deadly, beings is a good first step. And if these beings thrive on destroying connection, the most important work of today is to regrow our connections to nature and community, such that we repair the broken loops that create oppression, pollution, and destruction. As activist Joana Macy has said in her revolutionary programs, we must do "the work that reconnects."

In our Transformative Adventures programs, this is our key guiding ethic, our "North Star:" **we grow connection to nature and community.** Everything we'll show you in this book will be about building connection.

Stay open to
new
opportunities

Ask: "will my action
grow connection,
or disrupt it?"

Vibrant, sustainable
connections must be
mutually beneficial.

The diversity of our
connections increases
our resilience

The guiding principle
of transformative
action:

Invest in the people
and ecosystems
around you

Fossil energy,
exploitation, and
centralization destroy
connection.

Invest in
growing
connections
with nature and
community

Cooperate, don't
exploit. Every person/
element involved must
get a fair yield.

To increase yields,
increase
connections.

Take yourself seriously!
Set measurable goals.
Measure outcomes.
Adjust.

Each element should be as
whole, resilient and self-
sustaining as possible.

There is no
waste, only
under-utilized
resources for
new connections

Connect with
local, sun-and-
people-powered
resources.

And so we find ourselves now at the heart of the wild wood.

Cool air,
The scent of pine, earth, and deep memory,
Utterly still peace thunders through the trees.
Here we must blow the ram's horn, paint our faces with mud and make a
strong tea of moss and lichens.
Wait and be very still now.
Breathe.
The Green Man and Woman, the warrior ethos of forest, will come to tea.
Together, they can teach us how to change the rules of the game, to recruit
the help of powerful forces to aid in our quest: mother nature, biology,
physics, practicality and sensibility.
Sensibility is a stake in the heart to imaginary corporate monsters and the
deeply silly day-dreamers who imagine them into reality.
Practicality is a wreath of garlic.
The Green Man, the Green Woman, together draw a circle in the sand, to
teach us a practical, sensible approach to redesigning our City system in the
image of nature. It looks suspiciously similar to the ecological food chain
network we looked at above:

Such a community, village, or city—designed like an ecosystem—becomes insulated from the energy-sucking attacks from outside entities, be they corporations or other communities. The BIG change here is that this city is structured to grow wealthier from within, instead of from outside imports provided by distant multinational corporations. The beings within leak value with each other so the whole environment grows wealthier. The community survives off of photosynthesis instead of predation, both literally and figuratively. It DOES capture outside energy sources, but it uses them to invest in building internal sources of wealth. Meanwhile, it limits losses to the outside, especially corporations, keeping this wealth and energy inside the system, and intentionally investing it into more assets that generate wealth. When we structure our communities in such a sensible way, we strike a death blow to the monsters.

I told you, sensibility is a stake in the heart.

The same applies to the household or individual economy. Remember, the conventional home economy looks like a linear system, money in one end and out the other.

Conventionally, we focus almost exclusively on brute force corporate solutions to life. We get make-believe jobs from the corporate system and do make-believe "work" helping it in its silly cruel game. If we can't meet our needs or pursue our wants with what it pays us, we look back to corporations for ways to meet our needs in less costly ways, cheaper products and services. Usually, corporations accomplish this by "externalizing costs onto ecosystems or other people" ie, pillaging, raping, murdering, causing climate change, and other monstrous behaviors, all in our names.

In this program, we will redesign the home economy so that it also looks like the forest food web. First think back to the basic linear system as I first drafted it. Instead, we want something that looks much more like an ecosystem, something like this:

We'll be going into this in more detail throughout the book, but let's look at a concrete example of "catching and storing energy."

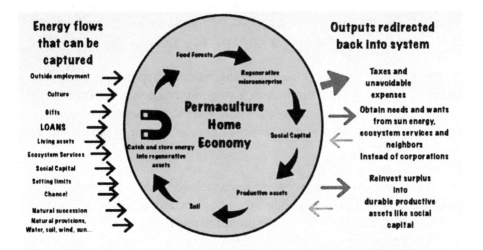

A home economy that naturally accumulates wealth and grows prosperity by:
1. Meeting needs in ways that build capital and wealth.
2. Catching and storing energy inputs into assets that grow wealth.
3. Grow wealth internally instead of being reliant on outside financial capital.

Polls show over and over that most Americans these days say they are "living paycheck to paycheck." Money comes in from work, and goes straight back out in order to meet needs such as food, transportation and housing. In/out, a dead-end losing game.

Instead, what if we take part of our yearly food budget and invest it in food, but in a way that also builds a permanent, perennial food system to catch and store energy for us. A "food forest" is a good example, since we'll be trying to grow wealth like a forest. Such a well-designed "transformative landscape" will pay for itself in the first year, providing as much food as would have been purchased from the corporate system. And beautiful, edible landscaping is known to be one of the best home investments you can make, so it's like putting every penny you spend on your forest garden into the bank. But more importantly, it is what we'll call a "regenerative asset," meaning it will continue to produce an increasing value of food for every year thereafter, decreasing the amount of money leaving your system and freeing up capital that we can reinvest. Eventually, it will likely produce an excess that can generate income or feed your friends.

We're not just talking about literal forests here. Similar approaches can be used to transform your housing, heating, transportation and virtually every "need" and want you're currently spending money on.

Again, when we use such a life-enhancing, practical approach to living and thriving, we fend off systems that suck away our prosperity. We start investing our life energy into assets and systems that generate more wealth for us and heal our communities, instead of ones that simply exploit and steal from us.

When we build communities on this principle, we finally have solid ground to stand on as we fight back against the vampires and wendigos. More importantly, we create a model of a beautiful, meaningful way of living and that doesn't require us to make up hideous monsters in order to have an exciting life.

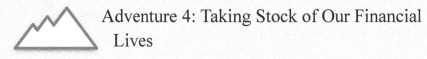

Adventure 4: Taking Stock of Our Financial Lives

Though this book, we'll be creating a new holistic design for our money systems. But to do that, we need to get an idea of what our current situation looks like. This is an absolutely essential part of the process that few people ever do. Consider this adventure your opportunity to flex some real muscle. When you've completed the adventure, do something to reward yourself!

Time required: Most people will complete this adventure in about 2 hours.

You'll need:

1. List all your assets. This includes any financially substantial items like art work, tools, your car, etc. It includes your equity, which is the current value of your home - your outstanding loan amount. It includes any investments, investment properties, stocks, or anything else of value.
2. List your monthly expenses, an average of 3 months will do. This includes your groceries, housing costs, insurance, utilities, monthly memberships, App purchases… get a full accounting of your monthly expenses.
3. List your liabilities and debts. You can think of this as your "negative money," the money you owe. This includes your mortgage, what you owe on your car, any credit cards or other lines of credit.
4. Calculate your "transformation fund," which is traditionally called your "net worth." We hate anything that implies that your worth is tied to a dollar amount, so screw that. But we do want to help you build a fund that you can use to transform your life and the world, so we'll call our total savings minus our total debts our "transformation fund." This is the total of the financial resources we'll have to create the lives we want.

Together, these give you a good visual overview of what your current financial situation looks like. It gives us a starting point for all our financial adventures. Everything we'll do in this book will be to improve this picture, to make it look more like a healthy ecosystem that will grow naturally in wealth, health, and abundance over time.

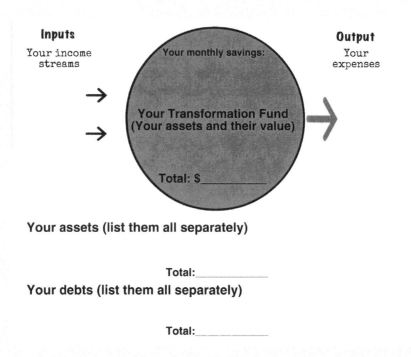

Your assets (list them all separately)

Total:_____

Your debts (list them all separately)

Total:_____

"The business of procuring the necessities of life has been shifted from the wood lot, the garden, the kitchen and the family to the factory and the large-scale enterprise. In our case, we moved our center back to the land."

-Helen and Scott Nearing

P6–Summary of Our Strategy for Societal Transformation:

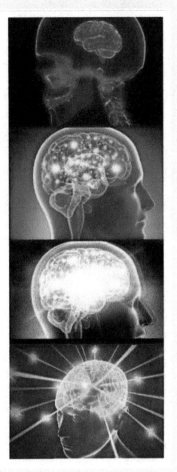

Let's fight climate change by changing our consumption and lifestyle patterns

Lifestyle and Consumption Activism is a distraction from the major systemic change we need. Lightbulbs and cold showers won't accomplish anything

Smart, targeted change to lifestyle and consumption is our single MOST POWERFUL tool for direct action against the most destructive systems, corporations and industries.

Transforming lifestyle and consumption can literally transform the underlying systems, values, beliefs and culture that cause climate change and most of our society's other major problems

A better life: a better world

One of the most toxic and ever present lies of our society is that you are powerless. You have no power to better your own circumstances or to have a positive impact on your world.

This is the message of those who'd like to make themselves, their political candidate, their idea, their organization seem absolutely vital to your life. You are powerless to improve your situation or that of the people you care about *without us*. Your power will be dismissed in a myriad of ways. You'll be told your belief in your own power is selfish, that it is privileged, "individualistic," misguided. When you believe you are powerless, you'll be easy prey for those who want to take your money and political capital to build their own.

And so, one of the fundamental ideas of this book will also be one of its most controversial for some people: that you are indeed powerful. You have more power over changing your day-to-day life circumstances than any thought leader or politician will ever have. And you also have enormous power to improve life in your community and to build a better world.

Despite what we often hear, meeting our own needs and creating beautiful lives for ourselves doesn't have to be a selfish endeavor that's destructive to everyone and everything else.

In fact, we believe that creating beautiful, abundant lives for ourselves can be one of the most powerful things we can do to to build a better world, if we do it in the right way. We believe the path to a better life is also the path to a better world.

Once we realize that it is the same systemic forces that are destroying the planet that are also keeping us from experiencing the natural abundance and beauty of life, then we see that direct work on these issues have big positive impacts on both. Your work to free yourself from these destructive systems and to stop supporting them is powerful.

Notice which media outlets are running 1,000 stories about how you are powerless and that your own consumption choices are a selfish distraction from their agenda. Because they're the exact same outlets that are running

Boycott and divest from the world's most destructive industries

Destructive energy

Corporate healthcare

The new housing Industry

Corporate food and restaurants

Banking

Corporate clothes

Concrete

Amazon

The auto industry

Landscaping

1,000 stories shaming millennial do-gooders for crashing whole industries with their idealistic consumer choices. These evil millennials are destroying malls, golf courses, fast food, the lawn-poison industry, and so on, by choosing not to support them. And they're telling us these corporate sob stories at the same time they're telling us our consumption choices don't matter. Meanwhile, you want to know what would happen if the same millennials organized a campaign to protest golf because of it's environmental footprint? Golf would see a huge national resurgence, that's what would happen.

But of course, whether or not our FREE work will build a better world depends on what our idea of a better life looks like. If you're still dreaming of yachts and bling while you're jet-setting around the world on beeches, then yes, you're just going to be making the world a worse place for everybody. There's no way around that.

But that's ultimately a very shallow and disengaged dream for how to live, in which the whole point of life is consumption. But when we create dreams for ourselves that involve thriving while contributing something positive to our communities and the world, and without making life for other people worse, then we will be creating powerful action.

Keeping this very simple and concrete, here is an outline of our economic strategy for change-making:

1. **Divest from destruction**. First, we seek to reduce our "corporate supervillain dystopia funds" by replacing our consumption with production. All those articles about do-gooders crashing whole industries? Let's add to those! Specifically, we'll need to do this in a planned and coordinated way to be most effective. In this book, we'll target some of the world's worst industries to boycott and divest our support from. If enough of us can do this on enough of a scale, we'll have a big impact.

2. **Reinvest in regeneration**. Invest in repairing connections to community and nature. That means reinvesting in regeneration, investing in just and sustainable systems in our own communities. We do this work as we create our own positive support networks for ourselves. In this way, we're directly "seizing the means of production" that we rely on in our communities.

3. **Escape the corporate rat race** and take back our time, then help others do the same. Once you're FREE, you can lead others to the same place. The worst of our economic system relies upon a work force that is stressed out, economically fragile, and worried they'll lose their jobs next week and die broke. A society where more people have more financial resilience is one where people have more power, and corporate supervillains have less.

4. **Community organize**. Community organizing means building durable power. It means that as a movement, we grow our own wealth and political capital, so that eventually we can flex real

political muscle, too. As we make each other wealthier, we grow our political might.

5. **Fund a DIY "Green New Deal."** We actually need a whole army of people out there in our communities doing this "work that reconnects." And guess what, the government is never going to pay for that. So our work to become FREE helps build a new Green Corps who can actually pay themselves to do this important work.

6. **Better support important activism**. We're not proposing that our path of "lifestyle activism" is the only way forward. We believe we need activist approaches, too. By doing our FREE work, we can help better support the activism we need to transform our communities. And we can help activists better support themselves, too.

7. **Change minds by changing behaviors**. We often think that to change people's behaviors, we'll need to change their minds. And so we set out to guilt trip people, lecture them, or frighten them into better behavior. But research shows this approach rarely works. In fact, this way of changing behavior often back fires, and causes people to care less about our causes! Instead, to change people's minds, we must first change their behaviors: behavior is the leverage point. If we can get people to take environmentally and socially responsible behaviors as a way of improving their own lives, then people will naturally feel more positively about these responsible actions. This is a research-based approach to building a movement for a better world.

8. **Make viral change**. Do it all in a beautiful, fun, creative, life-enhancing way so that we generate viral change and make this anti-corporate, pro-connection ethos the new norm. In doing this work, we're teaching people how to live for more than just consuming. We're showing people how to live for each other and for connection to our beautiful world. If we can create truly beautiful, abundant ways of living and being in the world, then we won't need to twist people's arms to get them to change. They'll line up for it like it's the new iPhone.

For more about our strategy for societal transformation, see pages XXX

Chapter 4: The FIRE Path to Freedom

So now that we've addressed some of the key delusions that lead us to ruin, examined the trap we all find ourselves in, and looked at our strategy for societal transformation, let's continue down this adventurous path to freedom.

The main tools we'll look at to plot our course are those developed by the FIRE movement.

Like many, I was introduced to FIRE (Financial Independence, Retire Early) by Vicky Robin and Joe Dominguez's classic book Your Money or Your Life. For me, YMOYL was a great piece of anti-consumption philosophy, that aimed to help the planet by reducing consumption, and used the carrot of "early retirement" as motivation. When my old mentor handed me this book, he changed my life.

Let's break that down as simply as we can. **Financial Independence** means that you have enough savings that you can quit your day job and spend your time doing the things that really matter to you, and live off your savings.

Remember our list of things we care about, the definition of a wealthy life we started this book with? Financial Independence (FI) means you get to spend your life focusing on those. If one of those things is to "retire early," then you're talking about FIRE.

The big shocker here is that regular people are doing exactly this, on much, much less money than most people could ever imagine, and in far less time, too.

While the mainstream idea of retirement promoted by gurus on TV is that you need to save at least a million dollars to retire, and that it will take at least 3 decades to get there, many people are getting there on a tiny fraction of that.

Perhaps the paragon of super fast retirement on working class wages is Jacob Lund Fisker, who wrote Early Retirement Extreme, so named because his model is indeed extreme. Jacob first achieved financial independence in just

5 years, while earning only around $40k/year. The key here is that Jacob reduced his expenses to just $7,000/year, which is in the range that I myself have achieved through many periods as part of my path. I think it's important to use that word "achievement," in this context, because it takes work, knowledge and skill!

That's right, if you can follow that model, and reduce your expenses to that low, you can potentially retire in 5 years of earning $40k per year.

Other less "extreme" folks have retired in just a few years by earning significantly more, or working a little longer, but the basic recipe is the same: **"spend as little as you can, save as much as possible, until you have enough to live off of."**

I myself have achieved my basic financial benchmarks while working as an artist and activist, keeping expenses low, and not worrying overly much about money.

How is this even possible? We'll look at many different benchmarks and approaches throughout this book that have given real people like you a great deal of financial freedom and resilience.

Most FIRE programs have a half dozen to a dozen "steps," that will include things like "getting out of debt," and "calculating your net worth," depending on where people are at. But breaking this down to be really, really simple, there are really 3 main steps to every FIRE program:

1. **Reduce your expenses to the point that it costs as little as possible to have a rich, beautiful life.** Following Bill Mollison's recommendation, that means starting with a goal to reduce your consumption by 10%, hitting that, and doing it again until you get to a good level. To give a very basic benchmark, using the tools in this book, I know many people who are living great lives on $10k-15k/ year. Jacob Lund Fisker has lived on $7,000/year in San Francisco and Chicago, some of the most expensive markets in the United States. The world of Permaculture is filled with people who live on less than that, and still have rich, beautiful lives. I myself have probably lived a much more extravagant lifestyle, while still being in this ballpark. Yes, there are many, many caveats to that, including

that it takes a lot of privilege to get expenses that low. We'll discuss those caveats more through the book.

The 10% Pledge

Life energy ($)

SUPPORT FOR CORPORATE SUPER VILLAINS GOING DOWN!

NUMBER OF DEGENERATIVE ASSETS WEIGHING US DOWN GOING DOWN!

FREEDOM GOING UP!

Corporate spending

(Corporate supervillain dystopia fund)

⁰ **Now** -----------------------------> **GOAL!**

(For many of us, the very first strategy here is to get out of as much debt as we can.)

2. **Save enough money to pay for your expenses, so that you don't have to work.** Once you know how much your new low expenses are you can save enough money to cover those costs. Now this part is a little misleading, because you can actually do this on a lot, lot less than it seems like. For example, if you live on $10k/year, and you're 30 years old, you might want to plan to live another 70 years. So if we spend $10k per year for 70 years, that's $700,000. But we can do it with far less than that, which brings us to…

The 10% Pledge

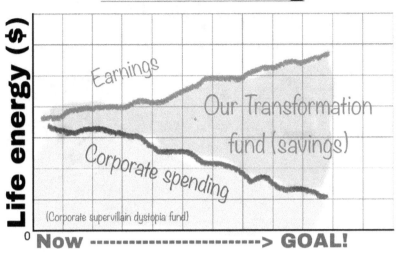

Life energy ($)

Earnings

Our Transformation fund (savings)

Corporate spending

(Corporate supervillain dystopia fund)

0 **Now** ----------------------------> **GOAL!**

3. **Invest your savings so that it securely lasts so you can live off it
    as long as you need it to.** The key to investing, is that you won't be
    living off the savings alone, you'll be earning income off your
    investments. On the other hand, you won't be living purely off the
    interest while your capital stays the same. You'll be strategically
    drawing down the capital so that you die broke and happy.

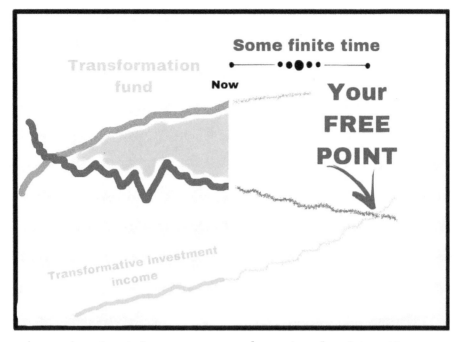

As your investments increase, your yearly earnings from interest increase and you get closer to retirement.
You can actually predict when you'll be able to retire and put that date on the calendar.

Well, how much does that take? Let's not beat around the bush. A rough rule of thumb discussed in the FIRE movement is the "25 times" or "4% rule," which states that you need about 25 times your yearly expenses to retire on. or in other words, you can safely withdraw 4% of your savings annually. So, if you need $10,000/year to live on, you multiply your yearly costs by 25 and that's how much savings you will need. With $250k in the bank, the theory goes, you would be free to put your full-time efforts into art, family, Permaculture, regenerative agriculture, cultural creation, or otherwise building a better world for yourself, your family and your community. If you can live off $5,000/year, and you don't want to work at all, you can retire on $125,000 of savings. (See Appendix 1 for a 4% rule table. Again, there are a great many caveats to this section, as well.)

So, looking at our $10,000 example, if you earn $40k year, and invest $30k, you can retire in less than 9 years.

Or, if you can reduce your expenses to Jacob Lund's "extreme" $7000/ year, and invest $33k, you can retire in less than 6 years, 5 with a little investment luck.

If you have enough information, we can do this right now:

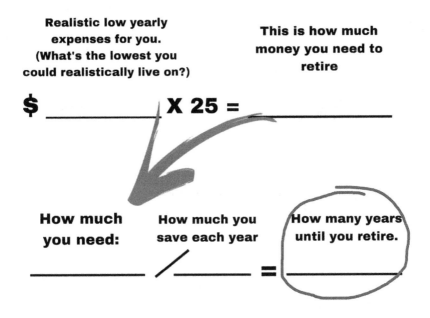

We've included some charts on page XXX to help you guesstimate your FREE point using the 4% rule.

If you're not happy with that number, you can do a couple things: you can learn to live on less, or you can figure out how to save more. That can tell you how long until you're Financially Independent.

At that point, you will be free from the rat race, free to devote your full attention to the things that really matter. You won't have to worry about losing a job, keeping a job, or going to a job you hate.

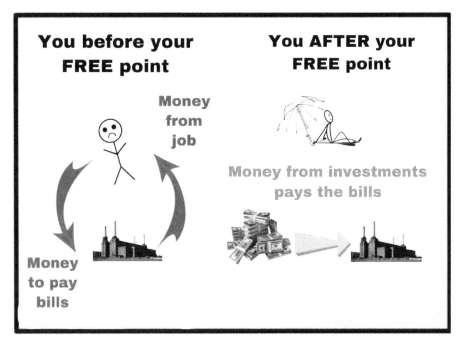

FIRE, basically. If this seems a little over-simplified, don't worry, we'll get to that.

But that doesn't mean you HAVE to stop working. It's actually very common that people who achieve Financial Independence actually start earning MORE money, because they are no longer forced to make bad economic decisions out of a scarcity mindset in the name of "security." But it means you get to decide for the rest of your life how, when, where, and why you will work for money.

In your "relationship with money," YOU are finally the one in charge. In FIRE circles, this is often called the "crossover point," but we'll call it the "FREE" point. The idea is we need to identify the point where we will be "Financially Resilient and Economically Empowered" to choose to spend our time the way we wish.

Now that may be fine for those who simply want to retire early and don't care about torching the planet in the process.

But from our perspective as artists, activists, and general hippie types, it might be helpful to analyze this paradigm further, to maximize how it meets the different kinds of goals that we might have when compared to other folks. For example, it's clear that we'll need to start out with a map that will get us where we want to go financially while accomplishing all the goals I began this article with in part 1: caring for people and the earth, while improving quality of life.

For example, do we want to be investing in the stock market, knowing we're supporting the very corporations that are destroying the planet and enslaving our friends?

So, can we have our FIRE cake and eat it without burning down the planet and ourselves too? Does a $250K, or $125k nest egg sound achievable for folks looking to simplify their lifestyles and pursue art and activism? Are there investments we can make that don't make the world worse off at our expense? Can we instead invest in the kind of world we want to see?

Chapter Resources

Note: within our group group, our two most recommended books on FIRE are Your Money or Your Life and Early Retirement Extreme. Those looking for an overview of basic alternative finance may enjoy Rich Dad Poor Dad, though some of that advice conflicts with what you'll se in this book. For a conventional FIRE resource, see the website, Mr. Money Mustache, Mrmoneymustache.com

1. Robin, Vicki, and Joe Dominguez. Your Money or Your Life 9 Steps to Transforming Your Relationship with Money and Achieving Financial Independence. Malmö: MTM, 2020

2. Lundfisker, Jacob. Early Retirement Extreme. Self-published. 2010

3. Hester, Tanja. Work Optional. Hachette, 2019

Adventure 5: Get out of (Bad) Debt

Once we start to see ourselves as being farmed in this linear system of the debt/consumption/job cycle, it becomes clear that one of the most important steps we can take is to dig ourselves out of any debt we're in.

Our liabilities, our debts, are a constant monthly drain on our FREEdom. They are the clearest manifestation of being chained into this system. If I were still in debt, there's no way I would have had the freedom to start my own businesses, write books, and invest in the properties that have created my FREE lifestyle. Getting out of debt was the first thing that had to happen before I could do any of that.

Hopefully, at this point, you've already started flexing some financial muscles by putting together a slush fund. Now, we'll need to kick those skills into high gear.

Unfortunately, it's easier said than done! Most of the money books I've read have the same exact advice for getting out of debt: just, you know, get out of debt! It's another "brute force" method, just stop buying lattes and pay down the debt. And if you can't that's a moral failing.

So let's take a more holistic and systemic approach to getting out of debt. Here are some tips and patterns:

1. Remember to think holistically and systemically, instead of just focusing on "brute force" methods. Remember that everything in this book is about creating the kind of financial situation where you'll be more likely to be able to get out of debt. You may have to prioritize some other adventures in this book first before you can directly tackle getting out of debt easily.
2. Make an "adventure" of it. One of the big keys to accomplishing any goal is to "periodize," or put a time limit on it. This allows us to feel like we're only sacrificing short-term. We can put up with anything for a short time! This helps us stay motivated and
3. Name it and claim it. Call this the "debt FREE challenge." This way, you have something positive that you are actively working on, instead of focusing on the negative of "not spending money." If

friends ask you to go on a group weekend in Vegas, you can tell them you're doing the "debt FREE challenge."

4. Pick a few other patterns or adventures from this book to work on for a short period of time that will help support your goal, such as improving your business, making a smart investment to increase cash flow, or work on one area of savings at a time.

5. Follow the leverage: if your expenses are more than $20,000/year, then you could save significant money by working on spending less and reducing your expenses. Find the areas with the biggest potential savings first and work on those. But if you're already spending less than $15,000/year, you might have to work very hard to reduce your spending much. In that case, you might work on the cash flow side of the equation.

6. Considering gamifying it with a wall chart or phone App. These can be helpful tools for some people to stay motivated.

Understanding Good and Bad Debt

In this book, the "back to the land" movement comes in for some heavy criticism for its ideas around money. But perhaps the worst money idea that I learned from that movement was the notion that all debt is bad and should be avoided at all costs. This idea is a barrier to people succeeding in getting FREE and it's a barrier to the kind of societal change we want to make.

Even today, this notion that all debt is bad is very strong in hippie and permaculture circles. Many people want to access land and start land-based livelihoods, but are strongly opposed to taking out a mortgage to do so because they're convinced all debt is bad!

The thinking in the movement is that debt is the opposite of freedom. This isn't entirely untrue. If you have debt, you have a monthly payment to finance that debt, and this adds to your life overhead. If you're trying to thrive in a privileged lifestyle as an artist or smallholder, then having an additional monthly payment can made the difference between success and failure. That monthly payment may keep you locked into jobs you don't like or cost your opportunities.

The the real problem to focus on is monthly cash flow, not debt. That's the real problem.

Here's an example: 10 years ago I was paying about $900/month for rent. I wondered, should I take out debt to buy a house? By taking out a mortgage on a triplex, I was able to rent out 2 units, completely covering my $900 of rent plus also paying the utilities. Because the house had rental units, I was able to include that projected income as part of my income when applying for the loan, allowing me to buy a much bigger house than I could have otherwise. And that asset appreciated over time, earning well over $60K of equity in 10 years. And it provided land for my land-based income streams, too. So taking on this debt actually eliminated my monthly housing costs, greatly increasing my freedom.

So for the purpose of this book, bad debt is debt that decreases our freedom. Credit cards, car payments, having more house payment than you need are all things that decrease your freedom.

Good debt is debt that increases our freedom and wealth. We shouldn't be afraid of this kind of debt. There's a very simple formula for weather debt is good debt: if it cash flows more than the monthly financing, it's really good debt! That's debt that will make you FREE!

Systems Leverage Points for Getting FREE from Debt

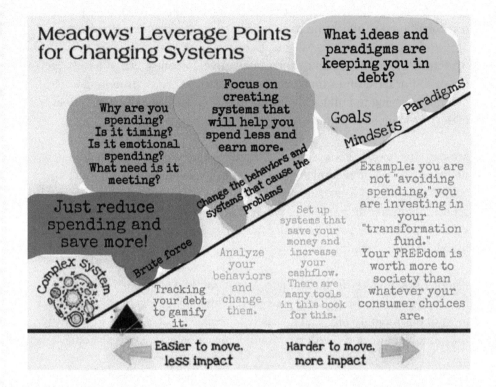

Since we've already seen that the standard "brute force" methods are usually poor ways of accomplishing our goals, let's think about how we can move up to higher leverage points.

Brute Force Methods. "Just get out of debt." Any sort of thinking that makes getting debt free a battle of your own will against your spending is very likely to fail. Even just switching to a mindset of "gamifying," in which you win by paying down debt, is a more empowered mindset that's more likely to succeed.

Behaviors. When and why are you spending money against your own values? Are you getting a cup of coffee everyday in the morning? Then get in the habit of making your own extra special coffee instead. If you make yourself something better than you can buy, you'll feel less motivated to splurge. Are you buying snacks all day long? Make your own favorite healthy snacks instead. Are you engaging in emotional shopping after a hard week of work? Plan special, enjoyable (and free) alternatives to help you reset emotionally, like going to a favorite park for a picnic by the lake.

Systems. A lot of books on debt basically give you one piece of advice: get out of it! For most of us, that's not really helpful if we're struggling to pay the bills or trying to build a business. Changing our whole money system so that we hold on to more money is what gets us out of debt.

Most of this book is about setting up systems that will help you meet your financial goals. For example, when it comes to saving money on food, you could create a food forest, create a buying club, set up a meal planning group, set up a dumpster diving group, etc. Instead of just trying to spend less, these systems will enable you to actually meet that goal, often without even trying to reduce your spending.

Another systemic fix is to automate your monthly payments. This can both be a big financial savings, and save you mental power and time. These days most of our monthly bills can be easily automated. Set aside an hour or two for this adventure and it will pay you in time savings for years to come.

Deep change. Again, many of the overall strategies in this book are about deep changes to how we think about money and our personal finances. For example, we can change the idea that we need money in order to have a wealthy life. We may even learn that hoarding money may get in the way of the things that bring us true wealth. If we can transcend the "money" idea, we may find it easier to achieve our ideas of a wealthy life if we're not chasing money all the time. What are some other examples you've seen already?

As we change the whole way we think about money, hopefully our debt will be replaced with growing abundance.

Choosing a Debt Strategy

Once we start bailing ourselves out of debt, there are two main strategies we can choose from. In the FIRE community, these are often called the Debt Snowball and the Debt Avalanche. The point is to choose the one that will be most motivating to you.

The Debt Avalanche

The Debt Avalanche approach is to invest in paying down the worst debt first. Pick the accounts with the highest interest rates and pay those down first, while making minimum payments on the other lines of credit! Generally speaking, all things being equal, this is the smartest financial strategy. As we pay off the worst debts, we have more savings each month, which means we can increase our debt payments over time, building to the debt avalanche!

The Debt Snowball

Some people will simply have better motivation if they can start knocking out some debts. The Debt Snowball strategy uses that motivating factor by prioritizing the smallest accounts first, lining the up, and knocking them out! It can be incredibly motivating to cross off a credit card from our ledger!

Gamifying Your Debt

Once you have a strategy, these days you may find many apps and tools to help you visualize and tackle your debt. If you're the kind of person who would benefit from them, we suggest searching for the newest and best rated tools available.

Chapter 5: Burned Out on Fire

At its best, the FIRE movement has taught millions of people to live for something other than to consume corporate crap before it goes into landfills. And it has allowed many people to retire and achieve a better lifestyle while doing that.

But, if we need to improve some of the downsides of the "back-to-the-land" movement, then we can also learn to avoid some of the pitfalls of the traditional FIRE movement.

And the biggest problem with FIRE is people get burned out on it. FIRE philosophy can lure us into making big sacrifices for the future, into getting caught up in the hustle, so we miss the things that are truly important right here and now in the present.

You: Why is this world so messed up?!?!?

Your stock portfolio:

Moreover, if we do our FIRE path well, we may be divesting from consumption, but we end up still supporting the corporate supervillains by investing in the stock market, or even joining the team in exploiting others and destroying the planet for our own "early retirement" of alternative consumption.

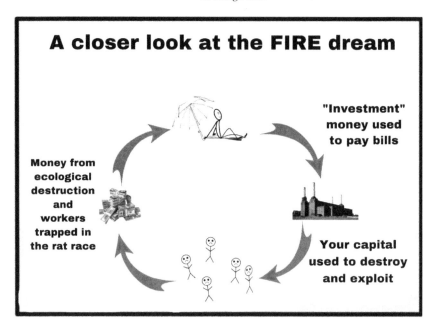

For some of us, this "new roadmap" as Vicki Robin called it, might be exactly what we need. But for many of us, the rich set of tools in this book for non-financial capital for spending less, and a bank of viable regenerative investment opportunities for investing can provide us with more options than the traditional FIRE scenarios. And find ones more in keeping with our values.

After I used basic FIRE steps to start freeing up my ideas around money, I realized I didn't want to follow FIRE in the race for FI and "retirement." I just wanted to feel FREE: Financially Resilient and Economically/Ethically Empowered. And I needed to be able do it here and now if I could.

There's a real need for us to be able to experience some amount of financial freedom and resilience ASAP, rather than sacrificing our time and values for a future that may never come.

I wanted to "catch and store" energies that would allow me to weather the storms of an economic system that appears to us to be failing. And I wanted to be resilient enough that I can survive even if important projects I take on fail, or if "life strikes" in some other expensive way. And I wanted to feel economically empowered. I wanted to be able to choose to start projects, organizations, or businesses I think are important. And I wanted to feel in control of my own economic destiny, rather than relying on other fragile systems for my livelihood.

But I also want to be ethically empowered, so that if an employer or investment opportunity ever conflicts with my values, I can afford to say "take this job and shove it." And finally, that word "empowered," I want to feel like I have the agency to invest in creating the kind of lives and society I want to see. Now that's feeling "FREE."

MORE than a fancy new name, in this book we'll combine some patterns and tools from Permaculture, along with some models for right livelihood to forge a path to freedom and community plenty, beyond mere retirement. So, we'll distinguish these FREE scenarios from traditional FIRE roadmaps.

So then the FREE dream might be to have a life with abundant time to spend on important things, with part-time, flexible, meaningful work we love. And instead of paying the corporate system for our needs and luxuries, we pay other happy, independent community members. Meanwhile, we have regenerative investments which provide our income, give us resilience, and allow us to be in control of our own lives. The question is, how do we do this? We'll look at many options and scenarios for making this work throughout this book.

Being FREE

Much like FIRE, our basic path is to reduce our expenses as much as we can, and increase our "Transformation Funds." But how much we need and how we invest it becomes the big difference.

And of course, it's important to keep our goal in mind. Folks who want to be FREE actually value having meaningful work in our communities, so instead of planning with full retirement in mind, we're planning to have some kind of income that we can make on our own terms.

Two of my mentors, Jerry and Stacy, come to mind. As a FREE couple, both are musicians who have created a life with a lot of flexibility to go and perform professionally when they have the opportunity. They have a lot of ease and space in their lives, and stacked, fulfilling livelihoods that help them connect with community.

They have their house and transportation paid off, have invested in energy saving, solar energy, and a strong local community network. They have a nice garden for food luxuries and enjoy cooking. She works part time teaching music lessons and offering holistic health services specifically to folks in the music community. She also teaches classes to others who wish to provide similar holistic health services. Meanwhile, he teaches part-time at a university, and hosts music community events and workshops at home. Their home always seemed to be filled with friends, music and art, good food from the garden, and a strong sense of love and community. When they wanted to travel, they could take performing jobs in different places around the world, and get paid to do it.

They might not have had great financial riches, but they sure seemed to be deeply wealthy to me in every way that really counts.

As a young person, I had the opportunity to meet quite a few people living lives like this, and each time, I thought "these people have really figured it out!" These people seemed truly free.

So, here's the trick with creating FREE benchmarks:

Let's say we can reduce our costs of living to $10k/year. It's honestly quite difficult to reliably make $40k-60/year as a small business owner or as a self-employed person unless you are in a high value consulting career of some kind. But, there are actually a lot of reliable ways to make that $10k/year. As a musician, I can reliably charge $30/hour to friends and earn about $15k/year teaching just 10 hours per week. I used to work with an artist doing live painting at art fairs on weekends who made significantly more than that just working weekends, while traveling around for fun.

My honest advice as someone in the industry for nearly 30 years, is that it's very difficult to earn $40k/year doing land-based incomes like farming, and most of the "gurus" who claim they're doing it aren't being fully honest about their numbers. And for 40 years, folks in our community have been predicting "very soon raising food will become highly valuable again!" Maybe! Or maybe not!

But, I know a lot of people who easily make $12k/year by working around 10 hours a week on sustainable market gardening businesses. I call this hammock income, because this is the sort of income people can easily make with light part-time work while spending most of the day in the hammock.

But, because farm labor follows the economic law of diminishing returns (the return on hourly labor/square foot rapidly goes down) it's nigh impossible to multiply that 10 hours by 4 and make $40k. It's far more likely to work 50 hours/week and only make $20k. At that point one has to wonder whether all the extra work is worth it. And, in this book I'll show you a lot of plans that use investments and stacked income streams to try to get as much income out of as few hours as possible. These work because they overcome that diminishing returns barrier. The benchmarks for our Landscape Transformation Program business, for example, can reliably get $40k off 20 hours/work per week by using these techniques. My own income after investments looked well over $60k when doing the Landscape Transformation Program business model.

But the point is, it's difficult to plan on $60k and reliable to plan on $12k.

So, if you can reduce your expenses to $10k and make $12k off 10 hours a week, the question is: are you already FREE?

Are we already there?

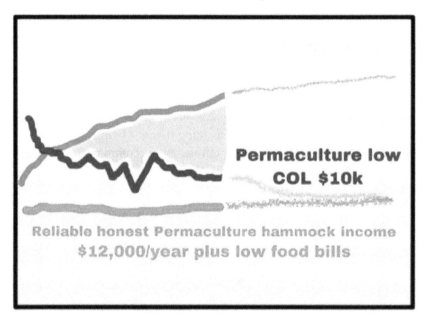

The answer is: realistically, probably not! (Though we may be closer than we think.)

The reason: life has bumps, and real freedom means having resilience and flexibility. Even if you can live off of $12k now, it doesn't mean you can sustain that into the future. And worse, there's inflation and taxes and wealthy people constantly sucking as much money out of us as possible all the time. And, many of us will often encounter family and community issues we wish to have a positive impact on, so it's good for those of us who wish to live regeneratively to plan to have some spare resources. Because of this, we still need that investment income to grow wealthy over time and be truly FREE.

For example, using the 4% rule, if we have $125,000 invested in transformative assets, we might reliably earn $5000/year. This way we keep pace with inflation, and continue to essentially "save" and grow wealth without having to struggle so much to make money.

In other words, at this point, our financial situation is "regenerative," and will continue to grow more secure and resilient as we live our lives. From a FREE perspective, it is once we have reached this place where our financial situations have become regenerative that we have reached our "FREE Point."

Again: if our financial situation is "regenerative," that means we will keep naturally growing wealthier over time. That's the goal.

Either this yearly "earning" can be compounded back into our savings, or in any year that $5000 could be drawn out to pay for emergencies, or take time off work for another opportunity. Of course, if a true emergency arises we might withdraw more than $5000 if we need to, and won't have to lose sleep over that decision. We might have the resources to co-invest with community members to make important new businesses happen. Of course, we may also invest in smart transformative assets that will increase our yearly income and our joy in our work as well.

Again, this level of savings and financial resilience is easier to accomplish than most of us imagine.

Some FREE scenarios

There are a lot of basic implications of this depending on where you are in your life and what your goals are. But some people are achieving a realistic FREE lifestyle with only around $120K invested in what we'll call "transformative assets."

FREE from Wage Slavery!

For one, if you're someone who's working an old economy job you hate, you may be much closer to retirement than you thought. If you're working that $40k job and can reduce your costs to $10k, in 5 years you could have $150k invested in transformative assets. Perhaps that's a fixer-upper house with enough land for a market garden paid off, with a DIY commercial kitchen. Perhaps that's a live-in studio with a commercial printing press or framing equipment. Perhaps that's a duplex that can generate $5k in income with land for a home herbalism business.

If their FIRE benchmarks were to live off $20k/year, they'd need $500k in investments to retire. But if they invested in $10-12k reliable hammock income, then they'd be able to retire off $250 K in total wealth, even with some of that tied up in a home or business equipment.

FREE Healthcare!

For some, especially Americans with our healthcare system that prioritizes obscene corporate profits over, well, health or care, insurance will be the big barrier to feeling FREE.

Many in this situation find greater freedom with a part-time job at one of the companies that give healthcare to all employees, regardless of the hours they work. Some of these jobs, like barista jobs, also put us in good positions to do community organizing and cultivate relationships.

Those on the FREE Healthcare plan (or it's equivalent "Barrisata FIRE") will work part time in one of these jobs and spend the rest of the week being FREE to do what they like with their time.

Some Companies that May Give Healthcare to Part Timers
Starbucks, Caribou Coffee, Aldi, Trader Joe's, Whole Foods, UPS, Costco, Lowes, Staples

FREE comes before FIRE!

Or perhaps you're someone who's been on the FIRE path, but your goals seem a long way off. But, maybe you already have a home paid off and were waiting to meet your FIRE benchmarks before you could retire. Maybe with some time and investment into setting up hammock income, you may already be past your FREE benchmarks, and ready to move into "working retirement."

FREE Opportunity!

Many in our society find they simply have a lack of real opportunities for achieving traditional financial goals. Whether it's struggles with mental health, or difficult backgrounds, a lack of family support, or many other issues that hold hard-working, conscientious people back in our society, the idea of making $40k/year and living off $7k is about as realistic as discovering billionaire Scrooge McDuck was your long lost uncle.

Yet, someone with part-time employment might invest time and money in setting up hammock income, passive income streams, and designing their incomes such that they can meet FREE goals while reducing their costs of living and increasing their quality of life. FREE benchmarks might be far more realistic to more people than the idea of saving up hundreds of thousands of dollars to buy a home in the country to start a money-losing organic farm.

Already FREE?

Meanwhile, there are folks with careers in arts, activism, and land-based incomes who might already be FREE if they simply shifted their financial design around a little. I actually know a great many of these folks who still live paycheck to paycheck, struggle with money, or take jobs they hate even though they've paid off or inherited homes with yards or have money in the bank. Many are farmers who own farms yet struggle to make ends meet because they're focused on a losing "market garden" business model or other model that requires long hours of work for very low wages. Many farmers I know work 40+ hours/week all year round and still only make $10k/year. They could almost all realistically instantly rearrange their businesses to still make $10k per year off of just 10 hours/week or less. They might even make

MORE money. Then, perhaps they want to work another 10 hours at a separate but stacked income stream to pick up another $10k. Most could do this, but they're stuck in their losing business models. Often, the most profitable thing they could do is just stop losing money by spending it on a business that has the whole game rigged against it.

Others do art or activism part time and work low-income wage jobs to make ends meet. Many of these folks, too, could quit their 20 hour/week jobs for Ronald McDonald, and make ends meet with some hammock income or transformative investments.

The Gift of FREEdom! (FREE Parenting)

For many parents, one of the biggest financial obligations is to their children's education and well-being. If this is important to you, then I would of course respect your choice and understand that will be part of your FIRE/ FREE plan.

But as an alternative, I have seen parents who passed on thriving small hammock businesses and workable FREE investments to their kids. One of my Permaculture clients inherited an art framing business, skills, equipment, and clientele from his parents, which has allowed him a great deal of freedom to do whatever he likes. His business can travel anywhere, can be scaled up or down, and he has the freedom to pursue degrees if he wishes, too. Their own "FREE" investments became his.

A neighbor of mine told me his father took him around to different construction sites as a teenager, so he could learn different skills by working on the job. He made sure the money was invested in tools and equipment, such that by the time he graduated from high school, he also had a basic FREE setup in place for life.

Yet another, one of my mentors, had his father train him in his house painting business. Again, he received the skills and the tools and investments to make the business work. It's an easy business to work part time and easily make hammock income. When he was 18 he rented a Uhaul to do his first job on his own and just used his dad's marketing tools to hire up a team of college painters to work with. He retired early as a very wealthy man, after working part time when he wanted during his life.

Sometimes our money is not the best thing we can give to those we love. Sometimes our time, knowledge, and wisdom can be more valuable than our money.

A beautiful environment and vibrant community is a form of wealth that benefits many. The gardens in my various Permaculture projects have all generated such a rich sense of community and abundance.

P7–The Patterns of being FREE:

The big difference between FIRE and FREE are the sort of goals we might have.

While those pursuing FIRE sacrifice in the present for the sake of an early retirement, those pursuing FREE may be more interested in gradually transforming their lives in a positive direction, starting as soon as possible. It's more about living in the present, instead of living for the future. They may focus on finding good work, rather than no work. They may prioritize having more free time and self-determination right now, rather than sacrificing their free time now for the hope of having more free time later. They may want to find rewarding, meaningful ways to contribute to their communities that feel good, rather than just "retiring early." They may seek the challenge and growth of doing something constructive to make a better world, rather than joining the leisure class in permanent vacation status, while living off corporate profits.

Beyond the goals, becoming FREE is a more personalized and flexible pattern-based process when compared to FIRE, which is like a plan based on the 3 main steps: Reduce costs, Save, Invest.

But as with FIRE, we could say there are a few main steps to FREE:
1. Reduce our costs of living as much as possible while raising our quality of life.
2. Grow our "Transformation Funds."
3. Invest in creating joyful, highly fulfilling "right livelihood" and "hammock income" from spending our time doing the things we most want to be doing.
4. Invest in regenerative and transformative assets until our financial situation is regenerative, highly resilient, flexible, and we feel very secure.
5. Keep investing in things that transform our lives and communities for the better.

But beyond those main steps, FREE is more like an individual recipe you cook up for yourself. Your own recipe may omit some ingredients, or use them in different amounts, but here are some common ingredients:

1. Compared to FIRE's philosophy of deferred satisfaction for future retirement, a FREE plan has to put the emphasis on the present and the path, and quality of life.
2. FREE prioritizes developing Right Livelihood, rather than joining corporate tyranny for an early retirement.
3. FREE might prioritize stacked, personalized income streams over corporate salaries.
4. The ability to take space from work when opportunities arise, rather than slugging it out for the end game.
5. Having a life and work plan where we're open to opportunities.
6. Being debt free, or only using debt to invest in our FREEdom.
7. Creating a holistically supportive environment, community, and landscape.
8. Investing in "regenerative assets," and more importantly, what we'll call "transformative assets."
9. Reducing the harm of our traditional investments, rather than just investing in corporate supervillains.
10. Learning valuable DIY skills to become a producer rather than a consumer.
11. Community organizing.

To follow that path, in the next chapter we'll look at a strategy for generating right livelihood that feels FREE and rewarding.

P8–Index Funds: Owning Destruction?

This is a good time for a reminder that we are not financial advisors, and this is more about patterns, ethics, and the history of the FIRE movement than financial advise.

When the FI movement first launched with the book Your Money or Your Life, the investment of the movement was Treasury bonds. That was the answer for 'what do I invest in?" Ethically speaking, it was at least a democratic investment, one that we all had a stake in as Americans, and which we all at least got a vote on. Certainly, we could believe that the downsides were worth cutting people free from the rat race and consumer lifestyle.

But of course, that was an investment from a different time, and that time will likely never come again. So today, we could say that THE investment of the FIRE movement is index funds.

This is because low-fee index funds equal the market, while only about 25% of intensively managed funds beat the market, and when considering fees, it's only about 23%. And it's hard to pick that 23%!

So first off, if you have money in Index funds, let's give ourselves a big helping of compassion. Especially if we're approaching retirement, and feel we need the security of that index fund, it's good to give ourselves self-compassion.

But, let's be honest about the drawbacks.

The down side of index investing is that it is arguably the least moral of all stock market investments. To put it plainly, if I own the S&P, then I personally own climate change, mass extinctions, ocean dead zones, plastic pollution, and child labor sweat shops. If I own index funds, I can't complain about "the system," because I am the system. The very decision I make, to profit from destruction, is the exact decision I am literally paying corporate executives to make. When we buy the S&P, we literally become that person making the choice to destroy the planet for a buck.

Index fund investing is investing in the status quo. It's investing in the past of the market, not the future. 12% of an investment in an index of the S&P 500 will go to direct fossil fuel production. A huge additional % goes to indirectly supporting climate change. An index fund has no mechanism to give us climate resilience.

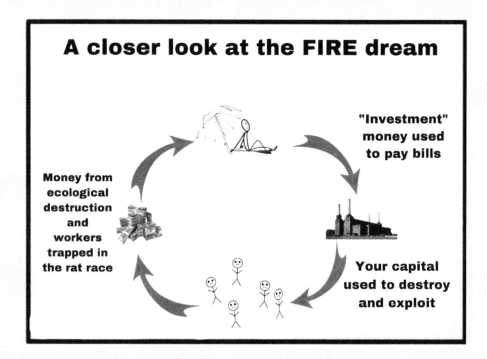

So an index fund investment is climate denial. Do you personally believe that fossil fuels can continue to be the energy that runs our economy into the coming decades, and that we should mine every last bit of oil and coal? Because when you invest in an index fund, that is what you are both betting on, and voting for. You may believe we need to develop alternatives, but you're putting MORE money into supporting the destructive old status quo than the future you'd like to see. When I invest in an index fund, I am literally the barrier to developing green energy, making it harder for new technologies to compete against the status quo.

But when it comes down to it, index funds are not even worth the destruction they cause. They're just not a great investment when it comes to meeting the sort of financial goals we have in this book.

Yes, index funds generally beat managed stock funds, but that's just not saying much.

The truth is that if you spend much time in online FIRE groups and forums, you'll see a virtually never-ending set of posts of discouraged people who have done the math, and if their only option is index funds, they've found that they cannot reach their FIRE goals.

Looking at the numbers on the previous page, a 30-year-old discovering FIRE will need to invest $5,500/month to get to the often-promoted goal of a million dollars to retire on by age 40. Let's be real, very, very, very few people will be able to sustainably save $2000/month right when they graduate from college. In fact, only about 5% of 20 year olds could do that, and frankly they're the 5% that doesn't need a money book. The most likely age to be able to achieve FIRE goals is age 30, when the top 25% of the population will earn enough to feasibly save $5,500/month, if they can live very frugally. Unfortunately, most of those top earners will live in areas where it will be very difficult to live off of $15k/year. Realistically then, 10-15% of people will have a brief window in their lives when a standard FIRE approach is possible.

No wonder that most people who hear about FIRE are discouraged when they run the numbers! For many, the standard FIRE formulas may be little more than false hope that tricks people into trading their real time and life energy for an "irrational exuberance" belief in index funds.

And, it's very easy to cherry-pick a given period of time, give or take a few months, to show that the index funds do very well. For example, over the last 10 years, as the FIRE movement has grown, the S&P 500 has made an earnest 14.8%. That looks great!

But the last few years, we could look at any measure of stock value, like the CAPE rate, Cyclically-Adjusted Price-to-Earnings ratio, also known as the Shiller P/E ratio. As of writing this sentence, the CAPE ratio is still close to 30, such that there have only been 2 brief periods in history when stocks were more overpriced, the peak of the dot-com boom and the eve of the Great Depression. With CAPE over 25, the next few decades are always erratic and poor performing, with 10 year returns between -4% and a high of 8%. When it comes to serious discussions of FIRE and getting FREE, these kinds of returns are virtually irrelevant. A FIRE movement based on that kind of performance is mostly going to mislead people.

10,000

How much you need to invest to be a millionaire by 40.

Age you start:

20,000

20: $1,700/month

25: $2,900/month

30: $5,500/month

35: $13,650/month

This is why the average age of people who've made a million dollars in the stock market is 70. Index funds simply aren't a realistic way to meet most FREE goals.

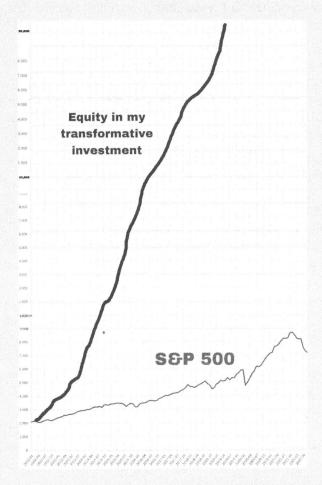

Let's compare index funds to the sort of "transformative investments" we'll talk about later in this book. These are a sort of investment that has a few very special properties, in addition to being societally transformative.

When I (Mike) invested in my first transformative asset, Lillie House Permaculture, my upfront share in around 2012 was $2000.

If I had instead invested that in an S&P index, I would have seen some of the best rates of return I could have ever expected from the stock market, getting in while the market was still reeling from the 2008 crash, and topping out with one of the highest CAPE ratios in history. With that spectacular rate of return, I would have made about $7,000, turning my $2000 into $9,000!

How did my investment in Permaculture work out? (You can read more details about this investment on page XXX.)

Well first, it allowed me to reduce my housing costs by about $3,000/year, helping me achieve a low cost of living. Owning a house will almost always save money on housing costs. But the attached rental property also helped to cash flow an additional $10,000/year after costs. And my personal share of equity over that same 10-year period grew to at least $50,000. That's realistically about $180,000 of profit, compared to the $7,000 I would have made investing in an index fund during a historically profitable period.

But the land involved also allowed me to quit my day job to spend my time playing with plants and cool people. Instead of investing in mass extinction and climate change, my investment helped start nearly 300 new gardens, created dozens of high quality habitat areas, bolstered local climate resilience, reduced my own carbon footprint significantly, and had countless other positive impacts. And that doesn't count the honestly tens of thousands of dollars of other assets I was able to pull out of that business (yes, even this book is realistically one of those investments.)

And the truth is, there's nothing spectacular about that rate of return on my investment. Some of the other authors of this book have reported similar outcomes, and I've seen many others do just as well off of transformative investments. Despite the emphasis on index funds in the modern FIRE movement, I personally know far more people who've grown FREE without the stock market. You'll find many potential investments in this book that can meet or beat those kinds of numbers.

That's par for the course. The only thing surprising is how poorly index funds perform comparatively, considering they're THE go-to investment of the modern Financial Independence movement.

The one big advantage that index funds do have, is that they appear to be one of the best places to store small amounts of money for short periods of time. But in the grand scheme of things, these rates of return are not going to be the thing that builds real wealth or leads to real FREEdom. So there are ethical alternatives to selling your soul for a definitively mediocre (index funds don't beat the market, they are the market —they are literally average) rate of return.

So in this book we'll focus on plans that will help real people grow more FREE no matter where they're at, ones that will be more accessible to far more people. That's going to require us to be more creative about reducing our costs and finding non-financial ways of meeting our needs. And it's going to require some different ways of investing.

P9–The Spectrum of Passivity and Livingry

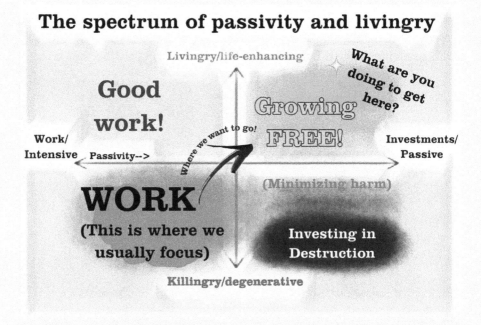

The spectrum of passivity and livingry

This tool helps us think about two areas of an income stream or investment that can be good, bad, or made better. SPOILERS: in a way, this one chart is a summary of this whole dang book. Giving this chart a complicated-sounding title with big unfamiliar words should help us all have to really interact with this idea and make meaning out of it.

First, one thing we need to think about is whether our livelihoods are life-enhancing, or destructive. A few of us writers have always liked Buckminster Fuller, so his terms **Livingry and Killingry** are useful here. "Bucky" was often surprised by how much money modern nations invest in things like "weaponry" and other technologies that are killing the planet. To make that connection clear, he called such tools **"killingry,"** which is in our bottom two quadrants.

But according to Bucky, we often have a choice. Often, we could solve the same problems by investing in things that made life better. Bucky thought that instead of buying weapons to kill people who were trying to fight to have better lives, we could just invest in helping those people have better lives, then they wouldn't want to fight us.

We could call that sort of positive investment "**livingry**," which is our top two quadrants.

So any of our work or investments can either be in "killingry" or " livingry." Often this is just a choice we can make. In teaching Permaculture courses and Transition groups I have frequently encountered people who had worked for weapons companies or oil companies, and they simply made the choice that they weren't going to do it anymore. (Of course, we can recognize that some of us may lack the privilege to simply quit, but we may choose to create an escape plan or use the tools in our chapter on "capitalism survival strategies" on page XXX to advocate from within the company.)

So we can ask: Are we investing in systems that make our own lives and world more difficult?

Are we truly "making a living?" Or are we "making a killing?"

Next, we can recognize that we can meet our needs in more active ways, which is basically work, and relatively passive ways, which is basically "investing."

Work, on the bottom left quadrant, is what most of us think of when we try to meet our needs. We have bills to pay and things we need to buy, and our first thought is usually that we'll need to work to get the money to pay for those things. Usually, most of us feel trapped into working to create killingry in one form or another.

Good work, on the top left, is a much better situation. Here, we have found ways to work for a better world, such that we work to create livingry, rather than killingry. Most FREE livelihoods will involve some forms of "good work." Again, my life is filled with people who simply made the decision they weren't going to work for killingry any more, and that they'd find good work. I'm proud of each one I meet.

But work isn't our only way to meet our needs. We can also meet our needs by investing.

Many people think of investing as using financial capital, money, to buy corporate stocks or so on, so that we can make money while doing nothing, off of other people doing work for us.

Because the corporate way of investing is so toxic, and we recognize that it's literally the #1 cause of climate change, of mass extinctions, ocean dead zones, plastics pollution, the seizure of indigenous lands, and etc. most of us may end up pretty strongly opposing that kind of investment.

Investing in Destruction is what we call that, on the bottom left quadrant. This is the way most rich people make their money. Investing is also synonymous with "passive income," where we earn income without working for it. Typically, most of the ways people talk about "passive income" are just more nuanced forms of investing in destruction.

But in this book, we'll use a different, more ecologically based definition, which recognizes that all organisms "invest." Through their actions they make their surroundings more abundant, more conducive to life. Birds invest in finding a good place to nest, with food, water, and safety. In fact, when birds find really good berries, they go back to the nest and "invest" by planting the seeds (yes, I'm talking about *pooping*) so that their home environment will have better food. And of course, they're also fertilizing those seeds. And then they invest their time and energy in building a nest, and raising the next generation. Nearly every activity of a bird is a matter of investing in a life-support system for itself and its family. Every organism does this same thing. So in this book...

Investing means to put our time, energy, money, and other resources into creating systems that will meet our needs into the future. Planting an apple tree is an example of a great **investment**, since that tree will pay you back in apples well into the future.

Growing FREE, is our final option on the top right. In this quadrant, we're investing in livingry, positive transformation, both for our lives and the world. This means we can set up streams of "passive income" that benefit us and our communities and planet. Even within much of the "regenerative movement" none of us ever talk about actively cultivating this quadrant.

We could say the whole main point of this book is to help us move out of the bottom two quadrants, especially the bottom left, and up into the top two.

But more importantly, the key advice of this book is that we also need to be thinking long term about *investing in creating the healthy systems of the future.* This book is about us together, investing in the future we want and deserve. So one major goal for this book is to help us find some ways to cultivate that top right quadrant.

That also recognizes that one of the most vital and life enhancing things we can do is have more free time in our lives. Investing in systems that will help us meet our needs can help us free up some time, helping us to earn more AND do more good while working less.

Perhaps one of the most important questions in this book is: *what are you doing to move towards this quadrant? What is your plan to invest in transforming your life and our world?*

And just as with livingry, we often have a choice about whether we're meeting our needs by working or investing.

For example, a regenerative farmer can have multiple ways to meet their needs. On one end of the spectrum, they could grow annuals, which require a lot of labor, and then take them to farmers' markets, which takes even more time and labor. That is choosing to work.

On the other hand, they could choose to invest in creating those perennial systems and food forests like I mentioned above, which is a move towards more passive income. And instead of going to the farmers market, they could start a CSA where their customers come to them. Or even more passive, they could start a You-pick business, where they don't even have to harvest. They could rent out the food forest to hunters, foraging classes, mushroom sellers, medicinal growers, and others, to generate passive income.

Artists could choose to paint pictures and sell them at art fairs. Or they could choose to invest in relationships with consignment where they could sell their art, a social media following, and a special niche market where their customers were coming to them online.

The thing is that both of those "jobs" could take the same amount of work. Someone could either put their time into finding and attending art fairs each weekend of the year, or they could invest that same time into consignment relationships. But the consignment relationships turn into semi-passive income, while the art fairs are committing to work. If you decide NOT to work, and you've only invested in art fairs, then you're not going to get paid. But the consignment operations will keep selling for you whether you work or not. It's a choice, and we often choose to work.

Herbalists could start a business growing and processing herbs into finished products, which is work. Meanwhile, Mike and Jason run "Transformative Adventures" home herbalism programs, in which people come to pick and create their own herbalism products. It's a more passive approach to the same livelihood.

Landscapers can choose to work to transform people's landscapes, but instead, you could replicate the Transformative Adventures Landscape Transformation Program, where you help people pick up their own plants, and design and transform their own landscapes—which is a much more passive model, and also one with a lot more *livingry*.

I could give 100 other examples, often, the choice between work and investing is just a decision we make.

So which quadrants are your income streams in? And which do you want to grow your livelihood in? Will you work for killingry, Invest in destruction, or find good work and invest in a better life and a better world? Make the choice, then let's make it happen.

Adventure 6: Start your Transformation Fund!

At this point, we've learned to flex some economic might. We've established a slush fund, paid off our debts, and developed and understanding of our own economic situation.

Now is where the real transformation begins, as we start to grow a fund we can use to create change!

Where do we put our transformation funds? Well, to start with, a checking account at your local Credit Union is a good choice. We'll need to have the funds in a relative liquid form. Once we have some cash saved up to work with, we can start investing it in the sorts of investments we'll learn about through the rest of this book.

But keep in mind, for the purpose of this book, we won't necessarily need cash in order to make investments! We can invest with little or even no cash. The point is to choose the sort of investments that will work for us.

P10–Patterns for Divesting From Destruction and Growing a Transformation Fund:

If we boil all our basic standard financial advice down to a few basic no-brainer steps, they'd be **Spend less, Save more, Invest wisely.** There, done!

The End.

And of course, in spending less, we are divesting our support from the corporations we know are destroying the planet.

Now, of course the trick is: how do we actually do that?

And of course, it's the first step of actually spending less that is often the most difficult for people.

Luckily, these days we have some communities we can turn to for support in accomplishing our goals. As good as this book may be, getting involved in communities that are working on these goals in real time is one of the most transformative "adventures" for accomplishing our goals.

When it comes to spending less, there are a few great communities I could recommend, and we'll summarize some of their key strategies. So, this list of communities also serves as a list of some of our major strategies for spending less.

Some communities that can help you on your adventure:

Permaculture. Globally, Permaculturists have been devoted to withdrawing support from the global corporate system for over 40 years now, which is a long time to figure out what works and what doesn't. Permaculture books and courses are often built on strategies for spending less, and getting more from connection to nature and community. A lot of the perspectives in this book are built on Permaculture Design. Permaculture communities may be portals to all of these other communities, too. That of course includes our Transformative Adventures communities locally and on social media.

Homesteading and gardening groups, though of course, this author believes many of these become very expensive lifestyle hobbies, rather than actual effective ways to save money and reduce our impact. Combining these with a Transformative Adventures approach focused on real economic practicality can help sort out the expensive hobbies from the actual savings.

FIRE, Early Retirement Extreme, FREE communities. There are many online communities, blogs, and social media groups devoted to FIRE, and many of these are good at helping regular people spend less money. We all participate in the Socially Conscious Fire group on Facebook, and in "FIREd Up" events on Zoom.

Frugal Living groups, groups devoted specifically to spending less. These are a great place to get inspiration and tips until you feel like you've learned the ways of frugality.

Buy it For Life, Buy For Life, or Buy it Once communities. This is a strategy that saves you money by making long-term investments up front.

Mutual Aid groups, FREEcycle, community lending/sharing groups. This is a major strategy used by Permaculturists for 40 years. Why own a commercial mulcher chipper if you only need to use it once a year? Why not own it with your community members and share the costs? There are many local groups that can help with these kinds of expenses.

Community Homeworks, house repair, DIY groups, and old house network groups. These can be a figurative goldmine for saving money on housing costs.

Simple Living and Minimalism groups. Perhaps the best way of all to spend less is to adopt a minimalist lifestyle. Luckily, there are many social media groups now to help you along the way.

By joining in with others who are interested in your goals, you can learn the basics, stay inspired, and get motivated by sharing your successes with others. When you've got the hang of one approach, you can get involved in another. It's a virtually sure-fire way to learn to live off less.

RESIST Capitalism
Like a Grandmother

Teaches subversive love
of nature in her garden

Pushes healthy snacks

Nurtures community networks

Darns clothes to fend off
hyper consumerism

Survived hyper-patriarchy
with time left over to bake pie

Cans like a mofo
to minimize waste
and maximize
resilience

Skillfully held together
an alliance of people
who'd otherwise hate
each other

Has cats

Pinches cheeks

Keeper of powerful
family knowledge

Fueled the informal
economy with
kindness

Some Systems Thinking for Spending Less Money

As we discussed before, when it comes to spending less, most experts just focus on brute force. Just spend less, darn it! But can we move up to higher leverage points when it comes to actually achieving this goal? What would some leverage points for behavior change, system change, and paradigm change look like?

Behavioral leverage points:

Invest in transformation, first! Each month, before you write a check to yourself, deposit money in your transformation fund. Again, this should be somewhat liquid, but not convenient to access. Doing this first will again remove the temptation to spend the money on other things. Go ahead and get excited about these payments. If you have a particular transformative investment in mind (we'll discuss these later!) you can chart your progress, and see how much closer you are to starting your Permaculture project or new business, for example.

Automate your reoccurring expenses and time the money to go out shortly after it comes in. Again, if the money isn't sitting there in the account all month, you've removed temptation, and placed a barrier of inconvenience between yourself and unwanted spending.

Replace unhelpful behaviors with satisfying helpful ones. If you find that each Friday you go out to the bar then go shopping, replace that activity with one that is a better investment in achieving your long-term goals. For example, get involved in a non-profit or networking activity that is fun and rewarding. This turns a negative feedback loop into a positive one.

Systems leverage points:

The envelope method, updated for the modern day. The big problem with budgets is that they're an imaginary barrier. In most cases, the only think stopping you from over-spending your budget is your will power, or "brute force." Back before the ubiquitous bank card, the "envelope method" was the solution. Each month, you'd pay yourself your "budget" into a few envelopes, such as an envelope for food, an envelope for entertainment, and you'd pay all your expenses in cash.

Of course, these days, few people use cash. But we can still create a digital barrier of inconvenience between ourselves and our money. The first step is to make sure any income is direct deposited into a holding account or slush fund that does not have a debit card. That last bit is the active ingredient. Each month, you "pay" yourself profit from that account into a checking account with no minimum balance, and that is all the money you get that month. The danger of a overdraft penalty should help keep you paying attention to your budget. And of course, in an emergency, you can still access your slush fund. But it puts a barrier of inconvenience and cool-off time between you and knee-jerk spending.

Profit First, if you're in business. Mike Michalowicz writes about a complete system redesign in his book, Profit First. This turns conventional accounting on its head. In a conventional business, our accounting looks like the linear systems we've discussed in this book: revenue - expenses = profit. This tends to turn businesses into money gobbling monsters, as business expenses grow to eat up all our earnings. So, Michaelowicz changes the system rules, to: revenue - PROFIT = expenses. In this case, we pay ourselves first, and use what is left over to cover expenses. This puts us in a mindset of crushing expenses, and actually making money FIRST, before we spend more money on expenses that might not even be worthwhile.

Paradigm change:

Changing paradigms is the most powerful leverage point, but is of course also the hardest to figure out how to do! And it will be very individual, and depend on your own paradigms around spending, pleasure, and money.

But I can give you an example that was powerful for me. It was to stop thinking of "saving" and start thinking of "investing in transforming my life." "Saving" sounds dull, and ascetic. "Transforming my life" sounds dynamic, focuses me on the lifestyle I want and goals I want to achieve.

Starting to think of money—not as something to either be spent or saved—but as a source of energy to transform my life, changed the way I thought about every dollar that came into my account.

The more we can align our thinking, the ways we think about things and the terms we use for them, with our actual values, the more likely we will be to accomplish our goals without having to use brute force to do it.

P11–The Transformative Adventures Targeted Thrift List

Really Save Money/Create a Better World

Several years ago when I was starting a new project, Permaculture designer Peter Bane stayed at my house for a Permaculture convergence. With the budget being tight, and the house being a fixer-upper, I was going out of my way to cut costs for my emerging income streams. As such, I had a huge stack of pre-cleaned but unusable mason jars sprawling into the corner of the kitchen. The jars were clearly becoming an obstacle to prepping meals, so Peter asked about them.

I explained that I didn't like the idea of not reusing them, especially when I'd have to buy new ones.

"Get rid of them!" Peter exclaimed. "They're recyclable, it's not like they're going in a landfill! If you had time it would be one thing, but washing that stack of jars isn't worth your time right now. You have higher priorities to focus on!" He was absolutely right. Even if I only paid myself $10/hour, it would have taken $50 of my time to wash all those jars, when I could buy them at a bulk price for $30.

Sometimes, being frugal just costs too much money!

This is especially true for a lot of the "hardcore" self-reliance and "green living" skills we see from social media celebrities. Spending hours to hand-make your own arrow heads? Cool! But calling that thrift when modern humane arrow heads cost pennies each, is "all cents no penny jar."

Therefore, we need to know when it's worth our effort to take the extra time to save money. This Targeted Thrift List was developed by looking at research on cost savings, doing some math, and running that by our personal experience. To make the cut, the work involved in these areas had to be worth approximately $30/hour in 2022 dollars.

The high-impact target areas: Housing, Home and Energy; Food; Clothing; Health; Recreation; Childcare; Transportation. These are the areas that consumers spend the most on, so they have the largest potential savings, making them good leverage points to focus on. These are also some of the world's most destructive industries, so the targeted thrift list is also targeted action.

In the Garden*.
Gardening can be one of our highest potential savings areas! According to US data, the average American household spends $4000/year on groceries. But as gardeners, we can grow high-cost, organic luxury items. Families eating an organic diet rich in fresh foods typically spend over $12,000/year.

So, if we can grow $10k of groceries/year and reduce our spending to $2-3000/year, that's a huge value. If we can do that 100 hours of work per season (this is a very realistic benchmark) then our time gardening is worth $100/hour. HOWEVER: if it takes your family 20 hours/week over the season to grow your food, then the time is only worth $12/hour, and if your family spends 40 hours/week, then it's only worth $6/hour! So, techniques to save time are highly valuable!

1. Spend a few hours per week on a family food garden. Even farmers should have food gardens for their families, as these will often be the highest value part of the farm.*
2. Decorate the landscape with plants instead of buying expensive materials like plastics and pavers.*
3. Invest in soil, mulch, and water direction, instead of expensive irrigation.*
4. Know which seeds to save and save them! (Save low effort seeds and specialties.)*
5. Use the holistic natural gardening practices, avoid spraying.*
6. Prioritize high value crops, these are often perennials like blackberries and asparagus.*
 7. Minimize expensive equipment, find used tools, maintain them well. Buy small and local.
8. Grow daily greens and herbs.
9. For winter, prioritize overwintering crops, cellaring, and saving Whole Foods over
processing, and plan to grow what you can actually use and save.*
10. Use "prolific plants" that are easy to spread and grow. (See transformativeadventures.org.)*

Housing.

The standard recommendation is that housing should take 1/3rd of your income! For me, that's a lot! But at that rate, housing becomes one of the biggest areas for potential savings. So for the median American family making $70k/year, housing usually accounts for nearly $24,000/year, or more in some markets! If the cost can be reduced to even $12,000 (doable while maintaining a middle-class standard of living in many areas) that's a savings of $12,000/year that can be added to our Transformation Funds. Many Permaculturists and FIRE fiends reduce their housing costs to mere thousands/year.

11. Practice wabi-sabi, or some other aesthetic based on simplicity.* See page XXX.
12. Prioritize energy investments with a short payback time. See our pattern on this.*
13. Buy used, invest in long-term quality.*
14. Aim low on square footage per person. This is also great for the environment.
15. Learn repair skills, keep old things working, use the internet!*
16. Aim to buy, but know when to rent and buy at the right time.**

Transportation
17. Get friendly with public transportation and ride sharing. Community vehicles.
18. Buying a new car may be the worst thing you can ever do for the planet.
19. Do your regular maintenance, learn the basics yourself.*
20. Regular oil changes, keep the gas tank more than half full.
Clothing, the world's worst industry?
21. Buy well-fitting, durable, clothes from natural fibers in classic styles.
22. The French wardrobe of fewer outfits with fewer pieces, more options, more accessories.
23. Enjoy thrifting and garage sales.*

Health

24. Learn home herbalism: forage, grow, and produce your own medicines.*
25. Eat fresh greens daily, perhaps the best thing you can do for your health.
26. Exercise: basic weight training 20 minutes 3 days/week, daily walking, mobility like yoga.
27. Connect with nature: regular gardening, hiking, forest bathing, pets, camping.
28. Daily meditation or mindfulness practice.
29. Doctor share?

Childcare:

30. Cloth diapers?
31. Childcare swap and investing in social capital and community. 32. Cooperative preschool?*
33. Host an au pair

Food knowledge from traditional societies.
34. Simplify, use staples in weekly batches, like soups, polenta, grains.
35. Grow corn, potatoes, sweet potatoes, amaranth,
36. Make "daily bread" a routine, keep a starter going, add flour daily. Use flatbreads.*
37. Eggs and milk are the cheapest proteins. The French style omelette is a time saver!
38. There are many keepable egg staples such as Spanish tortilla, cakes, crepes, quiche, tortes...
39. Keep the freezer full.

Recreation

40. Become a journey woman or man. Revive this old tradition and put your skills to use!*
41. Flex your network for travel.
42. WWOOF or join an ecosystem restoration camp.
43. Create recreation space in the garden and landscape.*
44. Invest in making home beautiful, the landscape regenerative, and community beloved.

Education*
45. Consider training in trades and skills.
46. Think of making investments instead of getting training for a job.
47. Become a journey woman or journeyman.(**)
Apprentice.
48. Avoid degrees in the new "hot thing" pushed by the universities or colleges.

Life
49. Take care of your teeth!!!
50. Avoid debt!!! Especially for degenerative assets. Debt is okay or may even be a positive if spent on regenerative procreative assets that cash flow.

Wabi-sabi and Other Aesthetics of Imperfection

In Japan, "wabi-sabi" refers to the beauty of the aged and imperfect, a flawed beauty that invokes solitude, nature, and spirituality. Instead of aesthetics based on being shiny and new, wabi-sabi celebrates things that age gracefully.

This is an aesthetic of what we'll later call "durable assets." It's a beauty that is as good for the wallet and our wealth as it it is for the senses. Ideas of "beauty" based on being new and perfect cannot last, and as soon as they are flawed, they're sent to the land fill. But things meant to show age and imperfection grow in beauty and meaning as they gain wear and flaws. Similar aesthetics are found in antiques, in "cottage core," in shabby chic, and English and French country styles.

This is extremely powerful, because it's another high leverage paradigm shift. More than anything else, Aesthetics drives our behavior. What we think is beautiful, fun, and makes a good life, drives virtually all our decisions! Changing our paradigms for what's good and beautiful in alignment with our goals and values, is one of the most powerful ways to change our outcomes.

For me, nothing is truly "beautiful" unless it helps build a better life and a better, more beautiful world.

We'll discuss these forms of beauty throughout this book.

Chapter 6: Open Your Eyes to Abundance

Have you fallen for the myth that you can only meet your needs by spending money? Capitalism sure hopes you have because it relies on you believing that and continually buying what it's selling.If you want to push back on capitalism's incessant efforts to turn you into a consumer, a powerful way to do that is to harness the wealth that surrounds you.

As much as corporations, the media, and even our government want us to believe that we exist in a world of scarcity, that is simply not the case. Certainly, resources are being hoarded, major systemic changes need to occur, and there are people struggling financially, but many of us are so caught up in the capitalist grind we can't see beyond our blinders to recognize the abundance around us.

We live in an abundant world. Maybe you've sensed glimmers of overlooked abundance in the way forests continually enrich themselves or how many still usable items end up in our "waste" stream. The world around us is literally bursting with productive energy, yet we are continually fed messages of lack and shortages.

Because those messages are pervasive in our culture it's imperative that we strengthen our ability to think outside the box about how to make use of things. To that end in his book *Stretch: Unlock the Power of Less And Achieve More Than You Ever Imagined* by Rice University Management Professor Scott Sonenshein differentiates between chasers and stretchers.

Chasers are often motivated consciously or unconsciously by keeping up with the Joneses and get focused on acquiring resources, overlooking what they already have at hand. The author points out that chasers tend to get caught up in functional fixedness (presuming that an object is limited to a certain function) and come to believe that having more resources leads to getting better results.

Stretchers on the other hand recognize that usually "better use of resources leads to better results." Typically, stretchers are more likely than chasers to view resources as capable of more than their primary use. As a result, chasers frequently get caught up in mindless accumulation and trapped in a job and lifestyle that leave them highly dissatisfied.

In other words, if you're a stretcher, you might do 10 jobs with one tool, while a chaser might need to accumulate 10 tools just to do one job!

Sonenshein also notes that almost anything, be it tangible or intangible, "has potential as a resource, but to become anything of value requires action." Stretchers more easily see the potential for beauty and usefulness in places where others don't and then take that required action to turn previously overlooked items into something of value.

Two skills that can be very helpful in unleashing all that unrecognized potential to transform things into resources are creativity and resourcefulness. I'm not creative in the artistic sense – I even find drawing stick figures challenging – but I do think creatively about how to live my life outside the rat race and use resources differently. And I strive to surround myself with others who do the same.

Here are three strategies that have served me and my friends well in our efforts to live more creatively and resourcefully.

"A stretching mind-set releases us from the anxiety of never having enough and teaches us that we can make more than enough with what's right here"

Scott Sonenshein, *Stretch*

Get more from what you've already got

My house has a garage that I don't park my car in. When my nomadic friend founded the Florida Fruit Co-op and needed a place to store his supplies between weekend markets I told him he could use my garage. Now in exchange for letting him use an underutilized resource of mine I receive free tropical fruits, fresh eggs, and a monthly massage, plus I see my friend more often.

Try perceiving everyday things differently

My neighbor is a musician and has a lot of social capital in our small town. One income source she has built for herself is hosting a bi-weekly local variety show on her inviting back patio. She interviews different local figures during each show giving them an opportunity to connect with the in-person audience as well as everyone who logs-in on Facebook to watch. It's such a fun and unique local experience. Supporters can make contributions via Patreon to fund the show.

Think outside our limited societal mindset

I'm a proud and active dumpster diver because I abhor waste and the financial benefits don't hurt either. In fact, there were a couple years when I earned several thousand dollars selling what I rescued out of thrift store, university, and grocery store dumpsters. These days I'm much more likely to gift, donate, or swap the non-food items I rescue and don't keep for myself through our local time bank or Buy Nothing Group.

My boyfriend and I are dumpster gourmets meaning we source about 70 to 80% of the food we eat from grocery store dumpsters. We supplement that food with items we've grown, foraged, been gifted, or bartered for. Thanks to my boyfriend's impressive culinary skills (I call him the Master of Umami) we eat some truly tasty meals that you'd never guess came from a dumpster.

The beauty of "stretching" as Dr. Sonenshein refers to it is that not only does this way of thinking about resources save us (and maybe even make us) money, it also offers us the opportunity to experience the satisfaction of creatively meeting our own needs and it's almost always a far more eco-friendly option.

So now that we've established the value of creativity and resourcefulness, how do we cultivate it? Because even if we are artistic we can likely still benefit from thinking more creatively about how to use and think differently about the resources to which we have access.

For me personally, one of the ways I unintentionally started exercising my creativity and resourcefulness was through cooking without a recipe, simply using whatever ingredients I have on hand.I wing it a great deal in the kitchen. Cooking with what's in your fridge and pantry is often mentioned as a great way to start flexing that creative muscle. But for those that don't enjoy cooking there are other ways as well...

No matter what situation you find yourself in, saying no to additional resources and forcing yourself to work with those at hand can often push us to be more resourceful. For example, Theodor Geisel, whom most of us know as Dr. Seuss, was bet by his editor that he couldn't write a book using only 50 unique words. The result of that wager is the book *Green Eggs and Ham*, so we know how that bet ended.

With all that in mind I encourage you to shake off your limited ways of thinking and open yourself to new ways of perceiving things. Start tapping your creativity, unleashing your unlimited human potential, and keeping more money in your pocket and out of the capitalist juggernaut. Ask yourself "What wealth am I overlooking that's already in my midst?"

Chapter Resources:

1. Sonenshein, Scott. Stretch: Unlock the Power of Less And Achieve More Than You Ever Imagined. Rice University Management.

P12–Patterns for Saving Money on Housing

That place where you hang your hat can either be your single biggest financial burden, or it can be a big piece of your financial freedom. It can be the proverbial money pit, or a giant live-in piggy bank. You get to decide.

For most of us, our housing will be our single biggest annual expense. The ol' timey financial advice was that housing should run about 1/3rd of our annual income. I call that ol' timey, because even pre-covid that advice was looking a little dated. But in the last few years, with rents and housing prices utterly soaring, I'm seeing major media articles noting that many Americans in many markets are now paying 50% or more of their income just to have a roof over our heads.

So, if you think about no other issue, just dealing with your housing costs can have a huge impact on your financial well-being.

For some of us, the savings may be obvious, and the real decision is about making trade-offs and priorities. Some of my friends pay $30,000 or more per year for their mortgages. There are opportunities to pay $5000 per year in the same market, within a 10 minute drive, and usually these lower-cost homes are closer to work than distant ritzy suburbs. That could be $25,000 that could go into the life-transformation fund each year. We must decide, what do we want more? Whatever benefits come with the big mortgage, or financial freedom in a few short years? Or is there a compromise between the two goals?

But at least in that case the money is going into a mortgage, building equity, almost always at a far better rate than we'd ever get in a stock market index fund. Others may be stuck in markets where it is simply very difficult to reduce our housing expenses much. In downtown Houston as I write this, the average rent is over $20,000 per year. And each rent payment just goes forever out the window, instead of building equity.

But either way, we can almost always improve our situations with regards to housing, and spending some time learning about some patterns for saving on housing can have a big return on investment.

Patterns for Housing Savings

Note: we'll have more patterns for "investing in housing," including more about coops and cohousing on page XXX.

Buy, if You Can

The first and simplest advice for saving money on housing is to consider buying instead of renting. We'll discuss strategies for investing in housing on page XXX.

In Houston, while it may be hard to find an apartment to rent for under $16,000/year, I can find houses available to own for $8,000/year.

More importantly, that $8,000 is going right into your own live-in piggy bank, where it will grow in value over time.

There are, of course, reasons to not buy. For example, if the market is unreasonably high. But even if the market is overvalued in Houston (which it may be) it's still better to pay yourself $8000/year than it is to pay $16,000/ year to a landlord.

Once we start talking about investment strategies, we'll see there are many very good investments that pair well with home-ownership, which can lead to very FREE lifestyles.

Pros and Cons of Home Ownership:

Pros

Live-in piggy bank forces you to save

Can be a great investment

Can pair well with other investments

Can provide land access for other streams of land-based income

Freedom

Lower taxes

Can more comfortably run around in underwear

Cons

Requires good credit

You'll have responsibility for maintenance

Harder to do while self-employed

May require a history of employment

Can "tie you down" to a place

Involves more risk, as you may lose the house or the neighborhood can go bad.

Saving Money on Buying a Home

(See additional Patterns on Housing Investment, Page XXX)

(This section is so important it could use an infographic/image.)

Open your Eyes to Abundance

"If you can see it clearly enough in your mind, then in the morning it will be there waiting for you."

Again, having a plan and vision for your life primes you to see opportunities you might not otherwise see. Multiple times now, I have sat down to create a real vision of where I wanted to be in my future, and then a few years later, realized I was exactly where I had envisioned. When you have a destination in mind you start actively looking for a way to get there.

And beyond that, you get clear about what things are really part of your plan. You may realize that you can accept the trade-off of a less expensive location for greater freedom. I myself have bought multiple houses with big holes right in the walls when I normally would have considered "functioning walls" to be the basic definition of a house! Holes can be fixed in a day, but the freedom that came with the affordable homes lasted for decades.

After setting his own vision, Jason realized that he could find an affordable home in a less gentrified neighborhood (and less "desirable" neighborhood in his region. Eric "upgraded" his life by deciding to spend his summers in a camper with a 5 star view of a lake and his winters in an affordable off-grid cabin. Jenny called the trailer she once lived in a "paradise" and now cohouses in a small permacultured home in Florida. None of these situations are on the mainstream conspicuous consumption plan. But with housing being such a major expense, it's no wonder that affordable housing choices were part of the FREE plan for all this book's authors.

Buying Distressed (without Gentrifying)

Even in 2022, as housing prices soar, it's possible to find houses in American cities for just tens of thousands of dollars, or even thousands or hundreds. Most of these houses will require a fair bit of work—in a lot of cases just to make them habitable. But for people with skills, and a willingness to enjoy a live-in work of art in-progress, it can be an excellent opportunity to "grow FREEdom." Buying a house for $10,000 that could be worth $150,000 if habitable is a huge opportunity for instant sweat equity, which can become an opportunity to access capital and big savings on housing costs. Every penny we put into such a house will have a guaranteed big return on investment.

"Sherif sales, county auctions, and tax sales." Most counties in the US manage the sales of properties confiscated by the state or banks to pay for debts or unpaid taxes. It's worth saying that this is something we should politically oppose, but once these properties have been confiscated, it's better that you or I, or others who live in our cities buy these properties. Usually, they're just bought for pennies by distant corporate bankers. So, buy the houses, then organize to provide better services and protections to people in economic need. Counties usually keep lists or webpages for these sales and auctions, so you can find these lists with an internet search for your county name and the terms above.

Foreclosures. These are often sold by banks when people fail to pay off their mortgages. These can also be found with an internet search for your local area and "foreclosures."

$1 Houses. IN a few of the most distressed American urban areas, municipalities have sold houses for as low as $1, with a commitment to live in and pay taxes on the homes.

Tips on Buying Distressed Houses

Beware the "money pit." Usually, you'll buy distressed houses without setting foot inside. There will be problems. Almost definitely you'll be taking responsibility for the previous owners' garbage. It could possibly be a hoarding situation. Be ready to take on infestations, electrical, and plumbing problems before you move in.

Some of the most expensive problems can be seen from the outside. Find someone who can help you identify flooding, landslide, sink holes, leaking water and sewer lines, fire or other problems in the landscape. Damaged roofs, crumbling foundations, or badly damaged siding can be very expensive. Beware of houses with no gutters, as these could have decades of water damage. In older wood sided Victorian homes, badly peeling paint could be a sign of improperly installed wall insulation, which could also cause black mold and other expensive problems.

Before buying, make sure to do a little homework to check records. Many can be accessed by searching for your county or municipality name and "GIS" or "tax records." GIS maps usually will show flood plain areas, utility easements, and property line issues. In urban areas some homes become virtually unreliable, because the driveway or part of the house was built on the neighbor's property, creating a legal nightmare you don't want to own.

Talk to neighbors to learn about the neighborhood first. I once ought a beautiful Victorian house with a finished mother-in-law apartment in the well-maintained barn, with 3 acres of grade A soil for a mere $70k.The neighbors had just sold their land to a gravel mining company, and other gravel mines in the region were dealing with lawsuits around lung cancer for silica dust. Some peace and quiet seeking friends of mine found a ridiculously affordable beautiful home, only to learn the property across the street had been approved for a bar and strip club.

The Buying Process

My advice is to find someone from your network who's done it before if possible. Your local Permaculture community might have folks who've made the journey before. Different municipality's may provide different levels of support, so call to see what guidance they offer. You may need a bank check to make payment at the auction.

Once you own the home, you may need to do the awful task of evicting the previous owners. Remember, you're not taking their home, the bank is, and the best time to solve this problem is BEFORE people lose their homes. Any offers or negotiations you make with the previous owners may become your own liability. Still, we can show up as people and be compassionate for those losing their home. It's best to initiate this process ASAP, as you will likely be unable to get full insurance on the property until they move out, and you may be liable for their injuries or losses while you own the property.

House Hacking

Consider cost sharing. What's better than owning your own home? Owning your own home and filling it with friends, family, and community, who can chip in on rent and other costs.

Rent out rooms. As with renting, it can often be more affordable to buy too much house and rent out a portion. Buying a duplex or triplex and renting out half can be a way to reduce yearly housing costs to nearly $0 while still storing money in the live-in piggy bank. It's honestly one of the best wealth-building tips I've seen work in the real world.

Buying (& living) with friends After her divorce Holly Harper moved with her daughter into an apartment. She soon realized though, that she'd like to live in a house again, but couldn't afford to make that happen on her own. It turned out that her good friend, Herrin, who was also recently divorced, found herself in a similar situation.The two mothers decided to join forces and funds to buy a property with multiple living spaces together. To ensure they were a good fit to pursue this cooperative venture Holly and Herrin had deep and honest discussions about their political outlooks, parenting styles, finances, and lifestyles.

Like other groups of friends, who've decided to buy property to live in together, Holly and Herrin purchased it as coinvestors instead of co-owners of a home - a technical difference that involves a few additional legalities while making it much easier for buyers to receive bank funding. In Holly's own words they essentially "live in a condo building with an informal, but legal, agreement between us."

https://www.yahoo.com/news/bought-house-another-single-mom-170756100.html

Downshifting

Another option for buying more affordable houses is to search in more affordable markets. Only you will know if this fits your holistic life design.

Buying Nomadic Housing

We called my uncle Ed "Turtle," because he took his house with him everywhere he went. He bought a distressed Airstream camper for around $1,000, fixed it up and decades later sold it for $15k. It saved him money on housing for years, and in the end was not a bad investment. New models will almost always depreciate rapidly, but older collectible models bought on the cheap will likely hold their value or appreciate well like uncle Turtle's did.

Buying Small or Even Tiny

Time will tell whether tiny houses hold their value and appreciate as an investment. The barrier is that such homes do not always allow families to grow. The upside is tiny homes may be a backstop against gentrification and soaring tax rates. If looking for an investment, find tiny homes with room for additions and growth.

Saving Money for Renters

Cost-sharing. If you find friends to live with, you can share on housing costs and other expenses as well. You'll also get to flex your community building muscles. I pretty much always lived in big houses filled with people and energy when I was young, and I still love that, today.

Rent and rent out rooms. In most markets it's cheaper per-person to rent a house than it is to rent a room. You may be able to reward yourself and your friends by taking the initiative to rent a house and—with your landlord's permission—rent out rooms to friends and fellow renters.

Work for Rent

When I was renting I had multiple occasions where I negotiated work for rent. This can be a great way to learn some building skills while you get low-cost rent. Such opportunities are often available in distressed downtown areas, for example, where landlords want to fix up properties but lack capital.

Websites like Caretaker.org can help you find long-term work exchanges across the country and sometimes even overseas. While most of the opportunities do require more than basic repair skills, a recent post was seeking someone to simply move a few horses from the barn to the pasture whenever the owners were away - no horseback riding skills required. Exchanges like these leave you with a great deal of free time to learn new skills, pursue a side hustle, work remotely, or just enjoy more leisure time.

Sometimes you can even find paid opportunities that include housing for positions like chef or innkeeper. With your living expenses covered you can stash more of your income to grow your FREEdom account.

Be open to opportunities If you want to jump start your FREEdom fund, work full-time remotely and are open to moving, consider relocating to Tulsa, Oklahoma. At the time of publishing this book the city is partnering with the George Kaiser Family Foundation to provide $10,000 grants to eligible remote workers, who move there from out of state through the Tulsa Remote initiative. New arrivals also receive a one year membership at a local co-working space, assistance locating housing, and access to regular community-building opportunities.

There's no requirement to stay in Tulsa more than one year, although it's certainly the city's hope that you will and it could just be that you find your peeps and desired lifestyle there. Check out TulsaRemote.com for more details.

Investing in a Place to Call Home

You may be reading this without a plan at all for where to "hang your hat." This has been the topic of many lengthy books, so it's more than we can handle here, but we can at least say a little about some of the major options and some of the debates around them.

Rent or Own (Or Squat!)

We've already discussed this big debate a little, but in a world of instability and climate change, there are a few more factors to consider. For most of us, ownership is the better investment and more affordable option if possible. But, as author Nicole Foss has pointed out, in a rapidly changing world, renting can allow us to find climate opportunities and avoid climate losses. Renting allows us to let other people take the risks of climate change and political instability for us. Those risks are likely to go up over time. As renters, we will likely pay increasingly more for the privilege of letting others take those risks.

Downshifting or Living Large

The quick path to a FREE life seems to be owning a home outright as soon as possible, so that we'll continue to grow in wealth while saving considerable money on housing costs. But this runs counter to the conventional financial advice. For those hoping to grow conventionally "wealthy," the advice is often "buy the biggest house you can afford." A big house in a good neighborhood is likely to be a good investment, and paying at least 1/3rd of your income on housing forces us to save money. Of course, this conventional advice is also a sure fire way to keep us trapped in the rat race, and feeling extra stressed about losing our jobs.

The Urban Vs Rural Debate (and College Towns,Too.)

An internet search or discussion in a Permaculture group will show that a great deal has been written about this debate, too. Much more than we can cover here. With decades in this movement, I've watched students, professionals, and big name leaders move back and forth, and back again in every which way. Often, they seem to feel that "there's only one option." Later, they may feel the other option is the only real option. The truth is, we can build FREE lifestyles of appropriate sustainable transformative action in the city, the country, the suburbs, or anywhere in between. If your choice is being determined because you think your choice is the only choice, you're probably choosing wrong. Each has its benefits and drawbacks and needs to be considered as part of a holistic life design. And so, a chart:

Urban	
Pros	Cons
-Culture, community, arts.	-Relatively noisy
-Land likely to appreciate well.	-Community!
-Lowest transportation cost.	-Expensive land and housing
-Lowest environmental footprint, highest sustainability.	-May not have easy access to land for incomes.
-High in opportunity	
-Near to amenities like healthcare, education, libraries, stores, etc.	
-Culturally permissive, less conformist, more freedom to do what you like.	
-Can build a beautiful, high	

Rural	
Pros	Cons
-Wide open spaces without people!	-Least sustainable lifestyle, unless highly self-sufficient.
-Solitude	-More pesticides and pollution, often lower biodiversity in
-Peace and quiet	farming areas.
-Possibly more affordable land	-Lack of community
-Space for conventional farming	-Lack of cultural resources
	-Lack of health care, schools, etc.
	-Often more conformist, less

College town	
Pros	Cons
-Best access to culture and amenities.	-Often more expensive than suburbs or rural. places.
-Great sense of community.	-May be a lot of competition for green careers.
-Often great public transportation.	-
-Culturally the most permissive.	

Suburbs	
Pros	Cons
-Cheaper prices	-Typically the MOST conformist and least permissive.
-a mix of urban and rural conditions.	-Expensive

P13–Energy Investments that Pay YOU

to Fight Climate Change

It's not just our house that's a huge potential for savings, it's what we do in it. Our homes are like big machines for containing people, and these machines require surprisingly large amounts of energy and resources.

And that of course makes our homes one of our biggest potential action areas for climate change, too.

Luckily, since all this energy is so expensive, we can actually PAY ourselves to save energy and fight climate change, and done well, this can be some real money.

Therefore, we should all have a plan to improve our home's sustainability, and a prioritized series of "adventures" to help us get it done. If we do this right, the first set of adventures will pay for the second, which can pay for the third and so on, such that the whole endeavor is entirely free to us.

Adventures to save money and fight climate change:

1. **Caulking and sealing. Payback time: < 2-3 months.**
For a few dollars of caulk and a few hours applying it, we can save significant money and have a more comfortable house. Make sure to get the right caulk for each job, not all caulk is the same. If it is going on surfaces that get painted, make sure you use a paintable caulk. It will say so on the package.
Savings: $20/year for new, "tight" houses, $100-150/year for older homes.
Priorities: Attic floor, ducts, light fixtures, wall sockets, storm windows.
Also: Door Strips, payback time: 2-4 months.

2. **Low Flow Shower Heads. Payback time: 2 months.**
You gotta go with the flow. Just keep the flow low, tho. Low flow shower heads can make the shower experience more comfortable in some cases. Some new shower heads have different settings that can deliver a fire hose worth of pressure, or a gentle rain. Others can shut off while you're washing your hair or otherwise not in the water. Cost $7-20.
Savings: Up to $250/year. Example: Evolve Road Runner II.

3. **DIY Indoor Storm Windows - NOT just plastic window film!!!**
   Payback time: < 1 year.

Vinyl window companies make a big deal of selling their products, but research has shown that well maintained old wood windows can work better, have less embodied energy costs, last nearly forever, and be nearly as efficient as modern energy efficient windows, so long as we have good storm windows. For extra savings, we can make interior storm windows for a very low cost. These can be made to be installed with compression gaskets and fish eye hooks for a good, tight fit.

Cost: < $1/window.

Savings: $20/window/year, but with diminishing returns

Priorities: bedrooms, main living areas

4. Programmable Thermostats: Payback time: 2-6 months

If you still have an old fashioned dial thermostat or other thermostat that isn't programmable, this is a no brainer. These can easily save $100/year, while making the house more comfortable.

Cost: $30

Savings: $100 - 150/year.

Smart Thermostats: Payback time: 4 years or more.

Cost: $350

Savings: $100 - 150/year, but may require hardware updates.

5. 2 Ceiling Fans (if used to adjust thermostat 10 degrees.) Payback time 7 - 16 months.

Savings: $100/year.

Priorities: 2 main living/sleeping areas.

6. Keeping Windows in Good Repair: Payback time < 1 year.

This means spending a little time to caulk or reglaze our windows. It's a good skill to have and makes for a great date night for eco-friendly FIRE geeks.

Cost: < $10/10 years.

Savings: Up to $20 window/year, > $100 - 300/year for whole house.

7. Insulate Canned Lighting. Payback time: ?

Canned lighting is just one of the absolute worst energy wasters in the home. You can buy insulating sleeves for these and save a load of money.

8. Water Heater Blanket and Insulate 10 ft of pipe. Payback time: < 6 months

Cost $15 - 30

Savings: $50-60/year

9. Duct Sealing and Targeted Insulating. Payback time: < 1 year

Cost: < $100

Savings: Up to 30%/year on poorly constructed and unsealed ducts!

Cash savings: up to $350/year

10. Attic Sealing and Insulating to 8-10 inches, R-40. Payback time < 6 months
Approx Cost: $130/100 SF of un-insulated attic space.
Potential Savings: Up to $1,000/year
Priorities: Seal first! Insulate around any attic penetrations, lights bathroom fans, etc.
Adding insulation up to 8 inches is a no—brainer! Up to 10 inches increases comfort.
Keep insulation in good repair!
NOTE: HOW TO FINISH ATTICS THE RIGHT WAY FOR COLD CLIMATES

MAXIMUM SAVINGS STACK:
So, if you were to only prioritize a few of these items in a standard American home, what should you do? These are some of our biggest ROI investments:
Cost: $200.
Gross Savings: $700/year.
Net Payback: $500 in first year!!!

—Water Heater Blanket: Cost: $20. Savings: $50
(Honorable mention: sink aerators.)
—Low Flow Shower Heads: Cost: $50. Savings $250/year
—Duct Work Seal and Insulate: Cost $100, Savings: $300/year
—Programmable Thermostat: Cost: $30. Savings: $100/year

Some Energy Saving Behaviors:

1. Heat the person, not the space.
2. Use your programmable thermostat.
3. 68 Degrees is the recommended comfortable Winter temperature for humans.
4. Turn off lights and electronics.
5. "Heat the person, not the space." One of the best ways to save money on heating is to not waste money heating rooms no one is in. Small space heaters by desks can have a huge increase in comfort at a minimal cost, for example.

Home Energy Investments for Renters

You don't have to be a home owner to save money by fighting climate change!

But the advice I'll give here may be a little counter-intuitive. We all have an ethical obligation to reduce our carbon footprints and save energy. But if you're renting, your first job may be to invest in getting FREE. Then you'll be able to afford to make big effective investments in a better world.

Therefore, we should prioritize energy investments that will give a good payback to renters, and those that help renters acquire their own "regenerative assets," which we'll cover in our section on investing.

1. Invest in improvements that will actually save YOU money on utilities first. For example, if the landlord is paying the gas and electric, and you are paying for water, go ahead and invest in things that will save water.
2. Invest in assets you can keep. For example, invest in low-flow shower heads, faucet attachments. If you're paying your electric, look into energy efficient space heaters, heat pumps, and window air-conditioners you can take to your next house. If you're paying for heat and you don't have a programmable thermostat, get one ASAP.
3. Invest in "heating the person, not the space." If you're paying for heat, this can save you money, and be a good long-term investment. And small space heaters and personal heating devices are an investment you can take with you to save money for decades to come.
4. When it comes to things the landlord is paying for, talk to them about trading rent for energy saving work. You can use the list above to pitch some investments. Let them know you have an idea for saving them money while fighting climate change and making the apartment more attractive to young do-gooder tenants in the future. See if you can strike a deal that saves them money and helps the planet. Do it well, and you might turn this into a side-hustle or job, pitching the same improvements to other landlords in your community.

P14–Reduce Spending by Getting out of Debt Prison!

And finally, another one of the big leverage points for reducing our spending? Debt.

While we already covered getting out of debt as one of the first "adventures" in this book, this is a good time for a reminder that giving up your interest payment is a good saving strategy.

The average median American, for example, spends $5000/year on interest payments. That's $5000 you may be spending for the privilege of being in debt and nothing more. The second we can give that up, it's a $5000 raise.

There are more patterns for getting out of debt on page XXX.

P15–Saving Money on Transportation

Since transportation joins housing and food as one of the top 3 expenses, putting some thought into how we get around is another high-powered leverage point.

But it's also one that comes with moral dilemmas for us authors. In David Holmgren's Retrosuburbia, he simply says to "do without cars," and leaves it at that! Cars are an environmental disaster, and a costly expense, so that seems compelling. But the truth is many of us will not have the privilege to simply forgo automobiles.

That said, reducing our reliance on them, or choosing not to own one, may translate to big savings.

This is especially true in 2022, as consumer reports now lists the cost of keeping up an average car at about $10,000/year.

That means that if someone wanted to go car-free, they could still afford to get an Uber every day of the year and rent a car for a week, and still save significant cash.

Walkable neighborhoods. Perhaps the biggest factor in saving money on a car is to live in a walkable neighborhood. If you aren't required to drive just to meet basic needs, the savings start accumulating, and the possibility for going car-free gets higher.

Car sharing. Again, for someone with an average car, it could be competitive to kick the car to the curb. How many Ubers would you have to take in a year to actually pay more than you are for ownership?

Public transportation. Cities with good public transportation are true luxury communities to me. Having lived in a few college towns with excellent public transport, I felt thrilled to not have to ever use my car. Then, if I wanted to take a road trip, I could afford a nice rental, and not have to worry about it getting damaged on my trip.

Buy used: Buying a new car may be the worst thing you'll do to the environment in your lifetime. And cars are almost always a notoriously poor investment. Buying used is a definite way to save for anyone. I have never owned a new car and can't imagine why I would want to.

Buy durable: There's a big difference in the long-term value of different cars, and it pays to know which ones will be durable and last. Paying a little more up front can save thousands of dollars per year over the life of the car.

Buy cycles: I mean, bicycles. Not only do you save money on transportation, you stay in good shape while you're at it.

Buy electric? I have environmentalist friends who'd rage if we didn't mention the possibility of buying electric cars. But the reality is: it depends. In some areas of the country, buying an electric vehicle will bring definite carbon reductions. But in others, where electricity comes from coal and oil, an electric vehicle may have higher emissions than a gas guzzling car. Either way, it's still best to buy electric cars used.

Green trip stacking. Some of the best advice for saving on transportation costs is simply to drive less! To make that happen, many of us like to stack up our trips. Instead of making many short trips, making one trip with multiple functions can save costs and wear and tear on the car. But we like to do this with a "green" twist. To offset the cost and footprint of our cars, we try to stack up green functions, too, like delivering plants, planting trees, foraging, or dumpster diving. For road trips, we'll include visits to Permaculture centers for learning. This way, we feel like we're using the privilege of car ownership for something more than our personal gain.

Chapter Resources:

Resources to help you live frugally and build your transformation fund:

1. Raiser-Rowland, Annie, and Grub, Adam. The Art of Frugal Hedonism, Chelsea Green. 2017.

2. Hoag, Michael. The Transformative Adventures Permaculture Design Certificate Course Pack, 2012.

3. Holmgren, David. Retrosuburbia. Melliodora Press, 2019.

4. Nazak, Jenny. Deep Green.

5. Freed, Dolly. Possum Living. The House Books, 2019

6. Greenfield, Rob. Dude Making a Difference. New Society, 2016

7. Yeager, Jeff, How to Retire the Cheapskate way. Currency, 2016

8. Zalinsky, Ernie. Retiring Wild, Happy and Free. Visions International, 2009

Adventure 7: Get Mean and Lean, Reduce Your Expenses

Perhaps the single biggest key to being FREE is to get as lean and mean as the thistle. The thistle can thrive anywhere, because it can make do on whatever little water and fertility it has access to.

In human terms, if we can reduce our expenses to the point where we can easily pay them off a few hours of work per week, then our lives will have an abundance of freedom. If you have $30,000 of expenses each year, then it almost doesn't matter how many assets you have, you'll always be in danger of failing to pay the bills.

The best way to reduce expenses is to make an adventure of it. Pick one or two of the areas in this book and work on those. Then pick another. In a year, almost anyone can significantly reduce their expenses. Set goals, make a plan, periodize it and knock them out!

Chapter 7: Waste to Value

There's no such thing as waste—there are only misdirected resources and poorly designed systems.

Having peered into countless grocery, thrift store, and university dumpsters I'm well aware of how much of what ends up in our "waste" stream is still usable. Maybe you aren't reaching into dumpsters like me, but if you are reading this book I bet you sense the value in the waste stream as well. Maybe you've rescued a table from the alley or yard sale leftovers from the curb.

Redirecting these still usable items from the waste stream can both save and earn us money, thus turning that trash into treasure. Waste to Value is especially impactful when we think of all of the energy and other resources that went into creating the product initially. Not only are we keeping items out of the landfill when we reuse, recycle, or maybe even upcycle them, we're preventing more energy and resources from being used unnecessarily in the production of the alternative items we would have consumed in addition to the energy that would have gone into handling those resources as trash.

Tapping the value in our trash often requires us to open our minds and look at waste in a different way. I ride my bike a lot and am constantly looking for excess fallen fruit to forage from alleys and sidewalks. Here in my part of Florida I can score mangos, litchis, longans, avocados, and more. I've even had success leaving notes on people's doors when I've seen fruit littering their yards offering to help them pick their trees in exchange for a portion of the harvest. That's also helped me increase my social capital when I make friends with those homeowners and then share my haul with my friends.

When my boyfriend saw this pile of dirt—he didn't see dirt—he saw darker soil and organic matter, which is hard to come by in our sandy part of Florida. He also recognized that he could use the corrugated plastic pieces for a future building project. He ended up loading it all on his truck, adding the soil to the food forest in his yard and using the building materials in his chicken coop.

Knowing how to repair and build things can be immensely useful skills in our efforts to keep things out of the waste stream and make those items usable again. With so many companies designing and planning products to have a finite life span in order to increase their profits, being able to fix things and extend their life is good for the planet and your wallet (and bad for corporate greed).

You already know my story of earning money selling things I diverted from dumpsters. Now let me share a few more examples of how people are profiting off the "waste" stream.

1) My friend Charlie Pioli from Orlando, Florida previously worked as a solid waste & recycling consultant, where he grew frustrated by all the waste he witnessed being generated and poorly managed around the country firsthand. Spurred to action, he started O-Town Compost to give his neighbors a sustainable and community based option to recycle their food scraps. O-Town provides composting services for households and events, sells worm castings and compost, and now employs several other people.

2) John Wilker from the Simplest Biz started out buying or being given pallets free by businesses that had no need for them and selling them to pallet yards. He eventually found other businesses in his area that were buying pallets and started selling the pallets directly to them. Later he started doing the same thing with crates, dunnage, corrugated boxes, 55 gallon metal drums, and wire reels. He now teaches a course instructing others how to do this.

3) Two college friends started a vermiculture venture, meaning they fed organic waste to worms and then sold the resulting worm waste as plant food. That business has since morphed into a multi-million dollar global company called TerraCycle, which collects and

repurposes hard-to-recycle waste. Over the years the company's mission has stayed the same – eliminate the idea of waste. TerraCycle has won over 200 awards for social entrepreneurship and sustainable business.

4) Emilie O'Brien lends a slightly different twist to this theme. Emilie paired her background in film and TV production with her passion for the environment to establish Earth Angel, which aims to reduce the carbon footprint of entertainment productions. Emilie and her team do this by helping TV and film re-think industry norms such as recycling materials from no longer needed set props that would have previously been thrown away ending up in landfills, setting up systems to compost much of the food waste created from all the catered food brought in for the cast and crew during filming, as well as improving the way hazardous materials are handled on and off set. Emilie has created an effective model that could be replicated in so many different settings — hotels, conferences, hospitals, universities, and on and on.

Whether you think about it as the problem is the solution or the obstacle is the way, our overflowing "waste" streams remain a perfect opportunity to apply our human ingenuity to address and profit from a most unfortunate situation.

Chapter 8. Designing Your Life to Thrive Like a THISTLE

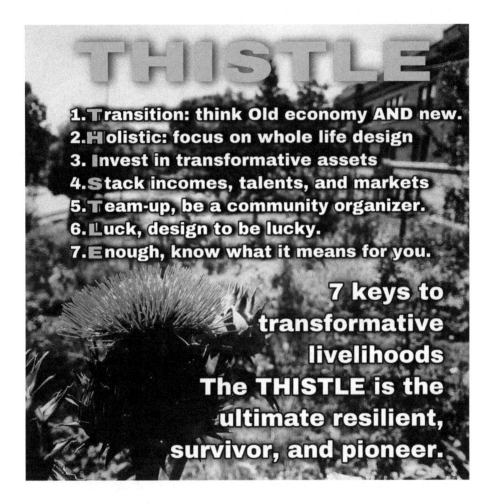

1. **T**ransition: think Old economy AND new.
2. **H**olistic: focus on whole life design
3. **I**nvest in transformative assets
4. **S**tack incomes, talents, and markets
5. **T**eam-up, be a community organizer.
6. **L**uck, design to be lucky.
7. **E**nough, know what it means for you.

7 keys to transformative livelihoods The THISTLE is the ultimate resilient, survivor, and pioneer.

To this point in this book, we've dismantled the money delusions that hold us back. We've outlined a holistic life strategy to get free from the rat race. We've understood that it all gets easier if we can reduce our expenses to the point we can easily pay the bills, and then we've given you a big helping of tools to help you do so.

Now, we're at a basic state of economic health, we can actually start designing our lives to grow naturally abundant over time, in the way that folks with the successful models for this book have.

Earning the Privilege to Live as You Like

One of my mentors in my university music program once taught me that being a musician is a privilege. Years later, that would echo with me when one of my farming mentors said the same of his profession.

Looking around at all the starving musicians and farmers in the world who are insanely talented yet underpaid, I wondered what kind of privilege this is! Yet, there are a great many people who would give up all their money to be able to live as musicians! And most of those starving rock stars wouldn't trade their lives for desk jobs raking in the cash. The same can be said for many farmers.

And that also goes for being artists, writers, small-holders and activists. if you're reading this book, that's probably you. In a way, we are all quite privileged.

And since there are many people out there competing to have the lives we have, we have to be especially resilient and clever about creating right livelihoods. Then, from that place of stability, we can help extend this privilege to others around us. As we do, it will get easier for everyone to live the same kinds of lives we are.

From our FREE perspective, one of the things that makes this possible is establishing what we'll call "hammock income."

In order for us to relax in our hammock, we have to be earning our living in a way that doesn't keep us up at night. So, hammock income is necessarily one type of right livelihood. It must be ethical.

But let's be clear that not all right livelihood is good hammock income!

For example, some may consider running an organic farm 60 hours/week for $3/hour to be right livelihood, once we get past the problem of self-exploitation. But, that doesn't leave very much room for hammock time, or for creating any kind of Financial Resilience and Economic Empowerment. It's not the kind of livelihood that will help us be FREE.

So, hammock income is income that we can earn part time, flexibly, without a lot of opportunity costs, and that can still realistically help us hit our FREE benchmarks for income by covering most or all of our living costs. My own personal number on this is $30/hour. Hammock income has to earn me $30 hour on average, or I'm probably self-exploiting and not moving towards my goals. Compare that to many farmers who report in studies that they earn around $3/hour!

And we don't want our hammock to get washed away in the coming storms, so good hammock income must be climate resilient, too.

What I've discovered is that everyone I know who has found this type of hammock income has followed some very similar rules to do so. So it's something we can mimic and copy for ourselves.

And being as we're all nature-loving hippie types here, this deserves a plant metaphor.

The THISTLE is the ultimate pioneer, finding its niche in difficult terrain, and thriving there, making the soil more fertile for everything else. We must also think like weeds in this economic system, resilient pioneers building the soil for the new economy.

TRANSITION
The first key to a regenerative livelihood is to understand that we need to TRANSITION. Most of us will need to be thinking of keeping one foot in the old economy, at least at first, and one foot in the new community and sun-powered economy we wish to build.

HOLISTIC THINKING
The next key is that everyone I know of who has been truly successful in creating a truly FREE lifestyle has focused beyond the career, beyond the job mindset, and manifested a complete whole life design. This means they don't just work. They build a beautiful place to live, a meaningful lifestyle, and a vibrant community. They figured out how they wanted to spend their time on this earth, and then they got very clear on their goals for getting there. Then

they designed a life path that led where they wanted to go. The more specific you are about where you want to go, the more likely you are to get there.

INVESTING

The third thing every successful Community Transformation Leader I know of has in common, is that they have escaped the J.O.B. mindset, and learned to see their work and their financial path as one of investment.

As folks on the FREE path, this is 100% of what we do: we invest our time and energy in creating better lives, landscapes and communities, by growing connection to nature and community. All we do is invest.

The best investment we can make is in ourselves. And in our futures. If we get this right, we may make a decent income up front, but where we really win the game is when all our investments grow in value and pay back years down the line. As we will discuss later, this is actually the great key that successful farmers have always known. If you are "farming" and you don't know exactly what your investment plan is, you're just growing vegetables, and you haven't started farming yet.

But when you start a Transformative Adventures program, you will be starting a path of wise long term investments that will grow your wealth long term.

Remember again the farmers earning $3/hour. Or even top farming earners making $10-15/hour. Do you think they'll create resilient lives and retire on that? The secret is that the ones who really make it work do so because they've made smart investments. And again, we're not talking about the stock market!

The truth is, for most of us who want to do privileged work, we're probably not going to be able to count on a big income for security or growing FREE. Most people won't do it as artists, activists, smallholders or doing good work in local non-profits. Review the charts in Appendix 1, and you'll see that only the top 5% of earners in any age bracket can make conventional FIRE work out. And most of the people I've met who've built beautiful, resilient lives dong this sort of work, have done so, in one way or another, through investing.

STACKING

A fourth key to success is to stack functions, just like an ecosystem does. In ecosystems, multiple species can fulfill the same role, and each species has many ways of obtaining its needs. This builds opportunity and potential for success.

We would be wise to do the same!

The smart community transformation activist will learn to stack income streams. Most farmers, for example, only generate one income stream from their work. But if we're clever, we could get multiple incomes out of the same hours of labor, by only adding a tiny bit of extra work. They also learn to stack audiences. Meaning for that work, they can appeal to different markets at different levels. Sometimes people would like to support us BIG, but we only offer small options for them. Or some people would be willing to throw us a few extra bucks, but we haven't given them options in the price range! When we stack these we connect to everyone where they are at. It's a matter of accepting everyone for who they are.

Finally, we are wise when we learn to stack our skills. The most successful businesses I know of are unique, targeted, and niche. The more we can make our work a unique representation of ourselves, the more likely we are to be successful. And to have a lot of fun doing it!

COMMUNITY ORGANIZING

The fifth thing all successful FREE folks have in common is that they are all Community Organizers. Period. Think of anyone in the arts, activism, or Regenerative Agriculture who has achieved success, and they did so primarily as community organizers—even if they don't realize it.

LUCK

Next, every Community Transformation professional I know of who has hit it out of the park has one very important thing in common.

Luck.

They got lucky.

It turns out, we can design to increase our luck, though.

How? There are a lot of key strategies. We can be open to opportunity instead of locked into plans. For most businesses, like most farm businesses, they over burden us with something economists call the sunk opportunity cost. This means if we have too many hours tied up by a job that MUST be done, there is a high opportunity cost. This program is designed to help you get lucky.

ENOUGH

Finally, the E in thistle stands for Enough. Knowing what it means to us in concrete terms frees up our life energy to pursue more important priorities, instead of accumulating more money. Some people get forever lost down the rabbit hole of seeking more and more money. But it's never enough to fill the hole. Hopefully, by the end of this book, you'll have a good idea of what it means to you.

The better you understand these 7 keys to success, the more likely you are to get lucky, and be profoundly impactful, and build the life you dream of. So for the rest of the book, we'll be looking more deeply into each aspect of the THISTLE.

Chapter 9: Transition

The thistle is a master of transformation. It is resilient, hardy, and of course, downright thorny. It can find its way through cracks in pavement, take root in the meanest soil, and then, through will and stubbornness it transforms the soil into someplace more hospitable for all.

Like all natural masters of transformation, which we call "pioneer species," the thistle is also necessarily a master of transition. Transition is of course a part of any transformation! And so, we would be wise to actually observe, recognize, and value this important process.

"Transformation" means growing from exactly what we are right now, into what we want to become. It doesn't mean we flip a switch and we're instantly there! This reality of ours rarely works that way.

That means wherever we are right now is okay. It's where we must be. If we have to work a corporate job. That's okay. If we have to have a conventional retirement account or stocks, then that must be okay, too. If we have debt, or need to buy Starbucks to get through the daily grind, we have to have compassion for exactly where we are, in order to realistically grow to where we want to be.

The Great Transition

If we want to transform our financial lives and systems, then there's one particular transition we need to be especially mindful of. This is the great transition of our day, from the old, dysfunctional economy that's destroying the planet, to the new regenerative economy we all want to see. As a species, and as communities we must all make this transition, and we must all make it as individuals, too.

As the old economy continues to fail us in shocking new ways, we may come to feel we're on a sort of fault line between the old and new. We may see the old economy is increasingly a poor bet to meet our needs, to care for the planet, and to secure a retirement or financial resilience. And yet, many of the new economy businesses we're trying to build may be out of sync with the financial realities of today—they may not be properly valued, or the market may only be in its early stages.

And so a strategy that will work for many of us during this transition will be to have one foot in the new economy, and one foot in the old. This way, as we straddle that fault line, if one side sinks at least we stand a chance of catching our footing on the other!

This might mean developing or holding onto conventional jobs and careers as we invest in our own transformations. Or it might mean having old economy investments, retirement funds, or less-than-perfect businesses or jobs. Again, we need to be compassionate with ourselves and others during this transition.

It's a good reminder that even in "Permaculture," the actual work to create this new economy, is (according to its founder) "not about how you make your money. It's about how you spend it and where you bank it."

Let's say that again, transforming your life and the world is less about how you make your income, and more about how you invest in that new life and new world. In fact, one could say that—within reason—taking from the old economy to invest in the new is radical and revolutionary. As filmmaker Michael Moore has said, "the capitalists will sell you the rope to hang them with," meaning we need to use the old economy to build the transition. The important thing is: how are we really investing it? Are we really investing in the world we want to see?

So as we make this great transition, there may be a few tools and patterns that can help us complete our transformation successfully. Many of these we could call "capitalism survival strategies," or even "escape plans."

P16–Patterns to Become a Financial Activist in the Old Economy

The unfortunate truth is most of us won't be able to just quit our jobs overnight. Many of us will have to work ourselves loose from the old economy.

The point of this book is that it takes a plan and a process. But once you have that plan, whatever your job is becomes part of your own personal work, which makes it all so much more tolerable. Even if you don't like your job, you're now working for yourself, your personal goals, and your own future. For me, that helped.

And while we're in the old economy, we may find some important opportunities to work on our FREE goals.

Workplace Activism

Many small and corporate employers could use some real help in becoming more just and sustainable, and the problem is your opportunity. You can help your employer grow, become better, and even save money, while bulking up your own resume, skills, and value. Keep in mind, if you want to build your value in the workplace, then make sure you build consensus and find projects that get your coworkers and management excited.

Transformative Landscapes: many businesses these days are upgrading their landscaping by including native plants, or food forests. The best can apply for Transformative Landscape recognition, giving the company an eco-friendly talking point. These can become great places to work, take breaks, or have meetings, too.

Recycling and composting: Many workplaces could use help creating a basic recycling or composting program. These could be opportunities for people in your local Permaculture community to start new composting businesses. Or you may already have people providing these services in your area. I've approached many restaurants and food service businesses for composting materials, and they've always been happy to connect.

Energy efficiency upgrades that pay to fight climate change: businesses can often use help with these, too, and save some money and earn some bragging rights in the process. The tips in this book would be a good place to start.

Anti-racism, anti-colonialism, anti-oppression work: Many regions now have organizations doing institutional work on dismantling systems of oppression. They might be able to help you organize workshops and training at your employer.

Permaculture Design Courses: Permaculture Design Courses or even just single introduction talks are great community building opportunities that can help get people together on the same page. Many places have local activists that would love to come and present for your workplace, and many workplaces have funds to help pay for such services.

Unionizing: Yes, organizing is one of the best things we can potentially do to create a better world right in our own workplaces. Your area very likely has activists who would love to help you do this work.

Finding a Better Old Economy Job

For some, the corporate economy will just become unworkable. We can seek out alternatives in the not-for-profit sector or cooperatives. These options come with their own sets of drawbacks, including sometimes difficult organizational structures, and lower pay, but may make up for it with increased flexibility.

I've known many FREE people who've achieved their goals at non-profits or coops that allowed them to work part-time or set the hours that they want to work. At the right place, and in the right position, it's hard to get more FREE than this! Some of these folks have livelihoods with great community organizations that do meaningful work, and they get the additional FREEdom of getting a paycheck for their work.

Of course, this is not the only path to growing FREE. I feel some sources over-emphasize finding jobs like this, when in reality these jobs may be very rare! But it's still good to keep an eye out for them. Usually, an organization like your local library or college will keep a listing of local non-profit jobs, and on an international scale, the biggest listing for non-profit jobs is Idealist. If you're not happy with your work, it might be worth a look!

Strategies for Earning More in the Old Economy

There's only so much we can do to increase our financial stability by saving money. The real potential comes from increasing our income. For those still working a conventional salaried job there are several tactics that could help you bring home more of that (vegan) bacon.

1) Negotiate when considering a job offer

The best time to negotiate your salary is when you receive a job offer. You'll want to do your research and know the salary range of others at your level of experience in your industry. Be prepared to tell them why you believe you deserve more and demonstrate how your strengths and track record will benefit the organization.

2) Don't forget the benefits package

Benefits can make up to 30 percent of your salary - which is not insignificant. And they're often negotiable as well. Some common benefits you might be able to negotiate include hiring bonuses, retirement savings plans, tuition assistance, a professional development stipend, relocation expenses, and more paid time off. A little time spent contemplating your needs and the benefits package offered by your (new) employer could pay big dividends..

3) Ask for a raise

Don't forget that asking for a pay raise is always an option, not just when you are accepting a job offer. Most employees don't ask for raises. That means they're simply settling for whatever small raises their employers may offer them and potentially missing out on additional income. Consider this -

research shows that the higher someone's annual salary is the more likely they are to have asked for a raise.

(https://www.careergeekblog.com/salary-negotiation-statistics/)(https://www.payscale.com/salary-negotiation-guide/8-surprising-facts-about-salary-negotiation/)

4) Hone those negotiating skills

Numerous books and YouTube videos are available for free to help you develop the skills and confidence necessary to negotiate your salary and benefits. It may also be worth investing some money in a few sessions with a career coach to build this skillset.

5) Consider getting a new job

The largest bump in salary tends to come when you change employers.Of course there are other factors to consider when contemplating changing employers than just the money, but all those other things appear to be at least equal than this may be worth pursuing.

6) Ask for a promotion

Just like you can ask for a raise you can also ask for a promotion. Even if there's no specific job opening you are interested in at the moment you can let the higher ups in your workplace know about your interest in a promotion and get suggestions for what you can do to qualify for open positions in the future.

7) Take advantage of free professional development

Be alert for opportunities to get on the job training in new skills that can increase your value to the company or a future employer (or yourself when you break free some day).

8) Take on more work

Yes, the goal of this book is to free you from your conventional life and job, but this option may be worth considering if it will help you gain your freedom faster (but not at the expense of your health and sanity). You could work extra hours to pay down some debt, accept extra shifts to more quickly meet your savings goal, or work overtime to pay for an unexpected expense.

P17–Healthcare for Americans?

This is a special consideration for Americans, who have a system that aims to make mega-profits off illness, and has the most expensive health care in the world, with the least government assistance in the world.

(Also see pages XXX and XXX.)

Patterns for Health Insurance: Know Your Options

Have you found yourself fed up enough to seriously contemplate quitting your J.O.B., but then choosing to stay in that toxic work environment because you didn't want to go without health insurance? If so, you are not alone. In the U.S., where the government does not provide universal healthcare and so many people rely on health insurance being included in their workplace benefits package, fear of lack of access to healthcare may be keeping many of you from breaking FREE.

With the extremely high costs of medical care and the fact that expensive medical bills are the leading cause of personal bankruptcy in this country, it's no wonder so many people attach so much weight to the health care benefits provided by employers. Educating yourself on the healthcare alternatives that may be available to you could be a helpful step in moving you that much closer to FREEdom.

And for those of you currently living without health insurance because you think you can't afford it or it's not available to you, the options I'm about to share may help you as well. All of us in the U.S. can benefit from being better informed about navigating our oh so confusing healthcare system. A welcoming space where you can pose questions to crowdsource answers from others, who are often more knowledgeable on this topic is the Harnessing Healthcare Facebook group.

ACA marketplace plans

The Affordable Care Act (ACA), also known as Obamacare, was a landmark piece of health reform legislation in the U.S. It extended health insurance coverage to millions of uninsured Americans and led to the establishment of the Health Insurance Marketplace. Eligible residents of all states can now buy regular private insurance plans through this marketplace..

To qualify to purchase health insurance through the marketplace you must earn between 100% – 400% of the federal poverty level (FPL). For 2022, that is $13,590 - $54,360 for an individual and $27,750 - $111,000 for a family of four.

Enter your zip code at https://localhelp.healthcare.gov/ to locate a trained healthcare navigator to help you through the enrollment process.

https://thefinancebuff.com/federal-poverty-levels-for-obamacare.html

Medicaid expansion

Medicaid is a program funded jointly by states and the federal government that provides health coverage to low-income adults, children, pregnant women, elderly adults and people with disabilities. One outcome of the passage of the ACA was the expansion of Medicaid coverage in thirty nine states including DC to nearly all adults with incomes up to 138% of the Federal Poverty Level ($18,754 for an individual, $38,295 for a 4 person household in 2022). The asset limits that apply to Medicaid recipients 65 years of age and older do not apply to Medicaid expansion benefits.

This option is not available to residents of the twelve states that chose not to adopt the expansion.(Alabama, Florida, Georgia, Kansas, Mississippi, North Carolina, North Dakota, South Carolina, South Dakota, Tennessee, Texas, and Wisconsin) To apply contact your state Medicaid agency or fill out an application through the Health Insurance Marketplace at Healthcare.gov.

https://www.payingforseniorcare.com/federal-poverty-level

High-deductible health plans & health savings accounts

Healthy individuals and families with a bit of a savings cushion, who rarely need prescription medicines, and aren't expecting to incur significant medical expenses may want to look into high deductible health plans (HDHPs), These plans cover basic preventive care before the deductible is met, but they don't cover anything else until you've met the deductible.

These plans typically have lower premiums and higher deductibles than traditional health insurance. Be sure to research your options and compare prices with other plans available through the Health Insurance Marketplace as sometimes the regular plans offer lower premiums and pay for non-preventive care before the deductible is met, which HDHPs cannot do.

Many people combine HDHPs with health savings accounts (HSAs) in which they can save money tax free to spend on any medical expenses they incur prior to meeting their plan's deductible. Monies not spent from the account during the HDHP coverage period remain in the account and can be used to pay for future medical expenses.

Catastrophic health insurance plans are not technically HDHPs, but function somewhat similarly with a few specific differences. To qualify for a catastrophic health plan, you must be under 30 years old or qualify for a "hardship" or "affordability" exemption if you're over 30. Since these plans cover 3 primary care visits per year before the plan's deductible is met they are not eligible to be paired with HSAs.

The application for all HDHPs and catastrophic plans can also be initiated online at Healthcare.gov.

Part time jobs with health insurance

There may be times in your FREE journey where it makes sense to take on part-time work to secure healthcare benefits (and income). Employers are not required to provide health care benefits to part-time employees, and many don't. There are some companies though, that provide health insurance to employees working 20+ hours per week and people seek out jobs with them specifically for the healthcare coverage. After working a certain number of hours with companies like Starbucks, Costco, and UPS you can find yourself eligible for their employee health care plan.

We discuss this more on pages (XXX)

DIY Healthcare

About ten percent of Americans lack health insurance and some of you may still choose to forgo coverage or find yourself unable to afford it. These days even those paying for health insurance are incorporating more and more DIY healthcare options into their lives such as at-home tests, medical devices, and a wide range of helpful apps.

Many smallholders and others living off grid without access to healthcare have long relied on books like *Where There Is No Doctor* and *The Green Pharmacy* to help them handle medical situations as they arise. They also prioritize maintaining a foundation of good physical and mental health and avail themselves of local members of Herbalists without Borders, community acupuncture services, local naturopaths, and other alternative health practitioners.

If you do end up going to the emergency room or otherwise incurring unexpected medical expenses, educate yourself on how to negotiate medical bills.. (Even those of us with health insurance would benefit from remembering this.)

https://www.aha.org/news/headline/2021-11-17-cdc-reports-uninsured-first-six-months-2021

P18–Patterns for Investing in a Better Old Economy

In our late stage capitalism mess the votes we cast with our dollars may be as much or more impactful than those we cast at the ballot box. Many of us are already prioritizing supporting locally, BIPOC, LGBTQ+, and women owned businesses whenever feasible. However, there are even more powerful ways we can flex our muscles as financial activists.

Because this section deals largely with managing our money I'm going to repeat our earlier disclaimer - I am not a financial advisor, economist, banking or legal expert, nor are any of my co-authors. The information presented here is NOT financial advice. It's what I (Laura) have learned along the way in my own journey to align my money with my values and I share it for educational and informational purposes only. Do your own due diligence before making any financial decisions.

Step Up to Earning & Managing Money

What would happen if those of us who would use money for regenerative purposes started earning more of it? What if you could afford to buy that piece of art you love by a local artist? Or move forward with that sustainable retrofit for your home that is more expensive up front - but will save you thousands of dollars in the future? Or perhaps buy a piece of land? Greedy billionaires don't need more money. And there's so much regeneration we could spark if reluctant capitalists like you and me were willing to learn about money and get more confident handling it.

The more you understand how money works and how you can wisely steward it, the more you can do to earn, spend, manage, and invest it as a force for good. Budgeting and debt payoff plans may sound boring or like deprivation, but they are some of the most powerful tools available to us as we start to grow FREE. Plus.you'll likely find that the more intentional you get with money the less you'll leak of it out into the entities and elements of capitalism that make you cringe. And the more you'll save to invest in our regenerative future.

Break up with Your Mega Bank

The Banking on Climate Change report clearly demonstrates that the major banks are using their depositors' money to fund the fossil fuels industry. If you are working hard in your life to reduce your use of and support for fossil fuels, your money is negating all those efforts if you are still banking with larger financial institutions like JP Morgan Chase, Bank of America, Citi, or Wells Fargo. (And fossil fuels aren't the only unsavory industry or practice those banks are upholding with other people's money.)

More ethical options are available by banking with local credit unions, CDFIs (community development financial institutions) that put depositors' money to work in low-income and marginalized communities, and fossil fuel free banks like Aspiration. You could even put your money to work supporting indigenous communities here in the U.S. by opening an account with the Native American Bank. Online tools available at banklocal.info as well as MightyDeposits.com make it easy to find a more socially responsible bank.

Invest Your Values & Vote Your Shares

The corporations we invest in through the stock market are many of the same ones selling us inferior products built to break, lobbying our governments to enact policies that benefit them and hurt the rest of us, and generally fanning the flames of the wendigo spirit. Some of us, though, have already or may still choose to invest in them.

Because of the rapidly growing interest in ethical investing, particularly among Millennials and women, there are more and more socially responsible investing (SRI) mutual funds and other products available to investors. They still keep your money in the stock market, but they screen companies based on their environmental, social, and governance (ESG) reforms as well as other criteria. Exchange traded funds (ETFs) made up of renewable energy companies have also become very popular with socially conscious investors.

If you have invested in the stock market through an employer based 401(k), ask the person at your workplace who handles the benefits packages what SRI or ESG investing options are available to you through that plan. For those investing outside the workplace, the screening tool available at InvestYourValues.com can help you find fossil fuel free, prison free, tobacco free, and other funds that divest your money from issues of concern to you.

Those investing directly in stocks (meaning you don't own fractional shares through a mutual fund or ETF) can flex your muscle through shareholder advocacy, a powerful and underutilized tool. That means you can likely cast a vote to elect or not elect) members of the board of directors and weigh in on other important corporate actions.Very few shareholders ever actually vote so there's potential for your vote and activism to make a difference. Organizations like As You Sow and the Interfaith Center on Corporate Social Responsibility can help you learn more about how to vote your shares.

Pursue Socially Conscious Investing off Wall Street

So much of our attention gets directed to the stock market that most of us have no idea that some really impressive as well as much more environmentally and socially conscious investing options are percolating off Wall Street. Instead of feeling conflicted about investing in beverage companies that produce unhealthy sugary drinks in single use plastic bottles or cross eyed from the excel spreadsheets that track your stocks, how would you like to feel proud, passionate, and excited about the things you invest in?

It's worth noting that when it comes to financial investments it's often the case that the higher the rate of return, the more extractive, harmful, and destructive the investment is. Expecting to achieve the same 10% rate of return from all of these socially conscious investments that one may have earned in the stock market is not realistic.These investments achieve a triple bottom line meaning that beyond financial returns they also provide social and environmental returns that at this point are just as valuable (or more) than any financial return you could achieve.

It would also be wise to point out here that these options often involve investing in start ups and small businesses. Since such a high percentage of new businesses fail there's tremendous risk in making these investments. Be sure to conduct the relevant due diligence before making any investment and don't invest more than you can afford to lose. My personal risk mitigation strategy is to make many small (dollar amount) investments in a wide range of industries and investment vehicles.

With all of that out of the way let's take a look at some of these innovative investing vehicles through which we can earn a profit while bringing about a better world.

1) Crowdfunding platforms

The JOBS Act of 2017, established provisions that allow early-stage businesses to offer and sell securities to the general public via crowdfunding platforms. This was a long awaited game changer for everyday retail (i.e. not wealthy) investors, especially those wanting to invest in the solutions instead of only the "less bad" options available through SRI & ESG funds on Wall Street.

Not all the businesses raising funds via crowdfunding platforms have socially responsible missions, but you can search for start ups on these platforms offering goods or services that align with your values and what you want to see more of in the world. For example, I've used crowdfunding websites to invest in a Native American owned food company, a software facilitating communications between farm managers and migrant farm workers, and an organization that makes loans for energy efficiency improvements..

You can often get started with crowdfund investing with as little as $100. Crowdfund MainStreet is a platform that specializes in helping mission-driven entrepreneurs raise capital. If you want to find opportunities to invest in climate solutions then check out Raise Green.

2) Social justice investing

Social justice investing is a way we can strategically wield the power of the dollars that pass through our hands to invest and inject much-needed capital into businesses and communities of color. These investments also divert our money from those companies that play a role in perpetuating and/or maintaining systemic racism.

The community impact funds that are managed by some of those same CDFIs that offer more ethical banking options are an example of a social justice investment. These funds, like Community Vision in California and Wacif in Washington, DC, have been using investors' money to lift up undercapitalized communities of color since well before social justice became such a buzzword in the Wake of George Floyd's death. And you generally don't have to be a resident of these areas to invest in these funds.

Sadly, black business founders only receive about one percent of all the venture capital injected into early stage businesses each year. So another way we can invest in racial justice is to search out companies led by people of color on crowdfunding platforms to invest in.

3) Investing in the solidarity economy

Similarly, the solidarity economy, in contrast to our current economic model, prioritizes people and the planet over excessive profit and growth while also building cultures and communities of cooperation. Cooperatively owned businesses that are democratically controlled by their member owners are an integral component of the solidarity economy (which also includes credit unions).

These coops sometimes need to raise investment capital from outside the company/entity. One such entity raising investor capital at the time of writing this book is the East Bay Permanent Real Estate Cooperative (EBPRC), a community-led real estate developer democratically run and led by people of color. Then there's the Cooperative Fund of New England, which has been using investor's money to provide financing for democratically-run businesses for over forty years..

4) Local investing

Everyone wants to live in a thriving, vibrant community, yet we usually spend and invest our money in ways that direct that money elsewhere. While we're often encouraged to embrace our role as consumers to buy local, much less emphasis is placed on our potential as investors in our local economy. In fact, it's sadly much easier to send our investing dollars off to Wall Street than it is to direct them to investments in our own communities.

Grassroots local investing efforts like Slow Money chapters and LION (Local Investment Opportunity Network) in Washington state have been trying to overcome those challenges with varying levels of success for years Those crowdfunding platforms mentioned above have been a great step forward in making it possible for non-wealthy investors to put their money to work strengthening local economies.

Michael Shuman's book *Put Your Money Where Your Life Is* is a great resource for anyone who wants to promote more local investing in their own community. My first local investment was purchasing an ownership share of a nearby permaculture farm. I found that investment by simply having conversations with people in my area about my interest in local investing.

5) Self-directed retirement accounts

To the extent middle class Americans are saving for retirement. they're mostly doing it by investing through 401(k)s, IRAs and other retirement accounts that limit them to investing in the offerings of Wall Street.I imagine most readers of this book would much rather be investing their retirement savings in some of the socially conscious investments I've outlined here, which is something you can do through a self-directed retirement account..

Of course you could make these investments outside of a retirement account, but the reason people prefer to invest through those retirement accounts is their tax advantaged status, which can decrease the amount of tax you pay on your investments and thus increase the amount of money you keep invested.

There are two types of these do it yourself retirement accounts - the self-directed IRA (SDIRA) and the Solo 401(k). Both require much more active participation on the part of the account holder than their conventional cousins. And there is a good bit to learn to successfully navigate these waters amidst the IRS rules pertaining to them. However, that shouldn't deter those of us who want to make investments that are more aligned with our values from considering these accounts because they unlock opportunities to truly make meaningful and impactful investments.

One of the most commonly held investments in these self directed retirement accounts is real estate. You can't hold a property you or your family live in, but for anyone considering real estate investing it may be a tax advantaged way to proceed. Think about the potential here for us to find ways to pool our retirement savings together to buy land to regenerate and establish agroforestry businesses!!

6) Investing in a livable climate?

One of the more controversial options in the green investing world are carbon credits. Carbon credits are offsets that can be sold to corporations or individuals looking to reduce their own carbon footprint. There are multiple ways to invest in carbon credits: by buying and then selling carbon offsets directly, investing in EFTs that specialize in carbon offsets, by investing in carbon futures, or by investing directly in projects that sequester carbon.

These are controversial because many environmentalists consider them greenwashing, or worse, a modern colonization scheme. Organizations including Greenpeace, the Indigenous Action Network, and many others have complained that carbon markets allow the worst polluters to claim that they are carbon neutral by buying credits, instead of doing the important work of actually reducing their own carbon emissions. Many indigenous rights organizations have complained that these schemes are encouraging western corporations to buy indigenous lands, converting them from management that actually does sequester carbon and increase biodiversity, to "carbon sequestration" schemes that may actually be less effective. And since most carbon credits are only available for pieces of land over 5,000 acres, carbon credits may be driving corporate centralization of land ownership, too.

Farmers also have to look out for predatory businesses that offer to "pay" them for carbon credits, but then actually charge them for agricultural products like microbial sprays that don't actually work. These businesses promise $10/acre in payment, then charge $12/acre for soil amendments that have no research to demonstrate that they actually work. Then these companies turn around and sell the carbon credits on the market, making money off both ends of the transaction.

All of this means that at present, carbon credits might not truly align with our values, and with growing political opposition, they may not be reliable investments, either. Still, these tools may be reformed in the future, and they may provide a means of funding important environmental or conservation actions. We don't currently recommend them, but perhaps some day carbon credits can become part of a truly green portfolio.

You can find a deeper exploration of the socially conscious investing opportunities available off Wall Street to everyday retail investors in the pay what you can Beginner's Guide to Regenerative Investing available in the online shop at RichandResilientLiving.com.

P19–Holistic Capitalism Survival Strategies:

Finally, some of the best of our strategies will be found in the cracks between the old economy and the emerging new one. These are the pieces of the non-financial economy that are showing through and available to us now. That might include the gift economy, barter, exchanging our knowledge, and other non-monetary ways of meeting our needs. This invites us to follow the THISTLE in behaving Holistically.

Chapter resources and notes:

1. Banking on Climate Change report (https://www.ran.org/wp-content/uploads/2022/03/BOCC_2022_vSPREAD-1.pdf)

2. https://news.crunchbase.com/venture/something-ventured-funding-to-black-startup-founders-quadrupled-in-past-year-but-remains-elusive/

3. Michael Shuman's Put Your Money Where Your Life Is. Penguin. 2020.

4. Hester, Tanja. Wallet activism. Benbella, 2021

5. Firpo, Janine. Activate Your Money. Wiley, 2021.

Chapter 10: Holistic Thinking

While some species in nature thrive off of just one life strategy, one rich niche, the rugged pioneers like the THISTLE that are masters of transformation behave more holistically. The thistle is capable of taking root on poor soil, and surviving drought and heat. But it is equally at home on compact and wet clay, or used up farm fields. It can even build more ideal soil over the generations. And it also has thorns to protect itself, inviting pests to feast on its neighbors instead! It produces many seeds which it can disperse on the wind, but it also calls to the goldfinch to come carry its seeds far and wide. The thistle thrives by behaving holistically, and we too would do well to think holistically, rather than only thinking about "the bottom line." Most importantly, this means realizing that money is not our only goal —a wealthy life and healthy society is a far more important one! Nor is money our only tool. And when we switch to other tools, we're more likely to meet our higher goals. Already, we've begun our journey with a deep discussion of our true goals and values. Now let's expand our holistic thinking...

We live in a society that has come to conflate wealth, security, and even individual worth with having lots of financial capital. Yet, as we've already highlighted, it's not the money we really want. Money is just colored paper and small pieces of metal (or digits in a computer) that we have all agreed upon as a means of exchange. What we really want are the things we can use money to access.

This heavy reliance on money to meet our needs though, leaves us fragile, vulnerable, and trapped in a scarcity mindset. But it doesn't have to be that way. In fact, opening ourselves to a more holistic balance sheet and expansive view of wealth increases our resilience, as well as our quality of life and connection to others.

The real alchemy begins when we move beyond believing the mainstream assumption that money is the only form of wealth to which we have access and that using it is the only way we can meet our needs. Then we can open ourselves to the opportunity to more deeply tap the resources and abundance that surround us, including our own creativity and unlimited human potential.

Financial capital is certainly the most well known and sought after form of capital. Yet, there are a number of other forms of capital that we don't tend to view as types of wealth. Admittedly, they are for the most part less tangible and fungible, but they are forms of capital that are convertible inputs into financial capital. While they don't necessarily fit easily into spreadsheets, recognizing these other forms of capital can bring us closer to true financial stability as well as a more joyful, meaningful life.

Plus, financial capital is extremely volatile, fragile, and speculative. Even the conventional wisdom in personal finance encourages you to diversify your assets. This more expansive view of wealth diversifies your portfolio exponentially, lending stability, agency, and resilience that just can't be achieved when relying on money alone.

According to the Oxford Dictionary, capital is "wealth in the form of money or other assets" as well as "a valuable resource of a particular kind." From an economics perspective capital also has the potential to generate more wealth.

Those of you, who have studied permaculture, may be familiar with the Eight Forms of Capital, a concept introduced to many permaculturalists by Ethan Roland and Gregory Landua. But this idea is not original to permaculture. For example, the Community Capitals Framework has been used in lower income rural areas to help communities identify previously overlooked assets and resources.

They are fantastic tools to help you see that you are richer than you think. So, let's explore these multiple forms of capital....

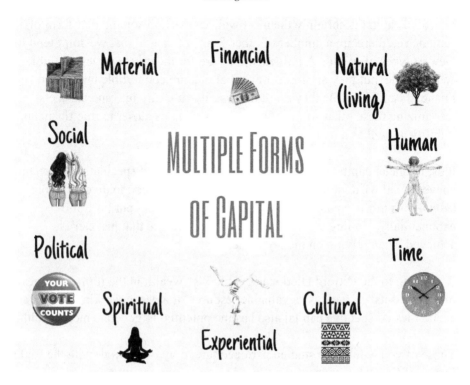

Financial capital is the one most commonly used in modern society. This consists of money, currencies, securities, and other instruments of the global financial system.

Material capital is non-living physical objects such as stone, metal, bridges, tools, and computers. This form of capital is probably the next most obvious, tangible, and sought after. One benefit to this form of capital is that it can be an alternative way to store financial capital that can be converted back into financial capital relatively easily. This form of capital can be especially advantageous if utilized in conjunction with an activity that increases one of your other forms of capital. For example, a jewelry maker invests in specialized tools that help her create high quality jewelry. Then she can sell this jewelry for money – financial capital, quickly recuperating the cost of the equipment and owning the "stored value" of the specialized tools should she ever want to sell them.

Living capital is made up of what we think of as our natural resources like water, air, land, parks, healthy soil, plants, and trees.Consider the shade provided by trees in your yard. It can help cool your house, significantly reducing your electric bill in the summer.

Many people want to establish a garden or food forest on their property because they grasp the value of natural capital. But it isn't necessary to have your own yard to access living capital. Nature is the ultimate model of abundance.Alleys, sidewalks, and other public right of ways are often littered with fallen fruit.

And don't forget about some of the edible "weeds" you may be walking over. Many people spend money purchasing the latest super foods such as acai, white mulberries, and chlorella. Yet right out your front door is likely a food that's just as nutritious, if not more, and free. Many of the plants we consider weeds are actually packed full of nutrients. Unlike the produce in grocery stores these plants haven't had the nutrition bred out of them in favor of a longer shelf life and large size.

Some readers are probably familiar with the concept of human capital. In this framework we can think of that as intellectual capital combined with experiential capital. **Intellectual capital** is knowledge, resourcefulness, creativity, and innovation. Society puts a great deal of value on this form of capital, emphasizing the importance of getting good grades in school and getting a college degree. It is certainly another capital that can be somewhat easily converted into financial capital. More higher education often (although, not always and possibly less and less these days) translates into higher wages. Learning new skills can often lead to a raise or an additional income stream..

Experiential capital is hands-on knowledge acquired by actually doing things – riding a bicycle, writing a grant proposal, drawing, fixing something broken, etc. There are many people who can repair cars that don't necessarily hold degrees from auto mechanics schools. They have experience working on cars and simply learned by doing.

Experience is just as useful as knowledge. Having a degree or reading many books can be helpful, but having actual hands-on experience can be just as valuable if not more because it makes you marketable. This form of capital goes hand-in-hand with intellectual capital, and we generally learn best when they happen in tandem. The richer we are in this form of capital the less we will need to spend paying handymen and others for their services.

Another form of capital that can eliminate the need to pay others for their services.is **social capital**. Wikipedia describes it as:

"a form of economic and cultural capital in which social networks are central; transactions are marked by reciprocity, trust, and cooperation; and market agents produce goods and services not mainly for themselves, but for a common good."

This is a fun and wonderful form of capital. You can accumulate it while attending potlucks, volunteering at a beach cleanup, attending a neighborhood association meeting and doing so many other things. True resilience stems from being rich in social capital.

For me the classic example of social capital is the Amish barn raising tradition, during which families gather at one home in the community to collectively build that property owner a new barn. These gatherings seamlessly combine socializing with a practical goal. As the locals gather to build the barn they strengthen their community bonds and reinforce the principle of mutual aid that's so strongly embedded in their culture.

One accumulates **spiritual capital** through religion, spirituality, or other means of connection to self and the universe. This includes our connection to something larger than ourselves, our sense of our place in the world, our religious or spiritual practices. The Buddhist concept of Karma is an example of a spiritual currency.

Cultural capital is exemplified by things shared by groups of people such as music, a common history, food, theater, and holidays. It is the only form of capital that can not be individually owned or cultivated. When thinking about where we want to live many of us consider the cultural amenities available in a particular city. Popular tourist destinations often have a strong sense of their local history and culture and create sites and attractions to share it with visitors and locals alike. Inventive entrepreneurs in the gig economy are finding ways to tap their city's cultural capital to create unique tours and other experiences for tourists.

There are three more forms of wealth that enrichen each of us individually and add tremendously to our quality of life that are worth mentioning here. They don't tend to beget more capital or value as the forms of capital previously outlined do, but they're invaluable for the well being and peace of mind they bring to our lives.They are also fundamental to our efforts to wisely cultivate, steward, tap, and appreciate the eight forms of capital.Yet despite all the amazing benefits they contribute to our lives, we are highly prone to taking them for granted and even squandering them.

Do you think of your health as a form of wealth or capital? Without **health capital**, a foundation of good physical, mental, and emotional health, nothing else matters or is even attainable.Healthcare costs are likely the major expense Americans worry about saving up for to cover in retirement.Yet we rarely discuss the long-term financial benefits of making wise health-related decisions (think food choices, physical activity, and positive social interactions) during our younger years. Nurturing a foundation of good health throughout our lives can reduce our medical expenses and greatly improve our state of mind throughout our lives.

And how about **time capital**? Since we know that what truly brings us happiness is autonomy over how we decide to spend our time, it shouldn't be difficult to grasp the tremendous value of your own time. Once you've chosen to spend an hour doing something, you never get that hour back.Time capital, unlike financial capital, is a finite resource. Are you filling your time with things that bring you joy and that move you towards your vision of a wealthy life?

Similarly, there are tremendous benefits to be gained by capturing people's attention.Our collective **attention capital** has been transformed into billions of dollars for media tycoons like Randolph Hearst and Mark Zuckerberg. Every waking moment you are choosing to direct your attention towards something. Be mindful as to whether you are directing it in ways that enrich your own life or only the wallets of others.

Another way you can design diversity and resilience into your balance sheet is by recognizing the stocks and flows of wealth that are already in your midst. *Gaia's Garden* author Toby Hemenway used the idea of his neighbor's wood pile to explain this concept. The neighbor had stockpiled enough wood to last 10 to 15 years. In addition to taking up a good bit of space in the neighbor's yard, Hemenway noted that any wood still in the pile after 5 years would begin to break down and not heat as well when eventually used so it was becoming an inferior product while it aged in that pile.

By accumulating such a large pile of wood, the neighbor was only focused on his stock of wood. In essence he was hoarding wood, losing sight of the flow of wood that was continually available to him in the surrounding forest. As a culture, we tend to focus much more on stocks, which has resulted in many of us being stuck in a scarcity mindset. We don't have faith in the flows. Nor do we give ourselves the time or opportunity to look at things deeply and clearly enough to recognize them as flows.

We do see a bit of the concept of stocks and flows in the proverb "If you give a man a fish, you feed him for a day. If you teach a man to fish, you feed him for a lifetime." Beyond that though, it's much harder for us to see the abundance in all the flows that surround us. We are much more likely to lose sight of those flows and focus only on the stocks. However, if we could start emphasizing the flows over stocks (or hoarding) it would lead to a more equitable, ethical, and sustainable approach to distributing our resources.

I had a joyful experience a few years ago recognizing a flow in my own front yard. It happened when I needed a new shower curtain rod and didn't want to buy a brand new one. One day I looked with new eyes at the slender bamboo patch out my window and knew I'd found my flow of free, beautiful, renewable, and sustainable shower curtain rods.

My boyfriend found a flow in the public beach one mile from his house. To finish his yoga certification training he needed to lead ten hours of classes. Instead of trying to find a studio that would let him teach there, which he doubted was likely, he started offering his class on the beach and announcing it on Facebook. He added elements that were very personal to him, like blowing a conch shell to indicate the beginning of class and offering vibrational attunement with a drum during shavasana. Eight years later he's still leading his twice weekly practice there and it's one of the most popular yoga classes in the area. He recognized the public beach as a flow of yoga studios.

Becoming more cognizant of the various forms of capital as well as the stocks and flows that surround you can dramatically boost your efforts to both save and earn money. And then there's the wondrous way these forms of capital and the flows can act as a hedge against inflation. As our money continues to lose value and purchasing power over time through inflation, you can reduce inflation's impact on your balance sheet by finding ways to bypass money and directly access these non-monetary forms of wealth, like I did with my bamboo shower curtain rod. The more you are able to meet your needs without spending money, the less you are affected by inflation.

Pondering these forms of capital as well as your stocks and flows can grow and shift your understanding of the world and the transactions you engage in. So now, when you take a closer look at your own holistic balance sheet you'll likely see that in many ways you are already truly rich beyond measure.

And of course it's in these additional forms of wealth that the true richness and meaning of life reside. The more we can bypass money and directly access these forms of capital, the more we interact with others and save our own money to meet other needs or invest in our community.

Adventure 8: List your forms of Capital

For our next adventure, let's list our forms of capital. We're actually wealthier than we think we are!

Start with the forms you have now, but then also include ones you have an interest in developing. For each of these forms of capital, do you have resources you can draw upon? Do people in your network?

Attention and willpower, ability to focus on a task:

Material Capital:

Living Capital:

Human Capital:

Intellectual Capital:

Cultural Capital:

Social Capital: (networks, connections, mail lists, organizations…)

Spiritual Capital:

Experiential Capital:

Time Capital: (hours we can put into something)

Political Capital:*

Other resources:

P20–Patterns for More Holistic Wealth

As we learn to move beyond the money economy, we get a better idea of how those real people out there are living a FREE lifestyle.

And we can understand why folks like the artists, activists, and musicians I've described had big gardens, big social support networks, and efficient, sustainable homes. To be successful in these privileged fields, they'd become masters at beautiful, abundant lives of thrift. In learning to produce their own luxuries, they'd extended their lifestyles to be truly beautiful ones, while supporting their good work.

So let's look a little deeper at some of the patterns that can help us grow this holistic wealth.

Living with the Land, Rather Than Off of It.

And now that I understand the value of holistic forms of wealth, I finally understand why all the best artists, activists, musicians, and community organizers I met in my youth had gardens.

The fact of the matter is that really smart gardening is one of the highest-value activities we can engage in. Considering the price of fresh organic produce, people who have really dialed in smart gardens often make up to $100/hour for their work. Or more! And in a lot of cases, they're getting health-enhancing benefits and rare luxuries, as well. Add in some effort to get free fuel wood and perhaps a part-time vegetable or plant stand for a little extra cash, and having some traditional land-based skills is just a great life hack.

But with that said, it can be important to draw a few distinctions here. For most people, having a gardening, learning to forage, or hunt can be a great value. But because land-based work follows the law of diminishing returns, the value begins to drop dramatically once we try to "go pro" with it. We can quite easily make $100/hour for our own family gardening work, but studies show it's exceedingly difficult to make $3/hour professionally as a full-time market gardener. And so we need to address some of the myths of the back to the land movement.

Back to the Land Goes Back to the Drawing Board

There is a great old debate in environmentalist and other activist circles, which we could call the debate over "lifestyle activism," or the idea that regular people can have a transformative effect on the world by changing our lifestyles. This belief has become one of the defining ideas of the modern "back to the land" movement.

Here's how Permies publisher Paul Wheaton expressed his goal, while weighing in on this debate:

"...I want to, at the very least, come up with the recipe (a list of things regular people can do) so that if everybody in the world did all of the things, then it WOULD make a HUGE and POSITIVE difference. It would truly solve most of the world's problems that we are currently discussing. And it all starts in our homes and in our brains. And I think this path of building good things is more productive than being angry at bad guys."

In other words, since most of the problems in the world today are caused by our lifestyles, if we could truly change those lifestyles by giving people better alternatives, we could unmake our problems. Very often, this approach is also called "simple living." It's living without the complex corporate systems that are causing our problems.

In that quote above, Wheaton was specifically responding to activist Derrick Jensen's attack on lifestyle activism in his piece "Forget Shorter Showers" published by Orion. In that piece, Jensen questions whether personal lifestyle changes (like showering habits) can realistically have an impact on the major problems of our time:

"Would any sane person think dumpster diving would have stopped Hitler, or that composting would have ended slavery or brought about the eight-hour workday, or that chopping wood and carrying water would have gotten people out of Tsarist prisons, or that dancing naked around a fire would have helped put in place the Voting Rights Act of 1957 or the Civil Rights Act of

1964? Then why now, with all the world at stake, do so many people retreat into these entirely personal "solutions"?

So there we have it, two modern leaders taking sides in one of the most important debates in the world today. And so, if you're opposed to lifestyle activism, you'll cheer when people say "100 corporations cause 71% of all carbon pollution." And if you're in favor of it, you'll respond that that statistic is misleading, and only counts energy companies, and that we consumers are actually the ones using that energy. If you're against lifestyle activism you'll point out that the beef industry is a major player in climate change, and if you're in favor, you'll point out that it's consumers who are driving the demand for that beef.

Which side is right? Since some could see this book as "lifestyle activism," or "simple living," it's time we address this debate and try to get to the bottom of things.

It's worth pointing out that Derrick Jensen himself advocates for simplicity and personal responsibility. His point is that it's just not enough. We also need the bigger political change.

And it's also worth pointing out that Paul Wheaton has said he fundamentally agrees with Derrick, that lifestyle activism—like changing light bulbs—IS usually just a distraction. But as he says in the quote above, he thinks this is because the standard list of personal actions we're taught—like changing light bulbs—is simply more about corporate profit than actual effectiveness. But, Paul believes, if the list of personal actions was good enough, if it included truly effective changes, then it COULD solve all the world's problems, and that this is better than the "angry" and unpleasant work of political activity. As he stated above, we just need a better list.

And that sums up what I have found to be a very common sentiment within in within large tracts of the "back to the land" and simple living movement. Politics is just a distraction, they say, which alienates people who'd otherwise take direct action. For example, there are huge numbers of people in red states who'd favor simple, local, resilient living, but they're put off by talk of climate change and social justice. So what we need is to forget divisive politics and to just focus on better direct action.

One might point out that Paul Wheaton lives in a conservative, rural area of a red state, while Derrick Jensen lives in one of our bluest states, more receptive to activist messages.

On the surface, Paul's argument makes a lot of sense. We all agree that it is the systems we use to meet our needs—energy, transportation, industrial food, corporate clothing, etc.—that are destroying the world. So, if we "drop out" of those systems, we will not be participating in the destruction. And so, if everyone just did that, there would be no more problems! No more demand for carbon spewing energy and products. Done! No need to get involved in bad-feeling confrontation that alienates our conservative relatives.

It's a notion I myself have found compelling, so I'd like to put it as ridiculously as I can, just to be disagreeable: it's the idea that if we all lived in the country and grew our own food and lived simply, all the major problems of the world would simply melt away and we'd all sit around campfires drinking kombucha and singing kumbaya.

Sound plausible?

There are two major glaring questions with this. First, would it actually work? Can we actually make a good enough list? How will we know if the list is good enough? And second, even if we had a perfect list, is it really realistic at all to think that enough people could actually do the list? In Paul's quote, he says "if everyone in the world...."

Sheesh, I can't get 5 people to agree on a restaurant! Can we get the whole world—or even enough of it—to agree on a low-impact lifestyle?

In other words, we have two things to think about: is this really good for the world, and is it really good (or at least realistic) for us as individuals?

Let's get very clear about Jensen's point above. People did indeed accomplish all of these positive things he mentions, defeating Hitler, and passing civil rights legislation! And they did it through coordinated, persistent political action. They did it despite personal risk and the icky feeling of confrontation. They did not accomplish these things by avoiding deodorant, making their own granola, and having epic hippie jam festivals with good feelz.

And perhaps we are now slower to accomplish meaningful political goals exactly because our system has taught us to feel icky and confrontational about asking to have basic rights and have our basic needs met.

I don't know the creator of this meme, but it was shared thousands of times on Facebook alone. It's a good representation of this particular back-to-the-land sentiment. One might note all the people appear white, they're growing food in row monocultures, using a cob oven and open fire pit which both probably emit tons of carbon and particulate pollution, they're all sitting on a lawn, and of course an old bearded white man is the one teaching. And so the meme unintentionally reinforces a lot of the critiques of the back to the land movement and lifestyle activism: that it's full of privileged good intentions, but weak on details, and may only reinforce problems.

Even if Paul Wheaton has the most epic recipe for granola EVER, granola still wouldn't have stopped Hitler, and the most epic hippie jam session in history won't stop climate change.

And yet, despite the apparent truth of Jensen's observation, there are also few sane people who believe that Germany would have so easily fallen under the dictatorship of Hitler, if the cultural and economic situation in Germany had not been so dire and conducive to fascism. Every single serious history book on the topic covers the systemic and ecosystemic situations that gave rise to Nazism. The end of slavery, the eight hour workday, the Civil Rights Acts—all happened within a broader set of conditions and circumstances which were favorable to those accomplishments, and—despite Jensen's observation—this is exactly the sort of stuff that historians take very seriously.

"Holism" matters. The environment and history matter.

So, we are convinced the work of personal action, of personal responsibility, and lifestyle activism can absolutely be a powerful factor in creating a better world.

In fact, counter to Mr. Jensen's point, many of our species' biggest historic changes have been the result—not of political struggle—but of lifestyle changes. Climate change itself has been largely driven by the car. It was not a direct decision decreed by politicians. And that didn't come about by activists convincing people to drive cars, it came about via viral lifestyle change. The industrial revolution, the expansion of agricultural civilizations, the evolution from the Stone Age through the Iron Age, the Age of Exploration…. All had profound impacts on people's lives and on the planet, and they did not come as the result of political struggle. They were the result of lifestyle changes. Does anyone think a political decree forced by political activists could undo any of these?

If we're going to be serious about affecting big systems then we have to go about it like systems thinkers. It will take big changes to our paradigms, our ideas, and the countless little daily actions that add up to big systemic impacts. And it is by changing people's behaviors that we change paradigms and ideas. That's about people like you and me changing how and why we live and what we live for.

"It is in this space of mastery over paradigms that people throw off addictions, live in constant joy, bring down empires, get locked up or burned at the stake or crucified or shot, and have impacts that last for millennia."

Donella Meadows, discussing deep paradigm change

Now, let us be clear that this is absolutely not the same as saying "we just need a better list for personal action."

We're not taking Paul Wheaton's side, we're agreeing that both are making important points.

What we're saying is "yes, we need political action, AND we need well-designed personal action." And the personal action can be as powerful or arguably more powerful than political action. And the best personal action is honest, vigorous, and effective, and designed specifically to support political action. The two aren't opposed, they should go together.

We can use personal action to help support activists and communities. We can directly "seize the means of production." We can build "durable power" for political change by growing real wealth and resource access in our like-minded communities.

If our action is vigorous, we can crash whole destructive industries. We've already talked about the hundreds of news articles about do-gooders destroying destructive industries. We should take these as a game plan.

We can use personal lifestyle action to grow movements, build political capital instead of just spending it, and even create the viral self-organizing change that lasts for centuries or millennia.

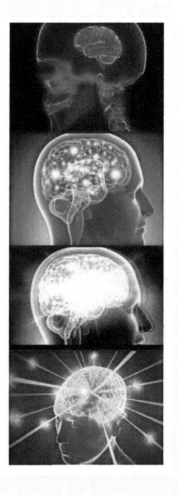

Let's fight climate change by changing our consumption and lifestyle patterns

Lifestyle and Consumption Activism is a distraction from the major systemic change we need. Lightbulbs and cold showers won't accomplish anything

Smart, targeted change to lifestyle and consumption is our single MOST POWERFUL tool for direct action against the most destructive systems, corporations and industries.

Transforming lifestyle and consumption can literally transform the underlying systems, values, beliefs and culture that cause climate change and most of our society's other major problems

So, we believe that lifestyle change CAN be powerful and transformative, but only if we take ourselves seriously about it, listen to the critiques and build better lifestyle activism.

So let's dig into a few of the major critiques of the back-to-the-land movement and its lifestyle activism, so we can make sure we're growing and moving forward.

Confronting Privilege

In 1954, Helen and Scott Nearing published "Living the Good Life," about their move to a backwoods farm in Vermont. Many give this inspiring book credit for giving birth to the modern back-to-the-land movement.

This is one of the books that has most inspired me in this life as well.

For me, the book's most profound message is that with simplicity and frugality, by returning to the land, one could work just part of the day to "earn your bread" and spend the rest free to work on more important things. I'd say that basic message underlies much of the movement today.

But what the book doesn't dwell on is that the Nearings were from a very privileged background, both inherited very sizable chunks of money that would be worth millions today. And they had their book sales, and free labor from likely thousands of eager guests.

This isn't a criticism of the inspiring way Scott and Helen chose to spend their lives! However, we simply must admit these are advantages that many who have tried to emulate the Nearings do not have. My experience is that more often than not, those who try to "live the good life" without huge stores of financial wealth find themselves in the insecure financial position this book was written to remedy.

So we can't just count on everyone withdrawing from destructive systems by going back to the land and becoming farmers.

If you've looked into "living off the land" at all, you've heard the stories and advice of those Regenerative Ag gurus who bought huge acreage (often with money made in the industrial destruction economy) took on massive debt, invested in thousands of trees with a 90% attrition rate, started experimenting on livestock, lived in hovels with dirt floors and tarp roofs for 20 years— until farm insurance speculators drove up their land prices enough that Real Estate website Trulia told them they were suddenly millionaires.

Their advice? Just do what they did and become millionaires! Easy!

Or perhaps you're more inspired by the intrepid entrepreneur veg-farm start-ups that managed to pull "$150k!!!" (fine print: that's gross, net is less than minimum wage.) That's only after staving off bankruptcy for 3 years by charging super-premium prices in upscale markets with no mortgages and lots of free money and labor. They SURVIVED! So now they cash-flow big money each year selling "profitable farming" workshops!

But most folks who jump in to emulate these gurus will never make it. Farm businesses fail at a higher rate than any other, and farmers have notoriously low incomes. And only a tiny percentage of people even have the resources and privilege to be able to even try it in the first place.

And so if we want lifestyle activism to be a serious solution, we need to get better at financial advice, and provide solutions that are accessible to more than a privileged few.

That also means our movement can't be one about ruralism. Or about owning farmland. Yes, there may be a role for some of us to live in rural places and manage landscapes there. But many people are simply going to continue to live in suburbs and cities, and a serious movement has to acknowledge that. Most of this book's authors, along with many leaders in the Permaculture movement, have chosen urban, community-based living. It's every bit as possible to find the good life in the city as in the country, and our "solutions" need to be accessible to city folks if they're going to be picked up by many people. Our solutions have to be available to those who grew up poor, and those who have disabilities, and those from marginalized communities, and people who live in apartments, and basically, our solutions need to be for everyone. Which is why the tools in this book aim to help people wherever they're at move towards whatever sort of life best works for them. We're not just out to help well-to-do people move "back to the land."

The Good Life is often Bad for the Earth

As a long-term advocate of the movement, I have been forced to come to the conclusion that a lot of our "personal solutions" aren't just ineffective, they can also be bad for the planet.

Many small farm businesses end up feeling pressed in a race to the bottom due to unrealistic economic expectations and the difficulties mentioned above. They can end up destroying soil with heavy tilling, using a lot of harmful plastics that cause health risks, using more fertilizers and poisons than industrial agriculture, and exploiting labor. Worse, we've had decades of policy supposedly aimed at local food resilience, that really just bolstered the profits of plastic companies selling things like hoop houses and plastic mulch.

Making sure we're financially free gives us the space to make sure we're actually healing the earth.

And if our movement is going to take itself seriously, then we need to actually be managing landscapes in truly transformative ways. For example, Transformative Adventures has created a Transformative Landscape Recognition Program to help us ensure that our management will be beneficial.

Lifestyle Activism Discourages Political Engagement

For me, one of the most frustrating things I see is when lifestyle activists like me act dismissively or even contemptuously of those pursuing political change. For example, the whole of the first meme in this chapter. A common feature of discussions in back-to-the-land communities online is "just plant a tree!" Or "if you were busy enough in the garden you wouldn't have time to worry about social injustice!"

These are standard responses to expressions of almost any sort of complaint, and it comes off as incredibly dismissive and clueless.

And also, it's bad gardening advice! Good gardening should be based on freeing up our time, not creating a privileged hobby that takes endless hours.

Even Paul Wheaton's quip about lifestyle activism being more effective than "getting angry at bad guys" might come off as dismissive and unnecessarily judgmental. Just because I engage in building new systems doesn't mean I can't or shouldn't get angry at injustice. And just because I'm going to protests, doesn't mean I'm emotionally immature or just "too angry" as the quip implies. Imagine if people had said the same about those who fought Hitler!

And while this attitude has become very common in parts of the movement, it's good to remember that the back-to-the-land movement itself began with rigorous political activism!

Many observers have cited Helen and Scott Nearing as launching the modern back-to-the-land movement with their book Living the Good Life. In the very opening of that book, the Nearings described their whole goal as to be able to have the free time and resources to engage in creating a better world as teachers, activists, and folks building political power to leverage political change. The Nearings weren't against "being angry about bad guys." Just as I'm stating here, the Nearings favored a "yes, and" approach. They certainly didn't believe that if they just grew pickles they were absolved from worrying about the rest of the world!

Even their hero Henry David Thoreau said much of his experiment at Walden Pond, where he was perhaps the first American back-to-the-lander, was to be able to live as a full-time citizen. Thoreau didn't stop at growing beans, he was willing to spend a night in jail for his political activism. And he had no trouble at all expressing anger at injustice! Later activists including Gandhi and Martin Luther King, Jr cited Thoreau's activism as an inspiration, showing that the man at Walden Pond had a big impact beyond growing beans.

I'll note that the contributors to this book all agree on this topic as well. My friend Jenny Nazak mentioned time for civic engagement as a major motivation in the introduction to her book, Deep Green.

And while folks on the "lifestyle activism" side often portray themselves as spiritually to developed to get angry at bad guys, we could even observe that the great teachers of all our religious traditions had this same balance figured out. Most of these got their groove by going back to the land, in a sense—by removing themselves from society for a time. But then they just didn't stay in the wilderness growing enlightened beans and pickles. They returned back to the world with their wisdom, to change people and build a better world.

Why? Why not just stay in their blissed out little bubbles to give an example of a better way of being human?

The Bodhisattva tradition in Buddhism perhaps gives some insight into an answer. The "Bodhisattva vow" is to "work for the freedom of all beings." It is often explained that this vow is important to one's own spiritual development. It allows us to "get over ourselves," move beyond our own petty dramas and shift our attention to the well-being of others. This allows us to finally experience true peace and relaxation.

Giving a crap about the world leads to greater peace and a happier life. This is why we see "compassion" is one of the three Jewels of Taoism, it is a major theme in the teachings of Jesus, it's a central tenet of every mystical tradition for a reason.

In my opinion, those who think it's enough to go to the backwoods and grow corn and stop worrying about the world—for the sake of their so-called spiritual development—have completely missed the entire point.

So, summing all that up, how do we listen to these critiques and respond?
1. We have to understand our inherent privilege. We need solutions that are available to everyone, not just a privileged few who can buy large acreage in the country and live off inheritances.
2. We also need to BOTH take personal responsibility AND act in ways that have a chance of creating real societal change.
3. We need to make sure we are doing our "personal action" in ways that are seriously better than the dystopian nightmare systems we're trying to replace. For example, with food and landscape management, we should be goinggoing being "organic," or even "regenerative," and meeting the Landscape Transformation Program Criteria.
4. To do a lot of this, we need to be more realistic about becoming financially secure and viable, and we need to build good financial advice into the movement.

If we get these things right, not only will we bebe be building a better, more trustworthy path for ourselves, we'll be more likely to build the kind of world we'd like to see while we're at it.

Discussing consumption and boycotting strategies to target the most destructive and vulnerable economic sectors

Teaching children about the sociopathic corporate system

WHAT PEOPLE THINK REBELLION LOOKS LIKE

WHAT IT ACTUALLY LOOKS LIKE

Comparing Molotov cocktail recipes for next tuesday

Watering crops with the blood of her oppressors

(Okay, now that looks a little more like real revolution.)

P21–Is "Living off the Land" Realistic?

This is a section for those contemplating living off the land.

I want people to succeed gloriously in creating beautiful, rich lives with greater connection to the land – living WITH the land, not OFF it.

And I think that goal is completely realistic. It is absolutely realistic to grow nearly all a family's food on just a few hours/week with a vegetarian diet, and have an omnivorous diet on just few more hours than that.

But many feel lured into quitting their corporate rat race jobs to buy homes in the country in an attempt to "make a living" at farming. Some even tell people they can get rich doing it!

Out of the fire and into the fryer. This is NEVER a good idea.

The fact is farming is one of the most stressful, high risk, and dangerous professions we have. Some may survive the heat, but that doesn't mean it was a good idea. Why not just get out of the fire?

Just because some profitable farming gurus survived wandering blindfolded through the field of pit-traps they set for themselves, doesn't mean blindfolds and pit-traps are good investments.

Everyone knows most new businesses fail, and the reality is the numbers for farm businesses are absolutely the worst of the worst. Read past the "think positive' hyper-optimism in online "successful farming" groups and you'll see virtually everyone agrees that no one is making money. And we have studies to back that up, in which most small farmers make very low incomes, often around $3/hour, and few farms ever make a profit.

Worse, I see many get into farming inspired by folks like the Nearings. They want to have connection to nature, heal the earth, help feed people, and have simpler lives. But reality sets in and they often find they're working longer hours, doing aggressive sales on social media, hustling to make ends meet— and instead of healing the earth and having connection to nature, they're in a death struggle with nature and stressed out every time they see an animal or plant in the wrong place! "Farming" took them in exactly the opposite direction they wanted to go in.

Anyway, none of this means you can't actually farm well or live with the land.

But it means that realistically, we'll need to think of production income as one part of our livelihood, and we'll have to be clever about that part.

And we may need to think very deeply about what our real goals are, so that we don't lose our true path in the struggle to "farm."

So why do you really want to homestead or farm? Is it:
To have a simpler but richer lifestyle?
To reconnect with nature and natural rhythms?
Because you love being around and caring for animals?
To find right livelihood?
To make a living OFF the land by exploiting the earth, animals and human laborers?
Or would you rather live WITH the land, in cooperation with your ecosystem and community?
Because you want to raise your family with connection to nature?

Because you want to take control of your family's food and health?
Because you want your children to be resilient, healthy and know how to
grow their own food?
Because you want to fight ecological collapse and climate change while
helping your community?
Because you want to prepare for the uncertain and dangerous future we
appear to be creating for ourselves?
Because you want to help feed your community?

You may well be able to design your life to accumulate all these things, and
have a higher positive social, economic, and ecological impact, without
farming. In fact, it's highly likely farming would only get in your way and
hold you back. Ask: Is it possible that our preconceived notions (or the
notions sold to us by digital farmers and University Extension services) about
farming and homesteading are just a blindfold?

What do I really want? How can I design my life to accumulate what I really
want? Answering these questions and daring to take off the blindfold, that is
the key.

P22–Mike's Honest Controversial TOP TEN RULES for making a right livelihood with Regenerative Enterprise

Yes, we all need encouragement, but in my opinion a lot of advice out there
might prioritize encouragement over honesty. I've been observing folks
doing it for more than 2 decades. Yes, it is 100% possible! But when you find
it, it probably won't look like what you thought it would.

10: It doesn't require owning land. There are many strategies that you can
use to make a living regeneratively that don't require you to own land, or that
don't have anything to do with land at all!

9. It probably won't be "farming," even of the "regenerative" kind. The
economics and realities just don't work out for most people without special
circumstances, like free land with grade A soil, a wealthy market, loads of
start-up money, and fame to drive volunteer labor and high prices. At least it
probably won't be animal, vegetable, or commodity farming. I grow and sell

produce and food plants as a part of my income, but it's never been something I would rely entirely on, and neither do any of the famous "farmers."

8. It probably won't be "landscaping," even Permaculture landscaping. The whole industry is about replacing home-owner labor with plastic, concrete, fossil fuels, and underpaid labor. It's really hard to make that system both regenerative and profitable. Besides, the two busiest times of year for landscaping are Spring and Fall, the two busiest times in the home garden, which can provide you with more value than cash from a landscaping business. So, I tend to take about 3 landscaping clients a year, and they're people who already have a relationship with their land and know how to take care of it.

7. It probably won't be a "Permaculture" or "farming" teaching business, especially not an online one. These days there are just too many online options driving down prices. And the PDC was never intended to be a career income! It was intended to be a local community organizing tool and to raise money for local regenerative investments. It's great for that. For most people, it won't lead to a great teaching business. And it probably won't be teaching online classes or workshops. There was probably a golden age where the first few to bring Permaculture to online classrooms had a wide open market, and they literally made millions. The first rule of farming is when people are rushing into a market, it's done, get out. We, the authors of this book, all do some online content, but it is ultimately to support local-scale organizing and business.

6. It probably won't be as a celebrity. All of the above options work really great if you are a celebrity. In fact, they work great if you're a celebrity, even if you don't have good content to teach! But there are a whole lot of us who want to work transforming our communities, and trying to become the next celebrity guru is a distraction from the things that will really make your livelihood. Check Google to find out what youtube celebrities, for example, really make. As of writing this book, it's usually not a living wage.

5. It probably WILL involve "stacking income streams." One of my mentors taught me that in any "privileged field," you have to be willing to do a variety of things and specialize in some to make a good living. In most modern markets, there are a LOT of people who want to live off the land, and

so wages will be low. But you also don't want to spread your time between very different streams like computer programmer/farmer/dancer. It takes too much effort to maintain those skills. So a "stack" means they are complementary and get extra income out of the same work: farmer/plantswoman/herbalist is a better stack.

4. It will probably involve holistic whole-life design. It means looking deeply at your goals and how you want to live and finding ways to be "FREE" Financially Resilient and Economically/Ethically Empowered.

3. It will probably mean having one foot in the old fossil fueled economy, and one foot in the new sun-powered economy--at least for a while. If you're focused on only one, you're on a fault line.

2. It will almost certainly involve being a local community organizer. Pretty much everyone who's successful at this is one, even if they don't know it. Which is great, because that is where the real transformation needs to happen, not--as much as I love you fam--on the internet.

1. It will definitely mean you have to stop thinking about it as a job, or even a career, and start thinking in terms of long-term regenerative investments. For the whole history of farming, good farming has always been about making investments. If you're not thinking about it that way, you're not even farming yet. You're probably the customer. Somebody else is probably farming you. "The poor have jobs, the middle class develop careers, the wealthy seek investments." That's how we have to think, only we want to do it without exploitation or destruction

P23–Informal and Gift Economies

While we're thinking holistically about alternative forms of capital, we could also be thinking about alternative ways of exchanging them.

On balance, money often gets a bad wrap in the lefty hippy community, as the "root of all evil." But many just and sustainable societies use currency! Currency can be quite helpful in accomplishing regenerative goals.

But also on balance, most just and sustainable societies have a lot less of their economic activity bound up by money, and what economists call "the formal economy."

Meanwhile, healthy societies have more opportunities to exchange and get needs met in an "informal economy," through direct barter and trade. These "informal" alternatives mean that on a very basic level, more economic interactions are happening, more value is being exchanged, and there is— without more "money"—literally more wealth.

And so it is beneficial for any of us to try to increase the informal economy around us in our families, friend circles, and communities. Some patterns for doing so include:

Time Banking and Time Sharing*

Time banks and time shares allow people to directly exchange their time for the time of other people in their community. For example, I have exchanged Permaculture consultations for painting, graphic design services, website help, and financial advice. Time banks help streamline the process and open us up to a broader "market" for trade. These days many communities have active, well-resourced time banks with hundreds of members. You could look yours up and get involved. If not, it could be that your community just needs someone to step up and help start one.

Local Currencies

While not exactly "informal," local currencies help accomplish many of the same goals as time banks, and in fact some of the best time banks are associated with local currencies, allowing people to exchange their time for local "dollars."

One of your humble authors, Mike, has been involved in starting 3 local currencies, he's such a fan.

Local currencies are especially useful where another community good or institution can be supported, like a farmers market or startup business incubator. The currency then acts as a sort of "collateral" that everyone believes in, to give everyone confidence in the currency. For example, if everyone believes in the farmer's market, or incubator, or community food forest, then everyone has an incentive to use the currency, which builds trust and buy-in. Using the currency, then, isn't just a matter of having a way to get your needs met, it's a way to support something the whole community believes in. In fact, it's Mike's opinion that local currencies work best when tied to a community good in this way, and currencies that don't are often not as engaged or used.

Mutual Aid Groups

One of the most extraordinary changes to come with COVID was the rise of mutual aid groups, groups devoted to stepping up and helping individuals within our communities.

As societal systems began to fail to help folks meet their needs, people began organizing online to step up and help meet those needs directly. This was one of the most inspiring examples of building the systems and economy of the future that I have seen in my lifetime.

In my own community, people spoke up because their childcare was unavailable, and community members stepped up to make sure they were covered. Suddenly unemployed people were unable to afford medications or toilet paper, and people in their communities stepped up. People needed help with house repairs while others needed jobs, and mutual aid groups made it happen.

Many of these groups began online, so you can find them on places like Facebook Groups. Others grew to have their own websites or forums. If your community doesn't have one, again, it could be the opportunity for you or one of your friends to step up* and get one started. Joining another mutual aid group to see how they work could be a good start.

FreeCycle Groups and Buy/Sell/Trade groups

FreeCycle groups are directly devoted to the informal economy of exchange. Often, all it takes to make these work is to give people an opportunity to advertise what they're trying to get rid of and to let people search for what they want.

Groups like this have also had enormous success and growth over the last decade, moving from a Permaculture fantasy to a very successful reality in a very short time. These groups have become a regular fixture on social media, especially Facebook and Reddit, so it's easy to get involved these days.

Community Tool Sheds and Other Sharing Libraries

The greatest skill of life is to want but little, as Thoreau said. And so I do not need much.

But, it turns out I do need a lawnmower.
And a weed whacker, I guess I need one of those, too.
And sod cutter.
Oh, and an infrared paint stripper is really nice when I have to repaint the house.
And I guess I could also use a tall ladder, a nice scaffolding, a nail gun, a hedge trimmer, a power washer….

But the thing is, I don't need them all the time. I'm not going to shower or do the daily dishes with a power washer. And, if I own a power washer, I've got to find a place to put it while I'm not using it, and just letting it sit around might actually increase the maintenance costs as it accumulates dust and old fuel goes bad and so on.

Sharing libraries and community tool sheds are the magical solution that allow me to have access to a power washer when I need it, but allow other people to use it and take care of it—getting FAR more value out of the investment—when I'm not using it.

The same goes for all of these sorts of tools.

And so a well-designed and trusted community tool library is a great source of wealth for all involved, allowing me to get access to a whole range of tools for the price I might pay for just one tool.

P24–Creating a Personal Gift Economy

Beyond these barter economy tools, the informal economy of healthy societies extends to generous giving, or a "gift economy."

Gift economies are economies in which items are given without expectation of a direct or immediate repayment or exchange. However, in gift economies, there is an implied debt or obligation, which we could at best call a feeling of gratitude. This feeling of debt is thought by some to encourage feelings of community and relationship, since giving someone a gift may imply a future interaction in which the gift is repaid in some way. And so it is thought that a culture with a strong gift economy has strong ties of obligation to one another, and that we could emulate those strong obligations by encouraging more gifting.

Even in the most capitalist of Western countries, we still have gift economies. Most of us operate on the gift economy within our close friend and family groups. We may host a party this month and pay for the food, with the understanding that one of our other friends may host next month. Or perhaps we host the party, and know that friends will gift the food for us to enjoy together.

Most of us do not charge our family members when it's our turn to make dinner.

And of course, that constant feeling of open giving within these groups does seem to encourage a feeling of closeness, connection, generosity, and a sense of a future together where the gifts will be reciprocated.

Observing the gift economies of healthy traditional societies, some Westerners (especially in the Permaculture movement) have argued that encouraging a gift economy more broadly outside our friend and family groups could make way for important work to be done that isn't valued by a capitalist system. For example, Charles Eisenstein in Sacred Economics and Seth Godwin in Lynchpin, seem to encourage us to give our own personal gifts to the world in the spirit of a gift economy. We all have important gifts to give, which may not be valued financially. But in a gift economy, we would simply give these gifts anyway, expecting that this spirit of obligation and relationship would help us to meet our needs when those needs arise.

We could see such a "gift economy" as an important way to build non-financial resilience in our lives.

However, this is an incredibly complex topic with a very robust academic literature, and it is often covered poorly in Permaculture texts. In that literature, it is clear that in traditional gift economies there are many nuances of how gifts are given, what types of gifts, rules that govern gifting, and so on. We don't want to continue to over-simplify the topic. Many of our well-intentioned and less academic discussions of the gift economy leave off many of those important details, and can lead to some significant problems.

Upsides to the Gift Economy (which gives us some hints about how to use it.)
1. It may encourage longer term relationships. (Though in my experience, I've had great feelings of relationship from more conventional exchanges. I often end up loving the businesses I choose to support with my money, and I love the customers who choose to support me by buying my produce, art, books, and programs.
2. It can help move people from "community member" status into our true friend circle. If you'd like to be friends with someone who's an acquaintance, it's pretty traditional to try offering them a thoughtful gift. Be mindful though, that this may not work, and if you're only offering a gift to get something in return, it's kind of manipulative.
3. Healthy gift economies, such as within family and friend groups, may help to create financial resilience. Folks who have that sort of gift economy in their circle know that they will be taken care of if something goes wrong.

Downsides to Working "in The Gift" (which gives us some hints of things to avoid.)
1. It often doesn't work very well.
2. It may encourage unhealthy, or coercive feelings of debt. Narcissists are famous for giving gifts and doing nice things that make people feel obligated.

3. It can encourage us to engage in manipulative behavior, similar to the behavior of narcissists. If we're doing something with an unspoken expectation, that may well be unhealthy, manipulative behavior. If you have an expectation that you'll be compensated for your time and efforts, then it may be more direct and less manipulative to simply say so, and put a fair price on your time.

4. It can more easily create inequality. It's often said that gift economies create greater fairness, by allowing resources to flow where they are needed, rather than being accumulated due to the imbalances of capitalism. But in reality, with no expectation of measuring "fairness," outcomes may be even more unfair. For example, I know of a few fairly privileged people in my sphere who are famous enough to operate on "the gift," who receive quite extravagant compensation! They have fairly large social media followings and are very good at asking for money as a "gift." They almost certainly make more money than they would if they put a fair cost value on their services and marketed them for a price. On the other end, they "receive the gifts" given of work, rather than paying for labor. The idea that they're being "generous" in receiving those gifts means they don't have to think about setting limits to what they actually need. Rather than operating on gifts, this person could provide scholarships to those in need, to get the resources where they need to go. Meanwhile, there are far less privileged people doing better work in the same field, who struggle to make ends meet. In these cases, the gift economy does not seem to be helping resources to go where needed, or to keep them from being accumulated by those hoarding them.

5. It can deteriorate the very sort of economic connections we're trying to build. In this case, I often think of the "gift" given by a member of one of my communities to a poor neighborhood in a food desert. Motivated to help this community, and hopefully create a livelihood for herself, this well-meaning person started a farmers market in the food desert.

She did this as a gift to the community, without asking the community for anything.

But with a closer look, it turns out her gift actually deteriorated functioning economic relationships. Just down the street from her new market, there was a member of that neighborhood who'd been organizing an informal market in the parking lot. His market had brought in some culturally relevant produce and goods, but also gave a space for locals to sell their own produce.

The informal market was well-attended and popular. But against the competition from a well-funded outside market bringing in outside farms, the small informal market dried up. Meanwhile, the bad relationships caused by the faux pas caused the new market to fail as well, leaving the neighborhood with less service than it started with, and with new resentments and broken relationships.

In other examples, I've seen well-meaning people offer "gift" classes on Permaculture, foraging, or mushroom cultivation, for example (these are all real examples in my experience) with the hope that these would turn into actual incomes. Meanwhile, there were already professionals making a living providing professional quality services in the community, at a fair price.

Operating on a gift economy model, the new "gifters" couldn't afford to offer a professional quality, resourced product. But the competition from a "free" service greatly devalued the services of these professionals, making it seem like something that should be offered for free, rather than as a well-paid service. And in all these cases I've seen, the result was that the new gift business failed pretty quickly, but in some cases took the old businesses with them, or at the very least, they harmed the old businesses.

While I appreciate the spirit of a "gift" approach, I would encourage our readers to be more thoughtful about the gifts they offer, and what the outcome might be.

A More Nuanced Approach to Growing the Gift Economy

1. Start with the places you already have it, like in your family. If your immediate family operates on the gift economy, try expanding that outward to your more distant family and friends. I just love households that open up their dinner time to whoever is around, including friends. These are always beautiful situations to be in, and of course, gifts and resources tend to flow from them easily.
2. Expand it in your friend group. This means expanding it in the other places it is most present in healthy cultures. Try hosting more parties

with your friends and pay for a nice meal, or for the entertainment. See if that doesn't help fill up your calendar with other fun activities hosted by your friends.

3. Use gifts to bring acquaintances into your friend group or to strengthen working relationships. These are also common uses for gifts in many societies, and they feel pretty natural within Western cultures, too.

4. With a little more caution, try expanding it to the broader community in the context of businesses or organizations. This closely mimics what is done in many healthy societies. An excellent example is the Eccentric Day party held by Bells Brewery. It is a free large party where food is included (you still pay for drinks,) offered as a way to "give back to the community." People show up and still buy lots of drinks, but it creates an enormous feeling of community and gratitude. These kinds of acts of gift giving can indeed help foster more free giving within the community.

5. Try starting things like community food pantries and little libraries. These may help create more feelings of open giving within your community, which may provide you (and everyone else) with more resilience in tough times. This is clearly something you have to do without expectation that it will benefit you directly, but instead, out of a belief that it's the sort of thing that simply should be done in a healthy community.

6. Don't offer gifts in a manipulative way!

7. Don't offer free "gifts" when others in your community are charging for the same thing, unless your intention is to undercut them for some reason.

8. If you want to expand your personal gift economy beyond these options, I'd suggest studying the topic in more depth before jumping in.

Chapter Resources:

1. Nearing, Helen and Scott. The Good Life. Schocken. 1990.

2. Hemenway, Toby. Gaia's Garden. Chelsea Green. 2009.

3. Mollison, Bill. The Permaculture Designer's Manual. Tagari Press. 1988

4. Fukuoka, Massanobu. One Straw Revolution. Rodale, 1978

5. Hayes, Shannon. Redefining Rich. Benbella, 2021

6. Olympia, Off the Map, Crimeth.inc, 2006.

7. Brill, Hall, et al. The Resilient Investor. Berrett Koehler, 2015.

A full-time food forest garden.

ADVENTURE 9: Permaculture's Most Powerful Tools

When it comes to the landscape, there is one set of Permaculture Design tools that are simply the most important and powerful tools in all of Permaculture.

This technique is our #1 tool for weeds, our #1 tool for pests, the #1 way to save water, time, money, and energy, the #1 way to increase productivity, and to improve resilience.

And just as these are our most powerful tools for the garden, zone, sector, and element analysis are powerful tools for designing nearly anything.

Taking some time to do these design exercises can help us think and brainstorm creatively about our finances.

Permaculture Zones

Permaculture Zones is a way of helping us talk about how much energy something takes. In the Landscape, Permaculture Zones might refer to how often we visit an area of the landscape and how much time and attention a particular plant or garden takes.

For example, if a daily greens garden bed will be used daily, and these tender greens tend to require a lot of care, it would be smart to put them somewhere we can easily see t and visit them every day. For example, right by the kitchen door, if possible.

In the financial landscape, zones can help us think about a lot of different elements of our behavior.

Zones for Spending.

If we want to make sure our spending helps build a stronger local economy, which helps us have a wealthier environment to live in, then we can use zones to help us do so. We'd do well to keep as much of our spending as close to home as possible.

Zone 1: Shop at Permaculture and Regenerative enterprises, cooperatives, black-owned businesses or other enterprises you wish to specifically support.

Zone 2: Locally-owned small businesses.

Zone 3: Local franchise businesses.

Zone 4: Big chain stores.

Zone 5: mail order.

(Illustration should have space to list reader's ideas.)

Zones for financial behaviors.

In this case, we can also use zones to think about behaviors we'd like to encourage in ourselves. Often, we fail to make good habits simply because we've made things too difficult for ourselves to do. If we can think of our financial priorities, we can find ways to make sure they're "close at hand" to our attention, rather than "out of sight, out of mind."

Zone 1: Monthly bills and important statements that require your attention; important cost savings activities; priority tasks for your business: make sure these are easily accessible without much work. Don't put them in a messy bottom drawer somewhere so that they will require organizing just to do work!

Zone 1*; Daily costs. Do you buy a coffee or expensive, unhealthy snacks every day simply because you don't have inexpensive, healthy snacks available? Instead of using willpower to solve the problem, use zones, and make sure that these daily costs are conveniently taken care of. Make healthy snacks in advance to take with you.

Zone 2-3; What weekly tasks would help you create a better financial life or more successful business? Set aside a weekly time to do them.

Zone 4-5: what tasks can be automated? Not all our financial decisions need to have constant oversight. Can some bills or other tasks be set to auto-pay, so that you know they're taken care of, but you don't have to use up brainpower to do them?

Permaculture Sectors Analysis for Financial Design

Second among Permaculture's most powerful tools is "sector analysis."

Sector analysis helps us pay attention to and plan for external energies that impact our designs. For example, in the landscape, we might pay attention to floods, winds, fire, annoying neighbors, wildlife, or anything else that will have an impact on our outcomes.

We can do the same with our financial lives. What are some external energies and factors that will impact you and your ability to meet your goals? How can you take advantage of those energies or mitigate them?

Macroeconomics. There may be nothing more impactful on our situation, and also less out of our own control, than "the economy" as we call it. Growing wealth and abundance may be easier than ever in a "good economy," but it may be even more important in a bad one! Over the next few years, how do you see the economy going? How about the next decade? How about the next few decades? What will you do to mitigate your risks or take advantage of the opportunities this presents?

"A great economy!" This is what the talking heads call a period where GDP is growing, unemployment is low, but sizable enough to keep wages low, and wealthy people are raking in lots of money. It also usually means we're generating high rates of pollution, carbon, and resource extraction, and likely also that labor is being well-exploited in developing nations. In this book we talk about keeping one foot in the old economy and one in the new. Generally speaking, during these periods it's easier to find well-paying jobs, so this could be a time to focus on the traditional economy and storing up money in our transformation funds. On the other hand, prolonged periods of easy economic growth COULD be the opportunity for you to start that business, try to scale up a side-hustle, or take that risky move you've been dreaming of.

Hyper inflation. Inflation is a nasty condition in which the value of our dollars wittles away while they're still in our pockets. Often this is done by our governments, so that they can pay for things without a pesky and unpopular tax raise. Consequently, the cost of the things we buy goes up and up and up. At times of inflation, it may be wise to hold value in "durable assets" we'll discuss later, rather than in cash. Buying durable, valuable goods and tools at a low price to use or sell later can be a good strategy. Making necessary items like toilet paper, or providing necessary services like housing, may also be wise at times of inflation.

Stagflation. Worse, stagflation is the brilliant combination of high inflation and a stagnating economy with poor employment and low wages. Having a foot in the essential economy during stagflation is wise. Providing essential life goods and services may help us thrive during stagflation.

Deflation. The opposite of inflation, prices go down as the value of our dollars soars. While this SOUNDS like a great thing (lower prices! Higher wages!) it's usually accompanied by low employment and difficulty in obtaining goods and services. Everyone wants to hold onto their money, rather than spend it! If you're seeing deflation, watch out, big layoffs, high unemployment, and low access to credit are likely coming, if not a full on depression.

Recession. A temporary economic downturn, where GDP is down for two quarters or more. This means industrial productivity is down, there's going to be no job growth, no growth in wages, and fewer people have disposable cash so it's harder to start or operate a business. During recessions, informal economics, strong networks, trade, barter, and gift economics all do wonders to help pick up the slack. Valuable skills like repair, mending, building, etc. all become highly valuable as people may need services but not have cash to procure them. Our "non-financial" capital becomes our real gold. Recession is when we may be most forced into the new economy as the old economy fails people. This can be a tremendous opportunity! The biggest leaps in the Permaculture community I have seen have all happened during prolonged recessions.

Depression. Depression is typically defined as a deep and prolonged recession. These days no one likes to use the D word because it could strike fear in consumers, further harming the economy. Few experts give hard rules on what constitutes a depression in terms of length or size of contraction, just that it's bigger than a recession, and "they'll know it when they see it." We may never hear experts use the word again. But if talking heads start discussing the difference between a depression and a recession and telling us why what we're experiencing is just a recession, you know the economy is in for a prolonged and bumpy ride. It may be time to focus on developing your non-financial capital, while avoiding any unnecessary risks.

Uncertainty and Instability: the one scenario I think we're most likely to be able to depend on is that the future will be characterized by increasing uncertainty and instability. We are likely to get a combination of the above conditions, along with "bull markets" in which wealthy investors make oodles of money and the media celebrates the "great economy." Keep in mind, we've had many such "great economies" over the last 50 years, in which real incomes have gone down for most Americans, costs have gone up, and the quality of the goods we can buy with our money has plummeted. We'll likely get more of the same. Hopefully, the tools and patterns in this book will help you be more resilient no matter what comes.

Politics

After coming back from the Vietnam War, my step dad took a GI scholarship and got training in one of the industries the experts of the day were calling "HOT, HOT, HOT!"

And it was for a while. He was able to save up money working and eventually buy his own business. A few years later, he had expanded to multiple shops.

Unfortunately, politically driven changes to insurance law wiped out that industry overnight, gifting the whole sector of the economy to wealthy automotive makers, and leaving my step dad out of business.

It's good for us to consider how future political movements may impact our financial plans.

This is also why we say "Permaculture is necessarily political." Usually, the best resistance to such political changes are for us to act politically ourselves.

Background, Privilege, isms and schisms

In 2016, the median black family in the US had a net worth of about $17k, while the median white family had a net worth of $170k.

https://www.businessinsider.com/.../degrees-matter-black…

One major energy is clearly very impactful on our financial lives: relative privilege and class. Things like racism, sexism, homophobia and so on have a huge impact, and so the economics laws of the universe start functioning completely differently when you get into traditionally marginalized communities.

Take that massive whopping difference in the wealth held by white families vs that held by black families. Of course, that translates as wealth held by white communities vs black communities.

So if you're a white entrepreneur in a white community serving white families all with a high amount of resources, business life is just a lot easier. And so the median white entrepreneur is in the top 1/3rd of income earners. Meanwhile, black Americans start businesses at the highest rate of any demographic, yet the median black entrepreneur is in the lowest 1/3rd of incomes.

https://www.wbur.org/.../black-entrepreneurship-research…

So, how to fix the wealth gap? Well, we could expect black Americans to take out loans to go to university to become "more hirable." But the net worth of a median black family with a 4 year degree is $70k, while the median for a white family THAT DIDN'T GRADUATE HIGH SCHOOL is $83k. Meanwhile, without resources to begin with, black students take out significantly more loans than white families, and are likely to pay higher rates of interest. For example, 62% of black students entering medical school already have student loans, while only 35% of white students do. Without the background of family wealth, they're more likely to default and end up paying predatory rates.

Okay, how about black families take out mortgages to buy houses to grow wealth? Well yes, of course! After many decades where such loans were only available to white families, they are now at least MORE available to black Americans. But also, black families will pay higher rates on their mortgages, and black neighborhoods do not keep up with the growth in wealth that white neighborhoods do. If you buy a home in a black neighborhood, it will be artificially worth $48,000 less than in a white neighborhood on average. All totaled that's $156 BILLION dollars black families are getting swindled out of. Taking out a mortgage while white is a way better investment. https://www.brookings.edu/.../devaluation-of-assets-in.../

So should black Americans (and others in similarly marginalized communities) take out these loans to try to "catch up," or even just to survive, as the article suggests?
I really have no idea. As we say in the garden, "it depends."

But I suspect if we really wanted to solve this problem of inequality, the solution wouldn't be to make black Americans take out loans—just to compete in a rigged game—and pay back interest to wealthy white people.

Which is to say that, firstly, we need to be thinking holistically and that includes acting politically if we want to change these things. We can't or shouldn't expect marginalized communities to just do it on their own.

And secondly, if you're reading this and you're from a marginalized background, you may have to spend some time considering how that impacts your own financial design.

Resources and Notes:

1. Www.TimeBanks.org

P25–Investing in Skills that Build Holistic Wealth

Force has no place where skill is called for.
—Herodotus

"To win one hundred victories in one hundred battles is not the acme of skill.
To subdue the enemy without fighting is the acme of skill."
—Sun Tsu, the Art of War

The fool thinks "skill" is knowing how to do things. In fact, that is the definition of a fool. In today's very foolish times, the fool can now watch 10,000 Youtube videos on "how to" do many things in a quest to become "skilled."

But knowing how to do things is not skill. It is its opposite.

"Skill" is knowing how to NOT do things—on this point, the wise, experienced, and *skillful* always agree.

This is why we find a fool funny. To prepare for his first camping trip, the fool watches 20 YouTube videos, and buys each "must have" camping tool and gadget he sees. He arrives for his strenuous 3 hour hike to the camp site with 3 bags of heavy equipment, specialty clothes, and stiff new "hiking" boots that haven't broken in. Meanwhile, his more skilled friend has a single light bag, old jeans, and comfy shoes. It's just an overnight stay, afterall! When they arrive, their highly skilled cousin is already there relaxing and making dinner. She knew a parking spot just 20 minutes away, with a hike past exquisite views and a patch of flavorful berries.

Sun Tsu's skilled warrior wins without battle. The skilled artist has a greater impact with fewer brush strokes. The skilled musician can bring tears with the subtlest effect. The skilled gardener does the least work, while the fool learns 10,000 more things "to do."

On our journey towards a skillful FREE life, we may all begin as fools. We'll be tempted by 10,000 TikTok's on the "secret money tricks of the wealthy," and think we need to learn about 1,000,000 tax loopholes and investment "tricks" that we'll never actually use ourselves.

You might have guessed that I often see social media "how tos" as a "fool factory." In my areas of greatest skill, foolish videos on "10 things you can do" will get 100,000 views, while truly skillful videos on not doing get 7 views. Just as marketing ropes us into spending money on things we don't need, "how to" businesses rope us into doing things we don't have to do, so other people can make money.

100 times I've arrived for a Landscape Transformation consultation, and the completely flustered and overwhelmed land steward asks "How do I do find time to do swales, and hugelkultures, and a rain garden, and a pollinator garden, and have a profitable farm, and a food forest, and a hoop house, and regenerative cattle, and make biochar, and a rocket stove, and a chicken tractor, and on and on and on." It's the "technique of the week" approach, and the inexperienced steward thinks they must "collect them all." But when we talk, they may say their only real goal for the land is to steward it well and grow a little food to enjoy. They've learned from YouTube that means they're supposed to do all these different things! Then we observe. Already the old-field is transitioning into forest on its own, sequestering as much carbon and infiltrating as much water as we could with swales and holistic grazing. We find 10 high value edible species growing wild, all on their own already. Biodiversity is increasing, and "farming" would only set it all back. The best way to meet this steward's goals is to start with doing none of these fads. Now, with a few dollars and a little work, we can add a few plant guilds that will spread and flourish, tilting the process of natural development towards even more biodiversity and usefulness to humans. We've achieved far more, with just the teensiest fraction of the work.

So the path of skill in developing our lifestyle is to learn to do less and less, and have more room for abundance because of it. Keep that in mind as we think about developing skills to build holistic wealth.

We could also say "skills" are the unique and useful mix of non-monetary capital that help us not do unhelpful things, like waste our time and resources, and make mistakes and false starts.

It's worth thinking about this mix of capitals, as skill lies at the intersection of informational capital (knowledge,) cultural capital, experiential capital, and may well also include spiritual capital (such as the ability to focus single-pointedly on a task,) material capital (like the right tools,) and the right living capital.

The most valuable skills will usually be a true mix of the capitals that help us free up even more capital, like time, attention, willpower, and so on.

Cooking

There are few skills that will help us get more free time, more savings, and more enjoyment than cooking. A truly valuable skillset.

Cooking with true skill is always doing more with less. A skilled cook will free up lots of time, save lots of money, and get a great yield of joy and satisfaction.

In meeting to discuss this book, we authors all agreed the path to progress on a FREE lifestyle was about finding small little footholds to free up time, energy, and money to invest in transforming our lives.

We may come home from dinner after a long, frustrating day of work, and not have the time or energy to feel like we can cook. So instead, we get a six pack of beer and McDonalds. This costs us money, makes us feel gross, and doesn't take us towards our goals for a healthy body and life. This makes the vicious cycle of feeling bad and buying junk food to feel better even worse. Developing some skill with cooking then will be about getting a foothold that helps us actually free up time, save money, relax and enjoy cooking more, and enjoy better health for it.

Some Patterns for Skillful Cooking to Save Time, Money, and Enjoy Cooking More

Mike's Multiple Meals from One Prep Plan

This is an old world technology found in many of the world's smart peasant cultures, and it has been the biggest tool that Mike has used to turn a lot of garden produce into a lot of actual meals without spending hours and hours in the kitchen.

When Mike made it a goal to grow as much of his own food in his own garden as possible, he found that most of the "old timey skills" approaches emphasize techniques of spending endless hours meal prepping and preserving food. These were usually based on an American culture where servants or women were essentially exploited to make meals possible, and it was impossible to replicate these "old ways" of doing things without exploiting himself! But more egalitarian societies had farmhouse cultures based on skill, which made the most for the least amount of time, so that people could actually enjoy their lives instead of spending all their hours working.

This same sort of pattern is what allowed mike to turn more home-grown produce into more meals than he imagined on far less time than he thought possible.

Transformative Soups:

To give one example, **Jerusalem artichoke soup** is one of my favorite soups, but the same trick here can be done with potatoes. One plant will fill up a 3 gallon pot with soup for a week, and they can be left in the soil and harvested in my climate all winter long, which minimizes my gardening and storage work. I don't have to waste time harvesting, cleaning, and storing all at once, I can just do what I need when I need it, and the smaller scale makes all the work much easier. First, I'll make the soup straight and enjoy it that way as a main course. Then I may add roasted garlic for the second meal, and curry for a third or fourth. At this point, the soup becomes a side dish. Later in the week, the soup can become a sauce, a rich dip, and then later a gravy.

One fairly simple mail prep turns into a week worth of time and money savings.

Gazpacho, a tomato-based soup loaded with garden veggies and served ice cold, is another favorite that works the same way. The initial time making gazpacho may take 20 minutes. I love gazpacho and can eat it for multiple meals in hot weather, by simply adding more fresh veggies straight from the garden. It can be a main course, or move to the side to turn quick sandwiches or simple snacks into fancy, nutrient rich meals. It can be heated up, turned into salsa, made into hot sauce, used as pasta sauce, and then frozen in bags to be used later. That initial investment of time turns into time-savings for a whole week of home-cooked meals that can be thrown together in minutes.

Polenta is another favorite, which is traditionally made with corn, but may also be made with amaranth. Again, I will make a large 2-3 gallon batch of polenta with corn, the easiest grain to grow, store, and prep at home. Wonderful gourmet meals like this can usually feature as the main course at a few meals for me. Then, the solidified polenta can be sliced and fried or grilled or broiled in a toaster oven and served with fast sauteed vegetables from the garden (or a sauce from sunchoke soup or gazpacho!) for a gourmet meal in minutes. It can be sliced soaked overnight in almond milk and syrup for a gourmet breakfast or dessert. And it can be thin sliced and air-fried for polenta sticks, a fancy pants side dish for another quick meal. Since corn and amaranth are the easiest grains to grow at home, using them paired with quick garden veg fry-ups also can save significant money on groceries.

Risotto goes through a similar transformation in my kitchen, starting as a main dish on its own, being revived as a side dish or with different toppings, then getting sliced and grilled or fried as polenta cakes later in the week for fast meals that can be finished in minutes with simple steamed veggies from the garden.

Potatoes are a magical crop for lightening fast gourmet meals. They're one of the easiest crops to grow in a home garden without even tilling, just throw down newspaper, add a potato start, then cover over with some compost and mulch. Baby potatoes can be sautéed in a little oil on high heat in just a few minutes, then dressed with fresh chopped herbs of all sorts, a bit of olive oil, and a splash of lemon or wine. Greek potatoes are sautéed this way, then dressed with a "pesto" of chopped oregano, oil, and lemon. Basil pesto is also magic. Wilt spinach or other garden greens and add enough water to make them like a light sauce for a magic meal. Potatoes can be chipped or fried as a fast side dish or baked for quick baked potatoes topped with fresh garden goodies.

Simple bread skills are a major lifestyle level up. Again, the path to skill master is simplicity. If you study to be a baker in France, a country serious about baking skill, you may make a baguette every day for a year. Skill isn't learning to sort of bake 10,000 different breads you'll never bake again.

For those of us who are home bakers, skill is learning to a few consistent, flexible things very well. For me, the goal was one simple wild-fermented dough that can gain flavor for a couple days in the fridge, that could make an excellent flat bread for pizza or an excellent peasant style loaf for the week. I often keep a starter or batch of dough going at all times, which I can turn into flat breads to top with garden goodies, or make a loaf for sandwiches for the week. After practicing my one basic bread for years, I'd rank it with the best local bakeries in my region.

I have the advantage that all peasant bread-makers have always had. Each region traditionally had its bread style, and everyone practiced and improved and perfected it over years. Meanwhile, pro bakers may do a dozen different breads each week.

A good basic dough recipe is the Roman Pizza dough recipe in Peter Reinhart's American Pie.

Mike's Basic Flexible Weekly Dough Recipe:

This is not a beginner's dough, but easy enough, and flexible enough to be used as thin crust pizza, flat breads, foccaccia, or even a rustic peasant loaf. It should be chewy, and have a nice crisply crust, and full flavor.

Ingredients
1 1/2 tsp bread yeast, or try a packet of beer yeast for a slower rise but much more flavor.
5 cups Flour, unbleached. High gluten "hard" bread flours are best here. All purpose flour will do, but not get quite the same flavor or bite.

3 1/4 tsp sea salt.

1/4 cup Semolina flour (optional) or other home-grown or wild milled grains of your choice. These add texture and flavor.

1 3/4 cups luke warm water

Steps:
1. Sift flour into a large metal bowl, yes, this is an important step for the best texture.
2. Mix yeast and ¼ cup of flour and ¼ cup of lukewarm water until bubble and frothy.
3. Mix yeast, flours, salt and water and stir until it forms a dough ball. You'll notice this recipe does not require hours and hours of kneading. If you want to knead it a bit, it may give the final breads a little more chew.
4. Let the dough sit for 30 minutes or until slightly risen. Punch it down and place it in the refrigerator over night. This is where the magic happens, the long, cold ferment builds incredible flavor and texture, rather than the kneading.

Flat Breads and Pizzas:
1. Remove the dough from the fridge and and divide it into 6 equally sized balls. Avoid working them too much at this point.
2. Allow the separated dough balls to rise at room temperature for 2-5 hours. If you don't plan on using the dough within 5 hours, you can refrigerate them (for a few days) or freeze them for a few months. Keep in mind you can also cook the crusts and then freeze the whole crusts to be turned into fast pizzas later.
3. Press out the dough by hand with a little coating of olive oil (more flavor) or flour (more chew.) I'm a purist and insist that the pressing and stretching by hand will develop a better crumb than the more consistent rolling with a pin, but to each their own. This dough will make an exceptional thin crust pizza if patiently stretched thin. To do this, work with gravity, letting the weight slowly stretch the dough without ripping it.
4. Heat the oven as hot as it will go (up to 500 degrees.) A pizza stone is magic.
5. Bake for about 3 minutes until the flat bread is set, then remove, top with toppings, and return to the oven until it's "done" to your liking. The whole process should take about 10 minutes. Alternately, you

can top the crusts with light toppings and bake them about 10 minutes.

For a rustic bread.
1. Remove the dough and divide it into 2 balls.
2. Coat the counter with a sprinkle of flour, semolina, or other flours. Gently work the dough balls into the shape you like, keeping in mind they will rise to double the height if things go well. This dough will make a decent baguette-like bread, or a more conventional European style sandwich loaf.
3. Transfer to baking pan or surface. To keep the dough from spreading out too much, you can make "bumpers" of flour on each side to contain it as it rises.
4. Allow the dough to rise for 2 hours.
5. Heat the oven as hot as it will go. (500F is good.)
6. Place a pan of boiling water in the oven, or better yet, use a spray bottle and spray the inside of the oven with water as you add the bread.
7. Bake breads for 10 minutes or so, or when the crust looks dark and crackling. As it finishes, you may give the oven another spray of water and let the bread bake for another 2 minutes. This caramelized the dough surface, making it crispy and bringing out rich flavors and aromas you almost can't buy at the store.

Flash Fried Food Forest

The key point in Mike's meal planning is that there's whole abundance of super fast, incredibly gourmet better-than-restaurant meals awaits you in a home garden (or at the local farmers' market.) And super fresh, just-picked produce takes almost no work to turn it into amazing meals. The perennial vegetables and easy annuals found in a food forest type of garden will get the most food for the least work. Our favorite annual vegetables can easily be grown in such perennial systems with far less work than in a traditional garden. (For garden designs like this, see Beauty in Abudnace, by Michael Hoag.)

Turning the freshest vegetables into a gourmet meal requires just moments of cooking. In the Spring, fresh snapped asparagus can be sautéed with a tiny bit of oil and a sprits of lemon or wine, and a crack of pepper and salt, and become the star of a meal. Serve over risotto, polenta, or with a side of soup, and a sprinkling of chopped fresh herbs for lightening fast fresh meal. Turkish rocket is another personal favorite, a broccoli-like perennial veggie with an arugula-like flavor. Sea kale is another sweeter broccoli alternative, which can be served over a fast baked potato. A great number of "weeds" and perennial vegetables can substitute for broccoli and asparagus throughout the season. Since these are seasonal delights, I wait all year for fresh asparagus or Turkish rocket, I can eat them at several meals per week through the whole season without getting tired of them, paired with fast risotto, polentas, soups, sandwiches and flatbreads.

Taken together, these patterns give a view into the sort of old world culinary technology Mike used to eat very well while saving lots of money on very little time. In a given week, a single bread might be the fuel for several meals, and one other major item like a pot of polenta or soup. Then the focus of the meals was fresh, home grown herbs and produce. Flat breads or leftovers from the freezer can add a little fast variety here and there.

Meal Planning

Meal planning is another tool for building real cooking skill, which has helped many people save time and money while meeting other health goals. Meal planning involves an up-front investment of time that pays back the rest of the week. For example, some people dedicate Sunday night to meal prep for the whole week. An hour or two spent Sunday night gives fast meals that just need reheating or simple prep for the rest of the week.

The other big advantage of a meal planning approach is that there's a lot of support for it. There are meal planning books now for virtually every goal: vegan, vegetarian, how carb, low fat, and so on.

Adventures for Building Cooking Skill

The key adventure here is to periodize a new cooking skill for yourself, then commit to it for a few weeks, or a few months. Pick an adventure that will be fun for you and help you meet other goals, and one that gets you excited. If you love Asian food and want to eat more vegan meals, then find a vegan meal prep book with an emphasis on Asian food that looks exciting to you and has great reviews, and commit to trying it for a few weeks. If you have a garden and think more flatbreads and sandwiches would have a big impact on your time and diet, then commit to doing bread once a week for a few months. Periodizing is key to building new habits, so the most important point of the adventure is to commit to a set period of time, and stick to it!

Some adventure ideas:
1. Pick a meal planning book and try it for a few weeks or months.
2. Weekly bread baking.
3. Make one of the multiple-use dishes above, like soup or polenta, and try seeing how many meals you can get out of it.

Repair Skills

When it comes to repair and DIY skills, it's good to remember that skills are about doing less, not more. It's easy to fool ourselves into thinking we're saving money by doing every little thing ourselves, when it reality, we end up spending far too much time and money doing things without much value to our life goals.

That said, I've saved thousands of dollars by repairing my own appliances, and have helped many friends do the same. My personal cut off point is $30/hour for such work. IF I have the time, and IF it sounds fun and interesting, and IF I can "earn" $30/hour (in savings) then I will DIY the job myself. These days, as my own time has become more valuable, the cut off is much higher, around $60-100/hour.

For example, I've now repaired multiple washing machines and dryers, water heaters, furnaces, refrigerators, ovens, and in many cases the repair cost would have been $200-300+. Usually, for a few dollars in parts and 3 hours of time, I was able to do the repairs myself. It's rare to find a repair person who will do such a repair for much under $200. Typical appliance repairs take 2 hours or less, which means I've typically made $100/hour for this kind of work.

Usually the process is fairly easy.

Step 1: Identify your exact appliance model. You will need this.
Step 2: trouble shooting with the Internet. Search for your appliance and model and the words that describe your problem as best as you can.
Step 3: Get a second and third opinion. I never stop with 1 site. I always look for at least 3 different perspectives on the problem I'm trying to solve.
Step 4: Determine if the job is within your ability. Be honest with yourself, there's no shame in starting with a simpler task.
Step 5: Find your parts. There are now multiple online sites that sell appliance parts, so do multiple searches to find the best price. If you can't find it, I've had luck in contacting the manufacturer to ask for parts.
Step 6: Read instructions carefully! Complete the repair. Congratulations, you've just saved some money and built a new skill.

Basic Building Skills

Similar to repair, some basic building skills can be key to doing less and having more time. In 2022, there's an absolute crisis in finding qualified building professionals who will work for the wages being paid by local contractors, and meanwhile prices soar.

It has never been a better time to get handy.

For those who have a willingness to learn, each problem around the house becomes an adventure for learning new skills. Here are some areas that are particularly accessible to DIYers and highly valuable.

Basic plumbing is accessible to most people these days, in an age of easily built plastic parts that screw and glue together.

Simple electrical repair and wiring. This can include light switches and sockets, and other simple electrical. With the cost of an electrician, a few literal minutes of work can be worth hundreds of dollars.

Basic carpentry. Again, there's no reason basic carpentry can't be done as well by homeowners as it is often done by underpaid beginners working for contractors. You at least care about your home.

Flooring is accessible to most people. Just again, read instructions, get multiple opinions about how to do the job before trying to do it. Remember skill is NOT doing things, so focus on understanding what the possible common mistakes you could make are. Until you know the common mistakes, don't try a DIY job.

Scaffolding makes an excellent "generative asset" investment, as we'll discuss in the next section.

Chapter 11: Investing in Transformation

Permaculture Asset Class Analysis

The fundamental role of the THISTLE is that it invests. Like all pioneer species, the thistle isn't content to struggle endlessly in the poor soil it grows in. It works to regenerate and build soil fertility for the future, creating an environment where it will be free, and escape the hardships of its environment.

This section may be one of the most unusual and ground-breaking parts of this book for many people. It adds a new dimension not found in most books on simple living and back to the land lifestyles. Because—as we've said before—the reality is, for most people without big corporate incomes or trust funds, it's difficult to make those lifestyles work well off of income alone. And he same is true for artists, activists and other privileged lifestyles. Switching our thinking to "investing" is the trick that usually makes it work.

And this chapter is also a departure from typical "money" books.

Pretty much every money book out there will give a few very straight-forward and obvious pieces of advice:
—Reduce your spending.
—Save Money.

Then of course we're supposed to invest that money in things that make the people writing the books wealthier but ultimately do far less for us.

Which is why we throw out the idea of mere "savings" and focus on building our "transformation funds," to remind us that the whole point of us accumulating this capital is to invest it in things that will transform our lives, and our world.

So the big question is of course: once we have a transformation fund, what the heck do we do with it if we're not going to invest in mainstream corporate stocks in one way or another.

The best tool I have ever found for this comes from my studies of Permaculture.

Permaculture Asset Class Analysis

In his writings and teaching, Bill Mollison introduced these asset classes as a way of thinking about how we spend and save our money. Bill Mollison repeatedly called this "the most important part of Permaculture," and for me, this has indeed been the single most transformative and important idea in all of Permaculture. Hardly a single day has gone by since I discovered this way of thinking in which I haven't thought about these asset classes.

Which means that over the last 20-something years, I've had the opportunity to add some of my own nuance to the idea. And of course, I've developed it more with the our author team. So the version we'll present in this book will be a little different than the original 4 asset classes Mollison presented, and we'll add a 5th asset class, which is a high-powered sort of investment that can be very useful in growing FREE.

Degenerative (or Degenerating) Assets

"Take boots, for example. He earned thirty-eight dollars a month plus allowances. A really good pair of leather boots cost fifty dollars. But an affordable pair of boots, which were sort of OK for a season or two and then leaked like hell when the cardboard gave out, cost about ten dollars. Those were the kind of boots Vimes always bought, and wore until the soles were so thin that he could tell where he was in Ankh-Morpork on a foggy night by the feel of the cobbles.

"But the thing was that good boots lasted for years and years. A man who could afford fifty dollars had a pair of boots that'd still be keeping his feet dry in ten years' time, while a poor man who could only afford cheap boots would have spent a hundred dollars on boots in the same time and would still have wet feet."

"This was the Captain Samuel Vimes 'Boots' theory of socio-economic unfairness."

—*Terry Pratchet*

We've already hinted at the first asset class, which is the type we'd like to avoid.

The idea of these assets is that they exhibit entropy, they break down, often very quickly. This makes us poor. Recall the boot theory of poverty. If we buy boots that break down quickly, then we'll always be on the hook for buying new boots. Bad boots are like a weight we tie to our own economic lives. The more of these degenerative assets we buy, the poorer we become. Each one is a ball and chain weighing us down. And yet, this is exactly the strategy that corporations now pride themselves on: Planned obsolescence, crap made for the landfill. Each time we buy such an item, we are taking out debt that we'll have to repay in the future.

Meanwhile, pollution and garbage in landfills pile up.

Degenerative assets also tend to break down our connections to nature and community in favor of corporate products and profits, making them bad for our communities and the world.

The most obvious example is probably cars.

Cars! The second you drive them off the lot they depreciate by thousands of dollars. And without constant upkeep they will break down.

So, which of the following items would you classify as "degenerative assets?"

—Cheap clothes that only last a season or two.
—An apple cider press.
—Plastic dishes from Target
—Handmade ceramic dishes from a local artist.
—Antique tools from a garage sale.
—A new computer.
—A CD player.

The transformative key here is that now that I've started thinking about this, I became very aware of the difference, each time I bought something new. Almost instantly, I stopped wanting to buy a new link in the chain that was keeping me from my freedom.

REGENERATIVE ASSET CLASSES

So the alternative to these degenerative assets we could call "Regenerative Assets." Each time we invest in these, we're investing in our own freedom and in a better world.

Keep in mind, for something to be regenerative, it has to meet both halves of that criteria. It has to be regenerative to our lives, making our financial situations better rather than more precarious. And it has to be regenerative to the planet.

For many of us do-gooder hippie types, this is counterintuitive!

For example, buying $3000 worth of native trees to plant out on our 10 acre property MIGHT be regenerative for the ecosystem. Though of course, if we just stopped mowing trees would likely show up without us spending a single dollar. But, unless we have a realistic plan for those trees to earn their keep, this investment may leave us worse off financially, which might make it harder for us to keep the property, or it might mean we have to buy less expensive (and more destructive) food and clothes! So, those trees may well be a degenerative investment, afterall! So truly regenerative investments are good for us, and the planet.

We could further break these down into 4 different asset classes to have a very helpful analysis tool.

Durable Assets.

If degenerative assets are mostly made-for-the-landfill crap, the clear alternative is "made to last," durable assets.

If you said the plastic dishes from Target were degenerative, and the handmade ceramic dishes from a local artisan were regenerative, then we're on the same page.

The hand-made dishes are not only durable, able to save us money by lasting a long time, in many cases they hold their value very well, or may even appreciate in value, making us wealthier over time while we laze around in the hammock.

These days there are all sorts of Facebook and Reddit groups devoted to"buy it once," or "buy for life" strategies.

Each time you can buy something to meet one of your needs in a way where you'll never have to buy it again, you've removed a link from your chains.

Not only that, but many of these items are far more beautiful and satisfying than cheap plastic junk. Being able to eat meals off beautiful handmade plates or drink out of beautiful handmade mugs adds a whole character of richness to life. It's old, powerful magic to surround ourselves with such items of beauty. And once we are surrounded with a few items that are truly beautiful and add richness to our lives, we feel we need far fewer cheap trinkets. These well-made durable assets actually help defend us from consumption pressure and advertising.

Many of these items actually grow better with age, wearing in and developing "patina," beautiful signs of love, wear, and character that you just cannot buy new.

Speaking of boots, a well-worn pair of old boots takes on beauty, character, suppleness, and comfort that you cannot buy at any price. As in Terry Pratchet's example above, well-made boots often sell for as much—or even more—than when new! But the key is of course, the boots must be made well enough to last a long time!

All sorts of items develop character and improve with age: jeans, tools, homeware, furniture, and so on.

Like good boots, many of these will even appreciate in value with age. There are whole subcultures of people who will spend thousands of dollars on denim jeans and jackets from the 1900s and 1920s! Many of these could be expected to last for decades to come, with a little care.

As we write this book, durable assets are especially good investments! Due to Covid spending and war, we're already seeing rapid inflation, and expecting as much as 30% more over the next year. At times like this, I put cash in durable assets.

A year before Covid, I invested in a number of Okatsune pruners, amazing durable assets that will last a long time! I bought them all on sale for around $35 a piece. As of writing this, it's nearly impossible to find them under $60, with many offering them as high as $95. Think the stock market's the only good investment? That's a 300% increase in value in about 3 years. In this way I could make a good investment for myself, while offering my gardening clients an excellent deal on a valuable durable asset.

Later we'll talk about many other business and livelihood investments that revolve around durable asset investing.

But durable assets are only the beginning of our path to freedom. As we'll see in the next section, we begin to get real benefits when we switch to durable assets with a little extra.

P27–Patterns for Investing in Durable Assets:

Since most of what the corporate system sells to us is designed to break down and perform poorly, each time we buy one of these "degenerative assets" we're making ourselves poorer, while harming other people, and destroying the planet.

So one of our best strategies for a better life and a better world is to escape this trap by instead buying durable assets that maintain value or may even appreciate over time.

A General Buying Guide for Durable Assets

Buy things that are ethically made, or it's not a regenerative asset. That includes avoiding sweat shop labor, animal cruelty, environmental pollution, carbon emissions, and land fill fodder.

Buy things that can be maintained. Remember, "no maintenance" usually means something can't be maintained and must be replaced.

Buy older hand-made things. Many of these were designed to be maintained and made out of materials that you actually want to maintain.

Buy for "patina." Many of those older hand-made things actually grow more beautiful, and even more valuable over time. This value of beautiful, old things has been appreciated at least since Ancient Rome, when the world "patina" was first used to describe the beautiful, sought-after quality of old plates called "patinas." The word has gone on to describe that surface embellishment that only time can give us. High quality leather, wood, bamboo, architecture, cast iron, old tools, and even raw denim are all considered to grow more beautiful with age, so long as they are well cared for.

Buy Wabi-sabi. Similar to "patina," wabi-sabi refers to the beauty of age and imperfection. While "patina" is used to talk about a complexity and beauty on the surface of things that actually give them greater beauty with age, wabi-sabi refers to appreciating the imperfections and character that comes with age and use. Both can bring an appreciation and joy to old objects that can't be bought at any price.

Buy Classics. The classics never go out of style, and never use their utility. Every few years a new pruner design comes out and is all the rage, but nothing compares to the ease of use and durability of my old okatsune pruners. When we buy furniture, clothing, decorations, houses, or even fruit trees, it's good to remember the classics are classics for a reason. An outfit based on good quality leather boots and worn in raw denim looked good on Marlon Brando, Steve McQueen, George Michael, Brad Pitt, and all the stars of today.

Buy Multi-use things. The more uses a thing can perform, the more you'll use it and the more money it will save. Simple.

Buy brands known for durability. Some brands stake their reputations and build their whole business models on durability. Before buying appliances make sure to check which brands will be most reliable and long lasting.

Things to buy as durable assets:

Consider the following ideas examples to help you think creatively, not instructions on what to buy. And of course, the first rule is "Invest in maintenance instead of buying new."
Water filters
Clothes
Dish ware
Silverware
Decorations
Tools
Furniture
Art
Some appliances
Some housing
Musical instruments
Collectibles

Slow Fashion for a FREE Life

"The more time you spend worrying about clothes, the less time you have to grab life by the balls. You ever see a cheetah obsess over scarves and pocket squares? No. You see a cheetah bolt 70 miles an hour to take down a gazelle and shred it to fucking pieces. Be the cheetah."

—Henry Rollins

Well, I don't know about taking down gazelles, but I can say that Henry Rollins also has a reputation for being extremely generous with his time with fans, and that he's been a positive influence on a whole lot of people, myself included. Since he's famous for his work ethic, it's totally unsurprising that so many artists, activists, and Permaculturists have met and been inspired by Henry. And, at least in part, that's probably because he's not wasting time and energy on scarves and pocket squares.

But, on balance, even cheetahs preen themselves and take some pride in their appearance! And if we don't spend any time on clothing, we're more likely to buy cheap, planned obsolescence garbage that won't last.

What's more, the clothing industry is often called "the world's most destructive industry," so if we're not paying any attention to our clothing, we're almost certainly supporting a lot of environmental destruction, and exploitation of people. Our clothing choices are an opportunity to invest in the kind of clothing industry we'd like to see.

Good quality, well-made, artisan clothing that lasts can be a transformative investment that makes us wealthier, and makes the world a better place. Having beautiful clothes we love can be a very fulfilling way to express ourselves, connect with people, and tap into daily enjoyment and mindfulness. Appreciating the work of clothing artisans makes both them and us richer. Simple clothes can make us feel very wealthy, attractive, and empowered, and give us confidence when we need it.

So a middle path would have us not obsessing about consumer culture fashion, but also investing in clothes we will want to wear forever, and in a clothing culture that won't end life on the planet.

Dressing for a Better World: A Guide to Buying Clothes as Durable Investments

With the rampant inflation in 2021-2022, I also set out to invest in some new duds. Heck, if the economy was going to hell, I might as well look good for the apocalypse. In early 2022, many clothing manufacturers began hinting to expect a 30% increase in prices, and many had already started bumping their standard sale prices up a significant sum.

And since the average American spends $1800/year on clothes, and the average middle-aged American spends over $2000/year, a decade of savings could easily be worth $20,000. The average American woman will spend $125,000 on clothing over her lifetime, and the average man isn't too far behind. These days the largest share of our clothing purchases go to low-quality consumer clothing manufactured for the landfill, and much of this is only worn a few times, if that. Which means that by shifting to higher quality clothing we could realistically enjoy our clothing far more, dress much better, and save tens of thousands of dollars while we're at it.

In other words, I see clothing as a major leverage point for investing in our own joy while saving significant money.

Moreover, the clothing industry is often called "the world's most destructive industry" by sustainability experts. Fast fashion clothing is very energy intensive, often relying on long shipping distances to move clothing around the globe for different parts of processing. The materials are often highly unsustainable, like cotton, which is one of the world's worst crops for irrigation, pesticides, and fertilizer use. Dyes, breeches, and heavy metal processing is common and highly polluting. Many of these materials are non-biodegradable. And of course, the industry is famous for sweat-shop and child labor practices that could rightly be called slavery in some cases.

All of this also makes clothing a major leverage point for societal change, too.

And yet, many of us who bemoan that enough people won't pay a "true price" for locally grown beyond-organic healthy food (or invest in community art and culture) become indignant when asked to pay extra for organic hemp denim jeans made by a small company in the US.

There's a belief, as one farmer told me, that good manly workin' class clothes like they sell at the Walmart can't be part of the problem. Surely rugged manly man workin' clothes are too tough to be made by exploited little girls in sweatshops! This man was utterly convinced that his man clothes couldn't be a part of the problem, and believed that "all real working people can tell the difference."

Sadly, it is not high fashion that is the big problem. In fact, due to pressure from urban millennials, high end boutique fashion has become very conscious of social justice and sustainability. These days it's the low-cost clothing sold in big box stores that are more likely to be made in sweatshops out of unsustainable materials that are also harmful to our health. Even Carhartt, practically a uniform for outdoorsy folks including permaculturists, gets a "not good enough" rating from **Good On You,** the largest ranking for clothing industry companies. This company devoted to workers' clothes gets the lowest possible rating on labor practices.

So it pays to invest in better clothes.

Which means we need some tools to help us save money, buy better clothes that last longer, and make more ethical choices.

Some Clothing Patterns:

Grow connection to nature and community.
1. Dress better, buy less.
2. There's an order to ethical clothes=Make your own>buy local and regenerative>buy used/upcycled>buy from small or worker-owned ethically based companies>use rankings like Good On You to buy from more ethical companies, otherwise, I don't buy it.
3. "The French 5 Outfit Wardrobe." Or "Capsule wardrobe." These are approaches to clothing that minimize consumption by building "essential" clothes that are durable, functional, and look good. Then, we can buy accent pieces to have fun and spice things up. For folks who need to look good for work, and wish to reduce their consumption, these are great philosophies to look into and learn about. Men and women both can find plenty of articles on creating capsule wardrobes. (INSERT IMAGES ON CAPSULE WARDROBES FOR MEN AND WOMEN?)
4. "If you're not having fun, you're doing it wrong." I like to wear clothes that look beautiful to me and make me feel good about how I look. This also allows me to "obtain a yield" from the efforts I put into caring for the Earth and people. When we buy clothes we truly enjoy wearing, it helps create a life where we feel less need to buy consumer crap for satisfaction. It can also help us tune in to mindfulness and beauty.
5. Wear one weird thing. Wear conversation starters. I like to at least wear something fun and attention-grabbing to help me be approachable. It's kind and generous to help people who have trouble approaching people have an easier time making friends. Such pieces tend to also be better made, more durable, and made by artisans rather than sweatshop labor.
6. "Biophillia." I like clothes that connect me to a love of nature. I usually like natural fabrics that are hand woven or "slubby" (loosely woven to look more organic.) I love to wear floral patterns, especially because of the oppressive cultural BS that men shouldn't wear flowers. Sometimes I like to wear nature symbols.
7. Terroir. I like to wear clothes that root me in my bioregion and community, though I try to do this without reinforcing oppressive forms of conformity or implying there's a "normal" or "right" way for folks like permies to dress. I've noticed most Youtube Permie

celebrities wear a uniform of overalls and sun dresses, with country guitars twanging in the background. This makes the movement less accessible and implies only certain types of people are invited. I don't like that. I like to wear things like my Lizzo t-shirt to speaking gigs, because folks who like hip hop should also feel welcome.

Care for the Earth

8. Reduce, reuse, recycle. 90% of my clothes are "pre-owned"as they say these days. I think it's way more fun to "find" a cool piece in the wild than it is to pick something out of a catalog. This is probably the #1 thing we can do to ensure our wardrobes care for the earth.
9. When it comes to new things, I try to buy natural, sustainable materials in most cases. Synthetic materials have a much higher carbon footprint than naturals, even cotton (by about 1/3rd) I buy organic or regenerative if possible, especially with cotton. Hemp, nettle, and linen are good substitutes.
10. Buy once, cry once. I almost always buy things meant to last and "wear in, not out," meaning they get better with age. That includes things like real raw denim, linen, veg tanned leather (sourced from food waste streams) and other natural materials that "patina" with age. There are Reddit subs and Facebook groups devoted to these kinds of clothes, like the Rawdenim sub on reddit. The online magazine Heddels is all about clothes that grow better with age.
11. I avoid chemical processing and dyes like bleach and chrome dying in leather, favoring undyed whites, natural dyes like indigo, and veg tanning for leather. Metals for things like jewelry can be sourced from recycled materials.
12. I avoid cruel animal practices, especially with things like leather and wool. For example, the best leather companies have statements on animal care and source leather entirely from food waste streams. For wool, we can purchase from companies that sell "mulesing free" wool. Mulesing and tail docking are cruel practices and the best companies will be explicit that they avoid them.

Care for People:

13. Support small companies and worker-owned companies with good labor practices. These days there are many small start-ups manufacturing in first-world countries, or doing ethical manufacturing with good wages in other places. Many of these small

companies are at the cutting edge of sustainability and sourcing ethical materials. They're worth paying more for.

14. Good fashion should be accessible to all. Fashion has often been a code used to keep people of color and low-income folks from joining in society. I would hate to think that my clothing choices keep other people from my community or from seeing me as an ally.

15. Avoid cultural appropriation. Again, cultural appropriation isn't a good look and it can keep us from building connections to people from other cultures.

16. Buy local, artisan made, instead of sweatshops disposable crap. Buy from cooperatives.

17. Again, buy durable clothes that wear in, not out. Appreciate "patina" of things like raw denim, shoes, boots, etc.

18. I believe most of a wardrobe should come from thrift shops*. Not only does it reduce environmental damage, it ensures that "stylish dressing" is accessible to everyone.

19. Develop a minimalist style. This is a good way to reduce consumption.

20. Buy low-odor, low-washing clothes. Washing and drying clothes is a whole destructive industry we all participate in in our homes. But in this regard not all clothes are created equal. Well-made natural denim is famous for resisting odor and not needing washing. In fact, many brands of high-quality denim suggest their jeans should only need to be washed a few times per year, or may simply be cold soaked unless they smell bad. Marino wool is famous for resisting odors, while synthetics are famous for quickly smelling foul. All leather boots and shoes that are cared for well resist foul smells and may still have that "new leather" smell after years of wear. Meanwhile synthetic tennis shoes will often smell foul in a year.

A Buying Guide for Boots that Last

With boots being a great example of a "durable asset," buying good boots can be a real economic boon.

When I was working a university assistantship doing carpentry, my mentor there required all his grad students to buy a good pair of boots. "Don't buy the 'work boots' they sell today, those are for the kids who want to look like they're working. Get old fashioned "goodyear welt" (GYW) boots," he said, "those will be more comfortable and will last 10 years." The boots he recommended looked exactly like the boots my dad and grandfather wore. My grandfather wore the same pair of boots for decades, resoled multiple times, and they looked old (and beautiful) even in my earliest memories. These boots had aged to a rich, marbled deep brown, but probably had started a light tan color. He wore them for hunting, for farm work, in the garden, bumming around town, and hiking in the woods.

I wish I had listened to my mentor! Instead, I screwed up my first assignment and bought the "work boots" I saw other young guys my age wearing on construction sites. By the end of the year, the sole was falling off and couldn't be repaired. I went through a few other pairs of "work boots," each time at a more expensive price, and each time they only lasted about a year. Finally, I took my mentor's advice and bought a pair of goodyear welted boots with high quality leather. They only cost a little bit more, but then I wore that same pair of beautiful boots nearly every day for the next 10 years! I plan on wearing them for the rest of my life.

I've recently bought a few more pairs of good quality boots on sale for slightly different purposes, and expect that I will never buy another pair the rest of my life. I can wear them out on the town, as part of my professional attire for work meetings, and even get compliments on them paired with a suit at weddings and formal occasions.

On top of being highly useful as daily wear, multipurpose shoes, heirloom quality footwear that grows in beauty and quality over time just feels great to wear. I get a sort of pleasure and fulfillment from putting on and wearing boots that have a natural beauty to them. After a year or two, the leather begins to develop a depth of color and character you cannot buy at any price, and conditioning and care can make them look brand new—but with that rich added quality. This is part of the reason I haven't bought new boots for 10 years, I can't buy anything as cool as these old boots I've got. And if I feel the need for something new, a little care and conditioning can create an updated look without having to buy cheap new shoes.

And so it literally pays to know what distinguishes heirloom quality "buy for life" boots that have a good chance of lasting a very long time. And it's an excellent investment during times of inflation. At the time of writing this, it was common to be able to find very good quality boots at around $200 (often on sale,) though this was already getting harder due to Covid inflation. More expensive brands can go upwards of $1000, but offer little more than what you can buy in the $200-400 range.

Some key features to look for:

Goodyear Welt (or even better, hand welted) boots. This is the most important feature of boots—or any shoes—that are meant to last a long time. This refers to the way the sole is attached to the shoe, which allows a shoe to be resoled easily multiple times. These days, it is far easier, faster, and cheaper to make shoes by simply gluing (or "cementing") them together. However, this makes them far more likely to fall apart, and impossible to resole. So goodyear welting is reserved for the best quality shoes. It is a sign that the shoes are made with a high quality leather intended to grow better with age, and that it is made by skilled, often better paid workers. As such, many brands' GYW shoes are union made, or made in first world countries, even if the brand's other shoes are made in sweatshops out of glued-together cheap materials.

Who made them? The best boots will of course be made by small artisans, or worker owned or union shops. Country of origin can tell us a lot as well, as boots made in countries with labor laws are less likely to reward sweatshop practices. More just boots are more beautiful boots!

Sole type. This is a bit more subjective. GYW shoes are available in old-fashioned sole options like leather and cork, and with modern materials like rubber, and synthetics. Each has their place. While many poo poo a work boot with a leather sole, leather soles are long-lasting, and conform to the shape of your foot, becoming incredibly comfortable for daily wear on the street or on the farm. It's almost like wearing no shoes. Many reviewers note this is great for people on the lighter side, but as we get heavier, some padding becomes preferable. "Wedge" soles, then, give the most padding on hard surfaces and on the street, but less traction. Vibram and rubber soles give more all-terrain traction, while rugged "lugged" soles give the most traction in the woods and in the snow.

Leather Quality: After the welted construction, leather quality will be the single most important factor in shoes that last. High quality leather doesn't just hold its quality, it improves in beauty and character over time. See the pattern on leather types.

Some Brands to Consider:

Buying high quality footwear can be a research project, so it pays to know where to begin looking. While this info will change, some of the best boot makers have been in business for decades, or nearly a century in some cases.

Redwings Heritage. Redwings are perhaps the most often recommended boot in "buy for life" groups on the internet. However, not all Redwings are created equally. The Heritage lines tend to be all goodyear welt and be made in the USA with high quality materials.

Wolverine. Often considered the main competition to Redwings, Wolverine's 1000 Mile or "Heritage" lines are my favorite choice. Older reviews bemoaned Wolverine going through a period of quality control problems, having lower-quality leather, and only offering leather soled boots. All of these have changed, and 1000 Mile boots are now available with rugged Vibram soles for hikers and woodsmen. Wolverine now sources leathers from the best tanneries in the world, including high quality "veg tanned" leathers.

With those two brands being the most commonly recommended, there are other high quality options worth looking into. Whites and Nicks are often the boot connoisseur's choice, though at a higher price point. For those looking for very high quality rare leathers, Viberg is the fashionable option. Chippewa, Danner, and Georgia make lines with GYW, and some with high quality leathers. Canada West is another Canadian choice with great work boots comparable to Redwings. William Lennon is a high quality boot maker in the UK.

A more in-depth version of this buying guide is available at TransformativeAdventures.org.

Work Boots for Women?

If you're a woman, buying boots for life is apparently that much harder. Few of the companies that make well-built boots for men have lines for women. Those that do, often sell cheaper imported boots for women that emphasize fashion more than practicality. And finally, the boot makers that do have some high quality boots for women will often only have one or two lines, and it's rare for them to also have good functional soles, high quality leather, and also look good.

Finding high quality boots for women, then, may take a research project, but the value and joy that a good quality pair of boots brings is worth it. Look at the reviews of such boots, and you'll see many women used to low-quality over-priced footwear find their "work" boots to be so beautiful and comfortable they wear them all the time!

These things change all the time, but as of the writing of this book, here are a few places for women to start the search. This may change, so always look for "goodyear welt" (GYW) or "hand welted" in the description. If a boot has such a high quality feature, it will always say so in the description. (Mind you, EBay and other online resale shops may still be the best place to buy on a budget, and many men's boots fit women just fine, too.)

Redwings Shoes: Most of Redwings shoes do NOT feature high quality leathers that will last, or goodyear welts. However, their "Heritage" line for women is all made in the US and goodyear welt.

Caterpillar: As of writing, Caterpillar offered at least 2 GYW boots for women with beautiful leather and practical all-purpose soles good for work and daily wear.

Frye: Again, most Frye shoes no longer feature GYW and are made overseas of unknown materials. But their "Made in the USA" line, searchable on their website, all feature heirloom quality leathers, practical soles, and GYW. They also feature some lighter tanned leathers that will likely age to great beauty.

Double H: Offers two GYW boots, both in a Western style. Searchable on their website.

Whites: a staple of the Pacific Northwest, Whites Boots makes truly high quality boots, and has a few work boots available in women's cuts.

Nick's Boots: Another Pacific Northwest company with a devoted following, offering a wider variety of boots marketed to women, in women's sizing.

For a more up-dated, in-depth search, the Goodyear Welt sub on Reddit is probably the best resource available, with guides for women being updated every few years or so.

Buying Quality Leather Goods (Like Boots)

High quality leather, like this environmentally friendly veg tanned leather sheath from Okatsune, improves with age, growing more beautiful with each use.

These days, quality leather is a selling point, so most brands will say what kind of leather they're using, and where they sourced their leather if it's high quality. The best heirloom quality leathers for boots are:

—Vegetable tanned leather (veg tan.) In my opinion, (and my grandfather's, too) this is the highest quality leather for shoes, boots, belts, gloves, tools, jackets, etc. Veg tanned leather uses natural, biodegradable materials like olive bark to "tan" (preserve) the leather. This is important because "chrome tanning," the commercial alternative, is highly toxic and polluting, and is famous for destroying environments. The downside is that it can take months to tan a hide this way, while it takes just hours using chromium. So, it is reserved for the highest quality items. In addition to being the most environmentally friendly, veg tanned leathers are less processed, and so they gain color and texture with the sun, with oils, and use, developing that rich, sought-after leather quality that is nearly impossible to imitate. While these are usually the most expensive leathers, affordable brands like Wolverine do occasional limited runs of veg-tanned boots. Both of my new pairs of boots were made of veg tanned at just $200.

—Chrome tanned leather. Most leather today is chrome tanned. I certainly don't consider it a deal-breaker, especially for entry-level boots, but these are necessarily more environmentally damaging and tend to develop less character over time. But having one pair of chrome tanned boots over 10 years is better than buying a new pair of chrome tanned boots every year for 10 years!

—Combination tanned boots. These are basically chrome tanned boots as far as the environmental impact goes, but then they get an additional treatment imitating veg tanning, which allows the boots to develop a similar patina to veg tanned items. This includes some famous leathers like Horween's Chromexcel.

—Roughout leather. This just means the leather is used with the rough side out. Some people think that this makes the boots require less maintenance, but it may also mean they're harder to maintain for a long time. They are also far less water resistant. While "smooth out" leathers will gain character over time while still looking refined, roughout leathers will inevitably look dirty and rough. Some people, however, like this rugged look. Suede and nubuck are lower-cost leathers that look like roughout, but will be less durable. Many modern work boots are actually suede, which is the least durable leather for boots.

—Waxed flesh, or waxed roughout. These leathers are among the most durable for boots. Being waxed, they are naturally water-resistant, and the wax breaks down and adds character to the boots over time. While they will always have a less formal look than smooth out leathers, they require little care and will grow in beauty over time. My most recent boot purchase was a waxed veg tanned roughout.

Furniture as Regenerative Durable Assets

When it comes to keeping up with the Joneses, there are few things people feel more self-conscious of than their furnishings. In fact, many experts say furniture will cost 10-50% of their housing costs, and the average American may spend $50k-80k over their lives on furniture, depending on their income bracket.

These days, we're of course supposed to buy all new furniture every few years when the fashions dramatically change, and once-fashionable beige becomes the hallmark of "out of style" and all the cool kids are lounging on grey colors, or whatever.

And yet, smart, beautiful, comfortable homes have those hand-made classics that never go out of style and appreciate in value, and will always make any guest feel comfortable.

Many of these pieces hold value or appreciate in time, because they are so renowned. In fact, there are people who make whole businesses finding these pieces at garage sales and thrift shops, and reselling them for big profits.

Brands: The brands will come and go, so it's good to be connected to a buy it for life community for the current info. For example, a decade or two ago, La-Z-boy was famous as a low-quality made for the landfill brand, but now, tops many "buy for life" group recommendations. But small, handmade pieces like Stickley will almost always be sought after heirlooms.

General: In general, there are a few things we can look for, as always. For example, classic designs. Pieces with high quality woodwork will maintain value. Antiques of course, have often lasted 200 years, and seem likely to last another 200 with minimal care.

When it comes to upholstery, many people look for leather and velvet as materials known to patina and achieve a more desirable look and feel as they age. But any good quality, classic natural fabric is likely to age at least moderately well.

Avoid plastics, synthetic materials, and particle board which are all signs that the pieces will go to the landfill sooner rather than later.

If I'm making an investment, I often take the time to research and get up to date about which pieces are most likely to make my house feel like a home over a long period of time.

Durable Assets for a Sustainable Lifestyle

With an uncertain future, there are some durable assets that seem useful investments in resilience.

Good Water Filters. Within many sustainability circles, the Big Berkey filter is considered the best you can buy. Since they're portable and can be attached to large barrels, they're very flexible. Whole house filters might be a better get for some situations. A wise and worthy investment in a reality with PFAS rain, major city water supplies failing in "first world" countries, and toxic plumes spreading everywhere through our groundwater.

Rain barrels, cisterns, and other water catchment features. This may be especially useful for people who have land-based livelihoods or food gardens.

Solar panels. The future of energy may be bleak. Even the most optimistic energy experts base their optimism on the idea that some lone wolf inventor is out there working on the next energy technology in their garage somewhere. Materials for making solar panels are finite, and the US, we're lagging far behind other countries on buying them up. These may be incredibly valuable in the future.

Sustainable, affordable home heating technologies. With limited energy, we will still need to heat houses, and ideally do so without contributing to rapid climate change. Natural gas disruptions from wars with Russia and possibly proxy wars with China may make conventional furnaces less reliable and more expensive in the near future. Features like Russian ovens combined with sustainable forestry like coppice lots may be excellent investments in resilience. Rocket mass stoves may provide excellent sustainable heating for temporary and accessory structures like garages and barns.

Hydronic heating systems (More on page XXX) like boilers are my personal favorite home heating investments for their efficiency, sustainability, and resilient flexibility. Water is by far our most efficient thermal mass for storing heat effectively, typically providing 4 times the storage and heat as masonry. Plus radiator systems make circulating that heat around the house far easier.

It can be installed with wall radiators or floor heating. Most importantly, it can be endlessly adapted to different fuel realities and configurations. It's easy to add direct solar hydro or geothermal heating to an existing system, which can run off sustainable wood, and have an inexpensive natural gas or propane back-up. And it can be paired with smart wood technologies like dual use cook stoves that are more practical than Russian ovens.

Once installed, the radiator systems can be adapted to whatever the heating technology of the day may be. The cost will likely also be a fraction of that of a Russian oven. However, the Russian oven likely wins on durability over time. Then again, there are Victorian radiator systems and boilers that are over 100 years old that are still in use today.

Generative Assets

The next step up is to find durable assets that also can be used to provide a service for ourselves and others.

In other words, generative assets can be used to make stuff.

We could call these "means of production" if you like some revolutionary zeal. Investing in the means of production over things that we and our community members need is a major path to economic freedom and revolution against the corporate system destroying the planet.

Within our communities of creativity and regeneration, there are a multitude of generative asset investment opportunities that I have seen be extremely profitable and productive.

But there are a few keys to these generative assets.

First, they actually have to be, you know, generating something. A generative asset is only as good as it is actually useful, profitable, and something you're passionate about. This takes some thoughtfulness, honesty, and research.

Second, generally speaking (but not always) the larger the amount of capital, the more valuable the investment. So, a fancy printing press is going to be more profitable to operate on a local scale than having some screen printing equipment. This is because the fancy printing press will be less available to competition. But, in some cases, skill and creativity can make up for this, and I've seen people make good incomes out of low-cost investments.

And in the case of some business assets, regular folks like you and me can get business loans to buy higher value productive assets, allowing us to leverage "other people's money," as we'll discuss later.

Some Potential Generative Assets:

Art and music equipment and instruments
Recording studio equipment
High quality printing equipment
Videography equipment
clothing equipment (looms, etc.)
Transportation equipment
Drones
Regenerative Agriculture equipment like roller crimper
Activism tools like a community tool shed
Valuable specialized training
Commercial kitchen or food processing equipment
Nut cracker
Oil press
Cider press
Seed sorter
Thresher
Corn husker
Nut huller
Flash freezer
Canning equipment
Sustainably powered, large walk-in refrigerator
Wine cellar
Commercial land rezoning for mixed-use
Office space
Rental property
Art studio space
Maker space
Business start-up community space
Community green grocer space
Solar panels
Wind turbine
Photo booths

P28–Investing in Energy Independence

"I'd put my money on the sun and solar energy."
Thomas Edison

As it grows, the thistle invests in its own cellular power plants, which harvest energy directly from the sun, and it can even harness the energy of the wind to grow stronger, more durable stalks!

With the energy industry being one of the world's most destructive, and with the future of energy looking uncertain, investing in becoming producers of relatively green, renewable energy seems wise to us.

The Future of Energy?

Certain Buddhist and Taoist traditions have a story of a stingy monk, hoarding money and resources in seeming violation of good ethics. Seeing the monk's stockpiles of resources grow, the people of the village began to think this monk might in fact be too attached to worldly possessions! But one day, a flood came, destroying much of the town and washing out the bridge that brought supplies from the outside. To their surprise, the monk was nowhere to be found, and the monk's home, built safely on a hill, was untouched. The door was left open. Inside were enough resources for the town to completely rebuild, and to survive until the bridge was repaired.

When it comes to the future of our finances and, well, the future of humanity, energy is one of our most important topics.

Not only are fossil fuels the #1 cause of climate change, and a major cause of soil depletion, deforestation, pollution, war, and inequality, they are also a finite resource that may well become limited in the very near future.

According to research by British Petroleum, widely corroborated by other energy players, the world has about 50 years of oil and natural gas left, and about 100 years of coal left at current use levels. But even burning the remainder of that gas and soil would be a climate disaster, and the coal (the dirtiest fossil fuel) would push us beyond current "worst case scenarios" for climate. And of course, as we near the final decades of each fuel, prices will likely rise dramatically.

And energy experts, including those at BP and MP Mining, are saying that due to the limits of "rare earth elements," which are necessary for most renewable energy technologies, it will not be possible to transition all of our current usage to renewables. Research out of Stanford concurs.

And in my opinion, this isn't just oil company propaganda. It is highly likely that there are not enough components for PV, batteries, and wind electric to get to even a fraction of today's energy consumption. MP research projects that even by 2035, 1/3rd of projected demand for these materials will not be met, rising toward 2050, when renewable energy advocates would like us to reach a green power economy. Even the current path will not be met without some dramatic change to the availability of rare earths, let alone more ambitious goals of replacing oil and gas by 2050.

In other words, it is highly likely that energy will become more rare, more expensive, and more dangerous (nukes) in the future.

And so far, the US is dramatically lagging behind other countries, which means our national energy future may be very bleak.

Seeing what our future could bring, I sometimes wonder if that stingy monk has returned to this realm. I wonder if they're out there somewhere, quietly investing in solar panels and wind turbines.

Micro-Energy Investments

"Micro-energy" refers to home-scale energy production, that generates energy right near where it's used. Because it doesn't have to be transported (which comes with a significant loss) it is the most efficient form of green energy. This includes solar panels and wind turbines.

Home-Scale Biogas Digesters

One of the least known, and most interesting energy production systems is biogas, which captures the methane released from compost systems so that it can be used as fuel. Home biogas digesters can be built into septic systems and compost piles, and can be built for as little as $50 in parts. These systems are DIYable for experienced, handy folks, making them an excellent investment of non-financial capital! One study found that simple home compost digesters could provide all the fuel for cooking for farming families, proving their economic value. (Financial and economic feasibility of bio-digesters for rural residential demand-side management and sustainable development.)

Transformative Adventures community member Christopher Nesbit built his own, and wrote a thorough series of articles on the topic at PermacultuerNews.org.

1. Meyer, et al, "Financial and economic feasibility of bio-digesters for rural residential demand-side management and sustainable development," Energy Reports, Volume 7, 2021.
2. Nestbit, Christopher, "Biogas and Carbon Farming," Permaculture News, 2020. https://www.permaculturenews.org/2020/09/24/biogas-and-carbon-farming-part-1/

Energy from Forests (Wood Heating)

One of the most common forms of home energy production is wood-fired heating.

Because this is so common in "homesteading" and "back-to-the-land" circles, I feel the need to add a word of warning.

While wood is renewable, it is not necessarily sustainable. Wood heating cuts down forests, requires land that could otherwise be used for food and biodiversity, often comes with considerable particulate pollution that harms air quality, and in my opinion, usually contributes to climate change. In fact, we've already seen published studies showing increases in particulate pollution and reduced air quality in urban areas with increased wood fires promoted in part by us environmentalists! And while some dispute the impacts of carbon emissions from wood based on theories of potential carbon cycles, the fact remains pretty simple that if you are taking wood from the forest and burning it in inefficient burners you are adding to the current % of carbon in the atmosphere, period. Despite some back-to-the-lander fantasies of a utopia built around the fireplace, if everyone switched to wood heating using old fashioned fireplaces and stoves, it would be an environmental catastrophe.

And so we must think about 2 things, the fuel efficiency of our burners (how much pollution they release) and the heating efficiency (how much of the energy gets turned into actually useful heat.)

1. *Modern efficient fireplace inserts and wood stoves.* While the old fashioned stoves and open fireplaces many of us use are romantic, they can have efficiencies as low as 10-40% and be highly polluting to your home. Modern wood burners can have a combustion efficiency of over 90%, often into the high 90s. If you're going to heat with wood, an updated burner is a great investment for the planet, your health, and your wallet.

2. *Thermal mass heaters* like masonry heaters, soap stone stoves, Finnish stoves, and Russian ovens store heat in mass like brick and stone, then radiate it out afterwords, allowing us to turn upwards of 70-90% of the energy into useful heat! And these are beautiful home features which are considered to increase the value of most homes. While commercial models often cost $30k or more, I have seen wonderful DIY examples built for as little as $1000 in materials, though most professionals consider $5-6000 to be more realistic for most jobs. The safest and most efficient systems will use "cores" that are professionally made, and which generally cost upwards of $1,000 before shipping. These systems can typically heat a home with just one burn per day. Rocket Mass Heaters are another DIY possibility, though much more experimental and not yet accepted by EPA or residential building code. Though efficient and fun DIY projects, they will generally have a lower total efficiency than masonry heaters. And since they often require many burns, most professionals familiar with them recommend them more for heating recreational spaces, sheds, and greenhouses, rather than for reliable home heating.

3. *Hydronic or hydrothermal stoves, and back boilers.* Just as thermal mass heaters store heat in stone, hydrothermal systems store heat in the most powerful thermal mass we have: water. Water is 4 times as efficient at storing and supplying energy as most other forms of thermal mass, and it has the quality of being easy to circulate around the home, through pipes and into radiators. Radiator heating, while

sometimes considered "old fashioned" by many, is actually the most luxurious and efficient heating system we have! "Back boilers" can be installed on virtually any modern efficient wood burner, and some hydrothermal stoves are now available on the market, some which even feature cooking capacity. For most people, these are my favorite wood heating devices. Most permaculturists I know of are well versed in rocket stoves, but unfamiliar with these. Yet they will beat the best masonry heaters on both combustion and heating efficiency by nearly 10%, turning over 90% of the energy into useful, long—lasting heat. Best of all, these systems can be doubled up with biogas, geothermal, and solar systems, allowing us to use multiple renewable energy sources for the same radiant heating system, AND have electric or gas as a backup. Meanwhile, the cost of a DIY system can be as low as $2000, (or less for some very low-tech versions) compared to the tens of thousands for most masonry heaters. Outfitting an existing stove with a basic system can be done for just hundreds of dollars. As a DIY job, it is both easier and safer than Rocket Mass Stoves and Masonry Heaters. It's also more accepted by code and insurance.

Home Geothermal

Geothermal energy uses the energy of the earth itself! The most common form of geothermal energy is designed to use buried pipes to heat air or water, which can then be exchanged to provide heat or cooling for a building. Heat pumps or exchangers can concentrate this heat to provide low cost heating. Geothermal can then reduce heating bills by about 50% over the long term. But since commercial systems typically cost tens of thousands of dollars these high-tech systems only tend to ROI for very large homes or commercial sized buildings or compounds, or whole neighborhoods. However, it must be said that I have seen DIY systems that function as well as professional ones! The design and installation are not difficult, the barrier is the equipment to dig large deep pits to bury the pipes. Another downside is that the underground equipment is generally rated for a 25 year life expectancy, and will be costly to replace or repair.

Low-Tech Geothermal Options

On the low-tech side, this earth energy, "annualized solar inertia" can be harnessed to reduce heating and cooling costs or provide refrigeration and food storage.

Earth sheltered, and other thermal intertia houses, like the famous WOFATI design, are partially buried, taking advantage of the earth's constant heat, they will remain at about 55F degrees year round. While that's not a comfortable living temperature, it may be much easier to heat a home up to a living temperature from 55 than from -5. A downside is these homes may be uncomfortable for some, and may have issues with damp and mold.

Cellars, caches, cool cupboards, and under-ground storage all take advantage of geothermal energy to replace cooling. Because of the cost and climate footprint of refrigeration, these systems may be some of the best DIYable investments in home energy. Building a "cool cupboard," which uses solar energy to pull up the earth's "coolith" into a cupboard is an easy DIY project doable in an afternoon for a few dollars of materials.

Poor man's air conditioning can be installed by using the cool cupboard concept to cool off a small living space, like a bedroom. I've used this technique myself to great success at Lillie House, where we watched it quickly lower temps for our classes by 10-15 degrees.

Because these types of passive geothermal investments are built right into the homes, they can last for a very long time, essentially for the life of the house! So if I were a stingy monk thinking about the long-term future, I'd be looking into these as investments.

Home Solar Thermal

And stingy monks everywhere should also be thinking of home solar thermal for the same reason. "Passive solar" heating and cooling systems can be built into homes, and last virtually forever. While solar electric panels and wind turbines may only last a few decades, passive solar systems may continue on for hundreds of years. And while these high tech energy gizmos come with a cost of mining, and energy themselves, many passive solar installations will have no additional cost, they're simply a matter of laying out the parts we havc (rooms, walls, floors, windows) so that they maximize the energy intake.

1. Passive solar installations. Most basic passive solar installations are simply a matter of orienting the home to gain solar energy, and then not lose it! The key to these systems is storing the heat in "thermal mass," such as stone or concrete walls or floors.
2. Passive solar "generators" and "furnaces." These are add-ons that can be used to heat a conventional home. Generators like "trombe walls" are essentially south-facing attached greenhouses that can transfer heat into the home. Passive solar "furnaces" or "space heaters" are black solar panels that simply heat air then send it into the living space. I've seen these built for a few dollars of materials and recycled beer cans! While they're not going to provide all the heat for a home, they can provide some supplemental heat when it's needed.
3. Solar hydro thermal systems heat water, which can then be used as hot water or to heat radiant floors and radiators. Again, water is the best thermal mass, making these systems incredibly efficient. And water is generally very inexpensive! This is one of the most practical systems, as solar thermal panels can be installed cheaply, are DIYable, and there's research showing they can provide all the heat for a home in many climates. Best of all, they can be combined with wood heating, and have a conventional back-up. Many people use a conventional water heater system to provide the back-up for as little as a few hundred dollars. Even without the solar, these conventional systems will still be the most efficient conventional home heating systems available today. The solar guarantees very low heating costs in perpetuity, with very low maintenance. Since the average cold climate home will pay around $1500/year for gas heating ($3000+ for electric) a solar hydro system may pay for itself in the first year, and earn $15-$30k over 20 years. That's one of the best investments in this book.

Home Solar-Electric, Photovoltaic (PV) Solar Panels

The most practical and highest ROI micro-energy investment for most people will be home solar. In fact, depending on your local energy costs and sun availability, the 20 year return on a $20,000 investment in solar panels will be an average of $20,000. That's assuming an energy status quo. But in areas where energy is expensive and sun is plentiful, like in Hawaii or in Spain, that return could be over $60,000, which is not bad even compared to the S&P 500, which would return about $100,000. If energy becomes increasingly expensive, then the return could be even better.

Home Wind

Wind turbines become more efficient the larger they get, so small wind turbines generally do not pay for themselves. But the large ones sure do. At the large scale, they have a higher return than almost all solar. Because of the high costs, wind is often better as a community-scale investment.

Macro-Energy and Community Scale Energy

As we look to build energy security, some of us stingy monks may want to try to invest in community scale energy systems, and indeed I know some stingy monks who have even made a right livelihood off of this work!

On the community scale, neighborhood solar and wind farms may just be the next big thing. Where people have built them, they are incredibly successful as investments. Neighborhood geothermal is another option that might not be realistic on the single-family scale. There are some experiments with capturing energy from our public water systems by installing turbines in our water mains, but most responsible research on these shows these systems cost more energy than they produce, since they appear to require increased energy to pump the water! These systems may be realistic in areas with large natural water pressure reserves, but in other situations, I'd advise stingy monks to be cautious and look at the real numbers involved!

Green Energy "Flips"

For those who'd like to make a living as professional stingy monks, I actually know a few people pioneering the model. These folks are leading co-investing opportunities in wind and solar, by identifying ideal properties with a high ROI, buying them, organizing for the appropriate zoning, and then selling to groups of investors. Some simply arrange the sale, and do not buy the properties up front. These "green energy flips" can provide significant surplus cash to help stingy monks cash flow, while also allowing them to invest profitably in a better energy future. There are plenty of opportunities to invest in becoming experts and in creating the tools and techniques of an energy transition. Already, there are people making phenomenal livelihoods off of helping people create masonry heaters, set up hydrothermal systems, and install solar energy, both passive and electric.

Looking at the ROI of solar-hydrothermal systems above, if one could find a way to invest $20,000 in installing efficient neighborhood systems, it could return $300,000+ in 20 years, more than 3 times what we'd get from investing in the S&P 500!

An efficient Rumford fireplace at Lillie House is a beautiful generative asset.

Procreative Assets

The next step up in our asset classes gets us to a very special category that is powerful for wealth creation. These are necessarily durable, generative assets that can be used to provide a good or service. But, these special natural assets have an important quality in that they also procreate, or self-replicate.

For example, an apple tree can provide us with apples, so that we do not have to buy apples, and can potentially sell apples to other people.

But, an apple tree can also provide us with an infinite supply of apple trees, that will grow in their productivity each year.

Many forms of assets are procreative, though most (but not all) are natural assets, things like trees, plants, vermicomposting worms, and livestock.

At their best, these can (at least for a while) capture the power of compounding interest, and can be extremely powerful wealth-building assets. Many people have retired off the value of such procreative assets, and many fortunes have even been made!

But these, too, require some special consideration. Not all plants or animals are procreative assets. You may have chickens, or apple trees, but the chickens and apple trees might not be procreative assets! In fact, in most cases they probably aren't! This is a major mistake that many farmers and permaculturists make, assuming that they will be (whether or not they're thinking of the term specifically.)

So, we need to fulfill some specific traits to be procreative assets, or at least good ones.

First procreative assets, need to actually, um, procreate. I sometimes call these my "f-ing assets," because that's exactly what they have to do, they reproduce. If you have 10,000 chickens or 1,000 apple trees, you don't have a single procreative asset unless they are procreating and you are also selling those assets or otherwise obtaining a yield from them. An apple tree that isn't used to create and sell more apple trees is not a procreative asset, it is just a generative one. This leads us to a second trait.

Secondly, they must actually be valuable as natural capital. Meaning, the genetic material must actually be valuable. The chickens will need to be a valuable variety worth saving and buying for people, and at a premium, since they could get the chickens from a chicken mill more easily than from you. Same for the apples. Seedling apple trees, for example, rarely make very good procreative assets. Most seedling stock (except under certain circumstances) will not be very valuable. Heirloom varieties and rare plants then make the best procreative assets. I've seen people make great returns off of trading in unusual, valuable livestock like silk worms, buffalo, camelids for vicuna wool, yaks, alpacas, etc. Again, while standard modern breeds of common livestock don't have much value as procreative assets, these rare livestock breeds do.

Thirdly, recognize that procreative assets generally follow a "law of diminishing returns." I will tell you about some single plants that have earned about $1,000, just growing in a single square foot of space in a single year. That is probably the best ROI in this book. However, my time is limited, so there's a limit to how much I can scale that. It might easily scale to say $10-40k, but at that point taking care of all the plants and getting them to a market is a LOT of work, probably a full-time job. If I want to go beyond that, I've got to hire labor, and then they get a cut, and my margin is down to a few dollars per plant at best. So procreative assets are powerful, but their power diminishes as they procreate!

P29–Patterns for Investing in Procreative Assets

Plant Collections:

After selling my share in Lillie House, I moved a few times in quick succession, and really discovered the lasting value of a high-quality plant collection.

When I initially moved out, I took just a small handful of plants, one or two of each of the most important parts of my collection, and planted them into a very small, shady urban lot where I was living.

By the time I moved next year, those plants had multiplied to thousands of dollars of plants, which helped me instantly scale-up a very high value garden. Not only was I able to save thousands of dollars on plants, I made a few hundred dollars selling plants, too, probably enough to pay for the new garden, before the first growing season. It's hard to imagine many investments that can grow 5-10 times in value in just one year. Having developed that high value plant collection, it meant I had free gardens from then out.

Landscape Transformation Plant Collection

Over the last 10 years, my main income stream has been my "Landscape Transformation Program," which we'll discuss in more detail as an example soon.

The key physical asset for a profitable Landscape Transformation Program is a high value plant collection. When we develop the right kind of plant collection, a collection of locally-adapted, highly useful and valuable plants that thrive in our conditions, then we develop assets that are valuable to everyone else in our region and community. In my experience, given the high procreative value of these plants, this is one of the most profitable investments we can make.

The plant collection that powered my Landscape Transformation Program at Lillie House easily produced over $10,000 of food each year while also producing over $10,000 of plants sustainably on less than 1 acre, even when sold at a bulk discount rate through the program. With time and tweaking, a well-developed market, and perhaps more work hours, the system probably could have easily and sustainably produced over $40,000 of plants per season with no specialized equipment or expensive greenhouse.

Guild Matrix Plants or Allstar Plants

For most of us who want to help people transform their landscapes, there is probably no type of plant more valuable than what we in the Transformative Adventures community call "guild matrix plants."

As I mentioned, in the last few years I have created almost instant, highly productive, fairly mature ecological gardens in the first year with no tiller, very little digging, almost no imported fertility, with only one or two flats of seedlings, and minimal time.

In short, Allstar plants are procreative assets for the landscape! These plants have the special qualities of procreating very well on their own, spreading rapidly without much help, and—most importantly—being highly useful and valuable in large quantities.

For example, imagine walking into a forest that is filled almost entirely with edible plants. Well, that could be good or bad! If it's a plant you can only use or sell in very small amounts, it might not be very helpful! In fact, most plants in most forests are actually edible, but people aren't living or getting rich off their forests. So, here's where the magic is, this forest gives exactly the amount of produce you can reasonably harvest or sell, staggered all season long. And these aren't just "you can eat that" weeds, they are highly valuable produce, desirable and useful to you in the quantities needed for meals. And because the plants are vigorous, spreading and symbiotic with each other, 90% of the maintenance that is required is just harvesting to thin the plants and keep things in balance.

These are Allstar plants: spreading, easy, vigorous, highly productive, and highly valuable. And what makes then even better is when they combine well into a self-maintaining little community we'll call a "guild matrix." This is the "holy grail" of home gardening.

If you observe natural plant communities, you will see that most are characterized by a "community" or "guild" of players that seem to work well together, fit together in filling in niches, share similar needs, cooperate well and avoid competition. There is usually a basic matrix of a few plants that make up much of the ecosystem, with specimen plants appearing here and there like chocolate chips in a cookie. This is what we are going for. Only with Allstar plants.

It would be hard to imagine having too many of such useful plants. Luckily, they self produce rapidly, too! With careful harvest, it is easy to maintain populations of both by just letting them self sow and divide. Excellent guild matrix candidates.

Sorrels, for example, are delicious, productive all season long and provide a green for daily soups or salads and act as fortress plants suppressing weeds in the garden and creating a stable matrix. Alliums can easily grow vertically among sorrels, while sorrels spread and cover the ground to prevent weeds.

A wild and mild mannered mint might ramble around and fill in spaces too, and these have been known to both prevent weeds and encourage net biodiversity in the right conditions. Mints have been shown to be particularly good at eradicating field bind weed. Yet the effects of allelopathy are minimal when the garden is abundant and the soil is healthy. But if a weed is getting out of control, these vigorous allelopaths will crank up their chemical production and keep the system in balance. I know many people who simply can't grow enough basil, but are afraid of growing mild mannered basil mint in the garden!

Developing a collection of these high-powered plants that play well together in our bioregion makes us incredibly valuable plant wizards, able to transform properties with the wave of a wand, into highly valuable landscapes. It's a magic trick that can easily provide income wherever we are. It's also a model for understanding other valuable procreative assets.

Guild matrix plants will depend a lot on the climate and soil, so it's difficult to give a one-size-fits-all list. For more in-depth information on guild matrix plants, see Beauty in Abundance, by Michael Hoag.

Some Qualities of Collectable Plants

—They have to be unusually valuable for some reason. Either unusually useful, or unusually beautiful or interesting.
—They have to be somehow rare, or not easily available.
—Often this means they are not available from seed, or if they are, seeds are difficult to germinate.
—Otherwise they are likely procreated from vegetative cutting, which puts a limit on how fast they can be provided.
—There are some limits to everyone just easily propagating them. This can be intellectual property laws, or it can be that the actual knowledge for procreating them is rare.

Some Types of Procreative Assets:

Native plants
Edible perennial plants
Heirloom vegetables
Rare herbs
Valuable house plants
Bonsai species
Important rare ornamental plants
High value medicinal species
Heritage breeds of livestock and animal companions
New and unusual livestock
Vermicomposting worms
Microbial assets like fungi collections and beneficial microorganisms
High biodiversity native soil organisms
Building and craft materials plants including bamboo and willow
Coppice lots

Transformative Assets

Which leads us finally to our most high-powered assets, transformative assets.

To start with, these are assets which will be durable and generative.

And they also have two special features: they appreciate at a decent rate, replacing the interest we'd be expecting from the stock market, AND they can generate cash flow for us (giving us liquidity and sustaining us on a yearly basis.) This second quality would be similar to stocks that paid significant dividends. This allows our investments to potentially compound, by providing cash we can reinvest. That makes them especially good investments to structure our lives around, though not entirely necessary, of course.

This is important for those of us who are looking to achieve our FREE benchmarks without investments in the stock market because it is otherwise difficult to find relatively liquid investments that give us access to our cash on an annual basis without depleting our capital. For example, we might have $400k of wealth invested in our homes, but we'll need some thoughtful strategies if we want to live off of that without selling our houses!

So having assets that will help us cash flow is particularly important.

In most cases, these will not be "work free" or entirely "passive" income, (though there are some cases for that) but they should ideally be low-work income or "semi-passive" income, if we're prioritizing being relatively FREE.

Example, the Transformative Landscape.

Such gardens are often called "home gardens" by academics, or "forest gardens," or even "food forests" by enthusiasts. Of course, these things mean something entirely different to different people these days!

So, to avoid controversy and provide some clarity, within the Transformative Adventures community, we call the types of landscapes we try to create "Transformative Landscapes," because they truly transform ecosystem health, transform our lives, and have the potential to transform the world.

While "native plant gardens" just look to increase native plants, and "food gardens" look to cut us off from the destructive food system, these Transformative Landscapes formally aim to steward species, fight climate change, sequester carbon, care for water, restore forest, regenerate soil, and help us fight the corporate food system. For us, these are the ultimate in sustainable, life-enhancing landscapes.

As we've already discussed, high-value plant collections like guild matrix plants can be an excellent "procreative asset," growing in value exponentially at first.

These can also provide us with that highly important cash flow for a hammock income, while potentially continuing to appreciate in value over time.

But of course, we can "stack" these together into an even more valuable procreative asset, a whole home-garden or food forest garden system.

And we can "stack" together our products to create one very high value product. Instead of just providing produce, or even plants, the professional's Transformative Landscape provides food, plants, seeds, and materials. And they provide us the opportunity to stack together these with intellectual assets: consultation, community, and a class to walk people through the process of transforming their landscapes.

This is the basis for the Landscape Transformation Program, which has been our co-author Mike's livelihood for the last 10 years or so.

Now, we have a system that largely takes care of its own maintenance. The garden shown above generally required less than 2 hours of work per week on average to maintain, and yet easily provided well over $10k in hammock income cash flow, just on plants. Meanwhile, it provided well over $7000/year in food for the household at simple market value. And, of course, the whole business was stacked with a real estate investment that was carefully chosen to also provide real long-term value. As it was, my share of the real estate investment grew to over $70k in 10 years, while the plant collection investment continued to provide more than $10k/year in cash flow, even after moving on to a new home. The original plant collection, if heavily harvested, would easily be worth tens of thousands of dollars as well, while the initial investment was around $1000. And it returned a significant profit even in year 1, so it cost almost nothing up front.

This is a great example of a Transformative Asset, which built wealth and provided my hammock income while it literally transformed social problems and ecosystems, sequestered carbon, dramatically increased biodiversity, stewarded water resources, built community wealth and knowledge, built deep community networks and friendships, and had broad impacts on the community and world beyond.

For Mike, it was also the basis for transforming his whole life.

On a daily basis, he'd get to step out into his own home paradise, a place he considered more beautiful than any he could visit on vacation. And, unlike a vacation destination, it had special connection and meaning for him. He knew each plant. He watched the stories of each garden visitor. Guests would visit daily to buy plants or produce, and spend time chatting in the beautiful garden. Sometimes they'd stay for tea or lunch. Weekends were filled with life-changing programs that built a sense of vibrant community. If help was needed with a task, there were plenty of eager volunteers. This transformative landscape grew much more than plants and produce, it grew a truly beautiful way of life.

But of course that's not the only example of a transformative investment. We'll do dozens in this book. Examples include stacks with live-in rental properties, duplexes, art studios/equipment and business spaces. You'll notice that a lot of these do involve real estate PLUS some added elements. But I have seen examples that don't involve real estate, such as rare, high value antique equipment.

An interesting set of examples come from some clothing companies using antique looms to produce sought-after high-value clothing. Looms created by Toyota before they even made cars are now considered especially valuable, will likely continue to appreciate a great deal, and can be used to cash flow very well!

I've seen similar equipment sell in the US at high prices. Some well-loved antique farm equipment is also sought-after and worth significantly more now than just decades ago. Antique tractors that my step dad bought and fixed for just hundreds of dollars are now selling for tens of thousands, just a few decades later. This is yet another investment that beats the S&P! We'll talk about many other examples in the following chapters.

Remember the chart on page XXX? Now, we can see the sort of investments that real people are using to transform their financial situations, instead of just investing in index funds.

P30–Patterns for Transformative Investments

Transformative Investments are the most high-powered investments we can make when it comes to achieving the "FREE" lifestyle.

First, they are Regenerative, meaning they make us better off economically, and they make the world better off, too.

Second, they are necessarily durable, so they last a long time rather than wearing out quickly.

Third, they appreciate in value well, helping us grow wealthier passively over time.

Fourth, they provide us with cash flow, which acts like dividends and helps us to pay our costs of living in the present without having to sell off and liquidate the asset.

And finally fifth, at their very best, they allow us to invest with other people's money, and to do so at a favorable rate. This isn't 100% necessary for all our transformative investments, but it's honestly one of the biggest factors that allow people to grow real wealth.

This means that if you really want to be serious about growing FREE, low-interest home, farm, and business loans used to buy transformative investments is one of the most powerful patterns in this book. It's still very possible to see returns like on the previous page without debt, but it's much easier if you're investing with other people's money.

Important Note:

All the following examples should be taken as exactly that: examples. There are virtually infinite combinations and possibilities, so consider the following "patterns" to be an effort to inspire you to find the best "investments" for your individual life goals and interests.

Pattern: Real Estate as a Transformative Investment

One of the simplest examples we can use for a Transformative Asset is what we could call Regenerative Real Estate.

For most North Americans, as elsewhere in the world, home-ownership has been the single biggest opportunity for wealth-building we've had. Most of the last few generations were able to retire—not because of their wise savings or investments in the stock market—but because of the natural appreciation of their housing values and communities over time.

We call that "equity." Equity is the money stored in the value of your home. For example, if you have paid off a home worth $200k, then you have $200k in equity. If you bought a house for $200k, and now it's worth $300k, you have $300k in equity.

And because the real estate market is generally so terrible for the planet and people, it's also one of the highest leverage opportunities we have for investing in creating better communities and a better world. As we'll see in future chapters, rental property can be stacked with a whole variety of transformative investments, like transformative landscapes, plant capital, and other generative assets.

In fact, in an era where most of the rental housing and business real estate is owned by large out-of-town entities and corporations, buying back our communities is some of the most important and regenerative work we can do. WE need to own our communities.

Not only is this a deeply ethical way to invest our money, it is radical and revolutionary. This is how we peacefully "seize the means of production" of some of the most important needs in our communities.

And because in many of our internet circles, "landlords" get a bad name, it is necessary to discuss the ethics of this sort of investment directly.

Is Real Estate an Ethical Investment?

Yes, there are bad landlords. But the solution to this is not to stigmatize landlording generally. The solution is for folks like us, you know, people who actually care about ethics and argue over them, to get involved in real estate and providing housing.

In fact, stigmatizing landlords in general is counter-revolutionary and breaks down class solidarity! There are many small landlords who actively do the work of providing housing to people in their communities. They own the means of their production, the houses, and work them the same way farmers work their land or artists use their tools to create art. Attacking them is attacking members of the working class.

Take for instance, my friend Evelyn in Kalamazoo. As a black woman from Kalamazoo's Northside neighborhood, she was born with no inheritance or money. But she was able to start buying a few rental properties, and when she had equity, she bought a few more. Often these were purchased as distressed properties on the cheap. Evelyn works full-time managing her properties, does most of the repair work and maintenance herself, does all the organizing, showing, scheduling, and contracting herself. She has no employees, and when she hires help, she contracts with other local, small business owners, mostly sole proprietorships. She is doing well for herself, and is on her way to a FREE lifestyle, but she certainly does not have an exorbitant income! It's more what I would consider an appropriate living wage. Evelyn is a worker, and her business is worker-owned.

Within parts of the FIRE community, there are heavy attacks on landlords that are almost always used to defend heavy investing in the stock market. The argument as it goes is that if real estate is necessarily unethical, then that justifies the stock market (which we all know is unethical.) But even if real estate was necessarily unethical, that still wouldn't justify the stock market simply because landlords are also unethical! It's an illogical argument.

I take the position that if nothing unethical is being done, then nothing unethical is being done. This sounds obvious, but there are actually quite a lot of people who argue that landlords are inherently unethical. But there's nothing inherently unethical about being a landlord. There's nothing at all wrong with what Evelyn has chosen to do to make her living. In fact, it is revolutionary!

Usually, when people say rental property is unethical, it's just called "capitalism." But as we discussed early in this book, capitalism is considered unethical because it is exploiting labor. As we see from Evelyn's example, it is quite possible to have rental property without exploitation. Evelyn couldn't be considered a capitalist.

More accurately, landlords are critiqued with the term "**rent seeking**," or language associated with it.

But "rent seeking," which is a term for an unethical economic activity, does not mean "charging rent." Rent seeking means getting income without contributing anything. Having a house and renting out a room is never an example of "rent seeking." Having an extra house and renting it out is never an example of "rent seeking," (providing nothing) because one is providing a room!

But either way when people say "landlords don't work or contribute anything, they just sit around and collect money" they are making the argument landlords are rent-seeking.

"Rent seeking" is a technical term used by economists, including anti-capitalist theorists like Marx. "Rent seeking" means "making money without contributing anything." It means you're looking to increase your share of the pie, without increasing the size of the pie, which is considered to be stealing pie from everyone else. BTW, both anti-capitalist theorists and capitalist ones like Adam Smith consider "rent seeking" an unethical behavior. Like exploitation, rent-seeking doesn't get too many fans!

The classic example of "rent seeking" is someone who has a river running through their property, so they erect a chain across the river so no boats can go down it, unless they pay a fee. The chain and fee collector contribute no value to anybody, they are just charging for something that used to be free. It's the "bridge troll" archetype. In my opinion, this is also unskillful life design, since it's pretty obvious everyone is going to hate that bridge troll.

Some theorists argue that our modern western economies are actually dominated by bridge troll behaviors as the main economic activity of the wealthy. For example, planned obsolescence and user fees are examples of rent-seeking. Making light bulbs that last for 2500 hours so that they only last for 1000 hours is making money without contributing anything positive, yet as we have seen, we've based our whole economy on that sort of thing. Required software updates that eventually force you to buy new hardware are rent-seeking. Ever new ways of becoming middle men is rent-seeking. Bribing the government to pass laws requiring certain products or hindering competition is rent-seeking. Insurance is probably largely rent-seeking. Yes, white people passing laws that confiscated land from native Americans and African Americans and gave it to "homesteaders" were rent-seeking.

And it's true, much of the modern real estate market is entirely rent-seeking. Local land owners get involved in politics and collude to make decisions that drive up real estate prices in the neighborhoods where they own property. In this case, it is the collective work of the community, and of tax owners and so on that have made the prices go up, not anything positive contributed by these land owners. This is a huge business in our communities today, and the "wages" paid back to blue collar white suburban workers are little more than a bribe for political allegiance. My community, Fort Wayne, is extremely open that they use policy to promote the increase in real estate values, i.e., raising prices without contributing anything. Gentrification is the work of bridge trolls.

When we look at rising real estate prices and rents, we should be looking at these bridge trolls, not working-class Evelyn.

When smart revolutionaries write of "rent–seeking" this is the sort of activity they are talking about, where land is made artificially scarce or values are raised by manipulating policy.

They are not talking about Evelyn renting out a room.

There is no case in which "housing" as a service would be free without people providing it. Housing requires construction and maintenance at least, and practically speaking it requires work to manage the property, connect renters with housing and so on. Providing that service is necessarily " growing the size of the pie," creating housing that would not be available otherwise.

So what Evelyn is doing is neither capitalism nor an example of exploitation, and is also not rent-seeking. There's still a potential argument that landlords engage in "price gouging," taking more than a fair price for their product. Hypothetically, this is a problem that a free market should correct. So long as there are decent landlords out there offering rents at a fair price, they should outcompete the price-gougers, and the market should set a fair price! Indeed, we have plenty of data as to what landlords make as an hourly rate for their work, and it is rarely high! More often, it is not a huge hourly rate. Housing rental companies are nowhere near as profitable as banks, or energy companies, for example. There's little evidence that price gouging is happening either.

So, as I said, I'm of the opinion that if nothing unethical is happening, then nothing unethical is happening.

Even large apartment companies do not engage in "rent seeking." But they DO engage in "exploitation." They hire underpaid exploited labor to provide the service of housing, and essentially steal the labor value of their employees. They do not "exploit" their tenants," that is an incorrect use of the word. Again, they may "over-charge," but that doesn't imply that housing should be provided for no cost, since it requires a cost to provide the housing. Usually, when landlords overcharge it is in POC neighborhoods, for example. But most of this premium does not go to the landlords, it goes to rent-seekers in the insurance industry, who charge high premiums in these neighborhoods, and it goes to rent-seeking investors using boom-bust cycles to gentrify neighborhoods. Those are the people we should be critiquing and fighting against.

Arguments that providing rental housing "contribute nothing" or are "rent-seeking" or are "parasitic" are very difficult to defend. The idea that a black woman like Evelyn doing lots of work and accepting risk and giving up freedom to rent out a room or a house is "doing no work" seems just preposterous. And it's literally impossible to imagine any way to provide housing services to people without "landlords."

And of course, the real solution to the real problem of rent-seeking increasing housing costs is for folks like you and me to get involved in owning our own communities! WE need to own our communities, not the rent-seeking, manipulative land speculators who run our zoning boards. Believe me, in every community, these are currently the people buying up real estate, and making policy to make money without contributing anything of value. The solution to bad landlords and a bad housing industry is for us to seize the means of production and provide a better one, not for us to stigmatize hard-working working class folks just making a living by providing an important, and ethical service.

So not only is this a good investment, it's good for society.

Patterns for Investing in a Home

Since most Americans—indeed, most people in the Western world—build most of their lifetime wealth through home ownership, anyone looking to build a FREE lifestyle will need to at least consider building equity through home ownership.

In fact, I'll go so far as to say that you absolutely don't NEED to own a home of some kind, but if you don't I would strongly urge you to have some other plan for investing in transformative assets to make up for the lost equity opportunity. Real estate forces us to save around 30% of our income for each year we're paying a mortgage, AND it appreciates reliably at a rate that's better than the stock market. If you're not paying on a mortgage, to keep up with that, you'll need to plan to save over 30% of your income each month. That maybe especially difficult if you're paying 30% of your income on rent. So this will be something you'll need to mindfully figure out.

For example, if you own business real estate, that could take the place of owning a home. There are of course other ways to make up for it, the point is that you'll need to know which you are doing.

Of course, each of these options could deserve its own book, so we hope to just give you an overview to think about as you design your financial life. Do your own research, and look into your options thoroughly.

The Single Family Home

This is your opportunity to join Ward, June, and the Beaver, the Bradys, and a plethora of other sitcom families in living the "American dream." It has both its charms and its drawbacks. Those looking to age in place or manage edible landscapes will need to consider whether they can so without the help of live-in community, (which is considered in more depth in our "patterns for the later years." For this chapter, we'll just leave it at stating the fact that it's an incredible opportunity to easily get conventional financing and grow equity.

Duplexes, Triplexes, and Quadruplexes, Oh My!

Because Mike is an extrovert who loves living in a house full of people-energy, and he loves a good deal, this is one of his favorite investments. Buying Xplexes means you'll get both. You'll have the opportunity to build community in your home, potentially even find ways to help your renters invest in their own transformative assets, and get paid a small income to build equity for free.

Breaking down that last bit, at their Permaculture project Lillie House, Mike and Kim were able to get a very low-interest loan with a small down payment, on a triplex. They were able to keep rent low, live with like-minded friends, and the rent paid all the housing costs and at least a small wage for the landlord work Mike did. All while building over $100,000 in market-rate equity in less than a decade.

These are great opportunities to watch out for.

Condominimum Equity

Oh, well that's a pretty bad joke about the old wisdom that condominiums condo-minimize your equity potential. This may, or may not be true these days, and whether it is or isn't is its own set of tradeoffs.

Condominiums are essentially apartments you can own, rather than rent. The biggest upside is that you'll be building equity, and often "condos" are more affordable than houses, especially in expensive markets.

The biggest downside in terms of this chapter, is that compared to houses, condominiums are known to be not so good as investments. They tend to not hold value as well, not appreciate as much, and can require monthly fees that further detract from building equity.

You will also have little control over who your neighbors are or how they behave. Poor behavior and poor management are two reasons why condominium values may depreciate. Other condos will have strict rules over behavior, selling, maintenance, etc. These will potentially maintain higher equity, but at the potential cost of freedom, which may be a big deal to some of the readers of this book, especially gardening ones.

Equity in Cooperative Housing

For many readers of this book, housing cooperatives may be an excellent way to get affordable housing, actually become an owner rather than just a renter, and build some equity.

The other benefits are that you'll be living with built-in community, often of like-minded people, have people to share work tasks and housing costs with, and have a larger say in your own home than you do when you rent.

The downside is that you may not build as much equity in a coop as you would under other circumstances, but that may be considered a benefit, and at least you'll still be building some equity. To figure out how much, you'll need to know which equity model a particular cooperative uses. There are three main models: **Market equity** just follows the rising value of the market, which is the best opportunity to build equity, but may also be the most expensive to buy into. It can also cause problems when people want to sell their shares. **Limited equity** attempts to keep buy-in price low and may give residents a little more control over who buys in, but the downside is that it limits the equity you can build. **Group equity** may be the most affordable form of coop, and certainly the most common, but typically do not allow owners to build equity. Usually, owners get their deposit back, minus any charges to it. You will also be charged a monthly fee for upkeep, expenses, and utilities. In terms of equity it's the same as renting, but may or may not have lower rent, so do your homework to make sure the coop is best for you.

Ecovillages

Ecovillages are simply neighborhoods with a bit of eco-flair. Typically, they function the same way as any neighborhood of single family homes, so individual buyers will buy their individual dwellings. And for the purposes of this book, that means they will be growing equity.

A great deal has already been written about Ecovillages, precisely because they are such a potentially powerful way to change a destructive industry, from the inside. Those who invest in Ecovillages are often making incredible investments, since many of these actually appreciate far faster than regular neighborhoods (though some may experiment with limiting equity to keep prices low.) And ecovillage owners can be proud that they are also investing in a community asset and an important model for the future.

Getting Houses on the Cheap (Without Financing)

In privileged circles it's not uncommon for first-time home buyers to get family gifts of $100k to put towards their down payments.

For the rest of us, buying a house may not be a "privilege" we are given in this society. Remember, good credit is also a privilege that is given to those in upper classes, while the rest of us will have to struggle to get it.

And so it's good to know that there are options that allow us to skip giving money to evil Wallstreet banks, and buy homes directly at affordable prices.

In many of these cases, you'll be buying "distressed" homes that will require some TLC. That means you will also have to have some skills, or be willing to learn them. But it also means you'll have the opportunity for huge growth in equity. In my current market, even in 2021, it was possible to buy homes for literally thousands of dollars, that could be worth $150,000 on the market. That means there's a potential ROI of tens of thousands, or even hundreds of thousands of dollars over time. In that case, every dollar you put into the house is a dollar you save. I personally have friends who have bought houses for $1, which are now worth well over $100k.

HOW ON EARTH DOES ONE GET THESE HOUSES?!?!

In most areas, there are a few different institutions that sell off houses on the very cheap. See page XXX

Investment Patterns that Stack with Real Estate

In the next section we'll go into more depth on one important element of natural design: stacking. In nature, everything fills multiple functions, does multiple jobs, and has multiple ways of getting its own needs met. This creates a lot of resilience in natural systems. We would be smart to emulate this.

One thing that makes real estate such a powerful investment is that it can stack very well with other good transformative investments that cash flow and appreciate.

Best of all, because they're attached to homes, we can often get affordable financing, AKA, "FREE MONEY" to make these investments and start building real wealth.

The Permaculture Bed and Breakfast

Already the Permaculture B&B—with beautiful gardens, environmentally friendly quarters, and a focus on home-grown luxury breakfast—is quietly becoming an institution. These are some of the most successful Permaculture businesses I know of. In fact, this was a long-term goal for one of my projects, though I sold out of it before that income stream became a reality.

For those who want to regenerate land and real estate, and spend their FREE time meeting people, sharing a love of nature, spreading the word of Permaculture, and who love cooking, this is a winner of a life choice.

The best of these stack beautiful historic homes with transformative landscapes, and also create opportunities for light catering, produce and plant sales, landscape transformation programs, and event and meeting space.

B&B economic viability is heavily dependent on the mortgage and other costs, but many have made this investment a great working retirement.

Median cash flow income for a B&B manager is $54,000/year, for part-time work at home. For multiple-income families, a good Permaculture B&B will also offer produce and plant sales, space and garden rentals, and other programs. Sustainability themed B&Bs with a good home-grown menu may have a competitive niche to sell to an up-scale market.

A standard B&B host with 4 rooms could expect to earn over $40k/year, without offering breakfast or luxury accommodations. A great thing about this is that it can flexibly scale and allow the FREE host to choose when they want to work.

The downside is that you will be most likely to work on weekends and during local events. A live-in helper will be vital to making the investment work.

UnFarming Investments

This is to say yet again that I've seen people build really viable land-based incomes and livelihoods based on transformative assets, but that almost never has been "farming." Usually, when I've seen people buy land "to farm," it has not worked out well. Not saying "don't do it," just saying to consider it well in advance.

The key difference here is to think of long-term investments and regenerative assets rather than "farming" as an income. All of the land-based investments in this book are viable alternatives with much better proven profitability.

Therefore, instead of buying land to start a farming "job," invest in things like long-term agroforestry, tree crops that can also be sold as high-value lumber, valuable plant collections, and so on.

Home Aquaculture and Aquaponics

Like fish? Want to make some money off of them?

Aquaculture, generally, is the raising of fish and/or produce.

The regenerative power involved is that these systems can raise valuable protein at a higher rate than any other crop, do so sustainably, and while increasing biodiversity. While soy can produce 263 lbs of usable protein per acre, aquaculture systems can produce 300 lbs of protein per acre, at a rate of $12,000 of profit per acre, even in a cold climate like Vermont. (University of Vermont.)

Aquaponics systems are artificial indoor aquaculture systems, and even these can be profitable investments if done well.

Profitability outlook:

A study from the USDA is really our best information to date on the profitability of these systems, and the big take-home is: income from raising fish is comparable to small scale farming.

In other words, it is not a viable income for most people.

Gross income tended to be between $1000-4999 for the median respondent, with 10% receiving $50,000 or more.

However, the key to higher profitability and real livelihood was in stacking with other investments and income streams.

Keys to profitability

Real estate: Many of the most profitable operations use an aquaponics system to raise investment funding and financing to buy valuable real estate, often in urban areas.

Multiple revenues, fish and produce: In the studies, the operations that achieved real profitability didn't just sell produce, or fish, they sold both and benefited from the synergies between the systems.

Durable assets investments: the most profitable operations don't just sell fish and produce, they also offer services and products to set up home operations. This makes the fish and plants into "procreative assets," that go on to stock other fish systems. This provides other revenue streams like consultation, design, and sales of system components. Some very high end service providers design luxury ornamental home aquaponics systems in highly ornamental systems. I know designers who make excellent full-time livelihoods creating home ponds systems, koi pools, and natural swimming pools. Alone, these would probably be money-losing propositions, like farming, but combined with the transformative assets, these become viable livelihoods and paths to FREEdom.

Exergy or free energy. One of the biggest costs of aquaculture operations is the energy it takes. The most sustainable and profitable operations find ways to utilize waste energy from other industrial operations. For example, I worked at an aquaponics facility that ran entirely off the waste energy from an ethanol production plant. The aquaponics ran on free energy! Home scale aquaponics systems may run on waste heat from the house, or incidental heat from the living space. Other systems may run on heat from compost operations.

Small scale home setup profitability, (USDA):
Equipment Cost: $500
Lettuce yields: $432
Tomatoes: $86
Fish: $240
Total produce sales: $758/year*.

This was accomplished on just a few hours of hobby work per week. But combined with a business to install and sell parts, this can become a viable livelihood. Realistically, most of the income will come from activities other than produce sales.

Home Agroforestry Industries

Some of the most enviable people I know live like woodland elves in some fantasy realm, foraging profitably off of healthy, native woodland while keeping it thriving and healthy.

One particular client of mine in Northern Michigan had a livelihood of stacked incomes with plant capital, foraging, and agroforestry as the centerpieces. She sold lumber to a sustainable forester on rotation a couple times a decade, bringing in an influx of $30-50k each time. In Spring, she sustainably foraged and sold ramps, earning thousands of dollars per week off casual work in the woods. Visiting artists would stay with her to immerse themselves in nature, and could make extra money by joining in the harvest, there was plenty for more than just her. Through the rest of the season she propagated rare native plants for sale, and harvested medicinals like black cohosh. She made art and clothing of found objects in the woods to sell at the market. Others I know of make income streams off of wild blueberries, wintergreen, and native plant seeds. Still others spend part of the day in the woods and the other in the kitchen, turning the natural abundance into value added products like wild blueberry jam, pies and ice cream. Meanwhile, they are protecting and stewarding nature and biodiversity.

That's living the dream. These are real, viable incomes, available with the right investment. And in many of these cases, these pieces of land were purchased distressed, and in remote regions, for surprisingly little capital. With a good upfront business plan and natural capital inventory, it's possible to move right into a successful business as a sort of woodland elf.

However, these businesses take some development and networking. One must find or create viable markets for these materials, build relationships with vendors, and build a name for oneself in the industry. But with that work done, there are real livelihoods to be made by playing in the woods.

Home Agroforestry Establishment

What if you can't find your own elven paradise with abundant intact valuable woodland products just waiting for you to regeneratively harvest?

You can still invest in setting these up for yourself.

But fair warning, I have seen this go spectacularly well, and horrendously poorly! It takes more than the hippie good intentions often promoted within some of the Regenerative Agriculture community, as though "if you build it, the dollars will come!"

Most of these systems I have seen are created with no long term investment plan or economic viability analysis, and so they are never profitable, and require loads of unpaid labor of love. Few people can sustain that effort long, so most of these projects fail.

It's also worth noting that there may be low-cost loans available that allow you to make these investments with other people's money.

Systems must be well-designed with a clear plan for both profitability and regeneration, or they likely will accomplish neither goal.

Some numbers on potential profitability:
While I can't give you all the details of all the potential investments you can make, here are just a few.

Example: Black Walnut Based Agroforestry
Black walnut is almost the classic example, as it can be harvested for nuts and for lumber.
Commercial bulk market: $1000/acre profit after costs, labor, and financing.
You could do this and expect to "pay" yourself $4000/year in labor as well.
Potential per worker if self-harvested and sold direct to the market:
$19,000-24,000/acre at market value.
Lumber profit at 40 - 80 years: $100,000/acre or more.

This gives us the idea that someone could invest in black walnuts as part of a long-term agroforestry project expecting a sustainably managed harvest at maturity, while having a potential cash flow off nuts at around $20,000/year. Combine that with real estate value, and walnut based agroforestry is a great potential long-term regenerative investment that builds real family wealth.

But it can be combined with other short-term cash flow opportunities, like medicinals that grow well in black walnut forest:
Black cohosh sustainably harvested and shade-grown: $100k/acre/year.
Ramps sustainably harvested: $30k/acre/year
Ginseng sustainably harvested: $100k/acre/year

For early on in the project before nuts and medicinals are producing, we can plan for early succession crops.

Blackberries or raspberries can be grown along with black walnuts and harvesting can start in a few years. If the varieties are sought-after, plant sales can also add a line of profitability.
Blackberry establishment costs: $20-25/acre. (Less with good organic management.)
Blackberry proceeds: $30k-35k/acre by year 3.
Blackberry profits over 10 years: $280,000.

On a small scale, we could design a system to use a poly crop of different high value perennials over early succession, that have harvest times spread over a long season, including hazelnuts, asparagus, other perennial vegetables, berries, and some tree fruits, and expect to have a comparable cash flow and profit schedule.

Other trees like empress tree can be ready to harvest in just 7 years, and will generate $40,000/acre in proceeds. Bulk seeds are very easy to gather and germinate anywhere the tree is found growing. A ten acre planting could cash flow a decent income and end with a $400,000 return on investment in 7 years, enough to get "FREE" for many families, while establishing a long-term healthy ecosystem in the process, helping us make the transition to full-time forest elves.

A well-designed agroforestry system will choose trees based on our financial and life goals.

Home Agroforestry + Orchard

Some of the previous agroforestry models could be combined with orchard models, though it's important to say that most orchards will compete with low paid global labor and workers paid slave wages in the US due to labor law exemptions for farm workers. In other words, most of these will be comparable to other farm incomes, meaning they will not make viable livelihoods. Still, well-designed systems could integrate other long-term investments, agrotourism, you-pick operations and other income streams to create viable livelihoods on the path to being FREE.

Home Agroforestry + Plant Nursery or Seed Business

Again, like with orchards or other farming incomes, small scale plant nurseries and seed businesses done in a regenerative way are rarely viable incomes, looking at both the research on the topic and candid conversations from many folks in those businesses.

So it would be inadvisable to plan a livelihood with those businesses as the main income stream. But it can be possible to plan viable livelihoods based off other transformative asset investments, and use those to help fund a plant or nursery business.

And these can also be stacked with other income streams and investments, such as in the Landscape Transformation Program, to create truly viable livelihoods.

Stacked Home Investments for Artists, Artisans, Musicians, and other Makers

So far, many of our Transformative Assets have been geared towards land-based incomes for smallholders. But the options are nearly limitless. Or rather, as Bill Mollison said, the only limit is our creativity.

Makers in fields like art and music, can follow this strategy, too. There are a great deal of potential investments that meet all 5 of our criteria for transformative investments, including having access to loans to get started.

The Home Theater:

This investment is almost too common to pick a single example, since I've been in barn theaters, barn dances, home theaters, home music auditoriums, and even a live-in opera house with an attached apartment!

But one of my favorites is a little live-in concert venue built into an old attic in Northern Illinois. Here a couple of musicians converted a part of their home into a beautiful and unique music venue with excellent acoustics, and then started creating curated, custom small concerts for super fans of their favorite genres. Not only did this fill their home with music and friends, but it also provided great cash flow and a great set of investments. Visiting musicians would sign guitars and other collectibles, creating a high-value collection of durable assets, too.

Printing and Framing Businesses

High-quality hand-printed art, posters, and cards can provide a valuable peer-service to other artists in the community, if one has the space to host the tools and hardware. Such businesses can help artists make high quality digital scans, create unique artisan prints, and provide unique wedding invitations, and publicity materials. Some of this equipment is expensive, but highly durable, and it may hold its value well as an asset.

Framing is of course the same, and framing services can be a great way to cash flow while helping to build the local art community, and cut it off from corporate frames from Target. This again, can make a perfect home-scale business.

Home and Commercial Maker Spaces

For the handy-woman who's keen on collecting tools, a good workshop can become a community asset the way a home kitchen can. This can provide passive income as tool and space rental, but also provide an opportunity to teach classes, do workshops, and help new makers become experienced creators. Well chosen tools can be an excellent long-term investment, in addition to the opportunity for regenerative real-estate. The internet would be a good place to find many examples of folks making this Transformative Asset cash flow well into a right livelihood. I've seen local maker spaces funded by loans and local crowd funding, and advance subscription models like our "community supported" business models, making them great ways to leverage real wealth.

The Home Pottery Studio

My friend in Northern Indiana has a version of the maker space, dedicated to pottery. Again, wheels, kilns, and other tools of pottery make excellent long term durable assets which hold their value very well. Her live-in pottery studio is filled with color, friends, a pottery shop, classes, and fun. And in her off hours it provides passive rental income for other aspiring artists.

Artist Charcoals from Regenerative Heat

That's right, some of the home heating solutions mentioned in this book may be efficient enough to produce artist charcoals in certain conditions. Home kilns may also be used to create charcoals. For those with a network of artist friends, this could provide an income from an agriforest system, hedgerow, and home heating. Buckthorn, normally a weed species, is considered ideal for char.

Some Other Transformative Assets, Regenerative Assets that Cash Flow and Appreciate in value.

Plant investments that earn royalties

Housing or business property rentals
Businesses that can be made transformative, including some landscaping and home contracting businesses. Some of these can be purchased for just tens of thousands of dollars, and are eligible for business loan financing.
Generative asset rental, roller crimper, commercial nut cracker, oil press, that can be rented.
Intellectual assets like curricula, books, art, new business plans and models, etc.
Fame? Many farming gurus make most of their money off of this one asset, by selling endorsements and advertising. In most cases, I question whether this is done ethically, but I'm sure it can be.
You pick operations
Regenerative enterprises attached to real estate.
Landscape Transformation Businesses/Community Supported Permaculture.

Transformative Assets for Transforming Clothing, "the World's Worst Industry."

These high powered assets that are durable, appreciate, and cash flow can be found in many different areas of the economy, if one knows enough to know where to look.

In the US, there are entrepreneurs turning their clothing hobbies into livelihoods transforming this terrible industry, and bringing opportunities back home, by investing in the right assets.

As the "first world" clothing industry dismantled itself to ship production over seas 50 years ago, many of the old tools of highest quality skilled clothing were replaced by technologies that made cheaper clothes faster with low skill. Now, as more people recognize the lost quality, beauty, and durability of vintage and antique clothing and fabrics, these old tools are once-again sought after.

Exhibit A:

(Vintage denim, showing some signs of antique tools. Slubby fabric from uneven sized yarns and low tension weaving from an antique shuttle loom give the denim beautiful texture and the horizontal grain. Chain stitching with an antique machine contributes to the strong "roping" effect of light and dark at the seams. These artifacts of antique tools are highly sought-after by denim enthusiasts today.)

The "roping" effect seen in the pictured jeans is a result of a defect in the old sewing machines used to create this kind of durable "chain stitch." Today, most mass market jeans do not use this kind of chain stitch, in part because the machines to do so are now rare and expensive. And so this rope-like effect is now a sign of high quality, authentic denim for many "denim heads."

A few decades ago, the remaining machines were very inexpensive, and mostly sold for dollars to developing low-cost factories in Asia and Africa. It is said that the Union Special 43200 creates the most distinctive roping pattern, but other older chain stitching sewing machines are also very valuable.

Today, the remaining machines often sell for upwards of $5,000 to as high as $10,000 for machines in excellent condition. They are rare durable assets that will likely never be produced again, and the value is only likely to continue to soar as the remaining machines break down or are lost.

As a transformative asset, some seamsters and seamstresses have been able to find such machines in auctions, old factories, or yard sales have created high-value specialty denim-focused businesses. Standard hemming of jeans will prevent the legs from developing this roping effect, so those who can offer this authentic quality can charge 100% more and have a large market for their work.

These days, as people rediscover the high-value clothing of the past, there are many other transformative asset options. Antique generation looms for hemp, linen, and denim are now highly sought-after, and some enthusiasts have built strong new businesses off these highly valuable transformative assets. People are building businesses off sewing machines that can darn holes in denim in authentic ways, and hobbyists will ship their jeans across the country or around the world and accept long waits to have their jeans repaired this way.

As transformative assets, not only do these tools help us get FREE, they help transform a terrible industry, and bring textile arts back to the local scale. These tools also help create a demand and appreciation for repairing high quality clothing, instead of made-for-the-landfill fast fashion.

In recent years, it's worth pointing out that many small fortunes have been made by folks attempting to transform this industry. In an age of crowd-funding, multi-million-dollar businesses have been created with next to $0 in start-up costs. One example of a clothing business that has operated entirely on a crowd-funding model is Gustin. They've been able to become a major player in craft denim and menswear while funding all of their campaigns entirely with a crowd-funding model.

Textile Livestock

I've mentioned throughout the book that in my knowledge of the industry, most livestock operations are not, in fact, very profitable. Historically, livestock have almost always been a marker of wealth, because livestock provide benefits, but come with significant costs of time and resources. These days, conventional livestock like pigs, chickens, and cattle are extremely difficult to grow wealth from, unless you're stewarding rare heirloom breeds or have a rock-star reputation to charge rock-star prices.

The exception is have known several families who have created thriving lives around specialty livestock for wool, which can then also be used for value-added products. In the right location, Muskoxen naturally shed a high-value wool called quiviut, which can sell for $100-200 for a ball of yarn. Vicuña, camel, llama, cashmere, and other rare wool livestock are among the most profitable livestock of today, and since demand is likely to grow, they should make excellent "transformative assets," providing cash flow, materials for value-added artisan products, and "procreative assets" that will grow wealth naturally as demand grows.

Transformative Transportation

Another good example of people transforming their hobbies into assets can be found on 4 wheels.

Not everyone needs a car, but if you do, it could also be an asset. And it's worth pointing out that if you need a loan to access transportation, you might as well put that "other people's money" to work for yourself as a long-term asset.

In an era of internet ride sharing, any decent car can become a "generative asset," allowing us to make money by giving people rides.

But it's also possible to turn a passion for cars into transformative assets that appreciate and cash flow.

When I was teenager with from a car-loving family from a car city, it was still possible to find old antique cars from the days before planned obsolescence at a shockingly low price, hundreds or thousands of dollars. 30 years later, the same cars are worth many times that. Even a rusted out old cab of a Model T Ford alone sold for nearly $20,000. My uncle bought a model T for a few hundred dollars and fixed it up into a beautiful show car 30 years ago. Similar cars as his have sold for over $100,000 in the last few years.

Even fairly recent performance cars from the 90s went out of style, and have come back as collectors items, selling for big bucks. A 90s Supra might have sold for thousands of dollars a couple decades ago, and now they're generally listed from $45k-75k.

But of course, as transformative assets, these cars can also cash flow beyond just giving people cab service.

Making Money off Collectible Cars

Weekend Car Rental. Some people would pay big bucks to take your car out on a joy ride. Insurance required, of course. This can also work for trucks. We know of one person making nearly $1,000/month off of truck rental. The most popular app for this is Turo.

Weddings and events. There are websites to help connect car enthusiasts to people who can bring the bling.

Hollywood movie rental. Hollywood movies may pay well to rent the right car for their blockbuster. Again, the internet can help make the connections.

Other options: Others make money off local photo shoots, collaborating with photographers and artists, or off school events and visits.

Add Skills and Knowledge to your Transformative Car Stack

Collectible cars may take skills to keep them on the road. I've seen those skills grow into great livelihoods for many enthusiasts. Some will work doing specialized repair on a set of related cars, and may make full-time livelihoods working on their favorite cars and keeping them around into the future. Others learn how to find, repair, and sell these cars, like a regenerative automotive "flip" investment. Some simply help connect cars to sellers, and make their money off the connection.

Investing with Multiple Forms of Capital

Form of capital	Currency	Investment
Natural (living)	Plant material and collections	Landscape Transformation Program, Home herbalism program.
Cultural	Specific traditions and skills	Classes, specialty products and services businesses.
Political	Contact lists. Membership.	A member non-profit organization with a major donor program.

Once we've got the idea of transformative assets down, we can start to really make use of our multiple forms of capital. Until then, if we're using multiple forms of capital, we are probably just still stuck in a linear sort of system, instead of investing in long-term wealth.

Then the big insight is that we do not need financial capital in order to make investments!

But what kinds of investments can we make with our forms of holistic capital?

Just remember, anybody can make an "online class" for anything. 99.999% of these will take a lot of time and effort, but never make a single dollar. Without doing the other important design work in this book, my feeling is that this fad of creating classes and content will almost always be a big waste of time.

So it's important that the assets we invest in are indeed actual assets that are capable of generating real capital that can meet our real needs. It's far too easy to use "I'm gaining social capital" as a way of fooling ourselves that our class or other program is "growing wealth" while we're actually losing money by doing it.

Transformative Enterprise and the DIY Green New Deal

From looking at the patterns in this book to this point, you could get the idea that we authors believe that "business is a good business."

It appears to us that compared to investments like the stock market, "transformative enterprise" is both a superior investment and give us great life flexibility. We become masters of our own lives.

And frankly, what we truly need is a "Green New Deal," something like the Roosevelt New Deal, but focused on creating a just and sustainable economy. And we simply can't wait for "thought leaders" and politicians to do it, or count on them to get it right.

By investing in creating that new economy, we can fund a DIY Green New Deal, and actually pay ourselves (and each other) to do that work. We can transform the world with a whole movement of activists making a living off of the economic change we know we need.

To use some revolutionary rhetoric, "seizing the means of production" over the things that we need, and that people in our communities need, is both a good strategy for societal transformation, and honestly, perhaps the best opportunity we know of for achieving a really FREE life.

Owning a business is by no means required! But as we've seen in several of the graphics in this book (Page XXX) owning and operating some sort of low-overhead transformative enterprise is probably the most profitable and most reliable semi-passive investment in this book. Most of the people we've seen achieve a FREE lifestyle have done this in some way, whether that's making art, teaching music lessons, living in a duplex, selling plants, or any of the other examples in this book.

We've given many examples of transformative investments that can cash flow as businesses. And ideally, many of these can be done in "more passive" ways.

But investing in buying and transforming existing businesses is also a great potential investment. There are several online resources that list businesses for sale by region. A quick internet search for "buy business in (location)" should help you find some. Most of these will NOT be green businesses, but there's a lot of opportunity to convert existing businesses to sustainable ones. These come with the benefit of buying a proven business with an existing customer base, and then instantly growing the customer base and profitability by adding sustainability to the practices.

And of course, the best of these will include transformative assets that can appreciate over time. A good business itself will be an excellent transformative asset.

Some affordable and commonly sold local businesses that can be "transformed," include:

Flooring businesses. The opportunities for "green flooring" are huge!
Cafes and small restaurants. These could help create markets for local regenerative agriculture and Permaculture!
Housing services: gutters, window washing, pressure washing, etc.
Car detailing and cleaning. A real need to "green" these!
Pet care, grooming, dog walking businesses, can all be done with a "green theme" or even stacked with Permaculture sites.
Child care. Again, amazing opportunities to stack with regeneration.
Book stores. Huge potential for stacking with regeneration!
Landscaping. This is actually harder to make regenerative than one might thing. But even small improvements can be high-impact.
Schools. Permaculture magnet school? Sign me up!
Virtually any other business you find can be greened.

Eric Brown, the Second Act Entrepreneur

Now that we've got a full view of what a FREE life can look like, it's a good time to introduce you to Eric's story.

I (Mike) met Eric as a student in one of my Permaculture Design Certificate Courses. It was clear that he was in the middle of a life upheaval, rethinking what he really wanted to get out of his life. By the end of the PDC, he inspired everyone, by truly taking the challenge, and allowing the exploration of the PDC to transform his life. "This has given me my life back," he told the class at the final session.

Eric's story is more inspiring, since he has been a long student of the "money game," and is a successful businessman, primarily in real estate. As he says in his book "Second Act Entrepreneur," "our baggage becomes an anchor that holds us back, and we should focus on cutting it lose." Eric cut loose from his career in real estate, and has found a whole regenerative life of abundance waiting for him on the other side.

"I have 7-Income Stacks, and I have mostly focused on Passive Income, to expand My Free Time for reading, study, hiking and meditation. Here are the Income Stacks I have created for a steady cash flow.
My Income Stack;
   1. UrbaneFarm; HotSauces/Unique Gifts; Partial Passive Income
   2. Social Security; Passive Income
   3. RealEstate Holdings/Distributions; Passive Income
   4. Book Sales/Royalties; Passive Income
   5. BackAlley Eatzz Grill Trailer; Meaningful Income
   6. PictureMe Photo Booth; Partially Passive Income
   7. Adjunct Instructor; Drexel University; Become Your Own Boss; Meaningful Income

I chose to live in an RV in the Spring/Summer April-October, near my kids and grandkids, with Bert the Dog and Olive the Cat. I mostly get around on a Vespa Scooter, Bicycle or Walk, enjoying the SimpleLife.

In the Winter months I retreat to an "up north" off grid cabin in Northern MI, November-March. No electricity, no running water! I spend my time there chopping wood, reading, writing, studying and hiking. More simple life equals more abundance.

Housing is our largest expense, and I knew in order for me to live FREE I needed to flatten it. We fully recognize some of these choices are not for everyone, but this one works for me. The clipits of Joy have increased, with much stillness each day. It is quite decadent!

Chapter 12: Stacking Products, Markets, Incomes, and Talents

Next in our plan to emulate the wise and worthy THISTLE, is to learn to STACK our efforts towards resilience. Not only is the THISTLE hardy and drought-tolerant, it also is a prolific seed producer, and hit hast thistles for self defense! It stacks its strategies for maximum effect.

One of the key features of natural systems that make them so resilient and flexible is that every part can play multiple roles, and every necessary role has multiple players that can play it.

For example, the trees in a forest can provide fertility, can stop erosion, can help infiltrate water, and provide food to feed the entire community. And, of course, it needs to be said that trees do all these jobs particularly well.

But, if a tree is hit by lightning, or fire, the whole system doesn't necessarily collapse. Because there are other beings in the system that can step in to fill these roles.

If we were smart, we'd design our important systems—like our livelihoods, businesses, and personal finances—to function the same way. Permaculture designers call this "stacking functions."

Instead, most of us place all our reliance on one system, like one income stream, one job, one product, or one market. Then if something goes wrong with any of those, the whole system does indeed collapse. For example, a classic market garden business may rely entirely on growing produce for sale at a market. If the produce has a bad year or a competing market opens, or perhaps (as happened in one market I know of,) a non-profit opens selling greatly subsidized produce with some "save the world" marketing, we can get into a lot of trouble! Many artists, too, rely entirely on art sales through one or two markets, or just one or two types of products or income streams.

So as we learn to "stack" these important systems, there are three major areas we can focus on stacking: **Products, Markets, Incomes and Talents.**

Stacking Products (Or Income Streams)

I have attempted to work in Permaculture full time for 2 decades, since I first began studying it and believed it was the most important work to do in the world in an age of mass extinctions and climate change.

And for a decade, I failed to make that work. I was trying to do consultations, classes, online classes (following the trend of the day) plant sales, produce, a CSA, and events. None of these incomes really worked, and all together, they took a huge amount of time, and still did not add up to a full-time adult income.

Until I decided to stack them all up into one very high value product to create the "Landscape Transformation Program."

This program was like a Community Supported Agriculture program, where people buy their produce up front with a subscription, and receive produce throughout the season as it's ready.

The Landscape Transformation Program gives people everything they need to transform their landscapes, right when they need it, all season long. It packages together seeds and plants, right when they need to be planted, and a class on what to do, right at the right time to do it, and consultation, and a community to learn together with. Now, instead of offering all of these products separately, I was combining them into one highly practical program, with one big price tag.

And it sold out almost instantly, providing a basic adult income the very first season.

Think about it. Why would someone buy a bunch of strange perennial plants from me if they didn't know what to do with them? And why would they hire me to do a consultation if they didn't have the materials and resources to do the work? Why would they take a class on doing it only to find that it was going to require thousands of dollars of plants? But here, this package put all those things together, and used the power of procreative assets and guild matrix plants to help people grow their own plant capital. Now, it all made sense! People would get the plants they need, and the information and experience altogether.

Meanwhile, my Permaculture Design Courses would often create very excited new permaculturists, but many didn't know what to do after. This is a very common problem with PDC courses. People graduate, then never make a garden! Again, they don't have the right tools at the right time.

But the Landscape Transformation Program succeeded in creating lots of new permaculture gardens and plant collections that could be used to really grow out the project. Not only was it very profitable for me, it was highly valuable and impactful for the people taking it. And so, with that word of mouth, it continued to sell out every year I offered it.

There are likely a great many disciplines that could use this same redesign. I know of artists who have become successful by stacking together their art with engaging communities and interesting events, and chefs that made their businesses work by combining their food with cooking classes, and farms that have succeeded by packaging together produce with great enriching life experiences.

If you're not thinking about stacking products in this way, it's possible you're leaving money on the table, and not giving people a great way to support you.

Stacking Markets

The next way we can stack our livelihoods is by stacking our markets.

To start with, let's consider that market garden again. Most market gardens have just one market in mind. Perhaps they have a CSA, or maybe they sell at the farmers market.

Maybe they do both! But really, that's still just one market: mostly relatively affluent people who are interested in buying local produce and probably willing to pay a little extra for it. They likely have a yearly budget they're willing to spend on food, and both of this farm's markets are competing with each other for the same dollars. Those CSA customers are also probably their farmers market customers, and we're competing for their dollars.

But really this is common across all the folks I work with, and it's likely the #1 reason why I see otherwise great projects fail.

Avoiding Projects Designed to Fail

And that was exactly the path to failure that my business was on when I decided to use the design process to rework how we organized my efforts.

And without that change, I'm afraid my Permacultuer career would not have been long for this world, and I'd likely be back to working for some corporation I hate.

As I already said, I had poor sales of my nursery stock, design services and produce (which mostly got composted,) and poor attendance of the classes I was offering, even though I was offering them for free. On multiple occasions, I had a dozen or more people scheduled for a free class, which I would spend hours lesson planning and prepping materials for, and literally NO ONE would show up!

I'd struggle long hours trying to organize people to implement a single Permaculture project or engage in some environmental cause and never seemed to get anywhere.

I had designed for low engagement.

When I tell my new students this, they often say I'm reading their minds. Many have had exactly this same experience. Remember, it's a privilege to do what we're all trying to do, and we have to be good at it—better than some average schmuck on Youtube.

Now, I have a large, supportive community and I feel proud that we're supporting them in return. I've supported the creation of over two dozen forest garden projects just this year, and supplied them with thousands of dollars of plant stock and produce samples. I'm making a decent living charging for my programs, and many of them sell out!

My main business stream has profited nearly $200k in the last 6 years or so.

Largely, this is because I learned to stack my markets.

———————————

This is the most common type 1 error involved in project design, businesses, non-profits and activism efforts: the failure to engage that too often leaves us burned out and cynical, stuck blaming others for not caring enough, showing up or helping out. This is exactly the error I made in my programs.

But what if we can turn that blame around and accept the feedback that people didn't show up? Most of the time, people WANTED to show up, they cared about what we were doing, but when it came to prioritizing the time and resources, they simply had other priorities.

Let's face it, the modern world is tough, competitive, strapped for time and resources. People might love your paintings, your farm, your band, whatever it is you're doing, but they have to make tough choices about supporting you over everyone else they love in their communities.

So we realized that if we really want people to show up, we have to give them a good incentive, we have to make it so worth their while that they can't NOT show up.

You have to literally PAY people to show up.

In Permaculture, we call this principle "obtain a yield." We're not the only ones who need to put gas in our tank to get where we're going. We have to design things so that volunteers and supporters can put gas in their tanks, too, because without that fuel, eventually they're going to stop showing up.

When we get that right, we've super-fueled our project so that like the sun, or a wildfire, in burning it creates its own fuel. We pay people to show up by making them wealthier, and they pay in return for that.

Now, back to those projects that are destined to run out of gas. Look at this chart:

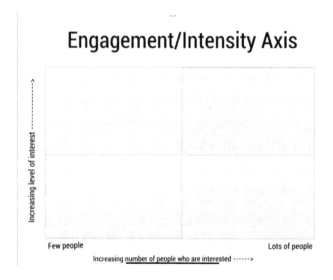

As you can see, the horizontal axis at the bottom is pretty simple, with small numbers of people on the left, moving towards increasingly large numbers on the right. The vertical axis is more interesting, Intensity of Interest, how much people want to support something.

When it comes to supporting our projects, there are really just two meaningful types of support we're measuring here: volunteering and donating. Are people actually interested enough to give the project resources or volunteer time? How much they're willing to give will depend upon how passionate they are about the cause or product. Low levels might be a few dollars or a few hours. Large levels of interest might equate to thousands of dollars or more, or perhaps people who want to make a living out of supporting our work.

Based on that axis, we can put any project or product into one of these four quadrants:

Engagement Matrix

Intensity of Interest (vertical axis)

Small group of passionate devotees willing to donate time and money

Congratulations, you have found the promised land.

You're on your own here.

Many hands make light work
Lots of people willing to "chip in"

People Interested — *More ---->*

Lets look first at the upper right hand box. This is the promised land, and very rare. This is where you'll have a large number of people willing to give a lot of time and support. For example: Houses. A very large number of people will actually work a significant portion of their lives for the privilege of owning their own home. And in fact, most* people in our society actually work providing goods or services in this category! Cars, refrigerators, washing machines… if you have a project or product that falls into this category, congratulations, you're pretty much guaranteed support and success. Unfortunately, endeavors that fit this bill are very rare.

Next, check out the lower right box. If your project is here, people might not be super excited about it, but they're at least willing to give you a few bucks here and there. But luckily, there are many, many of them. For example, Coke, Pepsi, McDonalds, Starbucks. There are very few people who are passionate about giving their money or labor to these companies, but millions of people are passionate ENOUGH about their products to give them small amounts of money on a recurring basis. This quadrant also defines a large number of non-profit endeavors, especially the large aid organizations.

Next, the upper left quadrant, where only small numbers of people are interested, but BOY ARE THEY EVER!!! In today's world this is the most interesting quadrant, and with the internet and globalization connecting people like never before, this is the quadrant that is radically changing how funding and marketing work, as has been pointed out by many critics. Innovative projects might not be able to find large numbers of people to support them, but if you want to tap into a few very passionate people, then you can accomplish a lot! These people may be "angel investors" willing to contribute large amounts of money, volunteers who'll invest a lot of their time, or even folks who want to turn your cause into their own source of right livelihood. Often these are professional or career organizations, or passionate hobbies tied strongly to self-identity and personal development. The fact that they are so niche actually helps them build identify, since we define ourselves most strongly by these narrow interests. You know, things like homesteading or Permaculture....

And from a Permaculture perspective, efforts in all three of these quadrants USUALLY allow participants to "obtain a yield" – often fulfilling multiple needs. They may help people eat, find housing, meet potential mates or friends with similar values, find personal development, and search for identity. (Hint: people invest a great deal in their identity, and people associate their identity with niche lifestyles, compelling brands, and inspiring people.)

And yet, most of our "good deed" efforts fall into the lower lefthand quadrant. This quadrant will have a small number of people with only a small amount of interest.

Basically, when we plan our efforts here, it's going to be us and, of course, our moms.

Worse, we design our efforts to be one-directional in terms of support, with volunteers and donors doing all the giving and us doing all the taking. We don't even make an effort to connect with their needs! There are a few people who may show up for an occasional meeting or donate a few bucks, but unless your project can survive on that level of support, your project isn't going to get far.

But when you think about it, this makes perfect sense: we look around, we see something that seems important TO US, and notice that nobody is doing it, so we see an opening. Meanwhile, most of the stuff that would be in those other quadrants is already being done! There's a reason why this stuff – even if it's important – isn't getting done. There's just not enough interest. Which is why business start-up teacher Ramit Sethi calls this sector the "Labor of

Love" sector, it only gets done with the love and sacrifice of one (or a few) individuals.

This is even more common in the days of the internet! Why? Because on the internet we can find many people who share our passions, whether they're community gardening or local produce, or climate change, so we start to assume there's broader, deeper support in our own geographic area than there actually is. Everyone in our online community might think that community food forests are a great idea, but do the people in the neighborhood where we want to build one? Are they passionate enough (or have access to the resources) to chip in their time and money, or put up with maintenance or social problems that may occur?

Most of the non-profits and community organizations I've ever been involved in or even personally organized myself have fallen into this lower left category! And in a lot of ways, this is exactly where my business was a few years ago.

So how do we change this?

1. We make sure we're offering people products of really high value. Stacking our products can help here.
2. We move our business out of the "Mom and me" zone and into someplace where we'll get some real support.

Realistically, we're probably not going to strike on an idea in the upper right corner. Which means we're looking at how we can move our products into the other two quadrants.

Here's the trick, this isn't an either/or proposition. It's a yes, and stack of both and everything in between awesomeness.

This is a matter of recognizing that we may have a lot of people who want to support us a little bit. So we need to give them meaningful opportunities. This might be a matter of offering plant sales or produce, and finding as many places as we can to connect people with that opportunity. And of course, making sure that we're connecting people with the ideas and messages we want them to support. For example, if we're doing regenerative gardening, we want people to know that buying our produce is supporting our regenerative work. For artists, this might be offering gift cards or stickers. And again, having a message or identity that is worth supporting.

Perhaps there are 1000 people in your region who would support you at that level. Are you actually trying to connect with those 1000 people to ask them for their support? If not, they're not going to magically send us $10.

Next, perhaps there are 100 people who will support us at $100. Maybe that's a small introduction CSA for the season, with a few packaged family events on pick up days. For artists, this could be a coffee table book or package of high quality signed prints for gifts.

Up from there, maybe there are 10-30 people who will support you at $1000/year. For example, many farms run successful CSA programs at this price point. Artists might sell snazzy party events with their original works.

...

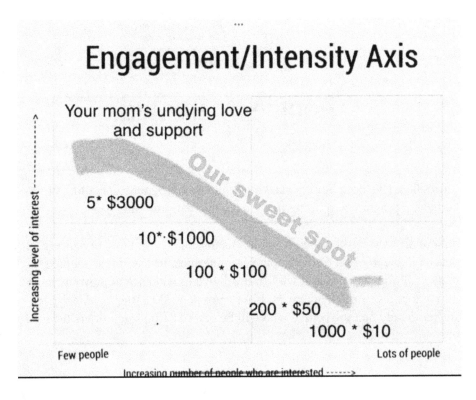

Engagement/Intensity Axis

Your mom's undying love and support

Our sweet spot

Increasing level of interest ----------------->

5* $3000

10* $1000

100 * $100

200 * $50

1000 * $10

Few people   Lots of people

Increasing number of people who are interested ------>

It was exactly this kind of stacked market design that turned my own income into an instant adult full-time income over night.

To be specific, here's what it looked like:

STACKED MARKETS BY ENGAGEMENT LEVEL

Intensity of Interest

MENTORSHIPS 3: $3,000–$5000+ $9,000+

PROGRAM MEMBERS, 10–15+ @ $1,200 $12,000+

INDIVIDUAL GUESTS IN CLASSES AND ONE OFF CLASSES. 30 CLIENTS @ $30–100 $1,000

INDIVIDUAL PLANT SALES 50–100 CUSTOMERS, $400–

PRODUCE SALES: $7,000 $10,000

SPEAKING GIGS, $7,000

CONSULTATIONS, ETC. $1,000+

CONNECT WITH THOUSANDS PER SEASON

People Interested   More ---->

TOTAL YEARLY PROGRAM INCOME: $25,000 – $40,000+

Since then, I've done similar stacking with other programs, including my herbalism program and professional development programs.

Best of all, this market stacking makes us instant "community organizers." It puts us in the mindset of developing communities, instead of developing markets. Folks who enter at the $10 level give us a chance to move them up into higher levels of engagement. If we can sell 1,000 $10 chochkies/year, we've already met the people who will be our 10 $1,000 supporters the next year.

Stacking Income Streams

Next, we can stack up our income streams to support our work better.

Note:

THIS IS NOT THE "SIDE HUSTLE" OFTEN PROMOTED BY FIRE GURUS. In fact, it may be its exact opposite.

For example, a lot of FIRE gurus will give people a list of different things that can be done to make extra money on the side. If you're a bank teller, fine, in your "free time" you can bake pies, and on weekends you can house site, and in the summer you can paint houses in the evening and soon you'll be retired early! Unless you're dead for overexhaustion.

This is not an income "stack," this is a haphazard pile of income streams lumped together in a way they might come tumbling down at any time. This author's humble advice: it's not worth it.

"Stacking" incomes means we put them together in a way where they work well together, such that we get multiple income streams from the same amount of work, OR there's good symbiosis involved.

For example, a pile might be "herbalist, home insurance sales, portrait artist."

Meanwhile, a "stack" might be: herbalist, plant illustrations, plant sales, herb-scaping garden design and installation.

Much of the work for our herbalism business might be growing our herbs. Now, without adding much extra labor, we can pot up seedlings and sell them. We'd be weeding them out anyway. While we're observing the garden, we could use our time with the plants to get better at illustrations of them. We can make cards, gifts, seed packages, artsy labels for our plants that allow us to sell them as high value gifts. Now, we've added on a stream that increases the sale price of our other products. And each one of these new incomes might help us attract new markets who will then become potential customers of the others. Someone who is moved by your portrayal of herbs might be particularly interested in your comfrey lotion.

Stacking Talents/Skills

Which leads us to our final way to stack for financial abundance: stacking our skills.

While this one may be the least obvious in terms of instantly increasing your earnings, it's almost certainly the most important for long-term success and abundance. It's the one almost everyone I know of doing this kind of work well has done right. It might be one of the most important things in this book!

And yet, it's one that almost everyone in the audience for this book has done wrong, or at least strongly contemplated doing wrong!

Again, this is like stacking income streams. We want a stack of skills that work well to build a really cool livelihood that really works for us, rather than a haphazard pile of skills that all make a mess and the parts sticking out everywhere get in our way.

Sounds logical! Why do we do it wrong all the time?

Because that's what society tells us to do.

Let's say you're reading this book because you're a farmer, artist, or activist type, and you're struggling to support yourself. What does VIRTUALLY EVERYONE say to do?

Go back to school and get a degree in something else.

Heaven help me I have seen so many really talented folks doing this sort of important work give up and go get a second degree. Usually, they're motivated by money now, so they get a degree in whatever the advisors say is the job-de-jour, coding, or social justice, or graphic design, or body work, or whatever is the fad. The problem is, everybody else is getting those degrees, too, so by the time they graduate there's a glut and there are no longer good jobs available. Now they've got two degrees, say music and outdated HTML coding, and they don't really go together at all. Any time spent on the coding career is costing the art career and vice versa.

All the people I know who are most successful have developed great skill stacks, period. IN fact, I'd say there are two paths to success in life and only two: Go really deep in developing specialized expertise in just one high value area, or develop a highly valuable novel skill stack.

For example, I have developed a lot of skills and knowledge with plants and farming, I've taken a lot of coursework in education and communication, I've studied writing at depth, and the "business" stuff to be able to turn those skills into an actual livelihood playing with plants. If it wasn't working out, I wouldn't go back and get a degree in some fad I hate just to make money, I'd think about how to add to my stack so that I could create a good livelihood that I'd actually love.

And of course, if things aren't working out financially, I'd go back and look at all of these ways I could restack my income streams, skills, markets, and products. All of these ways of stacking can build up to a livelihood that really works.

P31–Stacked Livelihood Examples

Since stacking income streams and skills is so useful, some of our best transformative investments will come with stacked cash flow streams. Here are a few models we can use to identify similar opportunities and build livelihoods around them.

The Regenerative Housing Activist

America alone has around a half million homeless. Not to mention an epidemic of rising housing prices, forcing many to pay 40-50% of their incomes on housing—a completely unsustainable situation.

Meanwhile, we have 16 million vacant houses, that will crumble into disrepair if not utilized, causing an environmental and social disaster as they collapse.

So what do we do?

BUILD MORE NEW HOUSES, of course!

And lest these new houses help alleviate the suffering of those trapped in housing insecurity, let's make sure these new houses are completely unaffordable. While the average house price in 2022 is a whopping $348,000, the average new construction is $443,300! That will put annual housing costs over $25,000/year, making the average new house unavailable to the average family, since that's 37% of the average family's income! Meanwhile, following the path of planned obsolescence, these cheaply made, oversized homes will have a shorter life span, and require more resource consumption to build, heat, and maintain. "Wendigohouses."

The embarrassingly simple solution to this preposterous situation is for us to invest in maintaining and occupying our perfectly good housing stock.

This has the added benefit of de-corporatizing the local economy. While new building is a corporate affair, with most building plans now coming from just a few large corporate firms, and most parts and materials also coming from massive, destructive corporations, rebuilding and maintaining is a local affair. Repair and retrofit work is largely done with existing materials, by small teams of small worker-owned businesses and artisans that the money goes to support, rather than distant corporate executives using exploited labor.

That means there's opportunity for folks like us to get involved in that work.

The tools and equipment, as well as the materials, can make for excellent stacked investments, and we also build highly valuable intellectual capital that can be transferred easily and profitably to others in our communities. There can be many opportunities to give classes and workshops, establish coops, and create books and pamphlets around these important skills.

Some Ideas for the Regenerative Housing Activist:

Lead Abatement. Perhaps one of the most important things we can do to revitalize our housing stock for the next generations is lead remediation. My god please let's not just bulldoze these houses due to lead, so that this dangerous material goes into the neighborhood soil! Many communities offer low-cost or free training on lead remediation, which can be done in safe ways by trained professionals. Much of the equipment is multi-use and durable, and can make an excellent investment. Equipment can be rented to start with, and a few thousand dollars of equipment can get a small operation going. Typical pricing is $15k for an urban house, and once equipment is paid off, most of that will go to labor. There is a LOT of room for growth here, and even for us to establish non-profits to promote this important investment in our communities. The fact that we give grants to white suburban contractors for new buildings but have few grants for lead abatement is frankly deeply racist.

Plaster work. Old houses are made with the best possible wall material we could ask for: lime plaster and lath! This is often called the "Rolls Royce of walls" for a reason: it has good thermal mass, great acoustical properties, is highly durable, and beautiful. The only problem is that there's a huge lack of people with the skill to do this work. Venetian plaster is an artisan form which is in high demand among wealthy clients. Repairing plaster is easy, far cheaper than dry walling, avoids waste, lasts longer, and practically no one is marketing this in our communities. Beyond getting the education, start-up costs are low, and the ROI would be high. I know multiple highly in-demand contractors doing exactly this kind of work and making good livelihoods doing it. Again, the money goes to labor, not to corporate materials cost.

Window Refurbishing. As an environmentalist, I love old wood windows. They can last practically forever, be easily restored, maintain their efficiency better over time, and when whole life energy costs are considered, they're more efficient than modern "efficient" windows we're replacing them with. Yet again, I know contractors making good money with window restoration as a big part of their careers, and this pairs well with regenerative investments in durable assets like old windows materials. Many of these durable assets are actually available for FREE as people get rid of them, and smarty pants folks snatch them up. Once you have the skill to put them back to use, they become instantly worth hundreds of dollars a piece. In addition, this builds intellectual capital. Some of my favorite workshops I've given have been on restoring windows.

Architectural Salvage. Once you begin to see old homes as worth valuing and investing in, the world is filled with durable assets that are ripe for "waste to value." We are literally throwing away well-made, artisan antiques that are often worth high prices at architectural salvage stores. These are some of my favorite places to shop, and my favorite business models, since they can often be started by simply connecting to folks bulldozing old homes and rescuing the materials before they go to the landfill. Of course, it does require a commercial outlet, which gives us the opportunity to stack with a real estate investment. Those who run salvage shops are well-positioned to find other income streams in Regenerating Housing.

Old Home Retrofit—AN URGENT SKILLSET! The downside of old housing is that it is often not so energy efficient as modern, tightly sealed housing. There are things we can do about this! But sadly, usually it is done in an entirely destructive way! Installing insulation in old wood-sided houses can be the death knell of old homes, causing paint stripping, rot, insect damage, infestations, and a high risk of mold issues. Many of the "updates" sold by careless contractors cause permanent—or extremely expensive— damage to old homes. For one example, insulation should never be in contact with the wood siding of old houses, especially ones with no sheathing. This is sure to cause rot and other problems. So, we must install spacers and barriers within the walls before spraying in insulation. Often, insulation in the walls is not even necessary, and sealing alone will get nearly as good an ROI without the damage to the home. Similarly, old home plumbing, heating, and electrical systems can require special knowledge. So old houses require a completely different set of skills and knowledge that appears extremely rare among professional contractors.

Stack Them Up! Some very interesting FREE lifestyles have been made by stacking up these opportunities, income streams, and investments together. They can also be stacked well for creative maker types, who may get real satisfaction from restoring tile flooring, or doing Venetian plaster work. Old pros may be happy to have enthusiastic help on the job. I've worked with an old school tile professional and spoken with a plasterer who seemed like he would be happy to have skilled help. Friends and family with old homes may be able to provide the opportunity to build a good portfolio.

Regenerative Commercial Kitchen Investment Stack

For folks who have transformative landscapes that produce food, and who like to cook, and are considering income streams from value added products, this is simply one of the best life moves I know of.

This allows us to get real value out of home grown produce, level up our sales to new heights, have assets that will hold value or appreciate very well over time, and get passive income from rental all at once. It's a great transformative investment.

The folks I know who are doing this well have also combined it with a real estate investment, building commercial kitchens into home or business spaces. They operate value added products businesses made with regeneratively-sourced produce, which can be everything from pasta, baked goods, pickles, jams, ferments, etc. but on a family scale, the kitchen doesn't have to be in use all the time! Which gives us the opportunity to rent out the kitchen to other regenerative enterprises and even share on other costs like marketing and promotion, together, too.

Folks who design their investment well and do their community organizing up front can easily pay for their kitchen install by financing and then renting out the kitchen to cover the financing. It's a transformative investment that could be free.

Costs: $5000-15000+, but possibly less with elbow grease and some good second-hand finds. Since restaurants often go out of business, kitchen equipment often gets auctioned or sold online. Friends of mine were able to do theirs for even less than $5000.

Rental profit income (assuming casual part-time operation.) $5,000 annually.

Rental profit income (assuming no carryover financing expenses and a more aggressive program to operate the rental kitchen or do classes and workshops) $12k+

That's semi-passive income in addition to using the kitchen to create value added products, making it a great potential investment. Income from value added products depends on a lot of factors and requires a full economical viability analysis. However, there is research literature on the profitability of such endeavors and it's not uncommon to see real, full-time adult incomes from these businesses, even on the part-time scale. Many seem to be making $60k+ in profit annually, working for themselves at home.

Active income from value-added sales:

Part to Full time, 1-4 workers: $10k-100k+

*Worcester Regional Food Hub study
*University of Florida cottage industry research.

Modern Regenerative Agro-tourism at the intersection of social capital and other assets

Agritourism remains a great life choice for those who love to be around people, build community, and share a love of nature and the seasons. The downside is that it is a very competitive market, and it requires a truly special place, a truly special product, or a truly special personality.

The real key is often a well-stacked and unique set of features to appeal to the target market. To give you an idea of some spectacular real world business models, here are some of my favorites I've visited or consulted on (given without names to preserve anonymity.)

Wherever I go, I try to visit such places, as they're always true joys to see and experience. The people who've put them together have built beautiful lives for themselves, and their communities.

The Agritourism Cannery:
One interesting model relies on a beautiful pastoral landscape and beautifully preserved farm architecture to create an event space, coupled with a professional canning kitchen for classes and value added products. A popular venue for weddings, catering can be done out of the commercial kitchen, and the barn used for the reception and for dances. Monthly dances and farm to fork meals bring potential customers out to the space and build community. The commercial kitchen is also used for a line of interesting jams and other canned products, and classes on canning are offered there as well. A small farm stand store allows guests to shop and buy produce and value added products. These "farmers" have created a FREE life with a whirl of beauty, community, and activity all around them. And it's all built into a set of transformative assets that will appreciate and provide deep security no matter what life brings.

Fair Trade Agrotourism:
Another favorite model stacks regenerative farming with the farmer's love of travel and fair trade durable assets. Ginger has filled her barns full of fair trade items, rugs, clothes, tools, instruments, and decorations from around the world. A visit is a real experience, walking around the beautiful setting and looking at all the hand-made items, and hearing the stories about them. You can also stop by the farm stand for some produce while you're there.

Art Farms:
I've visited several farms that doubled as art galleries, and the best benefit from stacking with other smart long-term, regenerative land-based investments. At their best, these can become gateways for other agritourism opportunities, with people coming to look at art and pick up holiday trees or decorations, pumpkins for the fall, and flowers in the spring.

The Cinnamon Roll Farm:

Cinnamon rolls don't grow on trees, but I visited one cooperatively owned and managed farm where cinnamon rolls paid the bills.

These cinnamon rolls had gained such a reputation that I waited in line over an hour just to pick one up, after strolling through a store filled with other farm produce, sandwiches, and baked goods.

I've visited other farms with highly successful specialty value added products, including vineyards, an elderberry wine farm, cider orchards, wood working farms, and other customized, interesting stacked income streams.

Often the key to making these work is one truly fantastic product with a great reputation. It only takes one to make the whole business work.

Natural Assets Stacked with Intellectual and other Assets

Because of the "procreative" power of many natural assets, these make some of our best possible investments for folks with an interest and aptitude for the natural side of things. For anyone looking to live off the land, these can make the dream a reality, and give us the opportunity to really thrive and meet our goals.

Combine that power with smart intellectual assets that "add value," and we have the path that many have used to get FREE.

Not all natural capital investments will work out, like with any investment. Later we'll call these sorts of investments, "higher risk, high reward," as many large fortunes have been made on these sorts of investments! But smart natural capital investors hedge their bets and make enough investments that some will work out well.

The Landscape Transformation program is an example of this intersection of natural capital and intellectual capital. It combines the right plant collection with the knowledge of what works locally and what to do with the plants. This is why it's such a successful program, while simple small-scale nursery businesses tend to struggle.

Since plant capital investments are hyper specific, I can point you towards some examples, but I can't really give you exact plants to replicate, beyond the Landscape Transformation Program. So we'll look at some models and how they made this special intersection work for them, with the right ideas, the right plants, at the right place, and the right time.

Natural/Intellectual Assets Model 1: Kalamazoo's Peppermint King, regenerative Ag pioneer and social reformer A.M. Todd.

The "Peppermint King," regenerative agricutlure pioneer, and social reformer,

A.M. Todd

A.M. Todd Black Peppermint

For those who care about building a better world while building a more financially free life, A.M. Todd makes a great example.

Albert M. Todd came from a humble background as the youngest of 10 children, to farmers who supported themselves on just 45 acres of humble soil in Michigan.

Early on, he had a fascination with peppermint, and began growing and experimenting with a small plot of it as a young man, with a mind to creating a value added product. He traveled Europe studying mint cultivation and products, and brought back several new varieties to the states, starting his collection of valuable plant capital for cultivation

Combining his work on mint variety cultivation and refining processes, he established the A.M. Todd company and began marketing its first product, the "crystal white" brand of peppermint oil. Quickly it became recognized as the best quality peppermint oil available and went on to find a huge global market.

Todd leveraged this business to acquire 2 large farms, on which he grew mints, spearmint, and other herbs for refining for oil, and eventually expanded to a global market. Even today, the A.M. Todd company is the world's leading producer of peppermint oils for candies and aromatics.

Todd used his fortune for public good, running for office as a socialist in the People's Party, advocating for busting monopolies, socializing utilities, and regulating big corporations like railroads. After losing re-election, Todd traveled Europe again, studying the more advanced public ownership of assets and tools to keep corporations and monopolies in check, and importing these ideas back to the states.

In addition to being a believer in the public commons, Todd was a collector of books, and donated the collection that began the Kalamazoo Public Library. His collections of rare books are now housed at several public libraries, where they enrich the public.

And it all began with the love for a plant.

The A.M. Todd Transformative Investment Stack:

—Perennial plant capital only available by root cutting, growing exponentially over time.
—Intellectual capital including plant selection, collection, and specialized processing knowledge and equipment for value added products.
—Other assets leveraged to buy land.
—A highly valuable business that was eventually sold by the family.

Natural/Intellectual Assets Model 2: Radiator Charlie and the Mortgage Lifter Tomato:

Radiator Charlie's Mortgage Lifter Tomato

They Call Those Big Tomatoes 'Mortgage Lifters'

M.C. Byles, better known as "Radiator Charlie" was famous for his depression era tomato, Radiator Charlie's Mortgage Lifter."

A natural businessman, Charlie was famous for his radiator shop, which he built at the foot of a steep West Virginia hill known for overheating radiators. "Location, location, location."

Byles came from a humble background and had no formal education on plant breeding, but simply collected together some plant capital, the 4 biggest tomatoes he could find, and bred them all together until he had plants that produced a consistently huge tomato. People would drive from nearby states to buy this special, highly desirable plant capital, which only Charlie could provide. The clever name for the Great Depression, probably helped, with many gardeners hoping to produce lots of tomatoes to can, and farmers hoping to pay off the mortgage with the trendy vegetable.

With his plant breeding success, Radiator Charlie was able to pay off the mortgage on his radiator shop in just a few years time, a story that no doubt helped him sell even more tomato plants.

The Radiator Charlie Investment Stack:

Intellectual capital: the developed variety "the Mortgage Lifter," clever marketing, understanding of his market, and of trends in plants and farming.

Natural Capital: the right tomato varieties to produce a huge, sweet tomato.

Other capital: the tools, seeds, and equipment to produce his tomato plants, and the real estate of his radiator shop.

Natural/Intellectual Assets Model 3: Madelyn Hill, the "Grand Dame of Herbs"

"Get rich farming" scams are old as the hills themselves, and the trend of Madelyn Hill's day was "profitable gladiola" farming.

Madelyn Hill's husband bought a Texas farm with dreams of gladiola riches in mind. But of course, once people are selling you "get rich farming" advice, it's already too late and there's no doubt already a market glut. And so it was with the Hills' gladiola business.

Luckily, Madelyn, with no college education on plants, had developed a love of herbs while visiting Europe, and began a hobby of collecting them and gardening with them. At that time, Americans preferred their food flavor free, and most Americans did not cook with herbs, let alone garden them. Madelyn moved into a wide open market with infinite growth potential and lots of transformative potential growing perennial plants that thrived on poor soil with no fertilizer.

Madelyn Hill became known for introducing Americans to many of the herbs we love today, and many of her own named varieties continue to be some of the best on the market. Some of her lesser known herbs are highly sought after among collectors. Madelyn was a regular contributor to The Herbalist journal and highly respected in the field.

Among some of her most successful (and profitable) introductions were: Mexican mint marigold, Hillltop Oregano, "arp" rosemary, Madelyn Hill Doublemint, and "Newe Ya'ar Sage." With her specialized combination of plant and intellectual capital, Madelyn was able to make Hilltop farm a success, afterall.

The Grand Dame of Herbs Stack:

—A locally rare and highly desirable plant collection
—Knowledge of herbs, cooking with herbs, and of the potential market for them in the US.
—Land.

More Models at the Intersection of Natural and Intellectual Capital

The Plant Lich Business Model:

Within fantasy literature, there is a notorious evil wizard who seeks to defy death itself, the Lich. Often surrounded by undead rotting things, the Lich is a disturbing foe.

But when we harness these powers for good, and use them to resurrect lost plants, everyone wins.

I know several stories of these plant liches, who have sought out and collected nearly lost plant capital and brought it back to life. That includes rare native species, long-lost native heirlooms, and family heirlooms of yesteryear. Some of my own plant investments are in this area, attempting to bring back perennial vegetable specimens that have been lost over a century of industrialism.

Not only are these excellent investments, this is truly transformative work. This is directly stewarding biodiversity and intellectual capital, and there are real opportunities here.

Designer Landscape Plant Collections:

I've said a few times in this book that nursery businesses are tough businesses with as high a rate of failure as farms. And the same is true of attempts to make landscaping regenerative. It's just incredibly difficult to do.

But, stack these two difficult businesses together, and you have a recipe for success I have seen thrive many times in the real world.

In fact, I've seen too many successes with this model to give just one example, though many readers may be familiar with "Dutch Invasion" celebrity landscaper Piet Oudolf. If not, you may want to look up his story online.

Oudolf, like many others, began with one of these two businesses then added the other to find real success. In Oudolf's case, he began with a nursery business focused on a specialized ornamental plant collection. But with his specialized knowledge of the plants, he came to believe he could do a better job at design than the landscapers buying his plants. This transitioned to a vertically integrated business where he could access specialty plant capital at a much higher margin than other landscapers, while still maintaining the natural capital of the plant collection.

This is very much like the Landscape Transformation Program business model, which combines these two business models into another successful business plan.

Permaculture, Natural Capital, and Land-Based Investments for Renters

While one could get the idea that you need to own land to invest in smart natural capital, nothing could be further from the truth.

In fact, we have created whole programs for renters to start transforming landscapes and building valuable plant capital investments. My opinion is that for someone who wants to do Permaculture or have a smallholding, it is never too early to start!

I'm certainly glad I had developed a high value plant collection, especially of guild matrix plants, WELL BEFORE I bought my first property. And I'm certainly glad I still had that collection as a renter before I bought my current project site. As I already said, this saved me thousands of dollars and allowed me to start cash flowing very early on my new site.

Meanwhile, other first-time home-owners, gardeners, and farmers will be stuck just planting their first annuals after buying land.

And you don't have to ever plan to own land to make this work, either. Plant capital can be a great asset even if you never plan to own land!

So let's look at some patterns that make plant investments work for renters.

Develop a "Permaculture Zoned" Planting System.

Permaculture Zones, as we've discussed already, are one of Permaculture's most powerful tools, and so it's no wonder it's highly valuable for renters! In fact, as it's the #1 tool for watering, weeding, pest control, fertility, it is also the #1 tool for renters to become food resilient, save money on groceries, and develop plant capital investments.

As you can see, the key idea here is that YOU don't need to own land. You just need to find it. Your own system, like mine has at many times, can include public land, waste places, public gardens, and collaborations with people who own land. All of these can provide you with space to start collecting high-value plant capital.

Indeed, wild spaces are the best places to seek high value rare plants like unusual sports* and color variations. Most of the most valuable plant varieties I know of were actually found in exactly this way.

Moreover, owning land and having to care for it may take time away from plant exploration, which is often the more valuable work! So here are some ideas to consider if you're a renter in love with plants, who wants to make investments that earn real "green."

Install Food Forests—Keep Some Plants

This is a non-destructive, actually regenerative version of the old business model of using other people's yards to farm.

While those models usually are terrible businesses, and rely on tons of tilling, fossil fuels, and plastics that make the world worse off, a food forest business model like the Landscape Transformation Program will make you wealthier and the world healthier.

In this case we create Transformative Landscapes, get some pay to do so, and also negotiate a "maintenance" plan where we get to keep the extra plants for our next job.

This is like a totally legal "ponzi scheme," where you take money from Peter to pay Paul, but in this case, you're just taking Peter's weeds and using them to start a garden for Paul. And you maintain control over the plant capital.

Transformative Guerrilla Gardening

There are countless waste places that can use a little investment of smart, durable, high-value native plants. And this also gives us an opportunity to grow our own plant capital for free. These thickets won't be the best places for valuable plants we could lose, but they're great for those weedy "guild matrix" plants we want to start developing, like sunchokes, elderberry, and selections of blackberries and black raspberries. These wild places give us an opportunity to grow the plant capital we can use to rapidly transform other properties as we have access. It's never too early to start these collections!

Food Mapping

I always keep a binder of my new communities of all the high-value food producing areas and what they're growing. I map out stands of sunchokes, juneberries, paw paws, apples, good quality crabs, grapes, etc. This allows me to generate some extra cash flow from tending the wilds. One year, I made over $3000 off of selling wild paw paws!

Foraging Tours

With good maps and knowledge of local edibles, you may also become the go-to expert for leading foraging tours and classes. Often, there's way more than enough to go around! In this way, plants on public land can become a cash flow opportunity, while you reconnect people to their own public infrastructure.

Patterns for Investing in Intellectual/Experiential Assets

You'll notice that many of the investment stacks in this book include a component of specialized knowledge or experience. This is because specialized knowledge and experience are one of the most valuable types of assets we can invest in! This is why people invest in university degrees, for example. I'd venture to say that most well-to-do people are well-to-do because of some intellectual asset they've invested in acquiring. That's important info, right there!

At the same time, much gets said about "intellectual assets" in these days when online classes are the next "get rich quick" scheme. And this is especially true in the circles of Permaculture, farming, and arts, where online gurus sell classes and books and things to teach you how to sell classes and books and things, and everyone's encouraging you to sell your intellectual capital.

The reality is these often don't work out well, and people invest a lot of time and effort into them and get no return.

So, there are a few patterns we need to keep in mind when looking to invest in intellectual assets.

Solve Big Problems, Have Big Fun

The first and most important key is that the best intellectual assets to invest in are those that solve big problems for people.

For example, if you could write a book that showed people how to eat whatever they like whenever they like and still lose a bunch of weight, a billion people will buy it! In fact, a lot of people have made a lot of money by just promising to tell people how to do that, without actually solving that problem!

Many of the most inspiring Permaculturists have made their mark by finding creative solutions to things like homelessness, indoor cooking without air pollution, how to have an easy productive garden without getting fines from the city, and so on. These are big problems that affect a lot of people. Solving them makes great intellectual asset investment!

If you can create a reliable business plan that artists can take and replicate and make a full adult living off of it while dedicating themselves to art full-time, then you'll have loads of people who will want to read your book, buy your business plan, or take your classes.

Many of the best plant capital investments will do the same. If you breed a banana that will grow and be productive in Michigan, congratulations, you'll be more than financially Independent for life.

Luckily, this tends to be the fun stuff! This is where we get the most creative. This is the stuff where we challenge ourselves, overcome our obstacles, and figure out how to thrive and live the lives of our dreams. If we can do that, others will want to hear about it.

Note, we've got to be realistic about what are big problems.

For example, generally speaking, a class about how to do conventional gardening or farming with plastics, poisons, and fossil fuels doesn't really solve a big problem. In fact, it probably just makes big problems worse. Investing in taking classes that teach you how to garden or farm by using plastics and chemicals are, in my humble opinion, not very good intellectual investments.

Figuring out how to garden and farm without plastics, poisons, and petroleum does solve an enormous, and difficult problem! (Which is why we have a Transformative Adventures Facebook group on that topic, and that will be the topic of the next Transformative Adventures book.)

The second important key is also the main reason why I've continuously discouraged mainstream approaches to farming in this book, in favor of things like Permaculture.

Since the Hoover Farm Bills in the 1930s that exacerbated the Great Depression, farming has been primarily a low-skilled job. That was one of the goals of the Hoover farm commission and later "green revolution" programs, to make farmers into low-skilled labor. Before that, farmers have primarily always been highly skilled market investors, and farmers thrived if they were knowledgeable and experienced. Today, that has been replaced by a system where the corporations and university extensions supply the highly skilled knowledge-based inputs, and farmers do the grunt work of simply implementing.

So, modern farming is a relatively low-skilled endeavor, while Permaculture systems are about returning the high skill trades to the land-based jobs.

I know plenty of fairly conventional low-skilled farmers who try to sell classes and get "interns" to come and do hours of weeding, digging, or tilling for them, then they're bitter and angry when nobody wants to do it! "Young people don't want to learn how to farm!" They complain.

Weeding, digging, and tilling are not valuable skills. You can learn all you need to know about weeding in an hour or less. And no smart farmer will pay somebody significantly more to do weeding work because they have 10 years weeding experience. Yet folks are literally trying to sell "educational programs" teaching people to weed and do low skilled yard work, and they're angry when nobody buys the class or sticks around for an "internship" once they've learned all they need to know.

2. **Intellectual Assets should be high-skilled and Economically Valuable.**

So, that's one of the most important factors. High skilled workers will be paid significantly more because they have good experience, that's one way you know it's high skilled. That's why it's valuable.

Some relatively low-skilled jobs:
Weeding
Mowing lawns
Watering
Assembling hoop houses
Digging
Planting
Removing pests
Going door-to-door or dropping off flyers
Making compost piles
Shoveling shit

Putting up electric fences

Some examples of high-skilled jobs for intellectual investments:
Design of programs, campaigns, farms, landscapes, polycultures, businesses, etc.
Arts, especially those in historic art traditions that are passed down through generations.
Artisan crafts, especially historic ones requiring special equipment.
High skilled old skills like hedge laying, dew ponds, masonry, etc.

3. Move up the Hierarchy of Development

A third key to look for is to follow the stages of development that most societies seem to follow in developing expertise.

In most societies, we develop people first as what we could call "operators." Operators use the information, tools, and systems to do work. For example, folks who operate machines on an assembly line, or in the modern farming system, folks who operate farms. So most people in a society will be operators at any time, keeping the society rolling. Generally speaking, even if you're an excellent operator, most people won't highly value your intellectual capital, because most people are on the same level themselves. They won't get a big return from just learning to be better operators.

Next we develop people as mechanics. They can 'fix" the machines or tools of a system. For example, they might fix the machines on an assembly line. On a farm, they would be the university staff, seed salesmen, and loan officers who trouble-shoot what a farmer should plant, how to fix weed and pest problems, and so on. These skills will definitely be more valuable to operators, so these types of professions generally are better valued.

As we move up from there, we become fabricators. These can make new parts in creative ways to solve new problems. Now we're starting to get highly valued forms of intellectual capital. These would include folks who can fabricate new parts to fix machines in factories, or the research academics who are teaching the university staff who work with farmers.

Finally, at the highest level of expertise, we have designers/developers, who can create entirely new machines, tools, and systems. These are our most valued experts, and these types of intellectual capital are the most valuable.

Here's the take-home:

One of the most common complaints I hear from clients who are farmers, or are trying to make livelihoods teaching "old skills" is that the market simply doesn't value their knowledge. Often they want to know "how do I get the market to value my knowledge? They look at it as a marketing problem. If only they could market their knowledge better, then they'd be rolling in the dough.

The market simply isn't likely to value operator-level knowledge.

I know a great many old-timer farmers of the back-to-the-land era, and they're quite bitter that people won't value their how-to knowledge. They'll watch new-comers with no gardening experience take a quick Permaculture course, then turn around and make $1,000,000 selling their own PDC (yes, there are now multiple examples of this) and it drives them completely mad.

But what they want to teach are things like "how to dig the garden with a rototiller" and "how to weed." But the fact is anybody can teach themselves these "skills" in about 1 hour.

But mechanic level knowledge and skill is more valuable. Mechanic level means you can rearrange the parts of someone's system to fix them. That might mean looking at somebody's farm business and why it's losing money, and fixing that so that it makes money. If you can do that and demonstrate it, you're going to find a market.

Jason's Skill Stack

I (Mike) also met Jason through my Permaculture work, as he was doing very similar community-based activism in the Pacific North West. He became interested in my "community supported permaculture" program and was one of the first people to try replicating it in his own region.

He loves teaching stuff. All kinds of stuff! This love of teaching and sharing things became the centerpiece of a personal skill stack with a strong basis in community organizing.

Jason grew up with a love of the outdoors and certainly never wanted an office job!

But like most of us, he followed the "standard old road map," trained in biomedical research and computer programming, which ended up paying the bills as he started his family.

Ultimately, the stresses of the modern rat race led to mental health challenges, and he realized that having time and freedom was more important than chasing money, and he set about finding a right livelihood that would work with his values.

Looking at his own passions and interests, Jason had a life-long love of science but also found himself drawn to older traditions and the paradoxically simpler yet more sophisticated work of caring for ecosystems as gardens, working with herbs, and foraging. This would end up being the intersection for his right livelihood, spending his time teaching "all kinds of stuff," with plenty of space for true abundance and family.

"With frugal living, we managed to get by with one or two of us working part time, so we had TIME. Time to learn how to work on cars, so we could afford to drive 20+ year old beasts. Time to save money by cooking food from scratch."

The next part of our journey is diversifying our income streams more.

Chapter 13: Team-up, community organizing beats marketing.

I once put together a pamphlet I called an "honest regenerative career guide." In it, every single career—whether they called themselves "farmers," "foresters," ocean farmers or whatever—was listed as "community organizer."

And that's the truth. Looking at all the paragons of the regenerative movement, they all make their living in good part because they're doing quality community organizing. We may call Joel Salatin a "farmer," but he's really made a good deal of his money off connecting people and ideas. Why is it that customers are willing to pay 4 times or higher than market rate for the produce of these "rock star" regenerative farmers? It's because of the people and the relationships, not because of the produce.

Community building is so important to land-based livelihoods that Bill Mollison made the first step in the formal Permaculture design process a community organizing phase. Before any of the land-based work begins, Bill Mollison had his students doing the work of building their community support networks. Until we've done that work, he said, we haven't started doing Permaculture yet!

And of course the same is true of any privileged livelihood. Why do people pay big $ for big name art? Because the artist has done the work to create a following with people. Once that work is done, the rest is smooth sailing.

Community beats marketing

Another controversial idea here, but if your goal is to create a community-focused, local scale business, then community organizing beats all the modern marketing best practice that folks are teaching in "marketing boot camps." Most of this stuff appears to have one real goal: "get famous, make bank."

But the truth is, not everyone can be famous. And more importantly, not everyone needs to be! Instead, most of the people who make the sorts of beautiful, abundant lives we're talking about in this book, are people you've never heard of. But they DO absolutely have vibrant community support systems for themselves in almost every case I know of. And this is why when you're looking for mentors, you shouldn't look for people who made their money by getting famous, because that kind of business advice works like a pyramid scheme.

Dunbar's support village

As we look to build a support system for ourselves, what we're really doing is trying to recreate the village sort of system of the past.

Researchers from the Robin Dunbar group theorized that we evolved in villages of about 200 people (with some debate on the exact size.) Within these villages, we met all of our needs and learned to thrive together. Even today, corporations and departments of this size are more successful and have happier employees with fewer conflicts.

People who wish to prioritize being happy then, will do well to make this Dunbar's Village the focus of their own businesses. For an idea of what that looks like, see the engagement matrix on page XXX.

So, how do we go about this work of building a vibrant community support structure?

 # Adventures for Building Village

A community organizing phase is a vital part of creating any kind of regenerative right livelihood. If you've never made a deliberate attempt to find your local village and connect with it, then you're selling yourself short.

Steps:

1. **Actually accomplish something**. This might sound obvious, but it's surprisingly common for people to start doing classes for things that they've never done themselves! The "demonstration principle" is king. Online, anything goes, but in your actual local community, if people can see what you've accomplished they'll be interested. If you grow fantastic produce, people will want to buy it. If you make great art, you're on the way to a livelihood.

2. **Identify your "fertile soil."** Now that you have something to sell, the next step is to start building a support village for it. So the next step is to identify "fertile soil" for our efforts. To do this, we'll use a tool from traditional community organizing.

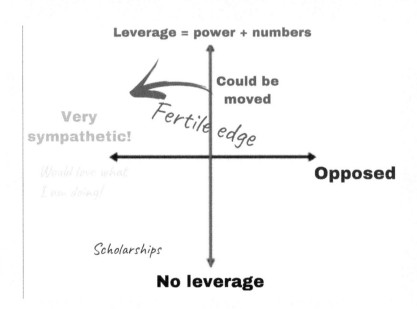

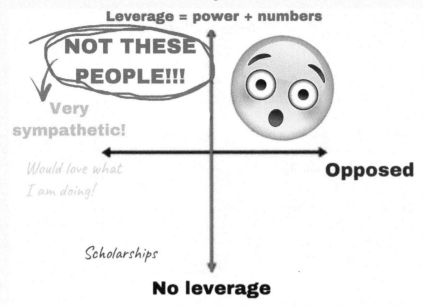

"Fertile soil" is about finding the people who will be the receptive audience for your efforts.

Again, this seems completely obvious, but this is exactly where 99% of people screw up completely. Let's take a look at this fertile soil chart to see where people usually go wrong.

On this chart, we've got people's resources going from bottom to top. So, people on the bottom have few resources to support us, and people on the top have plenty of resources.

So the first mistake people make is to focus their entire business or action on people on the bottom. Because these are the people we think are in need! The problem is, if we only work with them, the whole lot of us will have no resources to support each other. So we'll need to identify some groups of people with resources who can help support our actions.

But more importantly, the left/right axis shows how supportive and like-minded people are, or how opposed they are to what we're doing.

For example, if we want to make a right-livelihood off of helping Americans convert their lawns into gardens, we'll find some people are very supportive and other people are big fans of lawn, and they're going to be opposed to what we're doing.

Now here's the very counterintuitive thing people do wrong: they focus on people who agree with their message.

Wait, what? We're NOT supposed to focus on the people who strongly agree with our message? That's right, focusing on people who strongly agree with our message gets us absolutely nowhere, unless we're famous.

For example, most Permaculture oriented businesses fail because they focus entirely on the "permaculture movement." In fact, I know there are big name famous teachers who teach exactly to do this. Well, it works for them because they are famous! But their advise won't work for you unless you are also famous. What happens is we end up with 20 small holdings in the same geographic area, and they all are selling the same plants and the same exact services. Nobody's buying because they all already have most of those plants, and they're offering the same services. It ends up causing a "scarcity mindset" approach within the local community as they've all designed their businesses to maximize competition, and minimize any cooperation. Many times, people will try to get involved in their local permaculture communities and they'll find some resistance or hostility, and this is why! The whole movement is designed around scarcity and competition, of course nobody wants to have anything to do with each other!

Artists and musicians do the exact same thing. They'll think they're networking by doing a bunch of art-oriented events. But you know who doesn't have money to buy a bunch of art? Artists! And even if they love your art, they're just not going to be able to help you promote it, because they're busy promoting their own art.

So our "fertile soil" is NOT all the people who are already very interested in the sort of thing we're doing. If your a Permaculturist, that means we're NOT focusing on the local Permaculture movement and people who have PDCs.

Our fertile soil are the people who could be moved into the far left. They're POTENTIAL super fans. For example, for Permaculturists, that might be pagan groups, native plant groups, gardening groups, churches with "stewardship" mindset. If we're artists, then instead of going to art themed events, go to just about any other sort of creative event with people who care about culture: community theater, dance lessons, karaoke groups, any groups that could care about your art niche. THAT is our fertile soil.

This of course also has the benefit of "growing the pot," which allows us to cooperate rather than compete.

Now, we're mostly trying to identify groups here, because that's where we get the bang for the buck. If you have local pagan groups, churches, or clubs, you have the potential to turn on a big market all at once. But we could also identify people who are local "influencers" who come with a lot of social capital. Local celebrities and people with high social capital can go on the list. If we can turn them on to what we're doing, we'll have big allies! One such person can turn into a dozen or more contacts.

3. Start showing up. Once we have identifies the fertile soil, it's just a matter of showing up to events, participating, not being pushy, and just letting things happen organically.

Identify your groups, then set goals for how many events you want to attend per month, and get out there and do it. Remember, our goal is to grow a true vibrant community, not just do market our wares. But if you can become your villages "expert" on permaculture, or the source for really great produce, or whatever you're doing, then you'll be well on your way to a community supported livelihood.

For more information about community organizing as marketing, see the **Landscape Transformation Program Business Plan,** available through Transformative Adventures.

P32–Transformative Assets involving Team

Since TEAM puts the second "T" in THISTLE, this category of patterns could really include everything else in this book. But there are a few examples of investments and livelihoods that really put community organizing front and center.

For those of you who really thrive among people, and enjoy nothing more than networking and meeting new exciting humans and finding ways to help them, these are excellent livelihoods.

Permaculture "Green Groceries"

Within the Permaculture movement, this is one of our best examples of a business built on community organizing.

As we work to solve the problems of relocalzing food and building local economies, we often run into a number of major barriers. And among the largest barriers is there are few well established brick and mortar stores to really co-promote and sell locally grown produce and products.

And while the food Coop movement may provide this service in some markets, Coops (which are owned by the shoppers, rather than workers or growers) are beholden first to the people buying their groceries, rather than to doing the work of supporting local producers.

Within the Permaculture movement, Green Grocers have become an alternative. They look and feel in many ways like food coops, but since they are owned by local producers (or in some cases, investors aligned with local producers) they are a little more unique, more local, more rare, more experimental, and more focused on raising up local economies. At the best, these can work hand in hand with coops, while providing some services and products that won't be available at a coop.

Such businesses can become important "3rd spaces' for community members, operating as coffee shops, book stores, meeting places, and shopping places.

And if structured well, they can become the backbone investment for a number of aligned transformative small businesses.

The Landscape Transformation Program

While we've used the Landscape Transformation Program as a model in a few places in this book, it is at this intersection of social capital that we'll really dig into the service stack.

Because ultimately, this business is all about building strong local communities.

The Landscape Transformation Program Service Stack:

Individual Permaculture Consultation and Design Services
A plant and seed CSA program with the plants most necessary to transform the landscape
A class that provides monthly natural gardening skills, foraging info, and walks clients through a group Permaculture consultation process one step at a time.
A retainer on installation work.
Samples and recipes for making use of forest garden plants.
A community of peers engaged in the same goal.

The Permaculture Journeyman/woman Investment Plan

"Have Permaculture, will travel!"

Permaculture founder Bill Mollison was the first example of a true "global gardener," a Permaculture journeyman who built wealth based on smart investments over time.

Again, it's extremely important to make the distinction that Bill Mollison was not just traveling around Woofing or taking odd jobs. He was developing highly valuable intellectual and social capital (and also natural capital!) as he traveled.

But he was only the first. Many "global gardeners" have followed his path, building important clients, mail lists, networks, and skills as they traveled.

A Permaculture journeyman will have a variety of skills to develop and then sell while creating and facilitating workshops wherever needed.

I've seen these services include dew ponds, hedgerows, hedgelaying, natural swimming pools, herb spirals, Russian ovens, natural building, home retrofits, bicycle repair, beautiful visible mending workshops... the possibilities are nearly endless for someone willing to put in the time to develop an old artisan skill.

This specialized intellectual capital can then translate into books, online classes, speaking tours, or more localized brick and mortar businesses for some.

The Original Permaculture Business Stack

Looking at some of the earliest local Permaculture communities, early adopters of Permaculture often created a wake of local opportunity as they broke new ground. As the network establishes, it becomes apparent that there are many necessary pieces to put together to recreate a local economy. So many of the early local movements had a similar set of businesses which developed in cooperation to meet these goals.

Early on, Bill Mollison had people coming to him saying "I want a job! I want to help, please hire me!" And he would answer, that's not the business I'm in. I don't hire people. But I can teach you how to start your own business so that you can support yourself in doing Permaculture work with me.

To bring energy into the movement, there was an opportunity to create a "tour guide" and organization for local, regenerative tours. This created a business and an important mail list and network as assets.

The movement needed a way to buy and facilitate the transfer of land, so an early Permaculture livelihood is often the transformative Real Estate specialist. Many early Permaculture fortunes were built off connecting would-be regenerators with land to regenerate.

As materials develop, Permaculture movements often start presses to help get the words out. This creates opportunities for designers, editors, copywriters, and organizers.

Web design is of course necessary to all of this, and someone who specializes in an ecologically inspired design often does well in these communities.

And of course, marketers are necessary to make all of this thrive, too.

Ultimately, the aim may be to create a local "regenerative investment corporation" to facilitate co-investing together in transforming the community. Such corporations could set up maker spaces, help fund important regenerative projects, buy and sell or protect real estate, transform houses (the regenerative flip is an excellent business model) publish and distribute books.... And all of this can be done in a way that is profitable.

And it takes someone with a vision and the ability to do that community organizing work to make it all happen. For the person who takes on the challenge, the rewards are often forthcoming.

Political Asset Investments

Like farming, art, music, and all the other worthwhile endeavors in this book, political activism is often a very competitive and difficult career choice.

At least it is if you want to do something positive in the world.

If you're willing to shill for corporations, congratulations, there are millions to be made in doing that work.

But no, doing good in this world often goes unrewarded.

And yet, I have seen smart organizers find a niche, build durable power long-term, and most importantly, invest in developing the social capital to actually fund their activism well.

For the political investor, it is names and social/political capital that are the golden currency. It takes a plan to establish that network of support long term, but once established, this can be a great way to get a paycheck doing the work you want to do in the world.

My advice here is: "profit first." Or at least, invest in financial soundness first. Have a plan on paper for making the activism stable and secure. Use the market stacking tools to make sure you're getting a broad base of support.

Have a "major donor" program to target a handful of big investors who really believe in your message. But don't leave out all the others who would give you a small amount of money! So membership drives are also necessary.

Actually START organizing with this in mind, if you really want to be able to make it sustainable.

But there are many models of people who have done this work well, and turned their passion into doing good into a full-time livelihood.

Top 10 Worst Untraditional Investments

1. **Online classes** (without doing the necessary community organizing work.) The standard advice is just take whatever you're passionate about and turn it into an online class. "You should be able to make at least $3000/month off of each class" one famous author says. I could publish a whole book of laugh/cry emojis about that. I've seen literally hundreds of people fail at that over the 10 years since that became "the" business advice of the day. If you've done your community organizing work AND created a whole nuanced business off of real investments, then—and only then—I believe these classes can actually be good investments. But you need an audience, expertise, and probably other real world products, first.

2. **Social media influencer "careers."** Very, very few will ever make actual money. And it's nearly impossible to monetize these in regenerative ways. Most of the people who do monetize their influencer status do so through selling consumer crap. Yet, these ambitions require a huge time input and major sacrifices to your quality of life. Again, once you've done the rest of your work, social media can be an important modern marketing tool. If you have a functioning business, then being on social media can help you sell that better than any conventional advertising could.

3. **Any kind of "multi-level marketing"** or affiliate marketing program. These exist for one reason: to steal the time and money of people who start these businesses. That's it. Don't be one of them.

4. **Drop shipping businesses**. Just be another in the long chain of middle men selling stupid consumer crap to fill up the land fills and GET RICH. No, it doesn't work and it won't work for you. It's just

another game you can procrastinate on instead of doing things to build real long-term wealth.

5. **NFTs**. Just an investing fad that's already had its time in the sun. The likelihood that you'll get rich selling them is almost 0.

6. **Cryptocurrency mining.** This is a way to eat up real world resources while losing fake money. These can generate plenty of real cash, but in most cases the operating costs are exorbitant. You'll probably just lose money while making the planet worse off.

7. **Get rich quick scams**. Most of these are just praying on people who are economically desperate. Almost none of them work. Just do the real work of developing smart income streams and investments over time. It's not glamorous, but it works.

8. **Profitable farming schemes**, including hydro, microgreens, and growing weed. Yes, these businesses can be very profitable in a few special cases. I personally know people who became stupidly wealthy off of them. But these were special cases that involved smart investing based on "buying low, selling high." If you don't know what that means then you're not going to make a killing off the devil's lettuce.

9. **Personal "sustainability consultant" or coaching jobs**. I've been watching really brilliant people fail at this for 20 years. Now that there's even more people in the market trying to do this work, why do you think you'll succeed while all the others have failed. If you don't have an answer to that, I wouldn't try it.

10. **Starting a non-profit**. People are somehow still convinced that if they just start a non-profit organization, they'll live fat off of grant money. It rarely works that way. Unless you've done the other things in this book to build up social and political capital and have good mail lists and great donor game, you'll likely not make loads of money off a non-profit. If you've done all those things well, then a non-profit may be the thing that allows you to convert your capital into the lifestyle you want.

Chapter 14: Luck, designing our Financial Lives for Luck

And so now we have a plan to start saving and building our transformation funds, we've got capitalism survival strategies in place, and we've got ideas for how to invest our transformation funds to create the kinds of lives and world we want to see.

There's just one more thing we need to make it all work.

So ask yourself, are you feeling lucky?

Because all the people I know who have been successful in these privileged areas and created these really beautiful abundant creative lives all have that in common: They've all been very lucky.

You better believe that includes all the famous "paragons" of these fields, whether it's art, music, activism, permaculture, farming or so on.

Lucky for us, we can actually design to get lucky.

That's right, while many of us may see "luck" as some sort of superstitious woo fairy dust concept, there's actually a whole science devoted to quantifying luck, and luck, believe it or not, actually does appear to exist. And, we can learn from the lucky people who are loaded with the stuff.

For example, research has found that people who believe they are lucky tend to actually experience being lucky and having better results with "luck" related outcomes. Think lucky, be lucky.

Of course, that means on one level that if you see yourself as lucky, you'll likely interpret your experiences as the result of good luck. For example, someone could get in a car accident. If they see themselves as lucky, they'll be certain they got lucky by surviving. But if they feel unlucky, they'll instead focus on the fact that they had something bad happen to them in the first place.

But this goes beyond just their interpretation. First, the person who feels they were lucky will have an overall better experience of the situation, and deal with it with more resilience. They'll focus in with gratitude on how lucky they were to survive.

Meanwhile, the unlucky bastard will experience the accident and then also experience the emotional distress of focusing more on the bad event that happened to them. In addition to the accident, they'll feel somehow singled out by the universe for this heap of suffering.

In a real way, the unlucky bloke actually did have a worse accident than the lucky one!

But it goes further than that. People who think they are lucky actually do experience more lucky outcomes.

For one, people who can acknowledge their luck are seen as more attractive to others, are more likable, and more likely to get hired or included in opportunities. People who don't believe in luck tend to think all the good things that have happened to them are because they absolutely deserve it for their superior qualities, while anyone who has less, it is because of their personal failings, not because of luck.

This is not an attitude that is endearing to anyone. Researchers have found this actually contributes to people's behavior towards other people, it makes them less giving, less generous, and less understanding, and in turn, that contributes to how other people see these ungenerous people.

But it even goes further than that.

Those who believe they are lucky go into situations with their minds open to opportunity and "luck." They actually expect to get lucky, so they look for opportunities. In one now-famous experiment, the "Newspaper Experiment," Dr. Richard Wiseman tested this hypothesis. He asked subjects whether they were lucky or not, then gave them a newspaper and told them to count how many pictures were in it. When they were done, they would be paid $100. Early into the task, Wiseman placed two "ads," one that said "stop counting. There are 42 pictures in this newspaper." The second said, "tell the experimenter you've seen this ad and collect your $100 now."

As it turned out, those who considered themselves lucky tended to see one of these two ads, while the unlucky folks didn't and continued to slog through the task. The lucky people had a happier, more relaxed outlook and were looking for opportunities. The unlucky people approached the task with a sense of stress, and "put their heads down" to get through the task. Doing so, they completely closed themselves off to the opportunities that might arise along the path.

Add that up over a life time, and the lucky people have had countless more lucky opportunities to take, whereas the unlucky stayed locked into their lane, following where the path led instead of taking those profitable detours.

And that also has an impact on whether you actually risk those detours when they come up. Those who expect to be lucky are more likely to take the risks necessary to actually get lucky. "You can't win if you don't play," as the saying goes. Those who feel they are unlucky, even when they see the opportunities, may end up unwilling to take the risk, suspecting that it just wouldn't work out for them anyway. They put their head back down and keep slogging through the tasks of life.

And this brings us to design. By designing to get lucky, we can both increase our odds directly, and increase our experience that we are going to get lucky. It becomes a whole lucky positive feedback loop. We can design that self-fulfilling prophecy into our lives.

Which is why a whole suite of habits and attitudes go along with being lucky, and we can take those "patterns" and replicate them in our own lives.

And so we can make that the "L" in our THISTLE strategy: designing to get Lucky. As we design our lives for luck, here are some of the tricks in the luck person's quiver.

1. Do work that makes you feel happy and lucky. Do work where you'll say to yourself everyday, "gosh I'm lucky." Living at Lillie House, looking around the beautiful gardens, having cool and interesting people visit me every day, I said this to myself almost every day. Create a life that makes you feel lucky to be alive, and you'll be more likely to get lucky.

2. Don't worry, be happy. Build this habit. When you do tasks, slow down, be positive, take time, and be open to opportunities. If you're feeling rushed or like you can't stop, then you're out of the lucky zone. In the garden that means you might miss a pest or disease issue early on when it would be easy to get it under control!

3. Don't overfill life. If you're too busy to take breaks or to see or follow opportunities as they arise, then you'll be out of luck. A life with the space to go off the beaten path is one that will be lucky.

4. Develop "stacked" streams of cash flow. Again, stacking functions is one of nature's tricks for developing resiliency and making it through rough turns. Many of the people we see as being "lucky" actually just avoided failure! The truth is that most businesses simply fail before they make it. On a long enough trajectory, most of our businesses will find a big enough audience, evolve to meet their needs well, and end up being successful. Except for all the businesses that fail before they get there! So, being one of the lucky ones is often just a matter of being resilient enough to avoid failure long enough to make it.

5. Reduce your terminal risks. Again, being lucky is often just avoiding failure. This means keeping things like overhead and debt low. Having high overhead in businesses and in life is setting ourselves up for a terminal failure. If costs are low and we have no debts, we can tread water long enough to find land.

6. Avoid high opportunity costs. This is related to reducing your risk, this is a matter of opening as many opportunity doors as possible. That includes avoiding things like high debt, jobs like "farming" that keep us working long hours at home without the flexibility to take opportunities that come along. Many of our "profitable farming" gurus actually teach an anti-luck mindset, telling us we just need to "work harder," "be more committed," "put your nose to the grindstone" and work longer hours! This is the recipe for a life of bad luck. Unless you're the one getting rich selling this advice. Then you're pretty lucky people haven't wised up to the bad advice yet!

7. Consciously have a strategy to invest in resilience. What are some of the biggest risks to your business or financial well-being? What are some active steps you can take to mitigate those risks? If you don't have a strategy to build resilience, you're leaving yourself open to failure. If you do, that may help you feel lucky over time, potentially creating that self-fulfilling prophecy feedback loop.

8. Once you have that stable secure base established with low-risk bets, then use that secure place to invest in bets with a higher potential return. This is basically the standard investing advice of "diversify your portfolio with low risk and high risk bets." If you don't play, you can't win. And everyone in this book who has succeeded beautifully has placed big bets and won. That means actually assessing what the potential return of some of our opportunities are. Don't just bet blind, know your odds and the potential ROI. Some people take a big gamble on a business, only to realize the best case scenario is still just a minimum wage income. Ahem, farming.

So, now that we have some guidelines, how can we apply these to our life investment strategies?

As we said, we want to develop a stacked set of bets that includes a "solid base" of low-risk, but low-moderate reward bets to pay the bills and give us anti-fragility. That may include whatever our "hammock income" jobs are: a part time farm or art business, a landscape transformation program, or commercial kitchen business, for example.

We need to have that. If you don't know what yours are, you should try to figure that out!

Next we may have some moderate risk/reward bets in our stack, too. This is why real estate pairs so often with transformative investments, because it will have a very reliable ROI over time, giving us a hedge that we'll be alright in our later years and eventually get to a life of comfort, even if it takes us longer than we thought.

But that's not enough. I also strongly recommend that you develop some high-risk/high reward bets as well.

Again, everyone in this book, all the famous "gurus" out there in your field, they have all, ALL, 100% placed some high risk bets and won. Period. They probably don't even know it, but that is why YOU know their names.

And, it turns out, that this is actually the FUN stuff! This is where we get to invest in our dreams, be outrageously creative, do new and exciting things, and solve big problems. This means creating new, exciting business models, coming up with new ideas, creating cutting edge solutions, breeding great new plant capital, inventing new value added products, and creating a brand that really expresses who you are and your values, and that speaks to other people.

This is why we're working on building financial security in the first place: so that we can invest in creating beautiful, unique, abundant lives doing fun and exciting things we love.

Then it's just a matter of avoiding failing until you find a high-risk/high-reward bet that works out for us.

Where do your investments fall?

Low risk-low reward	Moderate risk/reward	High risk-high reward
Hammock income	Land	New business models
Provides security cash flow	Real estate	Cutting edge solutions
Market garden	Urban business model	New plant capital
Herbalism business	Intellectual assets Ebooks, etc.	Commercial products
Catering business		

Adventure 10: Lucky Investment Design

So how do we add this all up for a roadmap to the life we want? First, let's keep in mind that we need a transition strategy and to keep one foot in the old economy and one in the new, and that we need both cash flow streams and long-term investments.

So this is the time when we start choosing some investments and developing them. In my opinion, this is the actual process of doing Permaculture, choosing how we'll invest and then doing it. This is also the real key to meeting all of our transformation goals for ourselves and the planet.

We'll need to choose investments that work with our natural skills, abilities, and forms of capital. We'll ideally need investments that both represent "livingry," that will make the world a better place, and that are relatively passive. We'll need to choose things that can be stacked with our interests and with our local markets. Then we'll need to develop these into complex, flexible market and product stacks.

Then we'll need to do it, commit, follow through and see how our investments work out. And then we'll need to pick another that stacks well, and perhaps another, until we're meeting our financial goals.

And so we'll need to know:

1. What are your old economy cash streams (if necessary?) Is this a matter of improving your job, or finding a new one? Will you become the "permaculture" person at your organization and work for a better company from within?
2. What are your old economy investments (if necessary?) Do you have a 401k? Do you have stocks where you can get involved in shareholder activism? Are there "high risk" investments you want to make in supporting new companies that truly align with your vision for a better world?
3. What new economy cash streams are you going to work on building? Everyone needs these.
4. For each of these, how will you stack income streams, markets, and skills?

5. What are your stable, low-risk new economy investments? Again, my opinion is that everyone needs these today.
6. Do you have moderate risk/reward bets like real estate, durable assets, art, etc.? We can't be certain, but how much will they likely appreciate over time? For example, I know my share in my current project property is likely to appreciate to over $200k over coming decades. With luck, it could do much better than that.
7. What are your big bets? I suppose you don't need these, but, when it comes down to it, this is where the fun's at. What would you do with your life and your time if money were no concern? What big problem would you choose to tackle if you had the means to take real action on it?

Permaculture financial structure design

Old economy cash streams

Career development
Entryism?
Permaculture?

Old economy cash investments

Regenerative stocks?
401k?

New economy cash streams

Stackable streams, audiences, skills...

New economy investments

Low risk

Moderate risk

Big bets!

Adventure 11: The Overall Lucky Life Design

And here as we near the end of this book, we have the opportunity to put together everything we've learned, to make a new, more resilient, beautiful, and lucky path to becoming FREE.

Remember that when we began this adventure, most of us had life designs that looked like a linear system: money in one end from our jobs, money out the other to pay for our expenses. It's a system that keeps us firmly trapped in our need to earn to pay the bills.

But now, we've found that we are actually much richer than we thought we were. We can begin by reviewing our multiple forms of capital and resources, including our financial capital, savings, and total wealth.

We can add those to the worksheet on the left side.

Next, we can look at our expenses, and list those on the right. We can look for opportunities to replace distant corporate providers with cool ones in our communities, so we're "leaking wealth" and building a naturally wealthier local environment for ourselves. We can find ways to invest in things like owning homes and getting food from gardens, which meet our needs while returning money to us, rather than costing us. We can find ways to turn as many of our expenses into savings as we can, and reduce our other expenses.

Finally, we can list our investments, our accumulated wealth, in the middle.

Now this is a life design that looks much more resilient, much more like a natural ecosystem, one which will grow in abundance and wealth over time. Now, we have a "regenerative" life design, which will continue to get better and better each year, rather than leaving us worse off.

And hopefully, you also have a roadmap for where you need to go. You know the pieces you have, and what you need to work on. Hopefully, you have an idea of which you wish to prioritize as you build the life you most want to see.

And there we have it. Like all the good and beautiful things we wish to see and create in this world, it won't happen overnight like magic. But with a roadmap, and a plan, we can get where we need to go, one step at a time.

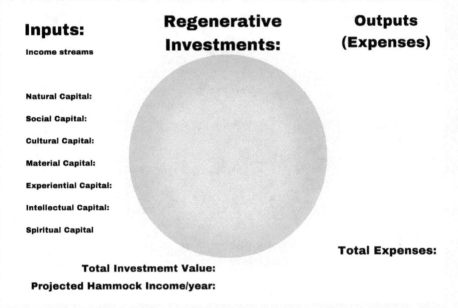

Inputs:

Income streams

Natural Capital:

Social Capital:

Cultural Capital:

Material Capital:

Experiential Capital:

Intellectual Capital:

Spiritual Capital

Regenerative Investments:

Outputs (Expenses)

Total Expenses:

Total Investmemt Value:

Projected Hammock Income/year:

The Home Economy Redesigned

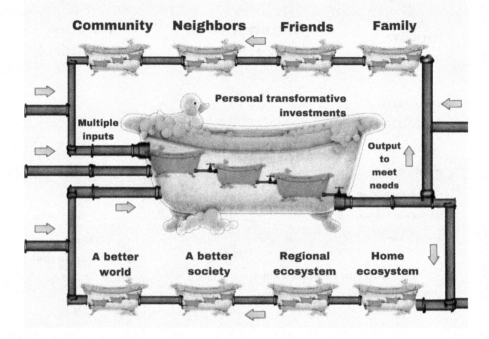

Chapter 15: Enough

And so we reach the final letter of THISTLE, and since it's the last, it must be enough.

And we've saved the best, and most life-enriching thing of all for last.

Because knowing what is enough, is the final powerful magic that wards off the wendigo spirit, keeps us safe from feelings of scarcity, and allows us to relax into contented life.

But it's far more than that.

Knowing what is enough for you, and setting a limit accordingly, is our greatest form of wealth.

Think of this: Jeff Bezos in 2022 is worth $132,000,000,000.00. If you decide you would be as happy as Jeff Bezos with $500,000 in wealth, congratulations, you just got the happiness equivalent of $131,000,500,000.00 for free. That's a hundred billion dollars you don't have to work for! And the world will be better off for you not hoarding that wealth.

We hope the patterns and adventures in this book to this point have helped you to create a vision for your financial life, and get a good idea of how much wealth you need to make those dreams a reality.

If you get nothing else out of this book, we hope that you now have a good idea of what "enough" is for you, because knowing this is the true key to being FREE.

Scale

If we are successful in our life designs, and we create lives and businesses that grow wealthier and more Financially Resilient over time, at some point we may face the question of "scaling up."

"Scale" is a major buzzword in business circles, which means a business must be able to grow indefinitely whether that increases happiness or value for anyone. Businesses, they say, must be able to scale!

In fact, the impulse to scale is so strong that there are a great many critics in Permaculture and regenerative agriculture circles, as well as art and activism circles, who vehemently insist that if a model can't "scale," there's no point to it. Such critics immediately reject all the amazing livelihood models we've discussed in this book, like the people who've found ways to make beautiful, abundant lives by playing with plants, healing the planet, and making art, just because they can't "scale" into stressed-out, overly busy lifestyles of destruction and exploitation.

That includes "greentrepreneurs" who think they need to "scale" their online green living or Permaculture courses to have 1,000; 10,000; 1,000,000 students. What's the point of teaching "green living" if we're modeling destructive businesses?

So it's important to remember that in almost all cases, "scale" is by definition accomplished by exploiting labor and resources, and externalizing costs like waste and pollution.

But it's equally important to remember that "scaling" is usually terrible life design.

Many of us have seen small, successful family restaurants and cafes, run as happy communities "scale" in to stressful businesses with high debt and unhappy exploited labor. Not only are the employees unhappy, but almost always the owners are, too.

They end up trapped by a similar linear logic as we have for our personal finances, where we look to solve all our problems by earning more income. With the business, "growth" becomes the answer to all our problems. Not making any money? Then solution is to earn LESS now, in order to invest more money into "growth," so that we can someday finally turn a profit! Only that day never comes, as we continue to endlessly chase growth.

Similarly, I've consulted on dozens of farms that went from happy part-time vegetable gardens that grew ample food for a family, with some left-over for a small, niche CSA. As we've discussed in this book, such businesses can operate happily on a part-time schedule. These people pretty much always got into veg farming to have healthier food, better connection to nature, better community, and to heal the planet. Then they decide to scale. In 20-something ears I have literally never seen this be a good idea. The farmers go from spending their time working land regeneratively and playing with plants to wrestling with irrigation hoses and plastic tarps that are polluting soil and contaminating food, and arguing with unhappy exploited labor. Instead of healing nature, they end up in a constant war with it. Instead of community connection, they're surrounded by unhappy workers. In all cases their hourly wages go down, this is a mathematical certainty. "Scaling" yielded exactly the opposite of what we'd wanted in the first place.

As Laura Oldanie has said, "E is the last letter of THISTLE, but it's also the last letter of SCALE," a reminder to know when we have "enough. The final consideration in scale is whether or not growth will truly help us meet our FREE goals.

Enough for Everyone

When we scale this wisdom of "enough" up to the whole world, it becomes a recipe for true sustainability. On a finite planet where all species must share in finite calories and resources, our ability to set a limit on what is "enough" is the single action that ensures there will be enough for everyone. Setting a limit on ourselves is an investment in having abundant ecosystems, happy communities, and a world of vibrant diversity. "Enough" buys us a community of peers instead of hierarchy of envious, bitter neighbors outside our walls. "Enough" buys us time for family, friends, and fulfilling hobbies. "Enough" buys us a closer relationship with the people we love. "Enough" buys us real respect, instead of false status. And "enough" can buy us true abundance, instead of a green paper symbol of it.

P33–Patterns for Our Later Years

What to do if and when you actually want to "retire?" Having enough means knowing we have a plan that will last us through the end of the journey.

And this wouldn't be much of a financial book if we didn't discuss the details of the end game: what we will do as we approach our later years. For many people, the two largest goals for their financial planning are to take care of their families, and to make sure that they have taken responsibility for themselves when they make the choice to stop working.

Here again, this book is provides a very different road map than the ones given in conventional "retirement" books. Those books seem to focus almost exclusively on using financial capital to buy and consume our own elder years. I find there's a prevailing sense—among virtually everyone—that this system is deeply, deeply flawed.

For those living in traditional societies with in-tact cultures, there are long-evolved systems for insuring that our later years are happy, secure and meaningful. Traditionally, eldership and wisdom were the capital of our layer years, and the young care for their elders and learn from them. The support system for elders was in family, friends, and community connection. In a society where these connections have been intentionally broken down for corporate profit, we can only count on being cared for if we have enough financial capital to make our care "worth it." If we want that sort of dignity and care that we'd get in a traditional society, then we'll need to create it for ourselves, using holistic forms of capital, rather than just money.

Of course, this entire book is about exactly these topics, and someone who is truly "FREE" will have the resources to not have to worry about working for a living, including in their "sunset years." And that includes forms of financial capital. But this raises a number of questions, such as how do I access the money I've stored in transformative assets? How do I transition my projects to other people? How do I do these in ways that don't undo all the good work I've accomplished?

Unfortunately, many transformative enterprises, projects, and livelihoods end up being reversed when their stewards retire. Regenerative farms get turned into subdivisions or bulldozed and planted with corn. Sustainable clothing businesses get bought and converted to sweatshop companies. Businesses that have stewarded endangered skills of the past, simply fade away, and the skills end up lost locally. So having an endgame in our transformation plan, one that successfully passes off our work, is an essential part of any transformative plan.

And, having a plan that allows us to feel secure, and to know that we won't become a burden on anyone is one of our most important elements in deciding what is "enough." For many of us, it is only then—once we have this plan—that we can truly feel we have taken care of all that is our responsibility.

According to the polls, millennials these days don't believe they will ever get to retire, and Gen Xers aren't far off from this. And yet, the reality is that as we approach our later years, we may want to relax into greater freedom, take less responsibility, empower younger people to take over for us, and essentially finally "retire." And of course, the reality is that some of us may be forced by life circumstances to take that step sooner than we would otherwise like.

And a major reason why we may want to be financially FREE is so that we do not become a burden on others when that time comes. And so that we have more control over our circumstances when it does.

And so we need a set of patterns for actual retirement, a permaculture design for retirement, if you like.

This means we'll need patterns to help us know how and when to draw down our various forms of savings, how to transition our work and our businesses to the next generation, how to cultivate relationships and get our needs met outside of the formal economy, and how to take our "transformative assets" and liquidate them to meet our expenses, without undoing all the good transformative work we've done. We hope these patterns will help.

Growing Eldership

For those of us who will have to create our own systems of eldership, we think that following the pattens in this book will help. But it's worth putting some mindful thought into what we'd like that to look like and how we'd like to get there.

In our society, the wisdom of age is an unused resource, and as we've said throughout this book "an unused resource can become pollution." In this case, that pollution manifests as our wisest community members feeling disconnected, lacking purpose, lacking respect, segregated off to ghettos with others their age. Meanwhile children are left lacking care, young families lacking help, young adults are left lacking mentors, and society in general appears lacking is wisdom and experience.

One cause of this break-down in connection is that our society makes us all "unskilled labor" in our own lives. Recall that in the old world, farmers have always been highly skilled investors, in charge of their own lives. But the modern world has taken away their skill and agency, giving it instead to "experts" in university extensions, farm credit agencies, and Ag corporations, leaving farmers as unskilled (and poorly paid) laborers on their own land. As we've pointed out before, much of economy has followed this model, so that even highly skilled laborers have their most valuable skills (what we called "mechanic" and "developer" skills) taken away, and institutionalized in the corporations. When the corporate banker or analysts retires, the young do not line up to train with them and learn their wisdom, because they get their training from the corporation.

So for many of us, we could think about "what kind of skills will young people really want to learn from me? As I become an elder, how can I really benefit the young? The patterns on different levels of knowledge on page XXX may help.

But keep in mind, that it's not just our informational capital that can help the young. All of our accumulated holistic wealth can help benefit future generations, including our social, political, and spiritual capital.

Scenarios for Happy Later Years

Prepared with a plan for cashing out your assets, the next step is to envision what you want your later years to look like.

My personal philosophy is that "retirement" as its usually thought of seems overrated, and people who have created beautiful FREE lifestyles with low costs of living will not feel like they have to spend $15k a year on cruises. They will have a more beautiful life around them then they could get on a buffet at sea.

But part of knowing what is "enough" for you is to be thorough in determining how much you personally want to be spending in your later years, not what we tell you to spend.

With a thorough vision for your later years, one of the biggest factors in our lifestyles will be housing. For many, this most basic need and how to meet it ends up as one of the major features: will you live with your children, will you live in an assisted living facility, will you find ways to age in place in your home, will you downsize?

To help you envision some options, we've put together a set of patterns we've seen successful retirees move into.

Aging in Place

Since we've already mentioned a few "downsizing" patterns above, where folks move into situations that are better for the later years, the alternative is staying in the home and community you've been living in.

For a lot of us, this will be a great option, where we keep our connection to homes, and perhaps can help them transition to the next generation.

But this may require some further thought and effort to make it work well.

Usually, aging in place is recommended for seniors who are healthy, financially resilient, have strong support networks, are connected to their communities, have their homes paid off, and adapted to require minimal maintenance and good accessibility.

So for those of us who would like to age in place, that is a good list of things to start developing.

For example, someone who has developed a modest sized, accessible home in a walkable city or town, with a robust support network, and nearby family and friends will realistically be able to age in place longer than someone living in a rural place with little support nearby.

Depending on how well we've prepared in those ways, aging in place can become increasingly difficult as health issues and financial strain increase, so for many of us a plan B for transition is also a good idea.

If you think you are in the last home you ever want to live in, then it's time to start planning for aging in place.

A basic plan to prepare for aging in place would check off these items:.
___Are you financially prepared to age in place?
___Is your home accessible if you face reduced mobility?
___Are your bathroom, kitchen, laundry room, safe?
___Do you have a list of home projects that will need to be done as you age in place as well as a timeline and the financial resources to get them done?
___What are your potential health challenges that could stand in the way of your independence? Do you have a plan for dealing with them should they become an issue?
___Do you know what services for seniors your health insurance will pay for?
___Do you know how you will get around if you can no longer drive?
___Do you know the available services for seniors in your area? Do you have an accessible list? There should be services in your area to help you figure this out.
___Do you have a list of home tasks that you may need help with as you age?
___Do you want to make arrangements for a live-in caretaker?
___Have you talked with your family and friends about helping out?
___Do you have a plan B?

Aging in Permaculture Places

For many permaculturists, land regenerators, farmers, and small-holders, who have developed land-based livelihoods, aging in place may require some special considerations.

As we said above, small, easily maintained homes in more urban areas near to friends, family, and help are the most realistic for aging in place. And so, those developing single-family homes in rural areas will realistically be more likely to have to transition as they get older.

This is something that should be considered carefully when making the decision between rural and urban areas.

As we've said before, the Permaculturist authors of this book have followed the path of Permaculture leaders like Toby Hemenway and David Holmgren in choosing to develop urban and peri urban sites, and aging was one major reason.

This may also be a reason why those committed to the rural life may seek to develop communities, eco villages, community farms, and other ways to develop support structures that will allow them to age in place.

Cultivating Intergenerational Community

Among the most enviable models I have seen for the golden age, are those who have cultivated beautiful rich multigenerational communities for themselves. So far, I've been lucky to say I've had a lot of this for myself, with many young people around with their energy, optimism, and ideas, and elders to bring their wisdom and experience. When we can grow connections between these two forces, we get the best possible advice and direction, and the best sort of communities, in my opinion. For me, this is what makes a complete social organism, and without this, we're cutting ourselves off from some of the best of what life has to offer.

Of course, this is exactly what our Western society is famous for: children left to be raised by professional caretakers while our elders are often left feeling like they've been ostracized to ghettos, disconnected and irrelevant.

It is certainly up to all of us to fix this within our own communities, rather than put it on our elders to to fix. And this is one of those examples where doing this work to fix a problem will hopefully benefit us as we ourselves become elders.

But, it also is probably wise for us to think of how we can help cultivate this for ourselves as we move into our later years.

A few of the best of these I've seen have been based on sharing of informational, experiential, and spiritual capital.

I think again of my friends Jerry and Stacy, whom I've mentioned before. Their home was always filled with this multigenerational energy, with everyone from high school and college students, to professionals, to other elders.

Because of this multi-generational energy, they probably were able to stay in their home while other people their age might have had to downsize or look to assisted living. Students were stopping by daily for lessons, which meant there were people glad to help run a few errands or help with things that were difficult for older bodies. Some paid for music lessons with yard work and help around the house. In my experience, it was common for younger musicians or other artisans to step into familial types of relationships with elder artists, as an opportunity to take advantage of their wisdom and advice on a regular basis. And I've seen similar energy and arrangements for others with special artisan and land-based skills, as well as for folks doing community organizing work.

I suppose the starting point for creating this kind of situation is to realize that it's a possibility, and to start figuring out how to intentionally cultivate it. Beyond this, it seems like it's necessary to try to accumulate some forms of capital that will be truly helpful to younger people. I must add a warning that I've seen some folks, especially homesteaders and farmers, who became bitter that no young people wanted to learn what they had to teach. Mostly, they seemed to want young people to come and do low-skilled labor like weeding, tilling, and mowing the lawn for them. There's not really much to be learned from doing hours of free weeding work, so why should we expect young people to invest their time that way? They may deeply want to help, but may not be able to afford to invest their precious time at an important phase of their lives into something that will build little informational or experiential capital. So these elder farmers, not recognizing the needs of young people became bitter, and that bitterness didn't really help with anything, either. So, it may be on us to recognize that we have to allow the people around us to really "obtain a yield" from their interactions with us, and offer actually valuable learning experiences, not just weeding and yard work.

Assisted Living

For many of us, as we get older assisted living becomes one of our most attractive options. It can allow us to get the care we need, yet maintain some degree of independence.

The biggest consideration here is cost. In the US, in 2022, the median cost of assisted living was $52,000, while the cost of a private room was well over $100,000 a year.

Options are available weighted to social security income and ability to pay, but these might not include features like a private room.

Those who want to continue as FREE a lifestyle as possible into assisted living, can do some things to plan accordingly. That can include coming to terms with a certain loss of independence, and finding new life-enriching activities appropriate to assisted living.

For many moving into this age, a Permaculture Design Course (one that emphasizes full life design) can be a great way to plan for the future.

Aging in Ecovillages and Art Communities

Ecovillages provide a halfway point between a village model and a neighborhood, and some of the best have been planning to help folks age in place, while simultaneously down-sizing and transitioning.

Some Ecovillages are now planning for whole life cycles, allowing young people to buy into small condos, or even rooms, building equity in place to own a home, potentially scale into a larger family home, and then finally, into village semi-assisted living.

If the ecovillage life appeals to you, you may look to find a model already doing this, or help bring these ideas into your own village.

Community Smallholdings and Other Informal "Collectives"

Another approach to cultivating community in rural places is the community smallholding, sometimes called the community homestead model (though of course, we encourage people to avoid this problematic term.) This somewhat informal model is often sometimes called a "collective" within some lifestyle anarchist circles.

Community smallholdings are usually developed by converting old family farms, which were often built with large families in mind, into community spaces.

Sometimes these, too, evolve into small, often somewhat rustic Ecovillages of a sort, as trailers, tiny houses, and retrofitted farm structures spring up on the space.

I've seen a few of these that also allowed some aging in place, and sometimes long-term community members will move into more accessible housing as they age.

The downsides of the model are that they are often owned by one owner or set of owners, and often buying into the farm is not allowed or encouraged. That means that only a few members of such a community have the real security of property rights and the ability to accumulate equity over time.

I have personally seen this end poorly for folks who were committed to a community smallholding for decades, then lose their home when the owners sold for some reason. The owners could count on their equity to secure their later years, and the community was left to fend for themselves. This has especially been common in parts of the back to the land movement, and even in Permaculture circles, where some would think it violates both our ethics of people care and fair share.

I recommend against such a model long-term, unless there are written agreements about buying into the property and building equity.

Aging in Formal Intentional Communities and Cooperatives

Compared to Ecovillages, which are essentially normal neighborhoods with individual home ownership, intentional communities are typically defined by collective ownership.

Retirement Communities/Senior Villages

A popular modern innovation is the retirement community, where seniors can go to live together. These often have many different levels of entry depending on the financial abilities involved, and level of care required. The downside is perhaps that these are fairly conventional in terms of their unsustainability. An experienced Permaculturist or Earth warrior may find opportunities here to improve the sustainability and make this innovation one that's good for society and the planet.

Transition Plans for Regenerative Housing and Permaculture Projects

For those who've made investments in building regenerative housing and landscapes, a big consideration becomes: how does the work I've done continue into the future?

We've said it before in this book, and we'll say it again, we need to start thinking about this right when we're designing the property! Design with the transition in mind.

That means creating works that will likely be valued into the future.
—Create landscapes that can be low maintenance and still provide useful yields!

—Don't create problems, like difficult-to-maintain landscapes or fruit trees that require spraying or else they only produce buggy wasp food. Standard fruit trees in regions with pest problems are unlikely to be tended, and very likely to be cut down.

—Don't expect the new owners to have to do hours of maintenance work to maintain the site.

—Design so that it will age constructively with little to no maintenance.

—For housing, make installations like solar panels that don't require lots of work. Complicated ''sustainability" features that require lots of upkeep and labor are unlikely to be valued.

—The same goes for business assets. If your business infrastructure (like orchards and perennial farms, as well as other home based assets) require large amounts of low paid labor, it's. highly unlikely they'll continue into the future.

When it comes to actually making the transition, it may help to sit down and come up with an actual plan, rather than just hoping for the best.

—How can the new stewards "obtain a yield" from their work? If we're counting on getting help with things like orchards and gardens, will this work actually allow people to pay themselves a living wage? If not, people may truly want to help, but may simply not have the "privilege" to actually sacrifice the time to help. This often leads ot problems. Aging farmers may hope to spend less time working by finding new managers to run the business, but if they pay too little, they may end up spending more time and getting stressed out by managing labor problems. But if we allow people to make a real living wage from their work, then we'll find people who can help.

—Cultivate long-term relationships with the end in mind. Instead of just hiring one person to train for taking over, try to make relationships with several, so we can find the right person over time.

—Be realistic about a plan that allows the new stewards to not go bankrupt during the transition!

Exchanging Youthful Work for Worthy Wisdom

As a senior earth warrior, artist, musician or whatever it is you do, you have a lifetime of experiential and informational capital to exchange for labor.

Like Jerry and Stacy above, we may be able to find ways to use our wisdom to build helpful intergenerational community for ourselves. If we can match the value of the wisdom to the tasks we need help with, this usually works out well.

For those of us looking ahead to our futures, this may say something about what it means to truly be an elder. And for me, that perhaps means there's a difference between being an elder and simply being old! It may imply that real eldership means having intention to grow into a person with real, valuable wisdom for our future community members. If we've spent our whole lives in corporate banking, and that's all we feel we have to offer, it doesn't mean we don't know things, but those things are primarily valuable to banking corporations. Outside those structures, that capital may not be worth so much. So we may also be wise to cultivate experience, knowledge, and wisdom that will be important to pass on to the community, but which isn't valued so much by the corporate sector: hand skills, artisan skills, small local business skills that need to be passed on. Eldering well means thinking about what will truly benefit future generations, and investing our time on this planet in acquiring some of that to pass on. And of course, it's never too late or too early to start becoming an elder.

Accessing your Savings to Pay Your Expenses

If we've done our financial life design well, and found a truly FREE lifestyle, we will have "caught and stored" a fair amount of money along the way. Some of this may be in conventional investments like tax-deferred retirement accounts or (regenerative) stocks (hopefully.)

But some may be in unconventional transformative investments, durable generative assets, successful businesses, land, housing, procreative natural capital, intellectual capital, and so on. We'll need to have a plan for how we'll convert those assets back into cash to pay for our expenses in ways that build connections to nature and community, rather than destroying the connections we've built.

Accessing Conventional Investments

This is the fairly straight-forward part. If you have significant conventional investments, then we highly recommend consulting with a professional financial planner. It is after all, what they do. And, these days there are many who are mindful of sustainability and transforming our dysfunctional economy. That would be a great connection to build and support!

They will help you with the main strategies required to accomplish our big objectives: avoiding big tax penalties by withdrawing money at a rate that avoids the taxes, not getting penalized on our social security, and liquidating assets in an order that sustains your capital as long as you need it.

For example, in the US, when you're retired, you'll have to pay taxes on your IRA "distributions" (the cash you take out) based on your tax bracket, how much you earn. In 2022, if you're over 65 a single person can "make" $11,950 without paying taxes. If you make more than this in a year, you'll have to pay some to Uncle Sam. If you've reduced your expenses to a fairly low rate, you may not have to pay much in taxes. For those with significant IRA savings, you'll have a minimum distribution you're required to take each year, and there's a chance it could kick you up into a higher tax bracket. In this case, giving some of your distribution to charity could help avoid taxes. Again, these things will likely change over time, and a financial planner can help you understand the ins and outs better than we can in this book.

And if you're working or getting IRA payments while receiving social security, this too, can affect your social security payment. Again, the person to help you figure it all out is a financial planner.

Accessing More Unconventional Investments

Where things get a little more complicated is when we need to access the cash we've stored in transformative assets.

We'll need to have a plan to convert these assets into cash in some way, so that we can pay for our expenses without working.

First, this will be a good time to review your options for sustainable or regenerative conventional investments, because as you liquidate your investments, you may need to store that cash someplace, and you probably have safer and more regenerative options than stuffing it in a pillow case or under the mattress. So this is one of the first things you'll need is a plan for what to do with the cash when you get it, if you'll be getting it in lump sums.

Withdrawing Capital from Housing and Land Investments

As we've said before, owning housing or land is far from mandatory and there are many paths to a FREE life. But the reality is that over the last several decades home ownership has been the most important way Americans (and others in the world) have built wealth and eventually retired. So we expect that this will be the reality for a lot of our readers.

The most obvious problem with getting capital out of your house or land is that then you no longer have a house and land! So, we'll need patterns that get us cash without making us homeless.

Downsizing

Many folks approaching their later years choose to downsize, which is to sell their larger houses—which may be too big and require too much care anyway —keep some of the value to live off of, and use the rest to buy an appropriately sized house.

Having grown up around many farming communities, I've seen this as a common pattern. Farmers usually age out of the hard and stressful work of farming, and end up wanting a smaller place closer to other people in a town or city. Over my lifetime, I've seen farms that were purchased for $100k have come to be worth $500k or more. I've seen farmers sell small farms in growing suburbs for over $1,000,000, give plenty to their families, use the rest to take care of all their needs, and have some left to secure their housing or assisted living for the rest of their lives.

Of course the details will depend on your specific circumstances and investments, but to get an idea of this, the average American home in 1990 cost $122,900. That same family-sized home today was worth $374,900 in 2020. The home owners could feasibly buy a new smaller home or condominium for $150,000 and have $200,000 (after costs) to cover retirement expenses.

Combining that with other strategies like co-housing, sharing with friends, living in eco villages, could help the money go further.

Land contracts should involve a lawyer to help make sure the contract is tight and your needs are taken care of in case the purchase falls through.

The Reverse Mortgage

A more conventional modern tool is the reverse mortgage, which allows you to tap your equity (the value of your home) while you continue to live there.You may even be able to arrange a monthly payment over time. And reverse mortgages last until the final owner leaves the home, so you don't have to worry about outliving the mortgage. You are eligible to pull out more of your equity the older you get, often up to 90% of your equity. So, that $374,900 home could be worth over $350,000 after fees, especially if it continues to appreciate, while you continue to live in your home, mortgage and rent free. That's about $12000/year in today's dollars, for 30 years, or $17500 taken over 20 years.

The down side is that a reverse mortgage means your regenerative property will return to bank ownership and be sold for profit, without your control. For those of us developing regenerative properties, this could be bad as the new owners may not value our work.

But this doesn't have to be terrible, if we've planned our regenerative projects such that they will be valued. Acreage of high value forest is likely to be valued by new owners, energy efficiency upgrades like solar panels, and Russian ovens are unlikely to be removed. Functional successful orchard businesses are likely to be kept. But our eccentric ornamental wide life gardens may not be valued by new owners.

Land Contracts

Another option for selling land is to use a land contract, in which both parties skip the banks, and the buyer directly buys the property from the seller through installments. This is often a rent-to-own situation, where if the buyer falls through, the seller retains the property.

In a good situation, this can be ideal for a seller of a regenerative property who's moving into full retirement, as it allows more control over the future of the property, while providing a reliable income over decades into the future.

The downside is of course the large risk, if the buyer should be unable to complete the transaction. That could lead to court time and costs before recouping the property. On the upside, if you have enough other forms of investments to draw on, it you may have the property to sell a second time, or to get a reverse mortgage on.

Getting Capital out of Regenerative Businesses

If you've established a successful regenerative enterprise with a good reputation and clientele, then you can convert that to cash as well, by selling it to the next generation. Businesses can be valued in multiple ways, but a common way to get a very oversimplified idea of the value of your business is that a good market value is *about* 3 years of predictable income (with some minor adjustments for inflation and growth.) So if your business hits the benchmarks for the Landscape Transformation Program, for example, by cash flowing $40k/year, then it is likely worth around $120,000 on the market. That's of course if you can find an appropriate buyer. Having an attractive business that is good for the planet and for quality of life should be a good one to convert to cash.

The most basic idea here is that we need to be able to sell the business in such a way that the person who's buying it can actually afford to take it over. You may find two types of buyers, one who has some capital already, and is looking for a good investment. For example, one of my students invested an inheritance in buying a hot sauce business, with an established market and reputation. For around $90k, he could buy a business that would cash flow $30k into the future, and with potential to grow, if he wants to put in the work. That's a great investment with transformative potential. If you have a great successful hot sauce business, you could likely find a buyer willing to take it over.

But the second kind of buyer may not have good access to capital, but they… might just be the right person. This is especially true with regenerative businesses. The key is that they will need to be able to buy the business in a way that allows them to not go broke while continuing to pay you. For example, if your business is worth $120K, someone could feasibly make pay $22,000/year over 6 years, and still make $18k. That's still potentially a good long term investment, especially if there's good potential for growth. I've seen people make contracts for this kind of arrangement, though it is exceptionally risky for the seller, and requires a lot of trust, or perhaps collateral. For that reason, this arrangement is more common within families, but I do know someone who sold a small resort business on land contract to a trusted community member, and benefited by the reliable yearly retirement income over a 15-year contract period. With a well-established permaculture site, or other land based business with good cash flow, this kind of arrangement could be possible and beneficial to both parties.

More often, buyers may need to access financing or capital to make that investment. If you care about the continuation of the business, you'll still need to price the business so that the new owner can reasonably meet their needs while paying their financing.

Selling Durable Generative Assets, or Business Property

Well chosen, durable generative assets used in a business may maintain their value very well over decades. Indeed, some machinery from the 1940s is highly sought after today, and not really available anywhere on the global market new. Well-kept antique tractors that cost around $1000-2000 when I was a teenager are now routinely selling for $15-16000 now. That's a larger ROI than most housing. Other machines like milling equipment or antique looms have appreciated just as much over the last 30 years. Some kitchen equipment, like Chambers stoves were being given away or sold for hundreds of dollars at that time, and now these same exact stoves are selling for $30,000-40,000 and up. Some specialty antique printing equipment also has a high value today and continues to appreciate.

Other assets recommended in this book include special sales inventory like antiques, collectibles, imports, etc. can be sold in bulk as a business, or auctioned off to liquidate the collection for retirement.

If you have invested in such high quality generative assets, it should be easy enough to sell them directly for capital, or as part of a complete business. This may change the type of valuation you do on your business.

Retirement Money from Plants

Plant capital and other procreative assets can be sold off in multiple ways.

If you have created plants that you get royalties from, these royalties can continue into the future to help supplement your retirement. Others choose to sell the rights to sole production of their plant capital to a nursery. Still others will sell their plant capital rights along with their own nursery businesses. There's really no one-size-fits all solution here, it will depend on the assets involved and the business. Cultivating relationships with the next generation of nursery businesses may help you make the most of your plant capital.

Cashing Out Intellectual Assets

Intellectual assets can take may forms, but for developing a FREE lifestyle, it's best to capture the capital into products like books which can provide income for years into the future. Because of the nature of "online classes," I'm personally doubtful that these will remain profitable over enough time to provide retirement income. Everyone expects the most recent and up to date content for a class.

Yet books, especially classics on topics that change little over time like gardening, can maintain their value for decades. The Permaculture Designer's Manual probably sells more copies each year today than it did at publication, and the same can be said for many classics on homesteading and gardening.

Yet, book sales will probably not be a consistent retirement income alone for most of us, even for full time professional writers with large bodies of work. But the passive income may help out!

Living off the inheritance you've grown for the next generation
Living off your children's inheritance may sound counterintuitive, so stick
with us. Sharing an intergenerational household is one of the oldest ways that
people have provided for their eldering years, and it is still arguably the most
common.

This old pattern is to spend our most productive years growing family wealth
in the form of excellent human habitat, "home." This means shelter, tools,
knowledge, culture, and community—set within a stable ecology providing
abundant food, medicine, fuel, fiber, and clean water. This is exactly the sort
of investment we've talked about in this book. By safeguarding and growing
that wealth, the elders give their children enough abundance to have the
means to care for themselves and *their* children. And the family has plenty of
time and resources left to offer full loving care to its elders. We could call
this intergenerational wealth, which each generation invests in when they
can, and benefits from when they can't. The broader the inheritance, the more
abundance is available for everyone at all stages of life.

In industrial contexts, the economically fortunate among us spend a lifetime
pouring equity into a home. But when we near the end of life, we often sell
the home to pay for ever pricier institutional care. All our wealth transfers to
distant corporate entities. This is not a good pattern for elder happiness, nor
does it benefit future generations, who miss the assistance they traditionally
would have depended on! It's our final example of traditional connections
and energy flows broken down to benefit banks and big business. We can do
better than that.

The central requirement to ethically live off the inheritance we'll leave
behind is to build a close enough working relationship between generations
that everyone wants it to work. Ideally this relationship is built consciously,
explicitly, and respectfully from childhood onward, by holding the ancient
value that "Elders provide for the young, and the young provide for the
elders." The second requirement is to go through a process of gradually
transferring responsibilities and control of wealth to that younger generation.
The young are raised to be responsible, competent adults the elders know
they can trust, and at the same time the young come to know from experience
that they will be treated with respect and dignity as equal members of the
family, and not as freeloaders or perpetual juveniles.

Jason's dear friend Rohit is part of a family of first generation immigrants who keep this approach to family and aging. When Rohit was young, his grandmother lived with the family, so he saw his parents live out this pattern. He lived with his parents until he got married, at which point his parents moved out of the master bedroom so he and his wife could use it. The parents were humble enough to give profound symbolic and material support to the idea that the next generation was entering the next phase of life, and that the parents were too. Even in a suburban neighborhood they are able to continue this ancient way that many of our ancestors kept. Of course it is not always easy sharing a household, but because this family has spent years skillfully honoring the different phases of life and the importance of respect, they make it work to everyone's benefit.

Their "retirement fund" was a lifetime of investment into the people they love. Perhaps that's a reminder that in the end, investing in the people around us are the best investment we can make. And if we get our designs right, all the tools in this book can be put together to grow Financial Resilience and Economic Empowerment for everyone we care about.

Resources

Chodron, Pema. When Things Fall Apart. Shambala, 2016.

Conley, Chip. Wisdom@Work. Currency, 2018

Enough Already

And just as we must decide "what is enough?" When it comes to our finances, so we too, must decide what is enough for our money adventure. We could spend our whole lives worrying and learning more and more about making more money—and some of us do. But when it comes down to it, how much knowledge and expertise do we need to meet our goals and feel confident that we've got this whole "money" thing worked out?

Hopefully, in this book, we've presented a path of adventures on money that will help you get to that point. And hopefully, that path is one where you can actually experience important growth and self-actualization, not just a bunch of worry over "money." But still, we hope that you will be able to periodize some of the things you want to improve, learn some things, grow more financially FREE, so that you can put this book down, stop worrying about money and live your life more fully.

And so where we're at now, you have a whole set of truly practical "adventures" that will undoubtedly make you more FREE. Someone who applies this book rigorously will have created a financial situation that is truly regenerative, so that they will keep growing in wealth over time.

The person who truly wants to be free will have taken the time to understand their financial situation, gotten out of bad debt, and worked on community organizing to establish a village of support for themselves. They will have invested in developing truly valuable knowledge at the mechanic or developer level, so that they're able to become information-rich members of their community. They will have shifted their mindset away from work, and found transformative investments that will naturally grow in wealth over time. Then they will have worked these into situations with good cash flow by stacking products, services, and talents together to create a unique and valuable set of products or services for their local region. They will have focused mostly on semi-passive streams of income so that they're not tied down to working long hours just to get by.

But beyond this, the FREE person will have invested in durable assets to give a low cost of living. They'll have durable, sustainable homes with low monthly costs. They'll be largely energy self-sufficient and food self-sufficient. With low cost of living but a high quality of life, it will feel infinitely workable to meet their needs with minimal work.

If you're not there yet, then you can ask why? What areas do you need to work on to grow your FREEdom? You now have all the tools you need to pick one, set a goal, and periodize improving on it. Then pick another, and another until you're where you want to be. Until you have "enough."

Any good garden grows over time until it finally "pops" and comes alive like an ecosystem. And any work of art will finally "pop" and come to life as it reaches a certain level of complexity. And just like that, we'll be able to feel our own life grow FREE. At some point, we'll just know we've achieved a way of living that just works for ourselves. And then we know we have enough.

And so we must also decide "what is enough?" For this book of ours. And we think this is about it. This is enough.

Thank you for reading it.

"A full moon rising." A shot from Eric's summer abode, an RV with a million dollar view. "By crushing housing expenses to under $3,000 per year, I have TIME, to experience spectacular full moons, sunsets, walks, reading, writing, study, and most of all, time to get my life back.

Adventure: The Beginning

Congratulations, you've now completed the first adventure we suggested in this book, which was to explore your life financial design and vision. We've started the transformative process, which is all about setting one periodized goal at a time, and completing it.

But the real beginning of your transformation starts now. The next step is to pick your next adventure, set a goal for it, set a time for it, and get it done. Pick something that's motivating to you, that will have a big difference on your financial freedom or free time, and get going! Don't let indecision get in your way, there are 100 ideas in this book you could work on, if you can't make up your mind just pick one and get started.

Because no matter how many books you read or things you learn, your life won't change until you commit to taking action. But once you learn that skill, then the world can't help but change. Remember, in this book, "skill" isn't knowing how to do things, it's knowing how NOT to. They key to this skill is to figure out what you're DOING that's standing in the way of getting things done, and then to stop doing those things. Recognize that you could have transformed your life 100 times over already, and accomplished countless goals, if you yourself weren't doing things that were getting in the way. The key isn't even to DO something. They key is to recognize the thinking and actions that are standing in the way of you transforming your life. The to let go of that.

When you let go, the life you want is already waiting for you to start living it.

Appendix 1: The 4% Rule Considered

One of the basic assumptions of the FIRE movement, and retirement planning in general is the 4% rule.

It remains constantly fiercely defended by mainstream financial advisors, and also continuously contested by a passionate minority.

As of writing this sentence in late September 2022, Vanguard itself, one of the "big 3" index funds, as published a new shocking analysis that with the Schiller S/P rate at a historic high, and estimated inflation to remain high for the next half decade, that the 4% rule would not apply to their main funds! This is important since Vanguard's funds match the market and perform better than 75% of all funds.

According to Vanguard's analysis, for the next few decades, they are anticipating a 2.8% withdrawal rate will be more accurate. Instead of a 25 times rule, this gives us a 36 times rule. This is a huge and significant change to FIRE assumptions. Of course, already there are many pushing back saying that this is just being overly conservative, and that the 4% rule is still safe.

For the purpose of this book, the safest approach will be based on transformative assets that produce cash flow and grow in value, with good opportunities to liquidate. And of course, working to create a resilient non-financial "solid base" to rely on. I'd note that looking at the 2.8% rule table, it makes mainstream, index fund based approaches to FIRE seem pretty unattainable, and really shifts my thinking in favor of FREE benchmarks with transformative assets, as in this book.

But we've included both charts with a 4% rule and this 2.8% rule to help with your calculations.

Resource: Vanguard Investment: https://investor.vanguard.com/investor-resources-education/campaign/advised-advantage/is-the-4-percent-rule-sustainable-for-retirement-withdrawals

Traditional FIRE Investment Table (Based on the 4% Rule)

Your Yearly Expenses	Savings you need:	Years @ $10k/year	$15k/year	$20k/year	$25k/year
$50,000	1.25 M			34	27
$40,000	$1 Million		34	28	23
$30,000	$750K	36 years	27	22	19
$25,000	$625K	31 years	25	20	17
$20,000	$500K	28 years	21	16	14
$15,000	$325K	25 years	15	11	9
$10,000	$250K	17 years	12	9	7
$7,000	$175K	13 years	9	7	6

This can help you figure out approximately how much you need to save and how long it will take at different savings rates, assuming you're getting about a 4% return on your investments while saving.

A big take home of a table like this is that if we're relying on conventional investments, we probably need to be saving at a rate of $15k or more per year to reach any kind of "early retirement."

Or, we need to focus on better forms of investments with much higher returns. With a high rate of savings over $25k/year, it's easy to hit FREE bench marks in a very short time frame.

A Traditional FIRE Investment Table (Based on the 2.8% or 36 Times Rule)

Your Yearly Expenses	Savings you need:	Years @ $10k/year	$15k/year	$20k/year	$25k/year
$50,000	1.8 Mil				29
$40,000	$1.4 Mil			35+	26
$30,000	$1.1Mil			30	23
$25,000	$900k		36	26	21
$20,000	$720		30	23	17
$15,000	$540K	30+ years	23	18	13
$10,000	$360k	23 years	18	13	10
$7,000	$252k	17 years	12	9	7

Note that this chart is based on the 9/2022 report from Vanguard, which many will think is very conservative in it's expected 20-year rate of returns on index funds. It get's less reliable after a few decades, which is why the numbers stop after around 30 years. If historic trends continue, after 20 years, we may return to the 4% rule, but this certainly isn't guaranteed. Some countries, like Japan, have seen numbers more like this chart for many decades. Again, the key in this type of economy may be to focus more on quality of life, rather than "early retirement," and transformative assets rather than the stock market.

Appendix 2: The Encyclopedia of Side Hustles

(IMPORT DATA FROM FILE 3)

CPSIA information can be obtained
at www.ICGtesting.com
Printed in the USA
LVHW081309111122
732865LV00008B/196